Iran Encountering Globalization

This book examines the current state of Iran, looking at a wide range of issues, including the economy, finance, politics, the media, population and the position of women. It discusses the uneasy balance between theoretic conservatism, and modernization and globalization. This is a key tension in Iran – one which has arisen following the revolution of 1979, since when the regime has worked to Islamicize the country, while at the same time international globalization forces have been pulling in a different direction. The book suggests that forces for change in Iran are currently building up.

Ali Mohammadi is Reader in International Communication and Cultural Studies at The Nottingham Trent University. His recent publications are *Globalization and Recolonization: The Muslim World in the 21st Century*, with Muhammad Ahsan (Taha, 2002), *Iran and Eurasia*, co-edited with A. Ehteshami (Ithaca Press, 2000), *International Communication and Globalization: A Critical Introduction* (Sage, 1997) and 'Electronic Empires: An Islamic Perspective', in *Electronic Empires* (Arnold, 1998).

Iran Encountering Globalization

Problems and prospects

Edited by Ali Mohammadi

Foreword by Fred Halliday

RoutledgeCurzon
Taylor & Francis Group
LONDON AND NEW YORK

First published 2003
by RoutledgeCurzon
2 Park Square, Milton Park, Abingdon, Oxon, OX14 4RN

Simultaneously published in the USA and Canada
by RoutledgeCurzon
270 Madison Ave, New York NY 10016

RoutledgeCurzon is an imprint of the Taylor & Francis Group

Transferred to Digital Printing 2005

Typeset in Times New Roman by GreenGate Publishing Services, Tonbridge, Kent

British Library Cataloguing in Publication Data

A catalogue record for this book is available from the British Library

Library of Congress Cataloging in Publication Data
Iran encountering globalization : problems and prospects / [edited by] Ali Mohammadi.
p.cm.
Includes bibliographical references (p.) and index.
1. Iran – Politics and government – 1979-1997. 2. Iran – Politics and government – 1997- 3. Islam and politics – Iran. 4. Iran – Economic conditions – 1979-1997. 5. Iran – Economic conditions – 1997- 6. Iran – Social conditions – 1979-1997. 7. Iran – Social conditions –1997- 8. Globalization. 9. Democratization – Iran. I. Mohammadi, Ali.

DS318.825 I64 2003
955.05'43–dc21

2002031778

ISBN 0-415-30827-5

Contents

Figures

Tables

Contributors

Hossein Adibi is Professor of Sociology at Queensland University of Technology, Australia. He has written many scholarly papers in Farsi and English.

Parvin Alizadeh is Senior Lecturer in Economics at London Guildhall University. She has published many scholarly papers, the most recent of which is *Iran's Economy: Dilemmas of an Islamic State* (I.B. Tauris, 2000).

Mohammad B. Beheshti is Associate Professor of Economics at the Universty of Tabriz. He has published various scholarly papers in Farsi and English.

Kamran M. Dadkhah is Associate Professor, Department of Economics, Northeastern University, Boston. He has published many scholarly papers, the most recent being 'An evaluation of progress toward European Monetary Unification' (with Michelle Casario), *Journal of Policy Modeling* 20 (1998), pp.741–65.

Stephen Fairbanks is a former US State Department analyst and currently head of the Farsi programme at Radio Free Europe. He has written many scholarly articles. He has a PhD in history and specialises in Iranian affairs.

G. Reza Ghorashi is Associate Professor of Economics, Richard Stockton College, New Jersey. He has published various scholarly papers. His most recent publications include 'Politics of trade policy of Iran: Offering of public goods in a global economy', in *Proceedings of the 25th Annual Third World Conference* (February 2000).

Barry Harper is Principal Lecturer in Economics at London Guildhall University. His most recent publication is 'Beauty, stature and the labour market: a British cohort study', *Oxford Bulletin of Economics and Statistics* (Oxford, 2000).

Homayoun Katouzian is Associate Member, Faculty of Oriental Studies, University of Oxford, and Honorary Research Fellow, Department of Economics, University of Exeter. His books include *State and Society in Iran*; *The Eclipse of the Qajars and the Rise of the Pahlavis*; *Musaddiq and the Struggle for Power in Iran*; *The Political Economy of Modern Iran*; *Sadeq Hedayat: the Life and Literature of an Iranian Writer*; and *Ideology and Method in Economics*.

Ali Madanipour is Reader in Urban Design and Director of Postgraduate Research at the School of Architecture, Planning and Landscape, University of Newcastle upon Tyne. His research interests include city design and development, culture of cities, urbanization and international urban change, social exclusion and urban governance. He has published many scholarly papers and books, most recently *Tehran: The Making of a Metropolis* (Wiley, 1998) and *The Governance of Place* (co-editor) (Ashgate, 2000).

Ali Akbar Mahdi is Associate Professor of Sociology at Ohio Wesleyan University. He has published a number of books and scholarly articles in Persian and English. His most recent book is *Iranian Culture, Civil Society, and Concern for Democracy* (in Farsi).

Ali Mohammadi is Reader in International Communication and Cultural Studies at the Nottingham Trent University. His recent publications are *Globalization and Recolonization: The Muslim World in the 21st Century*, with Muhammad Ahsan (Taha, 2002), *Iran and Eurasia*, co-edited with A. Ehteshami (Ithaca Press, 2000), *International Communication and Globalization: A Critical Introduction* (Sage, 1997) and 'Electronic Empires: An Islamic Perspective', in *Electronic Empires* (Arnold, 1998).

Hamid Zangeneh is Professor of Economics at Widener University, Chester, Pennsylvania. His areas of specialization are macroeconomics, money and banking, and international economics. He has published many books and scholarly articles, and most recently edited *Islam, Iran, and World Stability* (New York: St Martin's Press, 1994). He is currently editor of the *Journal of Iranian Research and Analysis*.

Foreword

Fred Halliday

The question of Iran's relation to globalization has two sides, both of them addressed in this important and perceptive book, a collection all the more interesting for the range of topics it covers and the very strong representation within it of Iranian writers. One aspect of Iran's relation to globalization is obvious enough: the ability of Iran to respond to the changes in the world economy, and in world politics and culture, that are subsumed in the broad term 'globalization'. As a country of 70 million people, with a history of three thousand years of statehood, substantial oil and gas resources, and a rich and influential culture, Iran faces a range of options, as well as pressures, within this international context. But the issue of globalization is not a one-way street: if globalization poses options, and some challenges, for Iran, the case of Iran also poses challenges for globalization, both in the sense of our understanding of, and debate about, globalization, and also in terms of where the world goes in the next decades. Iran, emerging from two decades of post-revolutionary transformation, is in a position to make its own contribution to the changing world, both in terms of its championing of an anti-hegemonic agenda in the world, and as an influential, and distinctive, participant in the politics and culture of the Islamic world. This contribution is all the more significant because, as the contributors to this volume make clear, there is no single Iranian voice on these issues: the debate, and at times conflict, now taking place in Iran concern both the future of Iranian society and politics and Iran's relation to the outside world. Our understanding of both of these themes is enriched by a reading of this book.

The challenges which Iran faces in regard to globalization are evident enough, and, in large measure, by no means specific to it. First, economics. Iran is a country whose economy has long relied on the oil sector, for most of its state revenue and for over 90 per cent of its export revenues. The problems this poses to Iran, as a '*rentier*' or 'distributive' state, have been present since the 1960s and have survived the fall of the Shah in 1979 and the post-revolutionary transformations. Yet the problems of this reliance on oil have been accentuated by the doubling of population since 1979 and by the inefficiencies which the Islamic Republic, like the monarchy, has incorporated into the distribution process. At the same time oil has, quite simply, bought time: Iran has not had to engage in the drastic transformation of its economy, manufacturing sector and, above all, educational system which others in Asia have – first in east Asia, more recently in India – because it has had a means of cushioning the pressures of the outside world. While oil has brought peace it has also, therefore, inhibited engagement with the world economy: Iran's main non-oil exports remain in traditional sectors – carpets and pistachio nuts – while foreign direct investment outside the oil sector is minimal. In any field of economic and social life, be it the law, the position of women in the labour force, or education, the unavoidable links between domestic change and future international engagement are evident.

The second challenge Iran faces is that of politics. Globalization, if it means anything, means pressure for greater openness in political life, a commitment to democracy and to the upholding of human rights. Iran is a post-revolutionary state, both in the sense that it was formed by the revolution, and the war with Iraq that followed, and in the sense that, slowly at first and more rapidly since the 1997 presidential elections, it has been the site of widespread debate and political conflict over where the revolution should go: the pressures of the external world cut both ways here – those advocating change see Iran as participating more actively and openly with the outside world, those opposed talk up the dangers of external pressure and conspiracies. The latter point to the fate of Russian leader Mikhail Gorbachev to illustrate how well-intentioned reforms in radical states may end by bringing disaster to their proponents, and their countries. These diverse views on post-revolutionary development are reflected in the debates within Iran on globalization: reformers allude to Iran's strengths in this field, especially in terms of mineral resources and culture, while opponents stress the dangers of 'cultural aggression' and the takeover by western economies. Much of this debate is phrased in Islamic terms, but Muslim tradition on this, as on almost all other issues, allows of varying interpretations: Islam can be presented as a universalizing doctrine, or, alternatively, as a cultural and social system threatened by its enemies. But there is in Iran a strong nationalist element in this too, born of Iran's experiences with external powers, of east and west, in modern times.

As many of the chapters this volume make clear, the debate, and the conflict, in Iran over the direction of the post-revolutionary state is far from over. Those who are threatened by a greater openness to the outside world and the political changes this entails may fight vigorously to prevent change from continuing. History does, however, provide some context for assessing the present chapter of state–society relations in Iran: it is the fourth such period of tension in modern history, after those of the Constitutional Revolution (1905–7), the Musaddeq period (1951–3) and the revolution (1978–9). In the first two the social challenges were crushed by indigenous rulers acting with the support of external powers. In the second two, and despite many a conspiracy theory to the contrary, the repressive state has acted without significant international support: the balance of forces has been a predominantly internal one. Iran's response to globalization will depend, in large measure, on the outcome of this conflict. Yet, as we have seen, globalization has contradictory implications for it.

Third, there is the cultural dimension of globalization. Iran is a society with a strong and diverse culture, be it in the linguistic and regional diversity of the country, the tensions between more secular and more Islamic currents in politics and culture, and the wide, very wide indeed, difference of interpretation of Islam itself. This diversity is located in a country where, as the first chapter of this volume makes clear, transnational cultural and social links with the surrounding world have existed for centuries, a country which itself has a long history of tension between autocratic state and social challenge. The debates in Iran today draw on this diversity and history, not least in the attempt to forge a political system that takes account of Iranian reality while, at the same time, moving forward to meet the expectations of the younger generation. The balances of pre-Islamic and Islamic, of lyrical poetry and austere theology, of clerical authority and individual judgement, are all part of these debates.

In regard to these debates, be they on politics or culture, the impact of globalization is contradictory: much of the history of modern Iran has involved a tension between challenging indigenous authoritarian power by invoking international standards, of rights, constitutional government and accountability and, at the same time, challenging the influence of external powers in the name of Iranian independence and values. The drive to modernization in Iran during the twentieth century, by the secular opposition movements and intellectuals as much as by the Pahlavi monarchs, invoked rational, international standards and goals to oppose the power of clergy, landowners and rulers; the critique of the power of the mullahs rests, equally, on international standards, including those of gender rights, freedom of expression by press and writers and financial accountability. That tension between two forms of contestation and legitimation is not, therefore, over, but its outcome may depend less on the impact of the Iranian past, more on the way in which social movements inside Iran can appropriate Iranian and international principles to challenge those in power.

The debate on globalization is not, however, a one-way street. If globalization challenges Iran, it is important to recognize the ways in which Iran poses a challenge for our contemporary understanding of globalization. First, history: most discussion of globalization in the western world operates within a very recent time frame, of the 1980s and 1990s onwards. What the Iranian case reminds us is how much of what is comprised by 'globalization' is of much longer-term character: Iran has experienced external pressure, financial, cultural and political, since the latter part of the nineteenth century. The first national protest movement was the Tobacco Boycott of 1891, organized to protest against the granting of a commercial monopoly to a British firm. Much of Iran's history has, as noted, been an attempt to respond to that pressure. Not only is this longer perspective the appropriate timescale within which to assess globalization, but it is this history, more than the trade or financial market liberalizations of recent years, which forms the Iranian perception of globalization. A country which has been invaded, and subverted, by external powers, and subject to external machinations of many kinds, is not going easily to trust the promises of global well-being associated with the current neo-liberal orthodoxy.

Second, Iran has, in its actions and in diplomatic terms, challenged the ways in which globalization is pursued. This is true both of the Iranian state in its post-revolutionary form and of the political and social movements that have, for decades, marked Iranian politics. The Islamic Republic has presented itself as an opponent of 'world arrogance' or imperialism. It has, in particular, criticized the predominance of a 'culture of exclusion' in the world economy and in world affairs and called for a more equitable distribution of power and wealth. Whether the Iranian state has itself lived up to the standards it espouses is doubted by many, but that it speaks with many others throughout the world in challenging the prevailing forms of globalization is indubitable. If Iran does participate in global institutions and seek access to markets, technology and capital, it does, at the same time, question the assumptions upon which these processes are based. Those opposed to the Iranian state may reject the instrumental ways in which the state uses such arguments to silence or discredit domestic critics, but they too may wish to see Iran pursue an independent, and critical, path within international relations.

Finally, there is the question of culture. Iran's relation to globalization poses, as has its cultural and religious influence for centuries, the question of how far a greater integration of states at the economic level can be reconciled with a diversity of cultures. Iran's combination of a variety of cultures within and considerable influence without gives it a special place in this debate, one that may take a specifically Islamic form, but which is by no means confined to such. The flourishing of Iranian secular culture in the US diaspora, and the influence of Iranian literature and language in Afghanistan and central Asia are parts of this process. The most widely read poet in the USA today is an Iranian, Jamal al-Din Rumi. If we are moving to a world of greater cultural pluralism, of shifting cultures within societies and diasporas, of a new global creativity, then Iranian culture, food, language, literature, not to mention film, will play a role in this.

The debate on globalization is not, therefore, one separate from political concerns. Many of the states and interests driving globalization wish to promote their own interests. The opponents of change within Iran want to use the debate on globalization as a means of conserving their authority, over the state, the economy, civil society, women and young people. Yet between these two poles there are possibilities which may broaden the benefits of globalization and to some degree meet the requirements of all societies who participate in it. The starting point for any such broadening of possibilities is an open, informed, discussion of the issues involved: one that includes perspectives beyond the mid-Atlantic consensus. To that end *Iran Encountering Globalization* makes an informed, and most pertinent, contribution.

Fred Halliday
London School of Economics

Acknowledgements

I would like to thank all the contributors for their cooperation and sincere support, particularly Hamid Zangeneh at Widner University, Chester, Pennsylvania, USA, and my colleagues John Tomlinson at the Centre for Research in International Communication and Culture, and Mike Featherstone at the Theory, Culture and Society Centre, both at Nottingham Trent University. Thanks also to Frances Banks, the secretary of the Department of English and Media Studies, for her usual support and sincere help. I would also like very much to thank Sara S. Mohammadi at the BBC for her editorial support and useful discussion.

Introduction

Iran is entering the twenty-first century with enormous development problems. The population has grown to over 64 million, with a literacy rate of 69 per cent, a GDP per capita of 9.6 million rials, inflation over 21 per cent and unemployment much above 15 per cent. The main industries include petroleum and petrochemicals, mines and metals, heavy and light industry, handicrafts, carpets and agricultural products. But more than 90 per cent of Iran's export earnings still comes from the sale of crude oil and petroleum products (Plan and Budget Organization Report, 1999).

There is a drastic shortage of houses, schools, hospitals, transportation and urban facilities, along with critically high levels of pollution. According to official estimates 25 tonnes of lead pollute the air quality of Tehran, the capital city, as a result of unecological, low-quality fuel. The recent official statistics indicate about 12 million people are under the poverty line, almost one-fifth of the total population. As a result of such social inequality 80 per cent of the nation's wealth is in the hands of only 20 per cent of the population. The average age of addiction has fallen to 20 years and the number of people with an addiction to drugs has increased at an alarming rate. Due to the social and economic conditions of urban life in the major cities in Iran the rate of divorce has increased rapidly too. The paradox between traditional forces and modern 'know-how' remains a stumbling block for the development of the country on one hand and the external forces of the globalization process on the other. Furthermore, the difficulty of reconciling free-market principles with the Islamic constitution would halt the participation of Iran in the global economy.

The crucial issues that remain unresolved are the lack of coordination between the executive legislative powers and the juridical system. There is also a lack of understanding of the modern banking system, capital market and deregulation policies and many others, and this has added to the problems that Iran is facing in the dawn of the new millennium.

The purpose of this collective work is an evaluation of rapid changes in the process of globalization and its impact on Iran as a restricted Muslim country. We are living in the age of transformation of capital into a global order, and the emerging new order will have an important impact on developing countries in general and on Iran in particular, located as it is at a strategically important crossroads between central Asia and the Persian Gulf.

In this context, the discussion of each chapter focuses on existing development issues within the Islamic Republic in the light of the rapid changes that have occurred outside Iranian borders since the revolution in 1979.

This text has been based on the crucial issues related to Iran's development as it encounters the globalization process.

Part I: Iran and the globalized world

The introduction of Part I is concerned with the problem of development, mainly in the context of globalization.

- Chapter 1 focuses on political development as a major stumbling block toward Iran's modernization process at the end of the twentieth century.
- Chapter 2 looks at Iran in the process of globalization, the rapid change of global forces and how those changes are causing tremendous problems for the Islamic Republic, particularly in the context of culture.
- Chapter 3 looks at the concept of globalization as it affects women and shows where Iran stands in regard to this phenomenon.

Part II: Globalization: an economic and financial approach

The introduction looks at the various aspects of the economic and financial approaches of an Islamic regime, which are analysed in three separate chapters.

- Chapter 4 looks at economic globalization and the prospects for democracy in Iran using provision of 'public goods' to describe the state's major functions. Economic globalization reduces a nation-state's ability to provide public goods. This process, which is harmful in cases of countries with a proper balance between the state and society, may enhance chances for democracy in Iran by modifying the state's structure and function.
- Chapter 5 focuses on the global finance markets and the stumbling policy of Iranian integration with international finance and investment issues. It provides a complete picture of Iran's options vis-à-vis international financial markets.
- Chapter 6 provides a policy appraisal of the Iranian economy since the revolution and argues how lack of development vision and economic leadership failed to attract investment to facilitate the process of globalization.

Part III: The global challenge for development

The introduction looks at the limit of theocracy and the reality of development problems in the context of the globalization process.

- Chapter 7 looks at the modernization of everyday life in Iran. In order to magnify the processes, the author employs case-study methods and argues that there has been a contradiction between revolutionary preferences for traditional life patterns and the actual modernization process.

- Chapter 8 looks at Iran's economic development and the requirement for structural change in human resources. In a society, access to development is possible if the minds, attitudes and behaviours of its people are oriented in the direction of development.
- Chapter 9's discussion focuses on the feminization of the labour force in Iran in general and after the revolution in particular, with regard to the globalization process.

Part IV: The limits of theocracy

The introduction looks at three issues in the process of development: the migration of the highly qualified to the west, lack of political parties, and the emergence of the new reformist group in the sixth Majles election which has raised the hope of democracy in the third millennium in Iran.

- Chapter 10 looks at the issue of migration since the revolution as an issue for development.
- Chapter 11 examines theocracy versus democracy in the context of new political parties as an issue for political development.
- Chapter 12 looks at the new emerging political groups known as reformist in the sixth Majles election and the hope for democracy in Iran.

Despite all the development problems that Iran is encountering today, there are strong possibilities for the ruling clergies to put aside their conflict of interests, resolve the differences of interpretation of the Quran and put Iran back on the road to modernity, which is the way it is going anyway were it not for the various obstacles placed in its path by conservative clergy among the ruling Islamists. Iran luckily has a great opportunity to play a leading role in the region, with the cooperation of the European Union and the USA, because of its geographical location, having borders with central Asian countries and the Arab nations of the Persian Gulf.

Taking into account all these opportunities and the quantity of qualified workers that has left the country as a consequence of the conflict between traditionalist and modernist groups in the past two decades, it can be seen that there is no threat from outside Iranian borders to jeopardise Iranian progress and prosperity: rather, the enemy is within, in the system of juridical administration, the lack of coherent and decisive government policies to safeguard freedom of expression, to check the balance of power and define the duties and responsibilities of policy-makers, and furthermore to recruit the 'know-how' to deliver the country to its deserved place in the international community, particularly with the initiative of President Khatami about the dialogue of civilization.

So far the evidence suggests that the disputes and conflicts of interest amongst various groups have not been resolved. President Khatami's success in improving the international image of Iran, in eradicating tensions over foreign policy and improving Iran's relations even with its adversaries is considerable. Nevertheless, it should be noted that his domestic policy, due to existing tension between traditionalist and reformist forces, has suffered to such an extent that the future direction of the Islamic Republic is unclear.

Part I

Iran and the globalized world

Since the 1990s when the Soviet bloc collapsed and capitalism with the expansion of communications technology rapidly extended its international borders to a global one, the nation-state has ceased to be an entity. Transnational corporations continued throughout the 1990s to increase their role in the world economy, in the markets for goods and services, and thus capital and technology. Their activities both broadened and deepened the economic interdependence of nations, to a degree that it is now commonplace to refer to the aggregate no longer as the international economy, but as a borderless global economy.

Now, at the start of the twenty-first century, we see the result of the globalization process that began two decades ago 'which referred to the multiplicity of linkages and interconnections between state and societies that make up the present world system. It described the process by which events, decisions, and activities in one part of the world come to have significant consequences for individuals and communities in quite distant parts of the globe' (McGrew, 1992).

Now global economic interdependence offers the prospect of higher productivity and living standards but it also links national economies to foreign financial institutions, which are out of the direct control of the nation-state; in the context of developing countries this trend will be dependent on certain economic circumstances of that country and its governmental relation to the big economic powers of the world. Any developing country, in order to integrate to global economy, needs to understand the pros and cons of international investment and the process of negotiating measures of deep integration to the globalization process. In the case of Iran, with its crucial geopolitical location, the leadership of the Islamic government has no comprehension of the globalization process, in particular the powerful role of international financial institutions, and the significance of the rapid brain drain of the highly qualified from the country, i.e. those who possess a more comprehensive grasp of the global economy.

In Part I the discussion of the first chapter centres around the experience of an ancient country entering the twentieth century. Iran is so confused about its past and unsure of its future. Chapter 2 examines how the process of retraditionalization of culture rejects the foundation of production institutions and the cries from international television and underground video clubs alike for a progressive, flexible and open approach. Finally Chapter 3 looks at women in the process of globalization and the struggle for civil liberty, equality, fairness and justice. The discussion in this chapter will be more concerned with the concept of globalization and will show where Iran stands with regard to the new global capitalism. The chapter then deals with the growing participation of women in non-governmental organizations, public activities aimed at increasing women's consciousness, and social groups established in order to protect women's rights. In contrast to establishing a theocratic state in Iran and closing its borders to outside influences, another process was taking place on the world scale which later became known as globalization. Globalization, as a social, political, economic and cultural force, has been able to penetrate the most isolated and closed-off area of the world. How then can the Islamic Republic of Iran avoid the forces of globalization emanating from the west? This chapter examines the effects of globalization on one hand and the process of Islamization of Iran and Iranian women on the other.

We are in the early stages of experiencing a one-world-system economy in a world that is multicultural. How should we evaluate the direction and the aims of the global economy if, as the advocates of globalization claim, the globalization process will eventually contribute to the improvement of the economic condition of the poor nations? Alex Inkeles (1998) argues that the process of convergence is accelerated by the activities of an increasing number of organizations that operate cross-nationally. The impact of cross-national organization is greatest in the case of those with some power to instruct or regulate, such as the multinational corporations. In contrast to convergence, he refers to divergence meaning the movement away from a given point. Again the process of globalization will eventually contribute more to those countries of the West as they did not previously have access to all developing countries; they will eventually have better access with no competition. Take the example of Europe after two world wars: European countries perceived economic unification as an antidote to nationalism, but now the companies and financial markets totally disregard the national economy when they want to make decision in terms of production and investment or marketing. According to the Institute for International Finance, in 1999 private capital flows were estimated at $136 billion to 29 countries while government capital flows were only $22 billion (Samuelson, 2000). Now many developing countries in general, and Iran in particular, are suffering the lack of 'know-how' with which they could otherwise utilize private capital for the joint development of various projects instead of borrowing from western governments. Globalization processes not only facilitate access to the market, but also provide flexibility and bring within easy reach private capital for joint ventures and partnerships for further improvement of the market and further development.

1 Iran and the problem of political development

Homayoun Katouzian

Iran is an ancient as well as a third-world country, an oil-exporting economy, and a Middle Eastern state which experienced two popular revolutions in the twentieth century.[1] What are its prospects for political growth and development towards a mature and democratic society?[2]

Iran came to the twentieth century confused about its past and unsure of its future – caught as it was between the traditional and the modern, the Asiatic and the European – and a helpless pawn in the diplomatic, economic and military rivalry between the Russian and British empires. The most important and immediate programme of its modernising intellectuals was to abolish the traditional system of absolute and arbitrary rule (*estebdad*), and replace it with the rule of law (*qanun*); hence their campaign for constitutional, constrained or 'conditioned' (*mashruteh*) government. The religious leadership and community generally supported their position, because there was nothing in Islamic doctrine which approved of arbitrary rule, the arbitrary state was not legitimate in the Shi'ah theory of government, and the *ulama* (religious leaders) would not alienate themselves from urban society – including landlords, merchants and the ordinary public – which was committed to the constitutionalist movement. A relatively small, but significant, group of the *ulama*, led by Shaykh Fazlullah Nuri, opposed the constitutionalist movement at its later stages, and advocated a vague notion of a strictly religious constitutionalism (i.e. *mashru'eh* as opposed to *mashruteh*). In the civil conflict that followed they sided with the existing arbitrary government which was supported by Tsarist Russia. However, they did not have the necessary strength, either among the *ulama* or within the religious community, to carry the day. The revolutionary programme was eventually extended by the more radical and intellectual leaders of the revolution to include democratic government, and a written constitution adapted from the Belgian model was established.

This, however, did not, and in fact could not quickly change the realities of a weak and traditional society, especially as Iran soon became a battleground for Russia, Britain and Turkey during the First World War. It emerged from that war – to which it was not officially a party – physically, politically and economically devastated, and on the brink of chaos and disintegration. The experience fanned the fires of the Iranian conspiratorial theory of politics which, since 1919, has often reached the scale of social paranoia.[3]

The Iranian conspiratorial theory of politics and government had been an inevitable product of a system of absolute and arbitrary rule where law and politics in the normal senses of the term could not, and in fact did not exist.[4] This was accompanied by a certain degree of xenophobia which – at least in part – was a consequence of frequent invasions of the border provinces and regions, and the occasional conquest of the whole country by her western, northern and eastern neighbours.

These two traditional features of the country's social psychology were heightened in the nineteenth century when Russia and Britain began their systematic intervention and interference in Iranian affairs. They were further strengthened by the Iranian Thermidor of 1911 when, as a result of a Russian ultimatum in which the British government acquiesced, the helpless Iranian government closed the national assembly (Majles) by the use of force, and ordered the expulsion of the conscientious and popular American adviser to the Iranian treasury. However more was to come. The invasion of the country by the warring parties in the First World War, and the disclosure of the Anglo–Russian agreement in 1907, put more ammunition into the cannons of xenophobia and the conspiracy theory. The 1907 agreement had divided Iran into three zones – Russian, British and neutral. Yet the conspiracy view and the fear of foreigners reached new heights with the disclosure of the much more sinister agreement of 1915 between Russia and Britain – known as the Constantinople Protocol – which was a secret accord for the dismemberment of Iran after the allied victory in the war.

Indeed, this disclosure (by the Bolshevik government) was the strongest and most immediate reason behind the great public outcry and agitation against the 1919 agreement between Iran and Britain. According to this agreement, Iran would employ British military and financial advisers, at her own expense, for a basic reform of her public finance, the creation of a uniform army, and the conduct of feasibility studies for the construction of railways and other public transport facilities.[5] The whole project was to be financed by a British loan of £2 million, against Iranian customs revenues, to be paid back at a 7 per cent annual interest over a period of 20 years. This agreement was received by the entire Iranian body politic (except a small group of politicians and journalists) with total indignation and rejection. They were convinced that it was a plot to turn Iran into a British protectorate.[6]

The Agreement was never ratified. The 1921 coup, which presaged its official annulment by the new government, was greeted by the modernist Iranian nationalists and radicals with joy and optimism. Yet it did not take very long before the large majority of politicians, as well as the political public, became convinced that the coup had been planned by the British government, and that its leaders – Reza Khan and Sayyed Ziya – were agents of British imperialism.[7] Ever since then, there has seldom been any significant (major as well as minor) political event, which (at least) a large section of the Iranian public has not believed to have been planned and executed by foreign powers through their Iranian agents.

To forestall misunderstanding it must be emphasised that foreign powers did in fact interfere and intervene in Iranian affairs in the twentieth as in the nineteenth century. I have already referred to a few earlier examples. To mention the other well-known cases, the 1921 coup was helped and organised by a handful of British military officers and diplomats in Iran; the 1933 Oil Agreement was ultimately reached as a result of British pressure; in 1941 Iran was invaded by Britain and the Soviet Union: the Soviet Union was behind the Azerbaijan uprising of 1945–6; and the American and British governments organised the coup d'état of August 1953.

On the other hand, the British government as such was not privy to the 1921 coup; a much better oil agreement could have been reached in 1933 had not Reza Shah been both jealous and suspicious of his able ministers who were in charge of the negotiations with the concessionaries; the invasion of 1941 could have been avoided through better diplomacy, and, in any case, Reza Shah would not have had to abdicate had he based his authority on some social foundation and a reasonable degree of public consent: the 1953 coup could not have been carried out without the collaboration and support of the Shah, conservative politicians and the religious establishment in Iran – besides, it could have been avoided or defeated if the popular government had not made some major mistakes.[8]

Yet, even if we assume that these events took place exactly as the popular theories claim, it would not follow that all the other major and minor events in the country were necessarily a simple product of foreign intrigue and machination. For example, the Qarani plot of 1958 was not a foreign conspiracy even if some foreign powers may have had advance knowledge of it;[9] the economic crisis and political discontent of 1960–3 were not the product of a foreign power; the uprising of June 1963 was neither initiated nor supported by any foreign government; the land reform was of the Iranians' own making, even though America and the Soviet Union may have indirectly encouraged it, and directly welcomed it after the event; the Shah's active role in the oil price increases of the early 1970s was not intended to please the Soviet Union, nor was it played on the orders of western powers, unless they are assumed to have taken leave of their senses. And the revolution of 1977–9 was manned, organised and led by Iranians themselves, even though, when the fall of the regime became apparent, the interested foreign parties began to hedge their bets.[10]

The conspiracy theory of politics and government itself was a product of the traditional system of arbitrary rule in Iran. This system was based on the state monopoly of property rights, and the concentrated – though not necessarily centralised – economic, bureaucratic and military power to which it gave rise. There could be no *rights* of private property, only *privileges* which were granted to individuals by the state, and which, therefore, could be withdrawn at a clap of the hands. There always existed social classes in terms of differences of wealth, position and occupation – landlords, merchants, artisans, peasants etc. However (and unlike European societies) the composition of these classes was changing rapidly over time, because the state could arbitrarily withdraw a privilege from a person, family, clan or community, and grant it to others. Consequently, there could be no established peerage or aristocracy, and there was an unusually high degree of mobility up and down the social ladder.[11] Lest there be any misunderstanding, it should be emphasised that a given Iranian regime, dynasty or ruler might be very different from another in some important respects. For example, rulers might be just, able, weak, generous, miserly, cruel or whatever. But, in all cases, government was based on an arbitrary system. Indeed, this was the most important reason why so much depended on the personal attributes of the ruler himself, and how power, progress and prosperity could be lost within a short period of time.[12]

The absence of law and politics was the institutional counterpart to this sociological base. Where there are no rights there is no law. Or, in other words, where the law is little more than the arbitrary decisions, whims or desires of the lawgiver, the concept of law itself becomes redundant, despite the existence of a body of public rules and regulations at any given moment. It is only dependent rights, not dependent privileges, which can form the basis for real economic and social power of individuals and social classes. Hence, the absence of rights results in the absence of law, and the absence of law must mean the absence of politics. It must be noted that it is not *just* laws and *rational* politics (usually associated with the rise of modern European society in the past few centuries) which are absent, but law and politics themselves – 'just' or unjust, traditional or 'rational'.

European society, whether ancient, medieval or modern, had always been founded upon some kind of written or unwritten law and contract, or deeply entrenched custom. This was very different in Greek city states and modern democracies, in terms of the scope and limits of the power of the state, the extent of its social base and political legitimacy, and the administration of justice as it affected social groups and classes. Yet the power of the state was subject to (varying but) definite limits which were determined by the rights of the social classes. These rights were different – through space as well as time – both among the social classes, and between them and the state. But they always existed, and hence there was always law and politics of one kind or another.[13] Modern European revolutions were not fought for law itself: they were led against existing legal and constitutional arrangements with the aim of extending social rights in scope as well as application.

In Iran, by contrast, the power of the state was not limited by any tacit or explicit law, contract or custom, but by the extent of that power itself. Absence of law did not mean absence of rules of conduct: on the contrary, it meant that the state could arbitrarily make or break 'laws' at will and to the limits of its physical power.

Estebdad literally means arbitrary rule, and where decisions are made arbitrarily, there can be no meaningful notion of law. Hence, while European revolutions had fought for *freedom from the traditional legal framework*, the Constitutional Revolution in Iran was fought for *freedom from arbitrary rule* – that is, for law itself. This incidentally reveals the differences between the concept of freedom in Iran before the Constitutional Revolution and the 'negative' and 'positive' concepts of liberty in Europe, as discussed by Isaiah Berlin: expressed in 'negative' terms, it meant freedom from arbitrary rule; in positive terms, it meant the right to a secure and predictable living guaranteed by an independent and inviolable legal framework.[14]

Therefore, the society was *pre*-legal (or *pre*-constitutional) as well as pre-political. That is how the state (*dawlat*) stood above, as well as opposite to, the people or society (*mellat*). It should be emphasised that while contract and politics exist even in dictatorial systems, they are principally absent in an arbitrary state. Hence, to speak of political processes or relationships in such a state is in fact inaccurate. Towards the end of the nineteenth century, when Iran had come into close contact with modern European societies, the terms *poltik* and *polatki* began to be used for 'politics' and 'political' in reference to *European* political events and entities. *Siyast* and *Siyasat*, which were later invented to denote these terms, had had no such meaning in their original usage.[15]

These sociological and institutional structures and phenomena – which contain an unusually strong element of insecurity and unpredictability – have been the main reasons behind the absence of feudalism (as it is known from European history) in Iranian society. Furthermore, they provided the strongest barriers against the accumulation of financial and (later) physical capital in industry and agriculture alike, for history and experience had shown that money and possessions could easily be lost, not infrequently together with the lives of those who possessed them.

The resulting social psychology and pattern of public behaviour is thus easy to discern. *Dawlat* is, in principle, regarded as the actual or potential enemy by both individuals and social classes, including its own servants. Both the systemic arbitrariness (*estebdad*) and the resulting individual examples of injustice (*zolm*) create an acute sense of fear and insecurity, mistrust, disbelief, frustration, resentment and alienation. There may be loyalty and attachment to one's own family and community, the popular (i.e. non-state) culture, or even the whole of the country, but once a given regime has managed to identify the arbitrary system with itself, it lasts not by consent or by sectional or class loyalty, nor even by otherwise overriding considerations for the defence of the realm, but merely by the dialectics of force and fear. Clearly the continuity of arbitrary rule does not mean that there has been no change in Iranian society since the fall of Adam. Indeed, compared with Europe, Iran has gone through too many changes – a fact which is at least partly due to the basic social features described above.

Furthermore, a characteristic feature of Iranian history is the cycle of arbitrary rule, public rebellion and disorder, followed by arbitrary rule. Since the state monopolised all rights it inevitably monopolised all obligations as well. Contrarily, since society had no rights it did not feel any obligations towards the state. In fact, when it was (rightly or wrongly) thought that the state was about to fall, the public reaction was such that it either helped bring about the collapse when it might otherwise have been averted, or shortened the death agony.

But rebellion was invariably directed against the government in power, not the arbitrary *system* itself, for which no alternative had yet been conceived. Thus, chaos and disorder appears to have been the only alternative to arbitrary rule in Iranian history. Disorder merely served to intensify lawlessness, and increase the state of insecurity and unpredictability. Therefore, before long, society began to yearn for order and discipline, and hoped for the return of another arbitrary ruler.

In the nineteenth century, a real alternative to chaos suggested itself through the window that was opened by European advancement. This, as I said before, was the rule of law. Thus, for the first time in Iranian history, the problematic became that of demolishing arbitrary government rather than just getting rid of an arbitrary ruler or dynasty. This led to the Constitutional Revolution of 1905–9. However the result was still a disorderly and centrifugal situation rather than a constitutional, let alone a democratic system of government. It is true that the invasion and intervention of the warring parties during the First World War played an important role in this, but it can also be shown that the main causes of disorder were indigenous rather than external. While constitutional (or even democratic) government had theoretically been discovered as a working alternative to arbitrary rule, there was no sudden change in the attitude of the public towards the state as an alien and coercive force. This was due mainly to the fact that the institutions of a civil, let alone democratic, government were almost entirely lacking.[16]

That is why when Reza Khan Pahlavi took over the realm, he was at first supported by a substantial section of the body politic. Yet, when he fell 20 years later, in 1941, his departure was greeted with unmitigated joy and approval by the vast majority of the people of all social classes, for by then his regime had changed from mere dictatorship to arbitrary government.

Between 1941 and 1953 there was a disorderly constitutional regime. The 1953 coup d'état brought a dictatorial government to power which was supported by landlords and the religious establishment. It was not an arbitrary regime, although gradually power began to concentrate. From 1960, because of serious economic difficulties and because of the decline in foreign support, there was a power struggle for constitutional government which ended in the riots of June 1963. This led to the concentration of power and the re-emergence of arbitrary rule in the 1960s and 1970s, which was greatly helped by sustained, rapid and eventually explosive growth of oil revenues which the state freely received and arbitrarily disbursed.[17] The relaxation of arbitrary rule in 1977 rapidly resulted in rebellion and disorder which ended in the revolution of February 1979. Once again the urban (and urbanised) society had rejected the claim of an arbitrary government that it intended to reform itself, and combined to bring down the state.[18]

The purpose of this rapid and rather sweeping brief about the character of state and society, and the logic and sociology of Iranian revolutions, is to pinpoint the dichotomy of arbitrary rule on the one hand, and chaos and disorder on the other, which would never have allowed sustained and cumulative political development, let alone the emergence of democratic institutions and government.

What followed the revolution of 1979 was familiar from other popular revolutions elsewhere in the world. In the French revolution, the period of argument, oratory and solidarity rapidly gave way to wholesale expropriation and indiscriminate killing, followed by the reign of terror – or *despotisme de la liberté* – in which many of the revolutionary leaders themselves, both Girondist and Jacobin, perished in the name of the very principles for which they had fought, a process which was helped and intensified by domestic strife and foreign intervention. In the aftermath of the October Revolution in Russia, similar events took place during the civil war and the war of foreign intervention, when not only liberals, but even Mensheviks and Social Revolutionaries ceased to exist as independent political parties.

One could scarcely have expected a significantly different outcome from the revolution in Iran, which in some important ways was less developed politically than the France of the late eighteenth, and the Russia of the early twentieth century. Almost all the dominant revolutionary forces and ideologies were absolutely certain of their own way, and the incorrectness or evil intent of the others, and convinced that they would be able to create the perfect society within a short period of time, once they had managed to eliminate all of their rivals. There was violence and terror, war and destruction, the mass exodus of some of the educated and skilled groups of the society, decline and dislocation of the average standard of living.

Yet it was not all in vain, for some highly important lessons were also learnt, which, if they are put into practice by all the major political tendencies, could result in lasting political development. It became clear that no individual, social class, party or ideology could resurrect the lost paradise anywhere in the world, let alone in a country where some basic rights and freedoms had not existed before; that even less ambitious, but still very important social and political achievements would not be possible by means of generalised (physical or verbal) violence based upon bitterness, hatred, rift and confrontation.

It also became clear that economic progress and social welfare are constrained by the country's economic, political and cultural resources and capacities; that while these resources could be put to efficient use for greater progress and prosperity, there was no magic formula or extraordinary act of will – through the ideologies of *étatisme*, the free market or any other – which would perform miracles in the field of economic growth and justice; and that productive performance is a much better indicator of economic progress than the level of consumption, especially if this is not wholly earned by the society's productive effort.

Indeed, it is becoming increasingly clear that political legitimacy and government by consent is not consistent with arbitrary rule, whether exercised by a central authority, or through a mob let loose in the streets, and that lawlessness – whether practised by the state, the mob or society at large – is bound to hurt all of the parties concerned in the long run; that while the existence of basic rights and freedoms, and of political tolerance and cultural pluralism, is one of the main pillars on which the democratic edifice stands, democracy is not a weak and ineffectual system of government; that unlimited freedom does not and cannot exist anywhere in the world; that democracy would not have succeeded as the most advanced as well as efficient system of government if democratic societies did not exercise their rights and freedoms with a mature sense of social cohesion and public responsibility; and that dictatorship is not only less developed, but also usually weaker and less efficient than democracy.

In the development of events a certain degree of realism in dealing with local and global issues had slowly begun to impose itself through rising politico-economic constraints, and decreasing revolutionary passion and resilience. This was strengthened by the cessation of the long hostilities between Iraq and Iran, and the death not long afterwards of Ayatollah Khomeini. The Iraq–Iran war could have been ended sooner by Iran with greater advantage to herself. However, overdue as it was, the ceasefire tended to diffuse the domestic and foreign situation to a significant extent, although a lasting settlement of the differences with Iraq is yet to be reached. Furthermore, and within a broader context, Iran's decision to remain neutral in the international conflict over Iraq's occupation of Kuwait was in line with previous developments.

From the political standpoint, the impact of Khomeini's demise was greater even than the ceasefire with Iraq, because it effectively ended the dynamic era of the Islamic revolution. Khomeini was a highly charismatic leader who had created and established his own personal legitimacy over and above both constitutional and institutional frameworks. Therefore, there could not be – and in fact there was not – a complete replacement for him from the ranks of the remaining religio-political dignitaries as a self-dependent and self-legitimising leader of both the state and society – both *dawlat* and *mellat* – and the personification of ultimate religious and political authority. In other words, there could no longer be *velayat-e faqih* as it had been theoretically conceived and actually practised by Khomeini himself. Ayatollah Khamenehi who succeeded him was in fact chosen by the standing constituent assembly, known as the Assembly of Experts: he did not carry the title of Imam, and was not regularly described as Vali-ye Faqih, but as Leader of the Revolution.[19]

Indeed, he tended to present the consensus opinion, over important matters, of the various Islamist factions, among which the leading collectivity of Islamist religious dignitaries carry the greater weight. A recent example (January 1995) was the disagreement on the position of the *Marja' al-Taqlid*, after the death of one *Marja'* Ayatollah Araky. Putting aside those of the *ulama* who reject the concept of *velayat-e faqih*, there were several opinions which – ignoring the minor differences among them – could be reduced to two alternative viewpoints. According to one of these – of whom the chief advocate and spokesman was Ayatollah Mohammad Yazdi – Khamenehi should have been recognised as the sole *Marja'*. This view was consistent with Khomeini's conception of *velayat-e faqih*, although – in practice – it had not been explicitly enforced during the latter's own *velayat*. The alternative view, espoused by several of the important Islamist *ulama*, was more in line with traditional theory and practice: the *Maraje'* usually emerged through consensus and adherence, as opposed to selection by the state or by a spiritual college, and there was usually more than one *Marja'* serving the Shi'a community. In the end, Khamenehi announced that he did not wish to be the sole *Marja'*, and that he merely regarded himself as the sole *political Marja'* for the Shi'a community outside Iran. This was consistent with the long tradition of Iranian heads of state being regarded as protectors of Shi'a communities in other countries.

Apart from the ceasefire with Iraq, and the disappearance of Khomeini's supra-constitutional power and authority, there were other important factors which concurrently helped reduce the high degree of revolutionary self-confidence, coercion and intolerance, and encourage a somewhat greater degree of realism in the formulation of both internal and external policies. The most important of these were the systematic collapse of oil prices since the mid-1980s; the breakdown of the Soviet Union as a superpower, quickly followed by its disintegration into a number of independent states; and the (partly related) worldwide decline in totalitarian beliefs and centralist state policies.

The financial burden and destructive effects of the war with Iraq, the considerable decline in gross as well as net investment, the rationing of subsidised consumption goods, the persistently high population growth, and the steady decline in per capita income and welfare – all in the face of rapidly declining oil prices and revenues, and increasing difficulties of obtaining foreign credit – necessitated the use of more practical economic and social policies. The extreme forms of *étatiste* economic and social policies were set aside, some state industries were privatised, and public subsidies of consumer goods and services were reduced in scope, amount and application.

Drastic changes in the regional and international situation made their independent impact on political developments in Iran. The disappearance of the Soviet Union as a superpower removed a countervailing power to the United States (and the Western alliance) which the Islamic Republic had used in defending its foreign and domestic policies. And although some such lever continued to be exercised through relatively better relationships with Germany, Japan, France and Italy, it was not comparable to what it had been before. In the same vein, the worldwide campaign for greater human rights and more personal and cultural freedoms was – in addition to the other factors mentioned above – influential in making the Iranian press relatively more independent, and those books and articles which were not regarded as being either offensive to Islam or dangerous to the regime, easier to publish.

No organised opposition of any sort (including peaceful opposition) outside the Islamist framework was, however, tolerated. The formation of political parties and professional associations independently from the state was not permitted. A recent example was an attempt by a group of more than 130 writers to set up a writers' association. This was given a hostile reception by the official press, and it was by no means clear that the writers would be able to proceed with their declared objective of forming a professional body within a legal framework.

The issue goes beyond the strict problem of organising political, social and professional parties and associations independently from the state. It reflects the exclusion of large sections and groups of society which represent (mainly, though not exclusively) the modern middle classes. They thus regard themselves as being dispossessed even of political and social liberties which are theoretically guaranteed under the Islamic constitution itself. Therefore, a real sense of alienation from the regime and the state is felt by social classes which are not only quantitatively effective and influential in the economic, social, cultural and educational sectors. It is difficult to envisage significant political progress so long as such important social groups are excluded from normal participation in social and political processes.

A general discourse on the problems of political development in Iran would be incomplete without a brief discussion of the country's ethnic and linguistic plurality and multiplicity, and the socio-political problems to which they have given rise (mainly) in the twentieth century. The subject has been made even more relevant – and perhaps urgent – as a result of the disintegration of the Soviet Union into independent states, some of which have had long associations with Iran in the past, and contain large numbers of citizens whose mother tongues are close relatives of modern Persian.

Iran is a plateau and a cultural region which makes up a number of independent countries including that which is known by this name. This cultural region was not always ruled by a unified state or empire. And when it was, it was not always governed by the people of the Iranian hinterland: it was ruled for almost two centuries by the Alexandrian Greeks known as the Seleucids; for more than two centuries by Muslim Arabs; and for several centuries afterwards by various native as well as Turkic and Mongol states and empires – some of which ruled at the same time in different parts of the region – before it was reunited by the Safavids not long after the fall of Constantinople to the Ottoman Turks, and at about the same time as the discovery of America at the close of the European Middle Ages. It was disunited once again for much of the eighteenth century, and both then and later in the nineteenth century lost territory to foreign or foreign-supported powers, until its present borders were established in the latter half of the nineteenth century.

It was inhabited (and is still inhabited) by ethnic, linguistic and racial groups and communities, which themselves were subdivided along regional, linguistic or nomadic tribal lines. For example, not only do the Persian-speaking people of the Khorasan, Kerman, Fars, Isfahan, Tehran and the Caspian provinces have different accents or speak a dialect which is not understood by the others, but they have (and often take pride in) their own specific provincial identities, ranging from poetical genres and styles to local cuisines. Furthermore, the typical Isfahani's character is clearly distinct from the typical Shirazi's, despite the fact that both of these cities belong to the heartland of ancient Persia. This being true of the Persian speakers among themselves, it is even more true between Persian speakers, Kurds, the Baluch, various Turkic-speaking communities, and so on.

Yet, as I said before, Iran is both geographically and historically a region which contains parts, or the whole of a number of countries. The group of Iranian languages – of which New Persian is the most widespread – includes many living and dead languages and vernaculars, ranging from the ancient Avestan, Soghdian, Khotani, Parthian and Pahlavi, to the classical and modern Dari, Tajiki, Persian, Kurdish and Lari. These languages are more or less closely related to each other, and make up a family in the network of the Indo-European languages. Apart from Dari and Tajiki (which, as it happens, are spoken outside present-day Iran), none of these other Iranian languages and vernaculars can be comprehended by modern Persian speakers. It is perhaps worth emphasising this point: modern Persian speakers understand Dari and Tajiki which are spoken outside of present-day Iran, but do not understand Kurdish and Lari, both of which are also Iranian languages and are spoken within the country's borders; they do not even understand the dialects of their own language which are spoken in the Caspian provinces.

I therefore propose a distinction between Iranianism in general, and Persianism in particular, although, as I have already suggested, even Persianism does not refer to a monolithic tradition – hence the uniformities and diversities of the broader Iranian culture, to which all the peoples of the Iranian region have made important contributions. Dari, Tajiki and Persian grew out of the Iranian languages which were no longer spoken, and they have been strongly influenced by classical Arabic and – to a lesser extent – old Mongolian and various Turkish dialects, all of which are non-Iranian languages. The Safavid Turkomans who reunited Iran under its ancient name for the first time since the Arab conquest, and rejuvenated the Iranian culture in a vast empire, nevertheless spoke a Turkic dialect at their court. There seemed to be no conflict between the uniformities of the looser and broader Iranian culture, and the multiplicity of its ethnic and linguistic parts.

Massive evidence for this broader Iranianism – which remained alive even during centuries of political disunity, mainly through the media of the Persian language and literature – is provided, not only by great chronicles and literary anthologies and works of criticism ranging from Bal'ami's *Tarikh*, Bayhaqi's *Tarikh*, Nezam al-Molk's *Siyasatnameh*, Nezami 'Aruzi's *Chahar Maqaleh* and Kaykavus ibn Eskandar's *Qabusnameh*, through Juvayni's *Tarikh-e Jahangosha* and Rashid al-Din Fazlollah's *Jame' al-Tavorikh* to Eskandar Monshi's *Tarikh-e 'Alam-ara*, Esterabadi's *Dorreh-ye Nadereh* and Lesan al-Molk's *Nasekh al-Tavarikh*, but even by classical Persian literature in the narrower sense. Here I shall give only two examples of what may take volumes to document comprehensively.

The great twelfth-century Persian poet Khaqani – who is especially well known for his odes which rival Beethoven's symphonies in their Olympian thunder – was a native of Shirvan, in the Caucasus, from a Christian (probably Armenian) mother, to whom he was exceptionally attached. When he received the news of the sacking of Outer Khorasan, which was then a part of the eastern Seljuk empire and was about as far away from his native land as central Europe, he wrote two long and mighty *qasidehs* mourning that catastrophe. The poems are in the form of elegies for Imam Mohammad-e Yahya, the religious leader whom the invaders had put to death by pouring dust into his mouth. He says in one of the poems: 'The heavens watched his mouth being filled with dust; although they know that dust is not worthy of his mouth.' And this is the *matla'* of the other poem: 'That civilised kingdom which you saw was destroyed; that sea of chivalry which you heard of became a mirage.'

My second example is from Sa'di, the thirteenth-century poet and so much besides, who, I presume, needs no introduction. He wrote in his *Golestan* that when he visited Kashgar, the Khwarezmian city in central Asia, he met in the college (*jame'*) a youthful scholar who was reading Zamakhshari's classic introduction to Arabic grammar. He quoted a short Arabic poem to the boy and was told that he should translate it into Persian so he would understand its meaning. When he told the boy he came from Shiraz, the boy asked him to quote something from Sa'di. Next day, when he was leaving the city, the boy learned that he was Sa'di himself, and there followed a moving farewell scene.

I have not seen any evidence in the vast expanses of the Persian prose and poetry that any of the peoples of this extensive land had ever thought of themselves as being inherently superior or inferior to any other on account of their ethnic and linguistic origins until we arrive at the twentieth century. Indeed, since the formation of the Ghaznavid state in the tenth century until the fall of the Qajars at the beginning of the twentieth, most parts of the Iranian cultural region were ruled by Turkic-speaking dynasties most of the time. At the same time, the official language was Persian, the court literature was in Persian, and most of the chancellors, ministers and mandarins were Persian speakers of the highest learning and ability. To demonstrate this point, it should be sufficient just to mention the names of Maimandi, Baihaqi, Nezam al-Molk, Nasir al-Din Tusi, the brothers Shams al-Din and 'Ata Malek Jovaini, Rashid al-Din Fazlollah, Eskandar Monshi, Mahdi Esterabadi, the two Qa'emmaqams, Amir Nezam (Amir Kabir) and the two Mostawfi al-Mamaleks – starting with the Ghaznavids and ending with the Qajars.

Turkic (or Mongolian) was the language of the rulers most of the time when Persian was the language of literature and of formal administration. But this did not convey any sense of inherent superiority or inferiority to any of these or other communities within the region. In the Indian subcontinent, which is another vast cultural region of Asia, Persian was the court and literary language of the so-called Mughal empire, and to know the Persian language and its literature in that subcontinent is still a prestigious cultural and intellectual achievement. To elaborate the point, India is a distinct as well as distinguished cultural region in its own right, yet its people did not, and do not, feel a sense of oppression or inferiority because of the exceptional status of Persian in their culture as a foreign language. Moreover, many more languages, vernaculars, religions and ethnic groups may be found in the Indian subcontinent than in the Iranian cultural region.

As mentioned above, conflicts over race, language and ethnicity in Iran are almost as new as the twentieth century itself, although their roots lie in the latter half of the nineteenth century, when Iran began to look at Europe through its own window, and look at herself through what she perceived to be the window of Europe. That was how a localised version of the modern ideology of romantic nationalism first made an impact on the psyche of a small group of modern Iranian intellectuals, and – after the Constitutional Revolution – spread widely as well as deeply among modernised Iranians, until it became the official creed of the Pahlavi state, from the 1930s until its downfall in 1979.

I have explained this process, its causes and its consequences elsewhere and the present limitations of space forbid but the barest allusions to them.[20] It had something to do with the economic backwardness and military weakness against the might of industry and empire in Europe; something to do with a sense of inferiority about the present, and a sense of superiority about the past; something to do with the contemporary power, success and prestige of Europe, and the decline, weakness and underdevelopment of Arabs and Turks who had conquered and ruled Iran in the past; something to do with the contemporary European theory and practice of nationalism, Aryanism and racism – with Gobineau, (Stewart) Chamberlain, and the Kaiser as well as Mussolini, Hitler, Rosenberg and Goebbels; something to do with intellectuals such as Akhundzadeh, Mirza Agha Khan Kermani, 'Aref, Farrokhi, Purdavud, Eshqi, Hedayat, Behruz and Shafaq; and something to do with public personages such as Dabir A'zam, Taimurtash, Generals Shaibani, Amir-Ahmadi and Yazdanpanah, Reza Shah and Mohammad Reza Shah.

The outcome was not just patriotism nor even the release of broader pan-Iranian feelings and energies alone. It was an eruption of deep pan-Persianist emotions which spread across the powerful, modern, educated community of Persian speakers and (many) non-Persian speakers alike, and was later sanctified as the state ideology. The country's history was rewritten to suit the Aryanist/Persianist theory, and state education and propaganda created public amnesia among the younger generations about much of Iranian culture as it had been known by their fathers and grandfathers. Arabs and Turks were blamed for Iran's backwardness, and were described as being inherently backward, unintelligent, aggressive and uncivilised. There was a terrible onslaught, not just on nomadic brigandage and outlawry, but on nomadic life and culture itself.

The provinces were remapped from their existing natural borders, and for some time were identified only by the numbers that were officially given to them – a policy that was intended to play down, as much as possible, the identification of particular ethnic and linguistic groups with a single province. The existence of Arabic-speaking communities in the country's southwest was all but denied. Azerbaijani and other Turkic dialects were forbidden to be printed or otherwise published and publicised in writing. The Kurdish language was officially described as a dialect of Persian. That, too, was forbidden to be printed and published. The provincial governors, military commanders and administrators were mostly selected from Persian speakers or Persianised non-Persian speakers, many of whom, even in the lower ranks, were sent directly from Tehran itself. There was general discrimination against all the provinces in the interest of Tehran, and in favour of Persian-speaking provinces in comparison with the others.

The policy that was supposed to safeguard the unity and integrity of Iran thus created deep divisions, frustrations and resentments across the country. It did not achieve much for Persian language and literature, yet it encouraged the non-Persian speakers – for the first time in history – to begin to regard themselves as subjects of discrimination, oppression and persecution. It served little the true interests of Persian language and culture, but it dealt a blow to the broader sense of Iranianism which had always existed, and for which the Persian language and literature had provided the oldest, strongest and most widespread channels. As a result, when the lid was taken off, once in 1941 and the second time in 1979, the centrifugal nomadic, linguistic, ethnic and provincial forces burst into the open and threatened the unity and integrity of a culture that had even managed to survive foreign invasions, conquests and rule throughout the millennia.

It follows that the interests, both of Persian language and literature, and of Iran and the broader Iranian culture, are consistent and complementary with each other, and are threatened, not by each other, but by the ahistorical racist and pan-Persianist theories and practices which swept over and controlled the land for 65 years. This was bound to encourage similar reactions by the non-Persian speaking Iranian communities, and so threaten the integrity of Iran and the solidarity of the broader Iranian culture. In other words, the reaction to this ahistorical pan-Persianism was itself greatly influenced by it. It was manifested in equally ahistorical pan-ethnicisms, the emotional rejection of the Persian language and literature, and the denial altogether of the broader Iranian culture and traditions.

If both these attitudes manage to grow strong roots, they could result in the breakup of the country, and this, in turn, would result in the cultural impoverishment, economic decline and political weakness of both Persian and other ethnic communities in Iran. It would also lead to the emergence of a number of small and oppressive states along ethnic or linguistic lines, fanning the fires of a historically and geographically alien concept of nationalism, getting into conflict and hostility with each other, losing the economic benefits of a larger and unified home market, and becoming weaker vis-à-vis greater local and global powers. Thus, political development in Iran would be incomplete without greater cultural as well as administrative democratisation, such that there would be no conflict between Iran's broader uniformity and integrity, and the development of her ethnic, linguistic and provincial parts. The use and development of the other languages and dialects would not damage Persian language and literature. Likewise, the use of Persian as the global Iranian language would not in the least hinder the other languages, while it would act both as a strong unifying factor, and a necessary medium for economic, administrative and social efficiency, as is done in India by the English language, even though English is a completely foreign, non-Indian and non-Asian language which was taken there as the language of the British Empire. Finally, Persian literature is a historical achievement of human civilisation, in which civilised humanity has taken pleasure and pride, and to which non-Persian-speaking communities of Iran have contributed down to the present time. What could they possibly gain by throwing away this unique prize, the greatest single achievement of the whole of Iranian culture?

Given the strict administrative centralism and the prevailing attitudes and policies towards the provinces and ethnic and linguistic minorities under the former regime, a considerable degree of conflict and strife was all but inevitable in the post-revolution period. The abdication of Reza Shah in the 1940s had been followed by unrest and rebellion in the provinces of Azerbaijan and Kurdistan, and among the nomadic tribes (notably the Qashqa'i confederation, the Khamseh federation, and – briefly at one stage – the Bakhtiyaris) in the south and southwest. It had taken more than 20 years for these revolts to be completely stamped out. The sense of grievance and alienation had, however, persisted beneath the apparent calm, and the revolution of 1979 once again brought them to the surface.

Immediately after the revolution conflict broke out in the Gorgan province which includes a large minority of Turkoman descent. However the main confrontation came in the Kurdistan province where a number of Kurdish organisations – of which the Iranian Kurdish Democratic party was the most powerful – demanded home rule. In the following years there was a certain amount of unrest among the Baluchi community in the southeastern provinces of Sistan and Kermam.

The Islamic Republic's response to these armed conflicts was swift as well as heavy-handed. On the other hand, it tended to pursue relatively less centralistic and more redistributive policies towards the provinces, and afforded a certain degree of latitude to ethnic and linguistic minorities for cultural self-development, including the publication of books and journals in the non-Persian languages and dialects. Such policies have tended to contain the extent and intensity of ethnic unrest, but a long-term solution would require a more fundamental strategy to ensure greater participation of the provinces and ethnic groups in local and regional affairs, within a firmly established framework of national unity and territorial integrity.

To sum up, the fundamental historical barrier to steady political development in Iran has been the repetitive cycle of arbitrary rule and public rebellion and disorder followed by arbitrary rule, which has been a product of the absence of law, and the lack of social legitimacy for the state. Therefore, political development would require the rejection of physical and verbal violence and intolerance by the state as well as by all other political trends and tendencies, and the repudiation of the conspiracy theory of politics in addition to the morbid fear and suspicion of foreigners. It would also require the rejection of pan-Persianist and other pan-ethnicist and racist ideologies, greater ethnic and provincial participation in local and regional affairs, the recognition of the uniformity and integrity of Iran as a whole, the toleration of the use and development of the non-Persian languages, and the confirmation of the Persian language as a highly efficient socio-economic as well as cultural medium for the country at large.

Moreover, the most important requirement, perhaps, for political development would be the extension of basic rights and freedoms to those social and professional groups – and especially the modern middle classes – which are, in practice, excluded from the social and political processes, and can (at best) present critical or alternative views as individuals, by writing books and articles which have a limited circulation. Furthermore, neither political freedom nor public discipline and social responsibility is likely to be established in the absence of social and political institutions, including political parties and professional associations. Political *change* would still occur as it did in the past, but steady political *development* would require a considerable extension of political rights and freedoms by the state, and a corresponding degree of public responsibility by society.

Notes

1 This is a revised version of the text of the public lecture delivered on 2 February 1994, in Berlin, at the joint invitation of Berliner Institut für vergleichende Sozialforschung and Haus der Kulturen der Welt.

2 See further, Homa Katouzian, *The Political Economy of Modern Iran* (London: Macmillan, and New York: New York University Press, 1981), Chapter 4.

3 See further, *The Political Economy of Modern Iran*, Chapters 5 and 6; and Homa Katouzian, *Musaddiq and the Struggle for Power in Iran* (London and New York: I.B. Tauris, 1991), Chapter 2.

4 See further, below.

5 The text of the 1919 Agreement has been published in a number of English and Persian sources, the oldest being J.M. Balfour, *Recent Happenings in Persia* (London and Edinburgh: Blackwood and Son,1922).

6 For the contemporary reaction to the 1919 Agreement see, for example, 'Ebtal al-batel' [Refutation of the falsehood] in Abdollah Mostawfi, *Sharh-e Zendegani-ye Man*. vol. 3 (Tehran: Zavvar, 1360 [1981]); Yahya Dawlatabadi, *Hayat-e Yahya*, vol. 4 (Tehran: Attar and Ferdaws, 1371 [1992]); Sayf-e Azad (ed.), *Divan-e Abolqasem 'Aref* (Tehran: Sayf-e Azad, 1327 [1948]); 'Ali Akbar Moshlr-Salimi (ed.), *Kolliyat-e Mosavvar-e 'Eshqi* (Tehran: Amir Kabir, n.d.); Hosain Makki (ed.), Divan-e *Farrokhi* (Tehran: Amir Kabir, 1366 [1987]). This view has persisted throughout the twentieth century. See, for example, Homa Katouzian (ed.) *Musaddiq's Memoirs* (London: Jebheh, 1988), Book 1.

7 For contemporary descriptions and interpretations of the 1921 coup see Mostawfi, *Sharh-e Zendegani-ye Man*. vol. 3; Dawlatabadi, *Hayat-e Yahya*, vol. 4; Poet-Laureate Bahar, *Tarikh-e Mokhtasar-e Ahzab-e Siyasi*, vol. I (Tehran: Amir Kabir, 1373 [1944]); Eshqi, *Kolliyat*; and 'Aref, *Divan*. See further, Homa Katouzian, *The Coup d'état of 1921 in Iran*, forthcoming.

8 For a discussion and documentation of all of the above points see Homa Katouzian, *Estebdad, Demokrasi va Nehzat-e Melli* (London and Washington: Mehregan, 1993, and Tehran: Nashr-e Markaz, 1994); *Musaddiq and the Struggle for Power in Iran: The Political Economy of Modern Iran*; and *The 1921 Coup d'état in Iran*.

9 See Homa Katouzian, *Khatarat-e Siyasl-ye Khalil Maleki*, Introduction, Chapter 2, second edition (Tehran: Sherkat-e Enteshar, 1368 [1989]), and *Musaddiq and the Struggle for Power in Iran*, Chapter 15.

10 For a discussion and documentation of the above points see Homa Katouzian, 'Oil and economic development in the Middle East' in Georges Sabagh (ed.), *The Modern Economic History of the Middle East in its World Context* (Cambridge: Cambridge University Press, 1989); 'The political economy of oil-exporting countries', *Peuples mediterranéens* (1979); 'Die politische Ökonomie der Ölexportierenden Länder; ein analytisches Modell', in K. Greussing and J.-H. Grevemeyer (eds), *Revolution in Iran and Afghanistan* (Frankfurt: Syndicat, 1980); *Musaddiq and the Struggle for Power in Iran*, Chapter 17; and *The Political Economy of Modern Iran*, Chapters 17–18.

11 See further, H. Katouzian, 'The Aridisolatic society: a model of long term social and economic development in Iran', *International Journal of Middle East Studies* (July 1983); 'Ein Modell einer langerfristigen Entwicklung in Iran', *Peripherie* (December 1980); *The Political Economy of Modern Iran*, Chapters 2 and 15.

12 See further, H. Katouzian, *Eqtesad-e Siyasi-ye Iran*, author's introduction to the second edition of the Persian translation (Tehran: Nashr-e Markaz, 1372 [1993]).

13 See further, Homa Katouzian, 'The execution of Amir Hasanak the Vazir', Pembroke Papers (1993).

14 See further, *The Political Economy of Modern Iran,* Chapter 4

15 See further, Homa Katouzian, 'Nameh-resani va Maquleh-ye Siyasat', *Adineh* (September 1372 [1993]), reprinted in *Chahardah Maqaleh dar Adabiyat, Ejtema' Falsafeh va Eqtesad* [Fourteen Lectures on Literature, Society, Philosophy and Economics], (Tehran: Nashr-e Markaz, 1995).

16 See further, Homa Katouzian, 'Demokrasi, diktatori, va mas'uliyat-e mellat', *Ettela'at-e Siyasi Eqtesadi*, 67–8 (April–May 1993).

17 See further, Homa Katouzian, 'The Aridisolatic society'; 'The political economy of oil exporting countries'; and *The Political Economy of Modern Iran*, Chapter 17.

18 See further, *The Political Economy of Modern Iran*, Chapters 17 and 18; and 'The Aridisolatic society'.

19 See further, Homa Katouzian, 'Islamic government and politics: The practice and theory of the guardianship of jurisconsult' in Charles Davies (ed.) *After the War: Iran, Iraq and the Arab Gulf* (London: Croom Helms, 1990).

20 See Homa Katouzian, *Sadeq Hedayat: The Life and Literature of an Iranian Writer* (London and New York: I.B. Tauris, 1991), especially Chapters 1 and 5; 'Nationalist trends in Iran: 1921–6', *International Journal of Middle East Studies* (1979); *Musaddiq and the Struggle for Power in Iran*, Chapters 2–4; *The Political Economy of Modern Iran*, Chapters 5–7; and *Khaterat-e Siyasi-ye Khalil Maleki*, Introduction.

2 Iran and modern media in the age of globalization

Ali Mohammadi

The dynamics of the 1990s were very different from those of the preceding decades, driven as they were by technological change in the modes of message delivery, specifically satellite and cable systems, and by global media deregulation. Today market forces and profit are the name of the game, rather than national development and political unity. In many ways, the rapidly changing media environment of the 1990s looked set to alter non-Western cultures more radically that ever before, but I think the kinds and directions of change are complex and contradictory. In this chapter the focus is on the issue of satellite television in Iran in the context of cultural and broadcasting policy.

The evolution of the existing organizational structure of broadcasting can not be separated from the various internal struggles for control of the revolution in the past two decades. The rise and the fall of Ghotbzadeh (the first director-general of National Iranian Radio Television), Bani Sadr (the first president of the Islamic Republic) and Bazargan (the first prime minister) can all be related in different ways to crises within and uses of the mass media. Some attempted to manipulate the media to gain popularity while lacking grass-roots support, while others concentrated on gaining grass-roots support at the expense of not controlling a major ideology-defining institution. It is not necessary here to analyse the early political struggles of the revolution, but only to note that the current shape of communications organizations and policy has evolved over these tumultuous few years and is still fluid and subject to alteration. We should remember that the revolution occurred within a specific set of possibilities and many conditions are carried over from the old regime; thus – revolutionary rhetoric to the contrary – post-revolutionary periods are likely to be as fraught with contradictions and tensions as pre-revolutionary conditions were, and the new regimes have their work cut out to institutionalize themselves, and to establish coercive forces as well as to develop new persuasive organizations. Gramsci suggested that all states require both coercive and ideological forces to maintain themselves; modern states clearly possess a variety of ideological institutions, including education and the mass media, with which to develop hegemonic control.

But in the Iranian context the notion of 'hegemony' should not be seen as a fixed and given situation but as a process, as work that the political system has continually to undertake in order to maintain itself. If a system is to survive, it must not only dominate but also lead, and the intellectual 'work' involves changing policies and discourses, appropriating ideas from popular movements, shifting positions and synthesizing ideological positions as necessary, in order to provide a dynamic and multilayered analysis of how the Islamic Republic has attempted over the past 20 years to develop a hegemonic Islamic culture, and the resistances to that prior to evaluating the current structure and management of radio-television (RTV) as the shape of the new communications policy. It is important to conduct an overview of the achievement and the failure of broadcasting policymakers after Ghotbzadeh in the context of Islamicization. In this chapter I would also like to examine the encounter between Islam and the modern media and the dilemmas of developing an Islamic television.

The major ideological concern of the Islamic Republic since the revolution has been the Islamicization of Iranian culture and media systems. I will review the process of Islamicization of the broadcasting media by looking at the organization of Voice and Vision of the Islamic Republic (VVIR), the Guidance Council codes for Islamic television production, and the weekly programme schedule of television since the new management took over from Hashemi. I will explore the prevailing set of symbols and images through which Islamicization is represented, and examine some particular problem areas such as the representation of women and the playing of music. I will also describe, based on my frequent visits, some countercultural tendencies increasingly visible in Iran since satellite dish piracy, particularly after the law banning satellite dishes came into effect.

Iranian broadcasting leadership since the revolution

One of the organizations that was crucial to Khomeini's regime was National Iranian Radio Television (NIRT), since it was very modern and rational in its policy-making and in its institutionalization of cultural organization. It was very efficient in production and progressive in cultural identity despite all the political and royal pressure from the court. One of the first and maybe the most crucial and critical decisions Ayatollah Khomeini made was to find a position for Ghotbzadeh, a long-shot political activist and supporter of Khomeini's opposition to the Shah's development projects.

Ayatollah Khomeini assigned Ghotbzadeh to be in charge of the NIRT. Ghotbzadeh was overjoyed and excited by this new authority. As the first director-general of its most modern and advanced organization, Ghotbzadeh's record of success and failure for the *velayat-e faghih* (supreme jurisprudence) regime that Khomeini had in mind can be briefly summarized as follows:

- In the style of a Mughal invasion he ordered the eradication and destruction of any sign or symbol of monarchism within the organization and froze programmes in production and development.
- He purged and cleansed NIRT's highly qualified and professional personnel in order to bring in his friends and to open space for the clergy.
- He closed some of the offices of NIRT and dismantled various research and

cultural projects which were fundamental to production and to RTV programmes in general.
- He ordered the destruction of files, records, documents and books of various kinds, finally eliminating any record that had the name of the previous regime on it.

The whole process shattered the professional pride and moral integrity of NIRT personnel. The bulldozer-style destruction had the following consequences:

- Contrary to Ayatollah Khomeini's recommendation – he substituted his imaginary *velayat-e faghih* for royal symbols which supposedly prevailed at NIRT. He consolidated his position and personal ambition by using NIRT organization and personnel to support his candidacy for election as the first president of the Republic.
- He employed all of his efforts to keep RTV in the hands of secular forces.
- He used NIRT to legitimize all forces of revolution by giving them equal prime-time access for debate about the future of the Republic.
- He created obstacles and excuses for not allowing religious groups, even Ayatollah Khomeini himself, to manipulate NIRT.
- He used prime-time television for the showing of hostages and gradually disarmed the forces of liberal democracy in the eyes of the masses.

Due to the growing tension between the US and Iran on the hostage issue, Ghotbzadeh left NIRT to be Minister of Foreign Affairs, in order to solve the issue. NIRT was without a director-general for some time. It should be noted that the damage to the infrastructure of NIRT and to the process of programme-making is incalculable and beyond the scope of this chapter. The very foundations of the organization, including the well-researched development plan put in place by founder-director Reza Ghotbi in the early 1970s, were smashed to pieces. Today, over two decades since the revolution, the renamed VVIR (Voice and Vision of the Islamic Republic) has once again been renamed to IRIB (Islamic Republic of Iran Broadcasting) and is now suffering from lack of 'know-how' and the ingredients of programme-making, and furthermore the basic lack of vision of national culture in the context of the globalized world.

After this period of crisis, then, NIRT had no leadership. I would call this a transitional process because the imaginary *velayat-e faghih* regime had no specific chapter on how to run a modern media system, and even in the various books of conduct of the Ayatollah Khomeini's code of practice there was no chapter on media and the media ethic in modern times.

In this so-called transitional period, the caretaker of television's day-to-day affairs was Ali Larijany, son-in-law of the late Ayatollah Mottahary, the trustee of Ayatollah Khomeini. Saeed Rajaie Khorasani became the caretaker of radio because he was a former student of Mottahary. These two temporary caretakers established an Islamic Committee for RTV personnel: Anjoman Islami Karkonan Radio and Television. The committee operated as follows:

1 They started to crush professional resistance to changing the content of radio and television programmes by adopting a policy of drastic reduction of the RTV budget, not only to get rid of the highly qualified and respected professional producers and writers, but also to avoid a likely strike by NIRT personnel. They also plotted to employ various means of deception in order to bring down the solid infrastructure of elite cultural production in NIRT.
2 This drastic and cruel purge achieved two objectives: first, the de-professionalization of the foremost modern organization in Iran and second, paving the way for new Anjoman Islami groups to take over NIRT and encouraging non-professionals to produce radio and television programmes.
3 Giving religious leaders and preachers air time to talk on radio and television, and using television instead of radio, eventually created a vacuum of skilled knowledge about both media. As a consequence of unjust and hostile attitudes toward elite culture, the shortage of producers became critical to an extent that instead of television programmes, audiences watched slides and listened to taped music every day.
4 Amid this wholesale destruction of broadcasting standards and policy, the most crucial blow was breaking the national sense of identity – the pride in being Iranian. This process and the extreme pressure to change television's outlook made the majority of its audience look for a different way to spend their free time.
5 Finally bringing the lumpenization of culture as hegemony into the cultural space of every individual Iranian's life.

Despite the rapid change in NIRT, Ayatollah Khomeini was not happy about the organization's performance. The Speaker of the House, Hashemi-Rafsanjani, in an attempt to reassure him, suggested his brother take charge under the direct supervision of the Ayatollah himself. The temporary caretaker director was re-assigned to take charge of the Revolutionary Guard intelligence unit and, as the war with Iraq started, Mohammad Hashemi officially became the second director general of RTV. The first thing he managed to do to was reinstate the development project planned during Reza Ghotbi's directorship. During the period of the war he managed to study whatever files and materials he could rescue from what Ghotbzadeh had packed and stored in various RTV buildings. It should be noted that Hashemi was the only director-general to appreciate the success and development potential of NIRT and he also gradually realized the importance of his job for the country as a whole and the image of the Islamic Republic specifically. He had no experience or expertise, but with the support and influence of his brother gradually gained in confidence and managed the organization for 14 years.

During Hashemi's directorship RTV was the first serious testing ground of tribal politics in the Islamic Republic which was in the making. Hashemi established his authority by bringing all the family, former schoolfriends and the friends of his brother into the management body in order to create a peaceful environment that would satisfy Khomeini and at the same time consolidate his brother as the first and foremost authority after Khomeini in the Islamic Republic. For example:

- deputy director for political affairs, Hemmati, was a close friend;
- deputy director of international affairs was the son-in-law of Mossavi-Ardebiliy, the former chief justice;
- deputy director of research was Haj-alimohammadi (nickname 'Zoragh'), a close associate of Khamenehi.

From the early 1980s until summer 1994 Hashemi was fully in charge of the broadcasting organization in Iran. He gradually and carefully looked through the previous records, strategy papers and documentation on how to run NIRT. During eight years of devastating war with Iraq he had ample time to study the organization, despite the pressures from various revolutionary institutions to increase religious programming. His primary achievements were as follows:

1 First he tried to bring back to work the former personnel who had been unlawfully purged, causing tremendous problems for the organization's production capacity. Second, he increased the budget and gradually expanded NIRT, based on the long-term plan of the former regime.
2 He changed NIRT officially to VVIR and extended television coverage by leasing a transponder from INTELSAT. He extended the two-year training programme of the School of Cinema and Television to four years' Baccalaureate and, on the demise of his administration, he was about to establish an MA programme.
3 He established a third TV channel to meet the overwhelming public demand for sports coverage.
4 He revitalized the Office of Satellite Research and Development established during Ghotbi's administration. This office under Hashemi employed all possible means to develop expertise to study satellite technology in close cooperation with the Ministry of Posts, Telegraphs and Telephones on the Venus satellite project. Conflict between the two administrations not only halted the cooperation, it also led to disillusionment among the handful of highly qualified engineers that had trained under Ghotbi. All left their jobs with the exception of one who survived with great difficulty. Despite the conflict Hashemi tried to keep the Satellite office alive and continued to fight for funds to expand its research projects.
5 During Hashemi's appointment, about 13 films were produced with the cooperation of the BBC and NHK. It was the first experience of joint ventures.

Hashemi also increased the number of personnel from 8,000 to over 14,000, more or less in accordance with the development plans of the previous regime. In an interview he revealed his appreciation of Ghotbi's contribution, and his honesty and integrity. He was surprised by literature produced by the CDI (Communication Development Institute) Symposium in Shiraz and Mashad. During Khomeini's era the major concern of the broadcasting media was to mystify Islam and to despise modernity: '*Islam-nab-mohammadi*' was the answer to everything without providing any strategies or plans. Hashemi-Rafsanjani, after the death of Khomeini, used all his efforts to adopt a policy that would demystify Khomeini's revolutionary slogan and relax the environment in which the broadcasting media operated by inviting the forces of the revolution to challenge the real development problems. In order to eliminate existing tension in the media, he pushed for further relaxation of the Islamic code on programme production, ignoring various forces – particularly those emanating directly or indirectly from the Office of Velayat-e Faghih. Hashemi tried very hard to reorganize the VVIR in line with the reconstruction and development plan of his brother, the president. In the summer of 1990, Khamenehi stepped in and he reaffirmed the position of his classmate Hojatolislam Duagu, former head of the Guidance Council, as the controller and head of VVIR programming again.

Stubborn and fiercely protective of his brother, Hashemi failed to see the close cooperation of factions within the Majles, who with direct support from the Office of Velayat-e Faghih, aimed to remove him from office and curtail the power and the influence of President Rafsanjani over RTV.

Having documented the achievements of Hashemi's administration, it is also important to look at his failures during his long incumbency:

1 During the entire period that Hashemi was in charge he did not allow any criticism of his brother Hashemi-Rafsanjani as president, regardless of the fact that he should have been impartial.
2 As head of broadcasting he refused to keep the balance between the Office of Velayat-e Faghih on the one hand and the Speaker of the House and the Office of the President on the other.
3 Ayatollah Khomeini's appointment of Khamenehi as his successor owed much to Rafsanjani's providing the right script and to all the cronies of Reyshahri in the Ministry of Intelligence – as was later recorded in a book of memoirs published by Reyshahri himself to get rid of Ayatollah Montazery and pave the road for Khamenehi to take charge of the *velayat-e faghih* regime. Hashemi was reluctant to let VVIR propagandize for Khamenehi as the leader of the world Shi'ah. Despite the Guardian Council's guidelines at RTV, Hashemi always refused to promote Khamenehi as 'saint'. The motive behind this was obvious: first, Khamenehi was lacking in charisma and political wit and second, through various speeches he made, and a few fatwa statements, he showed a lack of the sophistication necessary to a Shi'ah leader. As a result of the existing tension, Khamenehi assigned the surveillance unit of the Revolutionary Guard (*Sepah*) to keep a close eye on the whole broadcasting operation.
4 After the 1990s, satellite television dominated the footprint of Iran and Hashemi was keen to develop cable and satellite links with the new commercial broadcasts in the region. In the beginning he ignored the clandestine use of satellite dishes as a serious threat to Islamic media. He used satellite as an excuse to lure the very out-of-touch religious faction and reactionary clergy to the modern world and a relaxation of the Islamic code of television, in particular the production of serials and light entertainment programmes.

Directly contrary to his intention, the *Kayhan* newspaper (which is closely related to the Office of Velayat-e Faghih) started to provoke a public debate on the conspiratorial manner of this cultural invasion, while Mohammad Javad Larijany, a member of Majles and one of the ideologues of the Office of Velayat-e Faghih, suggested a Majles debate on banning the satellite dishes. Meanwhile, a few provocative speeches and a number of harsh demonstrations by Ayatollah Khamenehi pushed his conspiratorial approach to satellite in order to promote Ali Larijany, chief of the Revolutionary Guard's surveillance unit, as Minister of Culture and Islamic Guidance. As it was, the debate in Majles did not gain support, particularly after a very effective speech by Rajaie-Khorasani, Tehran's representative.

A new regime of cultural supervision is emerging

The banning of satellite, he said, 'is the worst kind of human rights violation', and compared it to depriving people of breathing. After some debate, and the failure to gain enough votes, the whole issue was shelved for the time being. All the papers, particularly those under the patronage of Khamenehi, started to provoke the debate again on moral grounds. Khamenehi and his cronies took advantage of the satellite broadcast act and during 1993 Majles authorized a set of charges against Mohammad Hashemi, director-general of VVIR, aimed at reducing the influence of Rafsanjani as president of RTV and at the same time preparing the ground for Ali Larijany to take over Hashemi's job as director. The accusation of Hashemi by Majles was quite unscrupulous. Some Majles deputies were very close to Khamenehi, and they criticized Hashemi for his administration's failure to produce effective programmes that would stop the cultural invasion planned by the west to corrupt their *Islam-nab-e-mohammadi*. For the first time, Khamenehi, in a lengthy speech, suggested satellite as a western conspiracy against Islamic culture. The removal of Hashemi in the summer of 1994 was very unfair, because during his 14 years' administration, despite a number of demonstrations by Hezbollahi mob forces against him, he refused the direct influence of conservatives in the Office of Velayat-e Faghih in the programming content of RTV. Nevertheless, mounting orchestrated pressure made Hashemi resign. This was a blow to Rafsanjani's tribal politics, and moreover it became an incentive for the powermongers behind the Office of Velayat-e Faghih to disarm Rafsanjani from political leadership for some time. On the advice of Khamenehi, the office took the issue to the Ayatollah Araky, who was in his death throes. The opportunist group in the Majles were in favour of banning satellite reception on moral grounds. Following extensive publicity in the mass media of Araky's fatwa on satellite broadcasts, the cronies of *velayat-e faghih* in the Islamic Council Assembly (ICA) reopened the debate and used Araky's fatwa as a coercive measure to bypass those who were challenging the bill. Consequently the law banning private use of satellite television equipment was passed (see Ayatollah Khamenehi's speeches on the assault on Islamic culture).

Satellite controversy in the media

Since Iran happens to be in the footprint of international satellite television broadcasting, over 60 channels can be received, according to an interview with the head of Voice and Vision of Islamic Republic in *Ettelaat* newspaper on 11 January 1995. Yet Iranians were fed up with the constant diet of religious sermon and homily in Islamic Republic television. They discovered it was easy to hook up to international satellite television broadcasts.

As a result, government control of film and video was restricted to domestic programming. Selector box and receiver equipment for satellite television became a lucrative business, and satellite dishes and other items related to satellite television piracy became rare commodities. In recent years, as a consequence of the bankruptcy of cultural policy on the one hand and boring and monotonous domestic programming on the other, people from all walks of life have become the victims of smugglers, paying high prices for satellite dishes, selector and receiver boxes in order to have access to programmes such as *Baywatch*, *Neighbours* and a few talk shows, whatever other channels they can zap into dependent on the size of their dish – such has become the hobby and entertainment of the average middle-class family in Iran. By recent estimates there are over two million pirate satellite receivers throughout Iran; more than half of these are in Tehran and the remainder in provincial capitals around the country.

A number of times in the past few years, satellite piracy has become a hot issue in the Iranian press and in the subject of Friday sermons at the University of Tehran. There are two dominant views on satellite piracy: one is for banning the satellite dish and putting a heavy fine on the smuggler and the users. The second is that satellite television broadcasting is very hard to ban and the only way to stop people watching is to improve domestic programming to be more competitive with international television. Recently the fundamentalist group, under coercive methods of campaigning, persuaded the members of the Islamic assembly to approve the law banning the use of satellite dishes. But it has not been set into operation, because the Guidance Council of the Islamic Republic had to give final ratification to the lengthy debate. The council asked the Speaker of the Majles to modify two articles of the bill and consider some minor changes before it can come into effect as law for Interior and Culture Ministries to act upon. For a few months people dismantled their dishes from the roofs of their houses and particularly from the rooftops of big apartment buildings; then gradually after two months they started to hook the dishes up in a clandestine way. Some made a secure shelter for the dish at the back of the roof or on the landing of their staircase. And business was as brisk as ever, but this time it was more covert.

The new director-general of radio and television, Ali Larijany, said in an interview that the Voice and Vision of the Islamic Republic was monitoring about 60 channels of international television for selection and dubbing into the Farsi language for rebroadcasting or for video use throughout Iran. At the same time, he revealed, they were negotiating with international television authorities for copyright, although he mentioned no companies by name. At the present time, Iran's capacity for film production is limited to 60 or 70 films per year across the whole country. There is no alternative but to import films and television programmes from abroad. Larijany also emphasized that some of the international television programmes were very useful and would be among those acquired, while some films or programmes did not fit the Islamic cultural code and would need to be modified.

It seems the new head of RTV will find a solution by negotiating with international television authorities for copyright or possibly franchise permission. So far the law stands as a coercive measure for responsible organizations to act upon, but in practice no one dares to act because they are afraid of creating mass protest and ultimately a serious challenge to government authority.

Due to the coercive tactics of the *velayat-e faghih* forces in the first six months of 1995, big satellite dishes were gradually replaced with smaller ones. Instead of protecting Islamic culture from western programming, the converse happened. With small dishes people could easily see porn channels from Turkey. Happy with the range of programmes that could be viewed with small dishes, they gradually started to put the large dishes back into operation in inconspicuous parts of their buildings.

Under new supervision

The new management came to power as a result of close surveillance of IRIB by the security arm of the revolutionary corps. Director-general Larijany had been in charge of the intelligence unit of the Revolutionary Guard for 15 years. He also was one of the associates of Reyshahri, the former Minister of Information and the mastermind behind the plot to replace Montazery. The new administration of IRIB took over a carefully written scenario aimed at ruining the image of Rafsanjani and giving the upper hand to the Vali-ye Faghih in everyday matters of government. The new management of Iranian broadcasting has security and intelligence experience, but they all lack experience in running a very complex broadcasting organization such as VVIR.

The present operational outlook of RTV resembles an army counter-intelligence unit, based on stringent security checkpoints and mistrust of all individual workers at RTV headquarters. When I went to interview the first deputy director-general on satellite policy, I heard one television director at the second checkpoint complaining: 'We are in the business of art and culture … In the morning they think we are urban guerrillas, when we go out from headquarters they think we are thieves.' The security measures are harsh and infuriating. He continued: 'I do not understand how they expect us to work in this atmosphere of horror and coercion.' The new deputy director for political affairs also said in an interview: 'VVIR is operating under close supervision of the Vali-ye Faghih. According to the views of the Vali-ye Faghih, the VVIR is responsible for the Islamic Revolution, which means we should not concern ourselves very much with the view of the public. We should look at what is useful for the revolution.' Then he suggested with no hint of a doubt that TV in the west is usually more persuasive and is more concerned with the commercialization of culture.

The present administration has, since the summer of 1994, adopted four distinctive policies: expansion, production, culture and broadcasting.

The expansion policy

The expansion policy of the present administration is mainly based on the long-term plan of Reza Ghotbi, the founder of NIRT, albeit in modified form. Hashemi concluded some of the unfinished projects of Ghotbi's era in a modest way. He dropped altogether the idea of having a separate symphony orchestra for NIRT and he gave up Isfahan, one of the important centres for RTV, instead developing Mashad very extensively because it is a holy city. This administration so far has not changed direction. The RTV structure continues to expand, based on demand from the public and various pressure groups. Rapid globalization and outside pressure from the World Bank and the IMF for privatization and progress in communication technology, such as internet access and distribution, have increased the pressure for further expansion to counter globalization, whilst the whole world is moving toward democratization of access and consumption. As a result of these global changes RTV administration and cultural policymakers have come under enormous pressure, not only to expand Iran's output but to make available the best of international television. So far, there are 18 television stations and 25 radio stations throughout the country. Since the 1990s, RTV external broadcast services have developed in various languages, Arabic, Urdu and Bengali in particular. At present the IRIB is broadcasting on short waves in 18 different languages for overseas listeners as well as on FM for domestic listeners. Beside radio, the external service of IRIB operates a television service in Arabic for neighbouring countries. The programme is about three hours and fifteen minutes of mainly news and public and political affairs. Since 1997 two new international television networks have been established in Tehran, Jame-Jam and Sahar; both produce news, sport and entertainment programmes for Iranians living abroad, but the Sahar network has multilingual programmes for other Muslim communities throughout the world.

Production policy

Since Larijany took charge of RTV with the direct support of Ayatollah Khamenehi and the Speaker of the House, Nateq-nuri, all budgetary constraints have been relaxed and an emergency session in Majles allocated a budget of about five billion toman (50 billion rials or $16,600,000) to RTV solely for film and TV programming, in order to combat cultural globalization or so-called cultural aggression via satellite television broadcasts. In the first year of his administration Larijany established a film company called Sima Film. This had three objectives: i) to accommodate the 50 billion rials in the private sector for the production of film and television programmes; ii) to change the ratio between production and broadcasting by mass production of TV programmes; iii) to ensure the aims of all TV programmes as well as film content remain within the framework of Islamic culture and the promotion of piety and Islamic ethics.

According to an interview with the manager of Sima Film, in less than a year, one and a half billion toman ($5,000,000) has been used to upgrade film and TV studios, and some has been granted to the private sector. So far over 823 projects have been reviewed: only 523 reached the censor board and 110 were approved.In conclusion, only 50 of these 110 projects are in the process of production. It is interesting to note that Ayatollah Khamenehi constantly criticizes the commercialization of culture in the west, yet in Iran Sima Film managers emphasize the private sector should cooperate with the public sector in film production. In less than a year, 60 private companies have been able to get loans from Sima Film for film production. The private sector has borrowed about 1 billion 200 million toman ($4,000,000) for making commercial films.[1]

So far the evidence shows that production policies are selective regarding Islamic rhetoric, very much the reverse of previous administrations. Careful examination reveals a lack of experience of television production in the private sector, together with a lack of technological 'know-how' and qualified personnel, proving the outcome has not been satisfactory.

The new administration of RTV is directly under the auspices of Ayatollah Khamenehi, and in a visit to RTV the editor of *Soroush* writes flatteringly that: 'the clear perfume of Velayat has filled the space of the headquarters of RTV. Everyone here wholeheartedly is waiting for the rise of Velayat sun.'[2] He believes that television's function should not be only pure entertainment: every programme on RTV should have a moral purpose, for entertainment is a western concept. Islamic RTV should be concerned more with the promotion of religious values.

The head of RTV in a report given during a visit by Ayatollah Khamenehi revealed the production of radio programmes had increased by 15 per cent and broadcasting hours had increased by 59 per cent.[3]

Cultural policy

In order to find out how the Islamic Republic encounters the modern media system and the expansion of global culture, it is crucial to examine its cultural and communications policies. There is a problem in piecing together statements and comments to tease out the policy direction of the Republic, for in the absence of explicit policy instruments, documentation of such areas does not really exist. To this is added the complex problem of evaluating current practices in terms of short-term and long-term social goals and development objectives and assessing how successful such policies might be, and in which areas.

Now what is the cultural policy under the Islamic Republic and how is it related to communications policy? Essentially, cultural policy can be summarized in a single word: Islamicization, this under the control of a new Ministry of Culture and Islamic Guidance.

Since 1980 and the proclamation of the Islamic Cultural Revolution, two essential principles have defined this cultural policy: one is '*Islam Rastin*' (pure Islam), not only as a spiritual guide but as an ideological orientation and a criterion for evaluating cultural content; the second is 'Neither East, nor West' and a non-aligned independence which helps the cultural sphere to underpin the opposition to cultural importation and to support indigenously produced material.

Clearly the Islamicization of Iran extends to political life and the suppression of secular organizations and debate; to economic life and the attempt to create a third way of economic development; in the social sphere to the delimited role of women, to taboos on alcohol, and general intrusion into private life. In the cultural sphere, the effects of Islamicization may be seen in the areas of book publishing and the press, film, theatre and the arts. The office of Amre be Marouf va Nahye az monkar in the Ministry of Ershad is in charge of the Islamic code of conduct covering all aspects of lives of Iranians. The 'office of surveillance for happiness' makes sure no one feels happy or so much as smiles throughout the land. There is no space to go into detail here about what wrong-doing they have committed in the name of religion.

Broadcasting policy

Unlike the broad definition of cultural policy which was soon articulated and implemented in various ways, the communications policy of the Islamic Republic is still evolving. In general, there are four major areas of communications policy-making that can be distinguished within any national system: i) centralized/decentralized patterns of organization; ii) definition of media scope and role; iii) regulation, control and supervision; and iv) access and participation.[4] While the Islamic Republic was swept to power on a wave of popular decentralized participation through traditional social networks of communication, the new regime quickly realized the enormous symbolic and ideological power offered by the mass media. The appointment of one of Khomeini's three disciples (Ghotbzadeh) as the first Islamic director of RTV was one indication.

The current formal structure, in place since 1986, has the director of voice and vision of the Islamic Republic (VVIR) directly responsible to the Guardian Council. This Council consists of three people: one from Majles, one from the judiciary, and one from the executive, all appointed by Ayatollah Khomeini. The aim of such a structure, described by former Prime Minister Moussavi, is that the VVIR should not be simply a direct arm of government, as in many parts of the Third World, but should reflect a balanced input from all three sectors of the system, supposedly preventing the creation of a dictatorship. The Council determines broadcasting policy, communications policy and the content of RTV programming, as well as making decisions about technical hardware issues, and broad budgetary policy. The council approved a new constitution for VVIR which allows for six deputy director-generals who deal with programming and education; finance; administration; politics; external broadcasting; and technical issues.[5]

In May 1986, the Guidance Council of VVIR, with the cooperation of the Ministry of Ershad, produced a document entitled 'Code of general policy, philosophy and objectives of programmes of VVIR'. This document describes the general orientation of Islamic broadcasting: the rule of Islamic revolution and its constitution should dominate all programmes within the framework of the slogan of independence, freedom and the Islamic Republic. In a long list of recommendations, RTV is supposed to bring the vision and ideology of *velayat-e faghih* to reality, broadcasting media is supposed to prepare the ground for achieving self-sufficiency and to promote the slogan 'Neither East, nor West,' within all spheres, economic, military and cultural, within the context of Islamic law and order. Each of those slogans is open to interpretation and little specific guidance is given on everyday matters of policy and organization.[6]

If the apparent point of the formal structure is to avoid dictatorship, it is highly ironic that many everyday issues and ideological matters are currently dealt with in a manner somewhat reminiscent of the time of the Shah, albeit within a totally different ideological framework, by using trusted political cronies. Under the Shah, sensitive political issues were entrusted to particular trustworthy individuals such as Homayoun (Minister of Information and former editor of *Ayandegan* newspaper), Jafarian (deputy director of NIRT and director of Pars news agency) and Nikkhah (head of research and news analysis at NIRT), who acted as the Shah's antennae, spotting sensitive news stories, and reconstructing events in a manner pleasing to the Shah without any coherent written policy. These royalist 'antennae' have been replaced by Islamic antennae, mainly close relatives of those close to Khomeini, which may be taken as an indication of the importance afforded such positions. For example, the deputy director of VVIR research, a close associate of Khamenehi and Duagu, was a class mate of Khamenehi and played the role of his eyes and his ears at VVIR; he was also the head of the Guidance Council at VVIR. Mohammad Hashemi-Rafsanjani, the brother of Rafsanjani, the president, is the director-general of VVIR. The family connection is very obvious. At the highest level, like many other government agencies, it has become a family business.

The Guidance Council consists of: i) a unit for programme planning for RTV which reviews and approves programmes and plans; ii) a political unit which determines news policy and the political 'line' of all programmes; iii) a department of control and evaluation which has essentially a censorship function; the political deputy-general of the VVIR has prepared a document on news treatment which gives strict guidelines on news presentation, including which names to include and exclude, how to address certain persons, etc.; iv) an operations unit which determines the function and duty of each component of VVIR; and v) an inspection unit which checks the costs and balance of the entire organization and also investigates any complaints, internal or external.[7]

Yet despite the positioning of trusted antennae and an increasingly formalized structure of command and responsibility, there remains considerable ambiguity as to what counts as acceptable content. Thus many television serials produced by VVIR personnel over the past few years have still been considered 'un-Islamic' by some of the members of the Guidance Council and were not shown. The portrayal and representation of women is an obviously sensitive issue but was supposedly resolved in January 1988, by the intervention of Ayatollah Khomeini himself, who gave a fatwa to the effect that current television serials were Islamic. When

Ayatollah Mohammadi-Gilani continued to object to the neck of a woman being visible under *hejab* in one serial, even protesting Khomeini's fatwa, Khomeini suggested that he control his passions.[8] In another case about the Islamic codes of TV programmes, the director-general of VVIR emphasized the *hejab* codes of women players in TV serials to such an extent it essentially meant the elimination of women from them. It is interesting that one of the members of the censure committee gives advice and instruction on technical matters to the producer of *Yousef and Zalikha*, a television series based on Biblical characters – for example advice on appropriate camera movements such as: 'Camera should not focus on the beauty of women'. Another sensitive area that has still not been resolved after a decade of Islamic media in operation is the question about the use of music among the *foghaha* (learned clergy). *Ghenna* is music which creates a happy mood, while *Tarrab* moves one to dance; the distinctions are hard to apply 'scientifically' and it is not clear which is worse. Imam Khomeini made a fatwa on certain music that he liked to be broadcast and emphasized in his fatwa that the musical instrument should not be shown. The board of censure then went one step further and said that, according to Ayatollah Khomeini, even the *nay* (an ancient Persian instrument) must not be shown.[9]

The director-general of VVIR, on the issue of how to make an acceptable television programme, emphasized camera movements, namely: 'In a *taziyeh* you should not zoom on the actor but you should show the crowd. You should not make a programme popular because of the actor or director. Avoid making a hero for the people.'[10] In a recent interview with three producers on issues of censorship and Islamic codes, all complained that even following the guidelines, some programmes would still not be allowed to be broadcast. When Duagu ran out of excuses he would say the language of the television serial or public affairs programme was too chic. Many of the producers expressed their doubts about the knowledge of the policy-makers.[11] The general principle of Islamization provides no very specific guidelines for media policy, and even *foghaha* (plural of Faghih), used to oral presentation, find themselves divided on issues of appropriate visual and aural media content. Many intriguing content issues were avoided for a long time because of the predominance of war coverage and propaganda in the media. Since the ceasefire with Iraq was accepted in the summer of 1988, these issues have resurfaced. When Rafsanjani became president, the first thing he did in order to secure his brother's position in the VVIR was to dissolve the Guidance Council, and VVIR became the monopoly of President Rafsanjani. During reorganization of RTV in the middle of summer 1990, Khamenehi stepped in and reaffirmed the position of his classmate Hojatolislam Duagu, former head of the Guidance Council, as the head of VVIR programming and control. The entire organization has undergone difficult changes in the past decade. However the struggle for clear guidelines and policies continues.

By looking at the development history of RTV, we can see that the function of radio and television during the Pahlavi era was concerned with promoting modernization and a western lifestyle for Iranians, and denying the traditional history and religious culture of the Iranian people.

During Khomeini's era the major concern of broadcasting media was to mystify Islam and to despise modernity, *Islam-nab-e-mohammadi* having the answer to everything without any strategies.

Rafsanjani was trying to demystify Islam and get the country back on the road of modernization and reconstruction. He was short on intellectuals' trust and the technocrats to define strategies and policies. Now, over two decades after the revolution, the lack of coherent policy and concrete aims for development are increasing the pressure on President Khatami to put Iran back on the road to development. Because the message of programmes produced, even today, by RTV is based on traditional models of communication, repeating specific angles on the history of Islam, denying the cultural heritage of Iran outside the context of Islam and failing to address the present issue of cultural identity in an age of rapid globalization, Iran has become a cauldron again, desperately in need of finding a way to participate in the international community. In this context it is crucial to explore the content of RTV programming.

The programming debate

During the 1984 Olympic Games viewers complained that the coverage of women's athletics was so limited, and asked why half of the population was being deprived of women's programmes. A few years later, the debate over the broadcasting of the 1988 Games was decided in favour of increased coverage. Certain articles in the press and magazines had openly articulated the marginalizing of women in Iranian Islamic culture, yet such debate has not yet flowed on to the television screen.[12]

The shifting role of the media was recently reflected in a heated debate when a young woman on a call-in radio programme admitted that she identified more with a character in the hugely popular Japanese soap opera *Oshin*, and took her as a role model more readily that identifying with the daughter of Mohammad. Khomeini was offended by the broadcast, ordered the head of radio imprisoned and the head of VVIR's Islamic ideology group sentenced to 50 lashes; only on the intercession of the chief justice, who argued that public opinion did not support Khomeini's overreaction, did Khomeini pardon the participants. Such occurrences are vivid instances of cultural struggle, and new Islamic television encounters such clashes whenever audiences are allowed to speak out and question the standards and criteria of Islamic broadcasting policy.

While this dynamic has existed since the formation of the Islamic Republic, what is important about these recent incidents is that they occurred in public, and concerned material already aired which was then criticized and retracted.[13]

Another controversial aspect of VVIR programming is news coverage: the political deputy-general of VVIR had prepared a document on news treatment which gave strict guidelines for news presentation, including the appropriate hierarchy of order of names and how to address certain persons, with a great stress on exact religious titles. The problem of news was covered during the war, as military propaganda flourished and little opportunity for criticism existed. But since the acceptance of the ceasefire in August 1988, a new critical mood has grown. The propagandistic nature of Iranian news was even criticized by the chief of news broadcasting, Hemmati. In an interview in January 1989 he described the dilemmas facing news broadcasters. He argued that news was the most important programme broadcast because it conveyed the beliefs and morals of the Islamic Republic and the way it saw the world – hence the considerable time allocation to news coverage on radio and television, so that 24 hours of radio carries three hours of news, while seven hours of TV has two hours of news. Hemmati argued that Western news coverage was subtle propaganda which was persuasive and helped to undermine other cultural identities. He indicated:

> in my view the Western method of news broadcasting is the best because they cover their propaganda in a complex, artistic form, in a very clever way, and are indirectly persuasive to the audience. So the BBC broadcasts news in a way that shows and feels how wonderful and objective the BBC is while in reality it follows the general British policy and influence. It attracts our trust.

Islamic broadcast policy is to awaken those nations that are under dictatorial and imperialistic regimes and to develop Islamic values. The deputy director-general for political affairs admitted that:

> we use direct methods of propaganda in our news broadcasts that have a negative impact; if we use western methods, we might have a better impact. Most people in charge of our communication system are not familiar with this medium and do not know the methods that other countries, especially the west, use.[14]

In line with political orientation of 'Neither East, nor West', and in opposition to the Pahlavi strategies, one of the major programming policy decisions in broadcasting has been to severely reduce the use of imported material, and to exclude materials containing sex or violence. However, some TV imports, even American, still appear: *Little House on the Prairie* was considered wholesome and family-oriented enough to be shown. Much of the imported material was from the eastern bloc and other Third World countries and some from Japan too. Most of the content was militaristic, militant and revolutionary by nature. From a cursory examination of the general content of the foreign-produced material, the distinction between political violence for 'socially positive' purposes and the anti-social violence of western television entertainment is quite obvious.

Over the spring and the summer of 1989, by far the most popular television programme was a Japanese soap opera, *Oshin*. Because of Islamic television's emphasis on values and the confusion of its management over what constitutes Islamic television entertainment, many of the domestically produced programmes are being censored without any concrete reason being given; consequently many television producers have resigned or applied for early retirement. As a result of the lack of a clear definition of Islamic entertainment, one could still find a large amount of foreign content, especially film, on television from a wide variety of source countries, including England (14 films); USSR (11 films); Italy, Yugoslavia, Germany, USA (4 films each); Australia, Hungary, China (1 film each); East Germany, Spain, Czechoslovakia, France, Canada, India, New Zealand and Romania. Up to the early 1990s foreign films predominated over domestic ones in the cinemas too, and indicated a remarkably eclectic cultural environment.[15]

Thus, despite the proclaimed intention of developing a new Islamic cultural and communications policy, the reality reveals serious conflict, contradictions and 'leaks' within the state system of official cultural production. It also remains very unclear to what extent RTV is generally accepted by the population at large.

In March 1987 a survey was conducted by VVIR's Research Division of Tehran businessmen's (*Bazzaries*) and shopkeepers' satisfaction with RTV programmes. The results showed that they watch TV or listen to radio for 2.5 hours in every 24 hours. Of those surveyed 51 per cent complained about the lack of entertainment and new films on TV, 33 per cent complained about the lack of informative programmes and 8 per cent expressed unhappiness about the lack of public affairs programmes. Regarding radio, the survey showed the majority of the population were not satisfied with radio programming, because of the lack of entertainment, information and social affairs programmes. Another survey conducted on a larger sample in Tehran revealed that 68 per cent were satisfied with foreign radio broadcasts in Tehran.

It also remains unclear to what extent Islamic cultural and communications policy is generally accepted by the population at large. Indeed there were very strong signs that there is both considerable cultural space in which 'alternative' material can be created and disseminated, as well as signs of popular resistance to Islamicization, despite, or perhaps because of, the harsh controls operated by the Islamic Republic. While extreme control is exercised in some areas, so that overt channels of collective political expression have been cut off, somewhat more passive and fragmented forms of cultural resistance are gaining ground. There are many signs of a broader cultural resistance to the fanaticism and puritanism of the Islamic culture and communications policy, even from those who would consider themselves good Muslims.

Video

Tired of the incessant war coverage and sermonizing, television audiences have turned to VCRs, preferring to rent videos. A VCR costs approximately 100,000 toman, about $1,000 at black-market currency rates, and they are now widespread amongst urban families. In big cities, especially Tehran, the numerous video stores of 1983 are still operating. Most current foreign films and soft porn and Iranian exile television are available on the extensive cultural black market, brought in via Dubai and the Arab Emirates.

Audio cassettes

There is a large market for audio cassettes, of both Persian and foreign music. Weekly news cassettes have also been created which provide information, analysis and music, and are sold by street vendors. Since the 1990s the market for video and audio cassettes has changed, first due to the relaxation of cultural policy after the war, and second, due to the fact that during the eight-year administration of President Rafsanjani, all government effort was directed toward reconstruction and development of the war zone areas of the country. The use of video and audio cassettes was legalized and the media environment of the entire country became slightly more tolerant. It is important to note that the cry for freedom of information and better RTV programmes exceeded that which government was able to provide. The impact of globalization on democratization of access to consumer markets on one hand, and the expansion of commercial and international satellite television on the other, influenced the conservative forces inside Iran to relax the Islamic code of programme-making for television. Consequently, the extent of network television and the variety of television programmes increased, but they remain far behind the basic standard of quality and content necessary to compete with international television.

Broadcasting structure and content

In the first decade of revolution, VVIR was running two television channels, Network One and Network Two, for approximately five-and-a-half and five hours daily respectively. The schedules were printed in *Soroush*, the weekly magazine of VVIR.

Contemporary Islamic television had a very different style from that of the days of the Shah. The sartorial elegance of the Shah's period was now considered 'oppressive' (*taghuti*), an expression of the old regime, and tie-wearing was a sign of westernization. Male announcers and newscasters wore open-necked shirts while women wore Islamic head-scarves and long sleeves. Another simple index of the Islamicization of broadcasting was the number of clergy (mullahs) seen on television, and the domination of religious content and language – hence the nickname 'mullavision'. Widespread exasperation often set in amongst viewers as one mullah after another used airtime as a pulpit, conducting prayers and sermonizing. Most Friday broadcasting was taken up with the relaying of sermons from the various assemblies around the country, the most significant being that delivered at Tehran University – another example of electronic media being used as a direct and simple extension of the pulpit.

Domestic Islamic (as opposed to Iranian) production was still at an embryonic stage. In the first decade the major productions, including serials, were: *Tanzavaran*, a satirical poke at Iranians in exile; *Badbanha*, which was a historic dramatization of the constitutional revolution and the role of an important leader, Modarres; and *Ethics in the Family* (*Akhlagh-e dar Khanevadeh*), which taught basic skills such as how to use cutlery and lay a table.[16]

During Friday prayers in Tehran over the summer after the ceasefire, Rafsanjani referred to Khomeini as a progressive leader of pure Islam, *Islam-e-Nab*, who had broken with certain dogmatic Islamic notions in allowing chess and music once again, and proclaimed that these were great steps for progressive Islam against the more traditionalist approach of the clerics. Television as a channel for war propaganda and maintaining religious fervour slowly gave way to a more diverse broadcasting schedule. I examined the schedules for selected periods during and after the war, to see if the suggestion of a relaxation in public atmosphere was really apparent in programming, although information was limited to programme titles and times, without any detailed description of content.

A typical day of programming during the war provided 1 hr 35 min of directly religious content, 2 hr 30 min of didactic educational and informative programming, and 1 hr of what might be called 'lighter entertainment' (slides, youth programming). I was interested to see if the programmes had altered at all since the ceasefire of September 1988, so I compared the above schedule with a week in February 1989.

It was readily apparent that religious programming had drastically declined, to be replaced by general-interest light entertainment such as *Images of Spring,* which was a slide and music programme. Another innovation was the presentation of a full-length feature film at 9pm. The new mood of openness was reflected in programmes such as *Negahi be Enghelab* (*A Look at the Revolution*), which had a discussion format and consisted of evaluations of the past and present processes of the revolution. There also appeared to be more imported programmes, such as *Years Away from Home* on Wednesdays. While there were again slight variations in daily scheduling, the overall week's programming was considerably more entertainment-oriented and less religious than that of the week during the war.[17]

Network One was directed more toward children and young people, but displayed the same general orientation toward lighter entertainment and away from didactic and religious content.

Network Two was also similar in general orientation and more geared to public affairs programmes.

Cultural policy and broadcasting vacillated on many issues, despite the rhetoric of Islamicization and the continued reaffirmation of the basic values of Islam.

The major problems facing VVIR today are the clash of values between the media profession and the new Islamic thrust, and the confusion of policy guidelines for the modification and adaptation of 1,500-year-old Islamic traditions, problems that alienated many fine and prominent media professionals.

A general national fiscal crisis created problems in the shape of Western embargoes on sales of equipment and film, so that Iran faced shortages of materials and was forced to buy on the international black market.

Another major issue was the extensive 'internationalization' of urban Iranian culture that took place under the Shah, creating a large urban population with sophisticated cosmopolitan tastes and interests. As research showed, Western media products were amply and cheaply available on international markets, and since the Islamic Republic was still not signatory to international copyright conventions, it was not surprising that considerable international cultural fare was available in Tehran: music videos, German soap operas, extensive Iranian exile TV products and up-to-date Hollywood videos. Evidence of the 'internationalism' of the cultural offerings in Tehran could be gathered by examining the listings in *Soroush*, *Kayhan* and *Danesh*, all government publications, not to mention private sector magazine such as *Adineh* and *Kelk* and many others. The film programme at the House of Culture of the Moztazafin Foundation over one week included Hitchcock's *Family Plot*, *The World of Laurel and Hardy*, *The Left-Handed Gun*, *The Human Condition*, *Jaws* and *Mirror*.[18]

The contents of *Soroush* magazine, the Islamic Republic's only TV guide, revealed this international eclecticism. Over 75 per cent of the magazine's content is international in focus, having little or nothing to do with the Islamic Republic. A typical issue at the time included a review of Umberto Eco's novel *Foucault's Pendulum*, articles on Virginia Woolf, Arthur Miller, Roberto Rossellini, Max Headroom, François Truffaut, and even Salman Rushdie, who was a favoured author before the publication of *The Satanic Verses*. Much of this material was translated from international film and arts magazines, often without acknowledgement.[19]

There was also a new atmosphere of public criticism and concern about broadcasting media and culture, again most interestingly expressed in the pages of *Soroush* and other cultural journals such as *Adineh*, and public confusion was evident. While the solution for many social issues was to be found in verses of the Quran, they hold no recipe for Islamic media policy. Beyond the broadest of value orientations, Islamic media was being invented as it went along, and differences of opinion once fought out within the media organizations were beginning to be publicly articulated. After the abolition of the Guidance Council at VVIR and Khamenehi's intervention in summer 1990 to ensure Rafsanjani no longer had total control, the organization underwent extensive change and expansion. In the second decade of revolution, approaching the end of the twentieth century, television networks increased from two to five channels. Audience interests and segmentation were the major concerns of programme-makers in their efforts not to lose audiences to international television.

The outcome of the various changes that have occurred in the past few years has stabilized as follows:

Network One covers 100 per cent of the population of the entire country and has become almost non-stop, offering social and political affairs as well as Islamic film series and sport.

Network Two covers 89 per cent of the population within about 18 hours of broadcasting, including drama series, current affairs, entertainment and feature films.

Network Three originally broadcast for only five hours and gradually increased to 16 hours daily. It covers 63 per cent of the population and focuses on youth interest, sporting events and entertainment.

Network Four began broadcasting in April 1996, offering 4 hr 45 min of higher education, art, culture, documentary, politics and economics. Broadcasting has since increased to eight hours.

Network Five, known as the Tehran Channel, broadcasts eight hours a day, documentaries on social and cultural failures and problems of old and new Tehran and other large cities, as well as news and political commentary.

Two other networks have also been added to the present broadcasting system: one is called Payam TV, which broadcasts in Farsi and English. Its main programmes are news information, science, history and Iranology. The daily production of this channel is about 180 pages in the form of teletext or videotext in Farsi and about 18 hours daily in English. In 1997 IRIB inaugurated a 24-hour satellite channel named Jame-Jam, transmitted by EUTELSAT (European Satellite Union), broadcasting news, information, entertainment, drama series, feature films, Iranian music and comedy with English subtitles. The rapid expansion of television networks has occurred without sufficient qualified staff and trained producers to create the quality programming that would attract international audiences or encourage feedback to improve provision. So far insufficient research and poor-quality production have failed to improve relations with Iranians living abroad or to arouse the interest of international audiences.

The director-general of VVIR in a recent interview complained that many government officials could clearly not tolerate criticism, after there were official complaints about some talk-show programmes that allowed the public to air their grievances, often over governmental inefficiencies. He couched the task of the media in very general terms: 'Our position should be carry out our duty, which is to be resilient, to carry out the principles of our constitution and to execute what the Islamic parliament defines as our policy.'[20]

Admittedly this was a retreat into generalization, with no concrete guidelines proffered as to day-to-day policy regarding content. And yet, for the first time, the ambivalent role of the media was being publicly aired and openly explored, namely that RTV is under the supervision of Ayatollah Khamenehi, the leader of the Islamic Republic and not of the elected president of the Republic, President Khatami – which contradicts the public interest, as the IRIB budget comes from the public purse. But IRIB has no responsibility to satisfy the people's interest or the president elected by the people.

Conclusion

In the first decade of the revolution, pressure increased for Islamic administrators to create cultural activities for leisure time, lest, according to an editorial published in *Soroush* magazine, 'drug addiction and the corrupt Western consumer culture will return because people have nothing else to do and nowhere to go during their leisure time'. The editorial warned against counter-revolutionary tendencies manifest in 'clothing, bad *hejab*, loose relations between men and women, and the social addiction to opium and heroin', noting that: 'In Tehran today heroin is cheaper than cigarettes and easier to find than a packet of Winston cigarettes.'[21] This was an astonishing admission for a major government magazine to publish.

During the second decade post-revolution, the arena for open political discussion and cultural relaxation gradually opened up under the initiatives of Rafsanjani. Since mid-1995 the Islamic Republic has been moving towards more active involvement in the diplomatic world. Under the initiatives of President Khatami, opportunities for civilized debate regarding reform for the election of the sixth Majles improved and dialogue became more transparent. But RTV, instead of supporting the presidential initiative of openness, moved in the opposite direction. As a result, audiences deserted RTV and showed more interest in international television and the free press, to the extent that traditional forces in the Ministry of Justice decided to close over 20 newspapers and renew their grip on power. Now, at the start of a new century, the masses in Iran are still struggling for basic democratic rights. The university uprising in July 1999 was a case in point.

There are powerful tensions at work inside the Islamic Republic and we need to examine not only the structures of repression of a powerful regime, but also the popular reactions and resistances to it and the new lines of cultural stratification which are developing.

Part of the power of the media lies not in any specific element of its content but in its relentless and repetitive presentation of a single vision of reality to the exclusion of all others. New generations are being socialized into the Islamic world-view formally by means of education and informally through the media, with little opportunity for debate. Whilst basic questions about the nature of Islamic development and the shape of the Iranian polity remain, one thing is clear: media plays a crucial role in the social formation of future generations. Yet at the same time, the dominant culture seems to provoke creative responses and alternatives. It is a period of great uncertainty at many levels inside Iran. It appears that fundamental contradictions in the encounter between media and Islam have not been solved either, as is best demonstrated by the sixth Majles election in February 2000. Coverage of the candidates was selective, yet the voters supported those candidates that RTV refused to publicize. The new theocracy which rules Iran appears more monolithic and dominant than the previous regime.

Notes

1 *Iran*, No. 170, September 1995, p.12.
2 *Soroush*, 1995, supplementary issue, p.4.
3 ibid.
4 See Edward Ploman, 'Communications policy and planning', in M. Tehranian, F. Hakimzadeh and M. Vidale, (eds.) *Communications Policy For National Development* (London: Routledge and Kegan Paul, 1977).
5 Personal interview with VVIR official.
6 'Code of general policy and philosophy of VVIR', Tehran, 1986.
7 Ibid.
8 *Soroush* 14, May 1985.
9 *Kayhan*, Tehran, October 1986.

10 *Soroush* 451, November 1988.
11 Ibid.
12 *Soroush* 431, June 1988.
13 Ibid.
14 *Soroush* 462, January 1989.
15 *Soroush*, 425, April 1988, and *Film Monthly* 48, 1986.
16 *Soroush* 431, June 1988.
17 Ibid.
18 *Soroush* 425, April 1988.
19 *Soroush* 462, January 1989.
20 *Soroush* 451, November 1988.
21 *Soroush* 425, April 1988.

3 Iranian women

Between Islamicization and globalization

Ali Akbar Mahdi

This chapter discusses the concept of globalization and shows where Iran stands in regard to this phenomenon. It demonstrates how Islamicization has limited and localized women's involvement in education, employment, health services, and family planning, and then goes on to deal with the growing participation of women in non-governmental organizations, public activities aimed at increasing women's consciousness, and social groups established in order to protect women's rights. The discussion of women's demands for participation in the global processes of democratic development and autonomous civil society are also focused on. This chapter also discusses the developments that have empowered women to demand a more meaningful share of decision-making in society and a curb on state's ever-expanding interest in controlling women's lives. It will demonstrate that despite the repressive and restrictive environment of the IRI, Iranian women have been able to gather enough energy to express their dissatisfaction with state policies toward women and to show their desire for inclusion in civil society. They have begun to articulate an interest in developing voluntary non-governmental organizations and social movements responsive to and reflective of their own interests and concerns – interests and concerns for adapting to the global changes taking place in the modern world. Finally, the chapter will show how the struggle for a civil society in Iran is a necessary step in enabling Iranian women to join and benefit from the forces of Iran in the past two decades that has experienced two contradictory phenomena: Islamicization and globalization.

The revolution of 1979 reversed the Shah's modernization and set in motion a process of Islamicization of Iranian society. Islamicization was meant to cleanse the country of decadent Western culture which had infected its body and soul. To the revolutionaries who toppled him, the Shah was a symbol of this Western decadence and cultural imperialism. Islamicization was meant to return Iran to its roots, to a traditional culture – a culture, of course, limited to its Islamic past and not a pre-Islamic one.

Around the time the Islamic revolution succeeded in establishing a theocratic state in Iran and closing its borders to outside influences, another process was taking shape on the world stage, namely globalization. Globalization, as a social, political, economic and cultural force, has been able to penetrate the most isolated and closed-off areas of the world. There is barely a culture and society it has not affected. How then can the Islamic Republic of Iran avoid the forces of globalization emanating from the West? What are the effects of these two contradictory processes on Iran and Iranian people, especially women?

Globalization

Globalization is an abstract concept which has gained currency since 1989, the year in which it became manifest. Generally speaking, it refers to a host of social processes taking place beyond, but having serious impacts on, national boundaries. As a sociological concept, it has several meanings, depending on the discipline, paradigm and perspective within which it is defined and embedded. To some, it refers to the expansion of communications and technology and the divergence of societal structures, to others it means the expansion of the capitalist mode of production and the subordination of peripheral countries to the industrial capitalist core,[1] and for still others it implies a combination of both of these processes which ultimately leads to promulgation of similar technologies but diverse values and attitudes about them. Some have equated the concept of globalization with internationalization,[2] some with Americanization,[3] others with transnationalization, and still others with privatization of economies through the multinational corporations and international financial agencies.[4]

Western economists and political scientists often use the term with the following in mind: a worldwide economic integration through market economies and free trade, the expansion of communications and information, and a desire by people around the world for normative pluralism and political democracy. However, such characterization is not shared by all social scientists. Political economists view globalization as a distinct phase in the world economy beginning in the 1970s and characterized by the increasing transactions and institutions outside of the interstate relations.[5]

In this chapter, I use the concept more in line with Harvey's (1989) notion of time and space compression[6] and Giddens' (1981) notion of 'time–space convergence.'[7] As such, it refers to the expansion of technology, communication, and science around the world and the fusion of markets, capitals and labor. A major corollary of these processes is a global consciousness resulting from the universalization of basic rights through time and space compression. More and more people around the world are being influenced by universal forces and values. More and more people desire to have material and non-material choices beyond those present in their own local communities. The logic of current it generates has influences beyond and above its temporal and spatial domains. The structures it creates acquire a logic of their own and generate reactions and relations much farther than their own times and places.

Actors at all levels, be it individual, regional, national or international, are impacted and feel compelled to relate and react to its forces. The movement of ideas, images, products and patterns of social relationships operates above the limits and boundaries established by the dictatorial regimes and isolationist states. Even in the most isolationist countries, products imported from other countries bring with them images, patterns and modalities which influence the local patterns and force the local actors to react to them either favorably or unfavorably. For instance, Islamic states like Iran, who are determined to stay away from Western influences, find themselves fighting not foreign armies and imperialist tanks and war machines but McDonald's sandwiches, Hollywood movies, Disney images and Western pop musical icons.[8]

Engineered, developed and exported by the Western capitalist countries, communications, information and industrial technologies have laid the groundwork for the expansion of individualization, consumerism, materialism, market deregulation, and a desire for autonomy and self-determination by individuals, groups, ethnicities, cultures and local communities. As a result of these changes, the desire for democratic change and participation in social, political and economic processes has been rising, especially in countries with non-democratic governments. More and more people view democratic processes as a necessary consequence of participation in global markets, communities and organizations.

Globalization has activated a host of processes that were either non-existent or in a passive mode in the past. International, transnational and non-governmental organizations have become the major conduits for penetration and diffusion of global products, values and processes. Of course, such development has been aided by the expansion of neo-liberal policies advocated by the International Monetary Fund and the World Bank by encouraging the borrowing countries to privatize their state enterprises, liberalize their markets and deregulate their economies. These processes have contributed to the development of local organizations, micro-communities and small businesses in the developing countries, thus helping the processes of localization of global demands initiated by those international agencies.

Demands made by the international financial agencies require the state to give up some of its distributive functions, cut back welfare programmes and give up some of its traditional communal tasks by transferring them to corporate and private entities. These demands force the state-run economies to transform themselves into market-oriented economies in which individual and corporate initiatives are rewarded and supported by the state. Along with such transformation, the state also gets transformed from being a guardian of universal interest to a guardian of particularistic interests of capitalist forces within the market. The transfer of state responsibilities to the private groups and citizens provides these entities with an opportunity to expand their roles in society and polity, thus expanding the civil society. Civil society, as the ultimate representation of the local interest, comes to be aided by globalization forces emerging beyond the terrains of local communities.

As both Harvey and McGrew[9] have noted, globalization, as a universal phenomenon, gives rise to opposite forces of particularism and localization. While promoting universal values, standards and processes, globalization provokes particularistic reactions along the lines of nationality, ethnicity and religious faith, particularly against Western cultural influences. While the globalization process has been regarded as rational, the reaction has been more emotional and often based on traditional sources of authority and legitimacy – as occurred when the global forces affecting the Iranian society during the Pahlavi period (1925–78) antagonized the traditional forces and structures, thus leading to the overthrow of that regime. Even after the establishment of the Islamic Republic, the global influences have come to problematize the traditional structure of family and gender relations advocated by the Islamic Republic. They have put pressure on local practices which limit the ability of women to participate meaningfully in the social world.

The two sets of processes of globalization and localization are tied together dialectically and work with and against each other at the same time. Localization channels the global energy, directs it to the appropriate destination and customizes it to the formats of the indigenous structures. In a dialectical process of give and take, the content and form of globalization shape each other to the local needs and demands. At the same time, the local demands and structures modify themselves to global processes and institutions appropriate to their growth and expansion. Global structures and changes, then, are integrated with local traditions and existing social structures.

Iran and globalization

In 1962, Mohammad Reza Shah Pahlavi, the ruler of Iran at the time, launched his White Revolution as a precursor to raising Iranian society to the status of a globally competitive country. In fact, he promised the Iranian people he would soon move them toward the Great Civilization (*Tamaddon-e Bozorg*).[10] Though his reforms were regarded by some as a ploy to undermine the landed aristocracy and religious stronghold on the Iranian society,[11] they generally resulted in the concentration of political power in the court,[12] transformation of much of the feudal class to a modern and dependent bourgeoisie,[13] modernization of social relations of production, incorporation of women in the labor force, secularization of Iranian society, and the expansion of the modern educational system.

All in all, this 'revolution' was meant to increase Iranians' consciousness of modern values, push Iran forward towards a modern society, enfranchise Iranian women by allowing them to vote and participate in the political process, and encourage the development of a middle class.[14] Of course, all these developments were dependent on the money received from the sale of Iranian oil and the friendly political support of the United States.

During the half-century rule of the Pahlavis, the socio-economic status of women improved over time, but within an apolitical framework in which they were to serve as a token of modernity not as modern individuals with equal rights and equal participation in social, economic and political arenas. Women's education and limited social participation were encouraged but women's liberation from traditional roles was opposed, even by the Shah.[15] Though the Shah's sister became spokesperson for women's affairs and represented Iranian women in various international forums on women's status, she did little to oppose patriarchal attitudes present even in the court. Most women's organizations established in this period were devoted to charity and welfare activities. The most successful and effective elements of Pahlavi's modernization plan for women were in the areas of education, family planning, enfranchisement and employment in the service sector.[16] This limited and managed 'emancipation from above', though nominally effective in removing some barriers to the improvement of women's status, somehow delayed active and meaningful participation of women in society and politics.

One of the consequences of the Shah's increasing alliance with the United States and reliance on the Western form of modernization, was the alienation of religious forces, the nation's bourgeoisie and most of the modern educated classes. While the religious groups were alarmed by the increase in the Shah's repressive power and affiliation with foreign governments and their ways of life, the intellectuals and educated middle classes could not tolerate his repressive politics and blind fascination with Western values. As a result, the Shah found most of his 'subjects', as he viewed them, opposed to his push toward what Iranians saw as Westernization of Iranian society.[17]

For Ayatollah Khomeini, a high-ranking cleric opposed to the Shah's rule, the Shah was a local puppet of foreign forces, particularly the United States. His opposition and successful overthrow of the Pahlavi regime in 1979 was meant to free Iran from the Shah's despotism and dependence on foreign powers. Once successful in getting rid of the Shah, Khomeini began his hidden agenda: Islamicization of Iranian society, establishment of a theocratic state, and eradication of all foreign influences in politics, economics, culture and society.

Iranian society was cut off from the international community by redefining it as a religious society with a theocratic state whose mission in global context was not to coexist peacefully with other states, religions and ideologies but to confront them with a new brand of Islamicism as the ideology of the oppressed. Immediately after the overthrow of the Pahlavi dynasty in Iran, Khomeini set himself to export this revolution, beginning a new globalization of a sort – an Islamic globalization.

With the establishment of the Islamic Republic of Iran (IRI), the process of globalization initiated by the Shah came to a temporary halt and a rough restart. From its inception, the IRI began a process of uncoupling Iranian consciousness from the globalizing values promulgated by the Pahlavi regime by reversing much of what the Shah had done in terms of integrating Iran into global social forces. Using Islam as a blueprint, the clerics dominating Iranian politics in the past two decades have done everything to move Iran away from universal processes and values in favor of particularistic, religious and local traditions. They have established an inward-looking ideology defending their localistic values, rejecting universalistic and hegemonic Western values, and navigating the world with a puritanical gauge separating right and wrong.

Women, who had a significant role in the opposition to and successful overthrow of the Shah, were the immediate losers in the newly established Islamic government. The movement against the dictatorship of the Pahlavi did not mean the liberation of women. During the revolution women were only used in revolutionary work, by all parties involved,[18] but not in revolutionary decision making.

In the development of the constitution of the newly established republic, women had no input. In the political institutions developed after the revolution, a few women were elected to the first parliament in a token ticket. Though in the first two parliaments these women initiated some legislation on women, by and large their presence in those early years, where the parliament was occupied with war issues, was inconsequential because they were basically 'ya-sayer' to the male decision-makers.[19] The Islamic Republic treated women as recipients of state policies rather than agents in the construction of the new state.

Such treatment left women out of the decision-making process regarding the new institutions, thus ignoring their needs and concerns at different levels of institution building and state formation.

In the economic arena, failing to maintain the semi-industrial economy of the Pahlavi era and a stable currency, the Islamic Republic has created a crony capitalism marked by low productivity, high commercialism, high dependency on oil prices, and runaway inflation and currency devaluation. Early in the 1980s, the IRI nationalized much of its private industry and business as part of a drive to free Iran from dependent capitalism and to ensure social equity. From the start, these industries and businesses were plagued by mismanagement, corruption and cronyism. Many state firms performed at a fraction of their capacity. With contradictory and often short-sighted economic policies, the IRI drove Iran's economy into the ground.

After the Iran–Iraq war (1980–88), the first five-year economic development plan was launched in which inefficient state firms were to be sold off. This effort also was marred by corrupt practices and many of these firms went to favorite members of the ruling elite, thus further contributing to the established clientalism.[20] Today, still over 80 percent of business and industry remains in government hands.

Privatization of the economy began in 1990 during the presidency of Ali Akbar Hashemi-Rafsanjani. After coming to power in August 1997, President Khatami's government took up the task of privatization again and around 4,000 state firms, many of them loss-making, were put up for sale or dissolution. In 1998, Khatami set out to salvage Iran's economy by improving conditions for foreign investment, increasing non-oil exports, accelerating privatization and reducing red tape. In the same year, Iran's economy suffered from the reduction in oil prices in global markets, thus cutting around half its total revenue and confronting the government with $6 billion revenue shortfall or one-third of its budget. As a result, most development projects were suspended and payment for foreign loans had to be rescheduled.[21]

Iran's post-revolutionary crony capitalism has created an excellent opportunity for growth of parasitic institutions, groups and individuals who utilize their access to the state for economic gain and exploit the economic vulnerability of the public for political ends. The Motallefeh Group (the rightist faction in the Islamic Republic representing the interests of Bazzari merchants and conservative Ayatollahs) is a typical example. Clerical groups and their functionaries controlling various foundations are another example. While Iranian society in the past two decades has gained a new class of commercial elite as extremely wealthy nouveaux riches (importers, traders, senior officials in various foundations and middlemen of all kinds), the income of the majority of Iranians has declined drastically. Rising unemployment, the increasing number of young people, and a declining economy have caused serious challenges for the well-being of the coming generations. Forced by the necessity of globalization and the demands of international agencies to cut public spending on the one hand, and the growing proportion of the poor on the other, the Iranian government has been seesawing between the rhetoric of monetary belt-tightening and actual increase in government provision and public spending for war veterans and poor people.

The third five-year economic development, to begin in March 2000 (Farvardin 1379), calls for greater foreign investment, the reduction of red tape, a boost in non-oil exports, and less reliance on oil production as the source of state income – goals that the IRI has had since 1980 and has failed to make much progress towards. The IRI finds it politically difficult to move away from its revolutionary rhetoric, thus continuing to subsidize the economy in order to prevent social unrest among the general public and economic hardship for those who fought in the war with Iraq and continue to remain loyal to the regime. In the current Iranian year which started on 21 March 1999, the government set aside 7.548 trillion rials in subsidies for basic needs such as bread, milk, meat and oil.[22]

These conditions do not fit well into the structural requirement of the modern global economy. The Iranian economy has lost its ability to provide jobs for its citizens, a decent standard of living, and foreign exchange for production.[23] Iran continues to rely on oil for some 85 percent of its hard currency revenues and roughly half the state budget. Though for most years the government has declared inflation between 15 to 20 percent, all experts and every Iranian knows that it has been between 40 and 60 percent annually.[24] Given the increase in population, from 35 million at the time of the revolution to 65 million now, Iran is facing serious crises in unemployment, drug use and alienation among the young. The official estimate of the number of drug addicts in the country is as many as 1.2 million, mostly below the age of 30.[25] Half of Iran's population is aged under 20, and 900,000 reach working age each year. Official estimates put the jobless rate at some 15 percent, while unofficial figures place the number closer to 25 percent. Today, half the population lives below the poverty line, with an income of less than $50 a month.[26]

To this bleak scenario should be added some two million Afghan and tens of thousands of Iraqi refugees. While the Iranian currency continues to be devalued (from 70 rials for one US dollar in 1979 to around 9000 rials in July 1999), foreign debt has also continued to increase to $22 billion or 21 percent of GNP (June 1998). These conditions have had devastating effects on the economy and the standard of living.

The failure of the Iranian economy is not just the result of mismanagement, war with Iraq and foreign boycotts. Much of it is also due to the way in which the economy and society are structured according to Islamic law. Interest banking is forbidden, while interest-bearing transactions continue to exist, albeit with ideological twists in definition. Foreign investment has been non-existent due to numerous factors: arbitrary conditions governing investment; changing rules governing export and import; fear of and negative attitudes towards Western financial institutions; a constitutional law limiting foreign investment to certain activities; not to mention unfavorable labor conditions, bureaucratic gridlock, widespread corruption, social and economic insecurity, and revolutionary rhetoric and factionalism affecting business activities.

After the revolution Iran's tourist industry, the point at which the local and global meet, collapsed as a result of the Islamicization and the war with Iraq. Islamic codes have made it very difficult for foreign women and even men to have a normal travelling experience in Iran. To travel to Iran, women have to cover themselves in Islamic veil, and avoid physical interactions with unrelated males altogether and with intimate males in public. All shops, restaurants, cinemas and government agencies are instructed to refuse to serve women who are not in compliance with the dress code. In the past two years, religious hard-liners have harassed foreign tourists by shouting anti-Western slogans. In August 1999, foreign females who travelled to the city of Isfahan to view the solar eclipse were attacked because they were not in full compliance with Islamic codes of dress and conduct. In recent years, attempts to attract foreign visitors have had limited success, earning only several hundred thousand dollars a year despite Iran's wealth of historical sites and its varied climate. Furthermore, constant high inflation, high unemployment and economic recession have given way to a mounting wave of kidnapping, attacks and armed robberies – a development that has kept foreign tourists and investors away. In the first part of 1999, several foreigners were taken hostage for economic gain. These crimes forced Khatami's administration to ask parliament for legalization of private detectives, bodyguards and private security companies for the first time.

Tensions between globalization and Islamicization

There were two inherent tensions in the idea of Islamicization proposed by the Ayatollah Khomeini. The first was the tension between globalization and localization. Khomeini's Islamic ideology advocated globalization of Islam outside of the country simultaneous with localization of societal norms and values inside Iran. Rejecting modern influences and foreign cultural invasion, his ideology promoted indiginization of values and faith while pursuing the idea of 'exporting Islamic revolution'. He opposed Western influence on social, economic and political aspects of Iranian life because they were 'foreign' and 'decadent'. He localized Iranian social life by disallowing most modern attitudes and behaviors whose sources could be traced to the West. The Family Protection Law of 1967, which had secularized marriage and put some limits on men's ability to divorce their wives wilfully, was cancelled immediately. The legal age for marriage, which had been raised to 18 by this law, was reduced to 14. The wearing of ties and short sleeves by men was banned, women were discouraged to wear skirts and jeans, even under the traditional veil, and Western music and films were disallowed on Iranian radio and TV. Islamic ideology advocated by Khomeini as a universal ideology had little patience with and tolerance of other cultures, values and norms.

In April 1995, parliament banned possession of satellite dishes as 'satanic dishes' bringing 'Western depravity' into Iranian homes.

The second tension was between nationalism and transnationalism. Ayatollah Khomeini launched his movement against the Shah and the West from inside Iran. His movement has remained localized in Iran despite its broad influences around the world. In the early stages of his return to Iran, Khomeini advocated an Islamic globalization which was not dependent on nationality and territoriality. He wanted to export his revolution to all Muslims around the world. He had no particular feeling about Iran as a national entity.[27] Once Iraq invaded Iran in 1980, Khomeini had no choice but to resort to nationalism as a means of mobilizing resistance to Iraqi intrusion. With the prolongation of the war for eight years, Khomeini found himself forced to forego some of his ambitious dreams for becoming the leader of Muslims around the world and accept Iranian nationalism as a necessary source of mobilization for the war. By the end of the war in 1989, he had failed on both fronts: in overthrowing Saddam Hussein in Iraq and in exporting his revolution abroad.[28]

Iranian women and Islamicization

The Islamic Republic claims that its approach to women's status in society represents one of the best global models present in the world. In fact, in 1995, then president Ali Akbar Rafsanji claimed that women in Iran had the most progressive status in the world.[29] Other officials in the IRI, even females, have uttered similar statements. On 4 July 1999, Zahra Shojaie, the advisor on women's affairs to President Mohammad Khatami 'stressed that Iranian women are considered as a model for other women throughout the globe'.[30] The reality is, however, very different. It may be true that the status of devoted Muslim women in Iran is far better than that of their sisters in Arab countries in the area or of women in Afghanistan and Pakistan. However, there are other Muslim countries, such as Tunisia, in which women enjoy far greater social and economic rights in general.[31]

Since the late 1970s the world has been more and more affected by global forces and countries have experienced greater pressure to open their borders, enrich their intellectual horizons and expand their cultural bonds to forces outside of their own domains. The Islamic Republic of Iran has resisted these forces and attempted to delink Iran from some of the global forces that previously shaped the social, cultural, political and economic aspects of that country. As far as Iranian women are concerned, this religiously motivated process of deglobalization has been accompanied by a localization or nativization process which has limited their life chances and social choices. They have been forced to abandon their choice of clothing, employment, education, and lifestyle for a more localized, normative system customized to the taste of the clerical establishment.

The establishment of a theocratic state in Iran was accompanied with the rise of numerous boundaries separating men and women in society: males and females were separated in higher education classes where classes had been mixed before; females were barred from some professions such as the judiciary and singing; female students were barred from certain university disciplines such as engineering and agriculture.

A decree dismissed all women judges and barred female students from law schools. Women were forbidden to participate in some sports and disallowed to watch men on sports fields. Erection and maintenance of these boundaries and limitations became a major part of the government's social policy and a permanent task of special forces within the state, both military and civilian. A female vigilante group (*dokhtar'an-e Zaynab*) was organized to maintain state codes of female appearance in public, and even some private, arenas.

Using Papanek's words,[32] the Islamic Republic viewed women as the 'carriers of traditions' whose existence was threatened by foreign forces of globalization. In the face of this assault, the stability and survival of the Muslim family was in danger. To protect the family and its central element, the woman, women were to be shielded from foreign forces and unwanted influences. To do this, it became necessary to keep a close eye on women's bodies, their sexuality and social activities.

Women's sexuality had to be limited to their husbands, their bodies to home, and their roles to a trustee of the family. This timeless and idiosyncratic notion of family is very important to the Islamic ideology, not only for its reproductive, social placement and maintenance functions, but also for its role in localizing female identity through socialization of girls. Family is viewed as the natural arena through which gender identity is formed and operationalized, gender stratification is fortified and women are protected from all that is deemed unnatural to them. This Shia vision of family is based on a nostalgic and idealistic notion of Imam Ali's family, in which Fatima Zahra (the prophet Mohammad's daughter) dedicated herself to both her husband and the Islamic cause. Other role models for women often cited by the officials and ideologues of the IRI are Khadijah, the prophet Mohammad's wife, and Zaynab, daughter of the first Shi'i Imam Ali. In fact, the IRI replaced the universal Mother's Day with Fatima Zahra's birthday.

To implement its localization policy with regard to women, the IRI tried four concurrent strategies. First, it began to limit the global mobility of meanings associated with women's rights by branding the idea of women's rights as Western and un-Islamic, thus demanding they be left behind the borders. Books advocating feminist ideas were either totally banned or partially censored. Western-educated women's access to public media was curtailed. Many female employees in the TV and radio stations were either simply fired due to their high-ranking position in the organization or demoted to less visible and less influential positions, thus limiting their access to the public. Magazines advocating Western feminist ideas were compelled to discontinue their practices or risk being banned or censored. In fact, even after the desired purification of the media, on several occasions the Islamically approved media found itself in the difficult and awkward position of defending the publication of an article or airing of an opinion found unfavorable to the Islamic ideologues. Even in the 1990s liberalized government of President Khatami, *Zanan*, a magazine devoted to women, was taken to court for publishing articles deemed favorable towards Western feminism or offensive to conservative religious establishment. On 6 April 1999, *Zan*, the only newspaper devoted to women, run by Faezeh Hashemi, daughter of former President Ali Akbar Hashemi-Rafsanjani, was banned by the court because it had published part of a new year message from the Shah's widow.[33]

Second, the state limited the spatial mobility of women, especially secular women. Women would no longer go anywhere at any time. Public theaters were separated into male and female sectors. University classes were divided into male and female parts. Buses also were divided into male and female sections. Females would risk an encounter with the moral police if caught riding bicycles or driving alone at night or on unusual routes. Several attempts were made to separate transportation according to gender – a policy in force in Saudi Arabia. In 1994, some 300 taxis were allocated for the transport of female passengers only.[34] However, the rising population, mushrooming urbanization, a shortage of transportation and popular opposition made such attempts unsuccessful.

Third, the state limited the interactional mobility of women by limiting and conditioning their interaction with male strangers, even young boys! Even as late as 1999, Khatami's liberal government was still expanding these limits. On 4 April the education ministry issued a statement forbidding 'the presence of women teachers in classes with schoolboys over the age of 10'.[35] Association with men outside marriage and marrying a non-Muslim are forbidden and punishable. If an unrelated man and woman are found interacting with each other in a secluded environment, they will be subjected to police interrogation and are forced to provide documents of marital or blood connection. In case of failure to do this, both are taken to the police station and punished for their immorality. Male and female students are not allowed to look at each other intimately or even exchange smiles in public places. According to a report by Agence France Presse (11 June 1994), Iranian police warned women against 'untimely' smiles to strangers and behavior that would provoke 'satanic desires'. In the same week, the *Jomhouri Islami*, a conservative paper owned by the leader of the Islamic Republic, urged police to pressure women and young girls to keep themselves covered 'before looking out the window'. The paper added that 'appearing without Islamic covering can arouse the covetous looks of the strangers and the satanic desires'. It also warned women about 'misplaced smiles' or behavior that could 'expose them to corruption'. The burden of these draconian rules becomes clear when one realizes that one cannot engage in these activities even in the absence of moral police. Often students are arrested unexpectedly on the grounds that they have been found secretly smiling, or interacting or coming into contact with an unrelated member of the opposite sex. These encounters do not always have to be real.

On many occasions religious forces use such accusations either to extort money from their victims or to settle personal scores. Even the state has used male–female relationships as a means of control and punishment against its opposition. Many members of political oppositions (i.e. the writer Ali Akbar Sirjani and the editor Faraj Sarkouhi) were accused falsely of intimate relationships with unrelated women.

Fourth, the Islamic state began to domesticate women by forcing many of them to give up their jobs and return to the home, thus limiting their occupational mobility. Domestication of women was a policy fit for the localization of female labor and its exploitation in non-wage activities at home. During the early years of the IRI employed women were specifically asked to give up their jobs in order to open up employment for their men. Domestication of female labor released both the government and private sector of responsibility to provide for the welfare of female labor. At home, these women are left to their husbands or their parents to care for. They become a source of free labor for the society without any cost. At home, they are tied to antiquated customs and traditions which channel their energies into reproductive, emotional and domestic work.

Although in terms of their goals and substance the two processes of globalization and localization worked against each other, their implementation followed a tumultuous road that was neither direct nor continuous. The implementation of each process was riddled with conflict, tension, resistance, gains and losses. The gains and losses were partially determined by the amount of repression the state used in enforcing its policies, partially by the degree of legitimacy the religious forces had established in overthrowing the Pahlavi dictatorship, and partially by the amount of resistance shown to these policies by local and international forces affected by them.

In the first decade of the revolution, the impact of the IRI's localization policies towards women was mixed. For religious women, who were practically banned from public engagement by their husbands and/or religious authorities during the Pahlavi period, their veiled public presence, something that the government was also interested in, was a symbol of liberation from social and spatial isolation. To them, the chador (an overall cover revealing only the face) is a form of protection against the unwanted and undignified looks of sinful men. Today, if they wish it, and their husbands and parents agree, they find it much easier to appear and engage in public life.

That such a public life is limited and controlled by religious men bothers these women less than if it had been a morally inappropriate one.[36]

However, the suppression of ideologies and Islamicization of society resulted in the wide-scale migration of educated and skilled sectors of Iranian society, including many women, either on their own or accompanying their husbands or parents. These families could no longer bear the impact of these policies and could afford to leave the country and launch a risky, but possibly freer life in foreign lands. Those secular forces who could not leave the country bore the brunt of restrictions imposed by the Islamic state. For Western-educated, middle-class women, these restrictions resulted in a loss of social status, meaningful employment and individual autonomy. To them, wearing chador against their will was an insult to their dignity. The chador represented imprisonment, imposition, backwardness and immobility.

Islamic policies applied to women have had devastating effects on the lives of Iranian women in general, and secular women in particular. Religious courts have condemned hundreds of women to death by stoning for adultery. Hundreds of women have been executed in prisons for their political defiance to the IRI. Numerous female prisoners have been raped prior to their execution. Thousands of women have been tortured in prisons for their political activities. Women all over the country are routinely harassed, jailed, fined and flogged for their violation of dress and behavioral codes.[37] The Islamicization of culture has pumped new life into the traditional patriarchy present in the Iranian society. Wealthy men have taken advantage of the new rule of temporary marriage (*sigheh*) and have extended their sexual harem beyond and against the wishes of their regular wives.[38] Finding the court on their side, abusive men feel they have a freer hand in imposing their wishes on their wives and daughters. These policies and the restrictive environment they have created, along with the activities of hard-line vigilantes as the hidden arm of the state, have resulted in a sense of powerlessness among most women, the resort to divorce by many others,[39] and suicide by those who cannot bear them any more. A study found that between 1989 and 1993 the suicide rate in the country doubled, most victims being women. The suicide rate has been especially high among women in the small towns and religiously charged areas where social restrictions on women are much higher and there is less room for escape from or defiance to these rules. For instance, according to the same study, between 60 to 80 percent of suicides in Turkemansahra, Ilam and Lorestan were committed by young women. Most of these women were illiterate and poor and suffered depression.[40]

According to Zahra Shojaie, President Khatami's adviser on women's affairs, a government study found young women in the city of Qum, the religious capital of Iran where moral restrictions are excessive, were more depressed than those in the more liberal capital Tehran.[41]

Women's resistance to Islamicization

The first and widest women's reaction to localization of the rules governing women's behavior was the widespread opposition to Ayatollah Khomeini's order for universal female veiling. On 8 March 1979, hundreds of thousands of women took to the streets of Tehran, and several other cities, in opposition to this decree. Initially, the regime reacted mildly by softening the language of the decree and trying to put a positive spin on its implications. However, finding women unyielding, the regime began a campaign of suppression which basically whipped any open and public opposition to veiling. By the summer of 1980, veiling became mandatory for women in all public institutions. Failure to comply with the strict codes was enough cause to lose one's employment, or for those registered in various levels of the educational system, one's educational status. This development took place in a context in which secular courts were replaced by religious and revolutionary courts and women's testimony in the court was downgraded to half that of a man's.

With the consolidation of power by the regime, especially in the early years of the war with Iraq, women had no choice but to turn to more subtle and quieter means of resistance. The first and most effective means of resistance was symbolic:

how to present one's body in public. How women dressed and handled their bodies and gestures in public arenas became a battleground for both suppression and resistance. The state became sensitive to the color, size, shape and thickness of the fabric used for veiling. The slightest hair left uncovered on a woman's head was subject to verbal and physical attack by Islamic vigilantes. The kind of stockings and shoes worn, the amount and color of lipsticks used, and the tightness of clothing worn determined conformity or resistance to state policies. This self-discovery and self-affirmation is one of the remarkable achievements of women in confronting the constraints imposed on them by the IRI. As defined by Esfandiari, 'through the dress code, the state endeavors to define and symbolically control the role of women. By flaunting the dress code, women not only seek to score points against the authorities; they also strive to assert autonomy over their own persons.'[42] These tactics continue to remain effective means of defiance and opposition today.

In the second decade of the revolution, women's reaction to state policies and Islamic ideology was different. While in the first decade of the revolution Iranian women lost their ability to fight this regime openly, and the war with Iraq allowed the regime to impose its universal control much more easily, in the second decade of the revolution women engaged in a new wave of resistance and demands that the IRI found harder to suppress. Demands for wider participation in society and the establishment of a civil society were the hallmarks of these years, especially latterly under the presidency of Mohammad Khatami.

After the war with Iraq ended, things began to change. Religious women who had accepted much of the rationale for their status in society offered by the religious elite and participated in various state-sponsored activities, including participation in the war by helping their brothers to fight the infidel Saddam, became impatient with the clerical establishment. There were several reasons for this. First of all, many of these women had given their lives, children, savings and energy to a cause that they were told would succeed. The failure to win the war devastated many of these families and made them suspicious of the divine nature of commands issued by the clerical establishment. Second, a decade of war had left most families poorer and demoralized. The economic decline had put extra pressure on women, who bore the responsibility of caring for all family members. The economic failure of the regime to lift the status of the poor and eliminate poverty also proved to these Iranians that the religious leadership knew little about the economy and had no intention of yielding power to skilled individuals at the expense of their control. Third, a decade of revolution had given the religious men time to prove their sincerity in what they preached: equality of men and women under the banner of Islam. In that they had failed.[43] It was not difficult for the religious women to see that much of what they were handed as religion came from religious men.

Fourth, a decade of division and suspicion between religious and secular women, often incited by religious leadership, began to break down. More understanding and compassion had developed between the two groups, especially as a result of discrimination and prejudices against the secular women who had continued to remain powerless and victimized.

Fifth, a decade of isolation of secular intellectuals and secular forces had pushed them toward cultural and educational activities such as translation of feminist literature and the latest intellectual works from the West. Finally, as the decade came to an end, globalization and change were in full swing.

Political changes and technological development around the world were having impacts on various social groups in almost all countries, especially women. Ideas of democracy, civil rights, women's rights and citizenship had become the topic of the day. Iran could not remain isolated from these developments, no matter how the clerical elite tried to prevent it.

These developments laid the ground for the reemergence of women's activism among both secular and religious women.

While the Islamic government's reaction to globalization has been in the form of localization of identity, culture, traditions and social norms, Iranian women's reactions have taken a course in between. Realizing the necessity of having access to the technological, scientific and communicational skills of the globalized world, and working against a localized but totalizing religious ideology and state apparatus, Iranian women have begun to demand access to global resources but at a pace and in tune with their local needs and concerns. They have begun to connect their local conditions to global forces of patriarchy and social inequality. They have discovered the role of local agency and its impact on changing global structures. They are pressing against and going beyond the narrowly defined Islamic codes of femininity imposed by the IRI. They are challenging the validity, universality and generalizability of religious codes concerning female status within family and society.

Realizing primacy of technology, science and economic development, they are interested to learn and receive education in these resources but not at the expense of denying their own cultural identity and historical heritage. In response to the government's demands for denial of their Iranian identity, they have emphasized their allegiance to their national symbols and cultural values. In response to its centralizing tendencies for power and control, they have turned to decentralization and diversification of women's participation in society, particularly in the form of non-governmental organizations.

Women and civil society

One of the hallmarks of globalization is the increase in the role of civil society – families, tribes, neighborhoods, associations, guilds, etc. Globalization reduces the role of national governments and demands a more active participation of forces of civil society, individual citizens, media, organizations and enterprises. As a crucial segment of the Iranian civil society, women have gained tremendous influence on government by promoting women's activism, stimulating politicians to react to women's needs, and fighting against religious laws denying them career opportunities and the right to divorce, custody, and equal inheritance. Iranian women have learned how to eat the forbidden fruit, cross imposed lines, neutralize the effects of draconian laws affecting their lives, and erect a dam of resistance in the path of a reactionary flood threatening their existence. They are taking their traditional society further down the road toward sexual equality. They are changing their socialization practices by sending their daughters to school, allowing them to have careers, teaching them not to be shy, and asking them not to defer to men who do not defer to them.

Since the early 1990s, four forces have become the most vibrant aspects of the Iranian civil society challenging the clerical state: women, youth, intellectuals/writers, and the press.[44] Since Khatami's election, press licenses have been granted much more liberally, spawning a proliferation of new magazines and raising the total of national daily newspapers to 26. The status of women in society has become a repeated theme of many of these newspapers and magazines.

Twenty-nine of these publications are devoted solely to women, of which the following have a longer history and wider circulation: *Zanan*, *Zane Rouz*, *Payam Hajar*, *Zan*, *Payam Zan*, *Payam Haajar*, *Jahaan Zan*, *Kousar*, *Neda*, *Farzaaneh*, *Al-Tahereh*, and *Mahjoobeh*.[45] Among these magazines, *Zanan* has had a special role in advancing the gender discourse among both religious and secular women. By reporting on various forms of discrimination against women and questioning many of the laws affecting women's lives, *Zanan* has been able to generate lively discussion about gender issues both within and outside the country. These discussions and dialogues, mostly carried out in the press, have created an empowering atmosphere in which Iranian women have been able to elevate their concerns for gender inequality to national issues.

Women's support for Khatami's call to establish a 'civil society' has been strong and steady. This support is indicative of women's desire for the establishment of an autonomous space in which they can regain responsibility for their social and physical well-being. In this respect, the desired 'civil society' is meant to secure a dignified social space for various social groups, including women. The new energy and creativity women have brought to Iranian civil society is fuelled by their hopes for freedom, equality and democratic pluralism.

By supporting Khatami's election, women have put enormous pressure on him and the IRI to confront the violence and indignities of Hezbollahis (vigilantes) against women in public and private spheres. Such pressures have forced the ruling clergy to distance themselves, at least publicly, from those street thugs whose physical attacks had been a major source of annoyance in women's lives. Forced to deal with these groups, on 28 August 1999, the intelligence chief Ali Yunesi, after stating that most of these vigilantes were pious and motivated by religious values, admitted that 'they are extreme, harsh, self-willed people headed for destruction'. He finally acknowledged that 'once, some of these people threw acid at the faces of women and deeply hurt the Leader'.' Of course, he forgot to mention that at the time of this incident the Leader neither acknowledged it nor did he do anything to prevent similar future acts against women.[46]

Religious leaders have often used the universalist tone of Quranic verses as evidence for the inclusiveness of Islam and the universality of its message. Women activists, both religious and secular, have started to problematize the vagueness of these verses and question the fact that the interpretation of these texts has often been monopolized by male jurisprudents. In other words, female

Islamic activists[47] have begun to deconstruct Islamic familism, the logic of gender separation, and the meanings assigned to religious texts by the ulama's androcentric interpretation. They have begun to expose the unequal division of labor, widespread domestic violence, dependency relations and the inferior position assigned to women within the Iranian Islamic family. While these Islamic women accept the family as a natural unit for sexual satisfaction and reproduction, they question its organizational and exploitative bias against female members. While accepting it as a natural shield against unwanted outside influences and as a protective unit generating meaningful religiously sanctioned relationships amongst its members, they point to the tensions, conflicts and inequality hidden within Islamic family relationships. These female Muslim activists have become so visible and demanding across the social and political spectrum, especially in media and politics, that they have forced Islamicists to come up with new strategies to limit their influence. They have been able to convince the Islamic clerics that gender does make a difference in the formation of public policy, especially as it relates to women's well-being vis-à-vis men.

Women's demands for an increasing presence in civil society have been in line with the demands of the general population for greater emphasis on environmental protection, sustainable economic development, gender equality, human and citizenry rights, rule of law and non-violence.

Both group interests and the general repressive conditions present in the IRI have caused women to support these values and treat them as women's issues. Women have discovered that their biggest enemy is ignorance caused by lack of education. Access to education and information have become the primary concern of parents, especially mothers. More and more women are realizing that education gives them independence and they are entitled to make choices. There are more women obtaining an education. Female enrolment in the educational system has increased at all levels. During 1999 close to half of the medical students and slightly over 50 percent of students entering universities were women.[48] Based on official statistics, from 1976 to 1995 the literacy rate among urban women increased 160 percent, while for men this increase was 120 percent.[49]

Alienated from a state which divides its citizens along the lines of 'we/insider' (*Khodi*) and 'them/outsider' (*Ghayre Khodi*) – a common distinction made by the religious elites – secular women and religious women who do not share the ideology of the state have to look outside the state for a sense of belonging and identity. When the concept of 'nation' is usurped by the ruling elite as a community solely of 'insiders' and the rest of society is characterized as 'outsiders' and denied access to political processes, those 'outsiders' have no choice but to develop their communities/groups of 'insiders' in order to gain a sense of identity and collective presence. Non-governmental organizations (NGOs), social clubs, and local associations become important sources of social identity. The number of these organizations has increased dramatically. A government report in 1998 cited 46 registered NGOs.[50] Most of these groups and organizations are nevertheless partially or totally tied to and/or dependent on the government. Their institutional ties to the state often cripple them in serving their constituency's interests.

If engaged in serving their constituency, they have to be careful not to offend the state or run against its ideology and interests. Still, the mere proliferation of these groups has increased women's confidence and determination to gain control of their own lives. The importance of non-governmental organizations for facilitating women's participation in social and political arena has been recognized even by the clerical officials in Iran. In a speech on 11 August 1999, Khatami called for women to take a greater political role in Iran, insisting that the sexes were equal under Islam. He called for the establishment of more civic and non-governmental organizations to benefit Iran's women. He insisted that 'even if women are engaged as homemakers and don't take on outside responsibilities, facilities should be institutionalized for their active presence in the political and social arena'.[51]

What is amazing is that despite the economic hardships which have reduced the lot of all Iranians and increased women's domestic and occupational tasks, women still find the time and energy to engage in collective activities of consciousness-raising, political rallies, meetings and social events. The demand by women for meaningful political participation has been there since the beginning of the revolution. Even religious women have been able to stretch the career limits established by the IRI. The number of women in the Islamic Consultative Assembly (Majles or parliament) has increased to 11, out of a total of 270. Today a female religious jurisprudent also sits on the Council of Experts, a body responsible for the selection and supervision of the Leader of the IRI. Women, whose number of eligible voters is four percent lower than eligible male voters, make up 40 percent of votes in most elections. In the last presidential election in 1997, Azam Taleghani, a religious woman and daughter of one of the close allies of Ayatollah Khomeini during the revolution, nominated herself for presidency. The Guardian Council, responsible for vetting candidates and insuring the compatibility of all legislation with Islam, rejected her candidacy. Taleghani's candidacy opened up a can of worms that the IRI had difficulty closing. Women across political and ideological spectrums and several male religious leaders argued that there was no religious decree barring women from the presidency.

These demands, plus women's support for his presidency, forced President Khatami to appoint a woman to his cabinet and appoint several more as municipal administrators.

Unfortunately, many of the gains by these women remain at advisory level and have not resulted in actual control at decision-making level. Representation at even these levels is both inadequate and skewed. First of all, there are not that many offices in which women are promoted to the higher ranks. Second, many of the cases are really token positions established to appease women and give an outward impression of participation, although this tokenism will still have some positive effect in the long run. Third, most women appointed to high administrative positions are religiously conformist and politically committed to the ideology of the state and its view of women's rights. Many subscribe to the misogynist ideology of the state and often show friendly reaction to policies which are blatantly against women's interests. For example, in 1998, two laws harmful to women's social and physical well-being were passed in parliament without effective opposition from the female representatives: a press law forbidding instrumental use of female pictures in the press[52] and another separating male and female medical facilities, with the stipulation that women have to be treated by female doctors unless authorized by their husbands. Fourth, nationalist, leftist, secularist, modernist women, who either are against or indifferent to the ideology of the IRI, are excluded from any meaningful occupation in society and position in the government.

Still, the presence of these women, even though mostly religious, in various layers of the government is an advancement on the early months of the 1990s when women were thrown out of these positions. We should not forget that women's employment, particularly in the industrial sector, experienced a serious setback between 1980 and 1986. While it did improve to some extent by 1991, it never reached the level it had achieved in the late Pahlavi period. The presence of these women in various government and social occupations has brought women's issues to the heart of the system. The views and concerns demonstrated by these religious women increasingly resemble some of the basic concerns and views of secular women. These achievements, of course, remain limited and constantly under threat from the Islamic state. In the most favorable scenario, when these efforts do come to fruition, the state often undermines them by political clientalism, corruption and co-opting. In the least favorable scenario, if found subversive to the state power and antithetical to its ideology, they are folded quickly and eliminated altogether. Iranian women still lack the organizational infrastructure for a sustainable civil society.

Participation of Iranian women in the election of local councils in February 1999 was the latest front for independent women to demonstrate their desire for social and political empowerment. Nationally, there were 5,000 women among 330,000 candidates running for almost 200,000 seats. Many women, including President Khatami's eldest sister, age 61 and a mother of six, from the central desert town of Ardakan, won seats on these councils. In a country in which women constitute only 0.3 percent of government managers,[53] women's presence in these councils can make a big difference in removing barriers to women's social and political participation. These municipal councils are new vehicles of social participation and empowerment for both men and women. Though provision for these councils had been made in the constitution, they were not implemented until early 1999 when Khatami decided to put this promise into action. A major goal of these local councils is to decentralize political power and empower local politics where individuals and groups might have a better chance of participation and involvement – a strategy well suited to the new women's movement in Iran.

Post-revolutionary women's activism in Iran

The post-Cold War international atmosphere has been highly saturated with the discussion of women's rights, human rights, the environment, ethnic violence, civil society, citizenship and democratization. These global themes have become so commonplace that it is hard to find any national setting not influenced by them. These themes have created structures of opportunity for the emergence of social movements across the globe. Given the vast opportunities and promises created around the world by globalization, Iranian women find themselves positioned by the IRI on shaky ground. To demand those opportunities in the midst of a repressive and misogynist state, Iranian women find themselves forced to be more concerned with their basic rights, security against the unyielding forces of fanaticism, and dignity in face of two decades of assault on their identity and status. In their battles with the structures of domination present in their daily routines at home, in the market and factory, in the street and office, and on buses and planes, Iranian women find themselves oscillating between contradictory tendencies: between the desire to defy and that to survive, between liberation and destruction, between achieving the peace of freedom and dealing with fear of violence.

A major aspect of Iranian women's desire for, and participation in, civil society is the dynamics by which these wishes are expressed and fulfilled. While there is no homogeneous women's movement in the country, there has been a rise in the number of organized women's groups in Iran. Since the death of Khomeini in 1989 and the presidency of Ali Akbar Hashemi-Rafsanjani in the same year, there have been concerted efforts by individual women in various professions, especially the film industry and journalism, and public arenas in Iran. All groups of women, Islamicist or secular, skilled or unskilled, educated or uneducated, old or young, have begun to show a higher level of awareness of their condition and to demand more control over the processes of their daily living, their relations with their parents, husbands, children and men outside of their kin. This awareness, and its subsequent activism, are aimed at ameliorating women's social conditions, denouncing violence against women, resisting repressive policies of the state, and opposing discriminatory laws affecting women's lives. These women, working in different arenas and with varied voices and tactics, are questioning power structures that engender inequalities between men and women. The importance of women's role in social and political change in Iran has caused some analysts to see them as the main source of the next revolution. Here are the comments of a CIA analyst:

> What is the strongest group in Iran from which the revolution could spring? That's an easy one: the women. They are a very vibrant group, very strong and they are influential within Iranian society. The women also hold one of the two last banners of the Islamic revolution by – excuse the expression – the balls: the chador. The other banner is hatred of the United States and Israel. The chador is the way in which the revolution is manifested in every square, on every street. Through the chador you create the feeling of an Islamic revolution in motion. Take it away, and bye-bye ayatollahs.[54]

While the strategy of women's groups in earlier periods was based on mass movement against the state, as expressed in anti-government demonstrations in the 1970s and early 1980s, the current strategy is to move in diffused directions, focus on incremental gains, empower local groups, and aim for smaller but sustainable changes. Women are concerned with tangible issues affecting their lives, such as the right of divorce, child custody, and inheritance. Suspicious of 'vanguardism' and the 'praxical rigidity' of leftist and nationalist movements of earlier periods,[55] the post-revolutionary women's activism has a 'self-reflective' dimension through which these women become active agents of their own lives by recoursing and reinterpreting the imposed structures and relationships. Women are less committed to totalizing ideology, grand theories and broad organizations. Instead, they devote more of their political energies to the localization of global values, which removes parochial obstacles to their growth, preserves their identity and dignity against the assaults by the totalitarian gender policies of the state, and prepares a taller stand from which they will make their next move.

Post-revolutionary women's activism is marked by much greater individualism than ever observed in the past century, albeit not as great as that found in the West. Certainly, the new individualism is reinforced by globalizing forces of modernity weighing heavily on a country pushed away from those forces for the past two decades. This new individualism balances between individual, social and global identities by emphasizing autonomy, nationalism and globalization at the same time. It balances the emotional and rational, faith and reason, traditional and modernity, and culture and civilization. The culture of this new activism can be best described as what Lubbers[56] has called a 'we-culture' against the Western 'me-culture'.

Two decades of ideological and political work by the IRI to force a collectivist identity on the Iranian women have not only failed to produce the desired outcome but have actually given rise to a desire to strike a balance between the extremes of Western individualism and Islamic collectivism. Women have become less concerned about political power, revolution and ideology. They are more concerned with control of their own lives within political, social and economic institutions, whatever the ideological configurations of those institutions.

Interestingly, in the same way that the IRI has targeted their bodies as an ideological battleground for control, women have also put an important emphasis on the control over their body. Their body has become the battlefield with the IRI. The government demands these women hide their physical and social identities. Women, in turn, are asserting their identities by peeling off layers of physical and ideological covers imposed on them. As one Iranian woman has observed, 'Lipstick is not just lipstick in Iran. It transmits a political message. It is a weapon.'[57]

The new Iranian women's movements have been able to articulate a far more multifaceted perspective of women's interests and concerns. These concerns include a greater awareness of human rights, individual rights, individual autonomy within marriage, family independence within the kinship network, and a form of national consciousness against the global diffusion of Western values. Their support for and desire to participate in celebration of the Iranian soccer success in the 1998 World Cup is one example of this nationalist consciousness. The wide participation of female activists and even ordinary women in the funeral of the victims of state-sponsored terrors, nationalist activists Dariush and Parvaneh Forouhar, and writers Majid Sharif, Mohammad Mokhtari, and Ja'far Poyandeh, is another example.

Iranian women's post-revolutionary activism can be best characterized as what Melucci has termed 'collective action without actors'.[58] In a movement of this kind, actors retransmit the domination of its own contradictions by reversing its imposed codes of meanings, subjecting its boundaries to pressures and inevitably contraction, and exposing its nature by personal declaration of its cruelty through various mediums available to them. It also can be argued that, very much as Rowbotham outlined years ago with regard to the feminist movement in a different context, these activities are structureless, directionless and without leadership.[59] These features can be both negative or positive, depending on what kind of politics is involved, what kind of goals a movement has, and how it produces the conditions of its own exhaustion. While it is true that there is little coordination between women's activism in different sectors of Iranian society, and thus little predictability associated with them, it would be wrong to underestimate their gradual and evolutionary effects on both women and the Islamic state. On the government's part, this social awakening/activism, accompanied by a high level of defensive self-activity, has increased enormously the cost of social control for the Islamic state. As a result, not only does social control require a higher investment of energy and social provision by the state, at the same time it has become less effective in gaining compliance from citizens. It has also reduced the internalization effects of the dominant ideology and has increased the necessity of resorting to external means of violence as a means of insuring compliance with state regulations and ideological stipulations. Many of the legitimation tools used by the Islamic government in earlier periods have lost their validity and become ineffective, thus forcing it to react to any transgression more lethally. Furthermore, the high activity, high visibility and widespread presence of women in social contexts will open greater space for them, thus reducing the patriarchal space.

On the women's part, their higher self-consciousness and self-activity have resulted in a creeping change in the public attitudes towards them, especially within the government and media. Women's activism and their higher level of awareness have put tremendous pressure on the Islamic state to ease its control and restrictions. Of course, technology and globalization have been important contributors in this respect.

The speed with which information has flown into the country, despite enormous efforts by the Islamic state to block it, has made it hard for the government to hide its corrupt practices and repressive measures. Another feature of new female activism in Iran is its reliance on women as the source of change. Learning from the unsuccessful experiences of the past, where women's emancipation would have come naturally and automatically with the success of a national struggle against dictatorship and imperialism, Iranian women have begun to form their own organizations, forums and groups, away and separate from men's organizations. These organizations, groupings, and collective endeavors allow them to discuss universal and national issues from their own particularistic perspective so that their specific concerns receive focused attention. Though these all-women organizations often help to promote the separatist policies of the IRI, it does have its positive side as well. In a traditional society where there is high sensitivity to male–female interactions, these new all-women organizations reduce traditional male sensitivity to women participation in organized activities outside of the home. This was an important factor among religious and traditional families during the Pahlavi era, whose women were not allowed to be active participants in public arenas due to male presence.

A major weakness of the emerging women's activism in contemporary Iran is its weak link with the international women's movement structure. Some Iranian women's organizations have participated in the Nairobi and Beijing conferences on women and have been involved with the UN commissions on women's rights. However, these organizations are either an extension of the state or controlled by it indirectly. The participation and agenda of all the groups present in these international forums were screened by the Islamic Republic. None represented secular women working outside the confines of the state. Non-government organizations participating in these conferences either enjoyed the blessing of the Islamic state or had to make sure that their words and actions in these foreign forums did not trigger Islamic sensitivity at home.

To be successful, women activists need to go beyond their current efforts and open a dialogue with labor, political factions, economic institutions and international human rights groups in order to inform them of Iranian women's concerns and needs and point out the various aspects of their policies and positions. Dialogue among women's groups, solidarity with women's organizations within and outside the region, and interaction with various agencies representing the interests of women are necessary steps in strengthening and expanding the scope of these women's efforts.

Notes

1 Jeremy Brecher and Tim Costello, *Global Village or Global Pillage: Economic Reconstruction from the Bottom Up* (Boston, Mass: South End Press, 1994).

2 See Paul Hirst and Grahame F. Thompson, *Globalization in Question* (Cambridge: Polity Press, 1996); and John Zysman, 'The myth of a "Global Economy": Enduring national foundations and emerging regional realities', *New Political Economy*, Vol. 1, No. 2, 1996.

3 Maurice Strong, 'The "New South",' *The World Today*, November 1995, pp. 215–19.

4 Richard J. Barnet and John Cavanagh, *Global Dreams: Imperial Corporations and the New World Order* (New York: Simon and Schuster, 1994).

5 James H. Mittelman (ed.), *Globalization: Critical Reflections* (Boulder and London: Lynne Rienner, 1996).

6 David Harvey, *The Condition of Postmodernity: An Inquiry into the Origins of Cultural Change* (Oxford: Basil Blackwell, 1989), p.204.

7 Anthony Giddens, *A Contemporary Critique of Historical Materialism* (London and Basingstoke: Macmillan, 1981), pp. 91–7.

8 Benjamin R. Barber, 'Jihad Vs. McWorld', *The Atlantic*, March 1992, pp. 53–63.

9 David Harvey, *The Condition of Postmodernity*, pp. 272–4; and A. McGrew 'A global society?' in Stuart Hall, David Held and A. McGrew (eds) (Cambridge/Oxford: Polity/Open University Press, 1992), pp. 61–102.

10 Mohammad Reza Pahlavi, *Besu-e Tamaddon-e Bozorg* (Towards the Great Civilization), (Tehran: Sherkat-e Offset-e Sahami-ye Amm, 1978).
11 James A. Bill, 'Modernization and reform from above: the case of Iran', *Middle East Journal*, 27 February 1970.
12 Marvin Zonis, *The Political Elite of Iran* (Princeton: Princeton University Press, 1971).
13 Bizhan Jazani, *Capitalism and Revolution in Iran* (London: Zed Books, 1981).
14 Ali Akbar Mahdi, 'The Iranian struggle for liberation: socio-historical roots to the Islamic Revolution', *The Review of Iranian Political Economy and History*, Vol. IV, No. 1, Spring 1980.
15 See the Shah's views on women in an interview with renowned Italian journalist Oriana Fallaci, *Interview with History* (Boston: Houghton Mifflin, 1976). Her article on the Shah is also instructive: 'The Shah of Iran', *New Republic*, No. 1, December 1973.
16 For a review of developments in employment in this period, see research by Kayhan Group, *Eshteghal-e Zanan dar Moze-haaye Tasmimgiri dar Bakhsh-haaye Khousoosi va Dolati* (Women's employment in decision-making position in government and private sectors), (Tehran: The Women's Organization of Iran, 1354); for legal developments, see Behnaz Pakizegi 'Legal and social positions of Iranian women', in Louis Beck and Nikki Keddie (eds), *Women in the Muslim World* (Cambridge: Harvard University Press, 1978); and Mahnaz Afkhami *Hoghoghe Zan dar Iran* (Women and the law in Iran, 1967–1978). (Washington, DC: Women's Center of the Foundation for Iranian Studies, 1994); for an overview in English see Guity Nashat 'Women in prerevolutionary Iran: a historical overview' in Guity Nashat (ed.), *Women and Revolution in Iran* (Boulder and London: Westview Press, 1983).
17 Nikki R. Keddie with Richard Yann, *Roots of Revolution* (New Haven, Conn.: Yale University Press, 1983).
18 See Haideh Moghissi, *Populism and Feminism in Iran; Women's Struggle in a Male-Defined Revolutionary Movement* (New York: St. Martin's Press, 1994).
19 For a review of developments in this period, see Parvin Paidar, *Women and the Political Process in Twentieth-Century Iran* (Cambridge, England: Cambridge University Press, 1995).
20 See Hussein Saffaar Harandi, 'Economic security from three perspectives', *Kayhan*, 7 Shahrivar 1378 (29 August 1999).
21 See 'Iran's economy: ailing, still' *The Economist*, 14 August 1999. US edition.
22 Quoted by a trade ministry official, Kar-o Kargar, 4 Shahrivar 1378 (26 August 1999).
23 See Sohrab Behdad, 'The post-revolutionary economic crisis', pp. 97–128, in Saeed Rahnema & Sohrab Behdad *Iran After the Revolution; Crisis of an Islamic State* (London and New York: I.B. Tauris, 1995).
24 Estimates of real inflation are hard to come by. Government officials often give contradictory remarks. In 1997, the President Akbar Hashemi-Rafsanjani said that the total inflation since 1989 stood at 595 percent. See his interview in the Persian daily *Jomhuri Islami*, 20 July 1997.
25 See Colin Barraclough, 'Iran confronts a long-hidden problem: drugs', *New York Times*, 29 August 1999.
26 See Eric Rouleau, 'Iran: an economy in need of reform', *Middle East Economic Survey*, Vol. XLII, No. 27, 5 July 1999.
27 On an Air France jet to Iran in February 1979, a reporter asked Ayatollah Khomeini how he felt about going back to Iran after 16 years in exile. His response then shocked keen Iranians who were wary of his political intentions, and later many Iranians who blamed themselves for not being able to read such an obvious sign early enough.
28 See Oliver Roy, *The failure of political Islam* (London: I.B. Tauris. 1994); Fred Halliday, 'The politics of Islamic fundamentalism: Iran, Tunisia, and the challenge of the secular state', in Akbar Ahmed and H. Donnan (eds) *Islam, Globalization and Postmodernity* (London: Routledge, 1994). It should be noted that historically Shiism has been a nationalist reaction to Arab domination of Iran. Khomeini's political Islam,

while de-emphasizing the division between Shia and Sunni, grounded itself in a Shii interpretation of politics in Islam. In the past two years, President Mohammad Khatami has tried more effectively to move this religious nationalism towards a more modern and secular direction. He has attempted to justify his call for an Islamic civil society by an appeal to the secular conception of nationalism advocated by the nationalist Premier, Dr. Mohammad Musaddeq.

29 Islamic Republic News Agency (IRNA), Tehran, 8 March 1995.

30 IRNA, 4 August 1999.

31 Valentine M. Moghadam, *Modernizing Women: Gender and Social Change in the Middle East* (Boulder: Lynne Rienner Publishers, 1993).

32 Hanna Papanek, 'The woman and the ideal society: control and autonomy in the construction of identity' in Valentine Moghadam, *Identity Politics and Women: Cultural Reassertion and Feminism in the International Perspective* (Oxford: Westview Press, 1994), pp. 42–75.

33 Early in the 1980s, when Ayatollah Khomeini was alive, Iranian Radio and TV found itself in the position of angering him by airing on a call-in show an Iranian woman's honest opinion about her choice of a role model. She chose a woman named Usha, a self-sacrificing and hard-working character in a Japanese TV serial aired at the time, as a better representation of the Iranian woman than Fatemeh Zahra, the daughter of the prophet Mohammad. The Ayatollah happened to hear this comment. To cool his anger, the manager of the program was sacked and efforts were made to keep the identity of the woman secret because in the Ayatollah's view her words had qualified her for a death penalty.

34 *Jomhouri Islami*, 6 February 1994.

35 Agence France Presse, 4 April 1994.

36 See Ali Akbar Mahdi, 'Reconstructing gender in post-revolutionary Iran: transcending the revolution?', *Middle East Insight*, Vol. XI, No. 5, July–August 1995.

37 A simple indication of the number of these arrests can be found in a statement by the European Parliament indicating that in one year (Sept '91–Sept '92) some 113,000 women were arrested in Iran for violation of dress code. See *Iran Times*, Mehr 1371 (September 1992).

38 See Shahla Haeri, *Law of Desire; Temporary Marriage in Shi'i Iran* (Syracuse, NY: Syracuse University Press. 1989.

39 According to a report by the conservative newspaper, *Resalat* (25 August 1999), in the first quarter of this calendar year (21 March–21 June 1999), more than 11,200 cases of divorce were registered, up 16 percent year on year.

40 Somayeh Askari, 'Women, main victims of suicide in Iran', *Farhang-e Tose'e* (a monthly cultural, social, political and economic journal published in Tehran, banned in 1999). Feb–March 1998.

41 Reuters News, Tehran, 29 August 1999.

42 Haleh Esfandiari, Reconstructed Lives; *Women and Iran's Islamic Revolution* (Washington, DC: The Woodrow Wilson Center Press and The Johns Hopkins University Press, 1997), p. 133.

43 For testimonies from Iranian women expressing their dissatisfaction with the revolution, see Haleh Esfandiari, *Reconstructed Lives; Women and Iran's Islamic Revolution* (Washington, DC: The Woodrow Wilson Center Press and The Johns Hopkins University Press, 1997).

44 See Ali Akbar Mahdi, *Farhang-e Irani, J'ame'eh-ye Madani, va Daghdaghe-ye Demokr'asi* (Iranian Culture, Civil Society, and Concern for Democracy), (Toronto: Javan Publications, 1998), especially Chapters 9 and 13.

45 See 'Majallaate Zanaan dar Iran', *Payaam Hajar*, No. 225, Autumn 1375 (Fall 1997). In a conference in Washington DC, as reported by the Associated Press on 18 March 1999, Ms Zahra Shojaie, President Khatami's advisor on women's affairs claimed that today 'there are 70 magazines and other publications for women' in Iran.

46 Reuters News, Tehran, 28 August 1999.

47 I have avoided using the label 'Islamic feminist' for these women. We have to be careful in labelling all Iranian women's social and political activism as 'feminism', either Islamic or non-Islamic, because many of these women themselves disavow the label even though their cause and demands are nothing short of feminist causes and demands.

48 *Zanan*, No. 51, Farvardin 1378 (March 1999).

49 *Tehran Times*. 12 December 1995.

50 These organizations are: Women's Solidarity Society (date of registration 1991), Society of Iranian Women for Sustainable Development (1993), Association of Women against Environmental Pollution (1993), Society of Women Church Supporters (1961), Armenian Women's Charitable Society (under the supervision of the Supreme Council of Armenian Vicarage, 1961), Assyrian Women's Society (1992), Society of Charitable Women (1981), Hazrat-e Khadijeh Foundation (1980), Hazrat-e Zeinab Foundation (1979), Hazrat-e Fatemeh Foundation (1993), Women Researchers Advisory Co-operative (not officially registered), Islamic Women's Institute of Iran (1978), Zeinab Society (1986), Women's Society of the Islamic Republic of Iran (1986), Women's Research and Study Centre (1986), Women's Baseej (Mobilization Unit, 1980), Women's Unit of the Labor House (1980), Yasaman Charitable Society (1983), Zahedan Narjes Islamic Science Centre (1966), Midwifery Society of Iran (1990), Theatrical Centre for Women (1985), Raad Charitable Women's Group (1994), Rural Women's Co-operatives (1992), Research and Engineering Society of Women (1993), Iran and Bosnia Women's Friendship Society (1994), Banoo Publishing Institute (1994), Jewish Women's Representative Office, Sajjadieh Noor Charitable Society, The Islamic Society of Physicians Women's Branch, Fatemieh Islamic Science School, Women's Charitable Society of Isfahan Province, Women's Esmatieh Institute of Ahvaz, Narjes Sabzevar School, Women's Social and Cultural Institute of Hamadan, Women's Islamic Science Centre of Hamadan, Jewish Women's Society, Sharif University Alumnae Association, Qum Fatemieh College for Women, Society of Zoroastrian Women, Domestic and International Marketing Centre for Women's Production, Society of Women Graduates of Al-Zahra University, Twelfth of Farvardin Foundation, Shah-e Cheragh Cultural Foundation, Sisters Unit of Co-ordinating Activities of Mosques, and Society of Nurses. Source: a government report of the status of women located on the internet at: http://www.salamiran.org/Women.

51 Agence France Presse, 11 August 1999.

52 The law states that, 'commercial use of women's images and texts declaring women's issues, humiliation, insult, propagation of formality, use of ornaments, and defending women beyond the bounds of legal and religious law is forbidden'. This law goes beyond a 1993 ban on the use of women in advertising. Women's pictures are not allowed on trademarks of any product.

53 This figure was given by Zahra Shojaie, the president's advisor on women's affairs, in a lecture in Zahedan, as reported by IRNA on 27 August, 1999.

54 Words of Reuel Gerecht, aka Edward Shirley, the CIA's top expert on Iran, 'Their man in Iran', *Ha'aretz Magazine*, 20 August 1999.

55 See Haideh Moghissi, *Populism and Feminism in Iran; Women's Struggle in a Male-Defined Revolutionary Movement* (New York: St. Martin's Press, 1994).

56 R.F.M. Lubbers, 'Globalization: an Exploration', *Nijenrode Management Review*, no.1, November 1996.

57 Quoted by Farzaneh Milani in 'Lipstick Politics in Iran', N*ew York Times*, 19 August 1999.

58 Alberto Melucci, *Nomads of the Present: Social Movements and Individual Needs in Contemporary Society* (London: Hutchinson Radius, 1989), pp. 75–8.

59 Sheila Rowbotham, *Beyond the Fragments: Feminism and the Making of Socialism* (London: Merlin Press, 1979).

Part II

Globalization

An economic and financial approach

In the dawn of the twenty-first century globalization is a process that spreads new technology and helps economies to grow faster than the national average, and it generally provides an incentive to increase the standard of life all over the world by equal access to consumer markets. However, this process can be an assault on national sovereignty, on local culture and furthermore on economic and social political stability. Developing countries have no alternative except to participate in regional integration in order to attract more investment. Integration with the regional economy is an important step for small and poor developing countries, eventually increasing their markets to the larger and more powerful neighbours; consequently regional integration is a survival kit for less-developed countries that have never been able to play an active role in the globalization process.

Iran as a developing country with large gas and oil reserves plus many other mineral resources can play an important role in the integration of regional markets as well as the globalization process. Unfortunately there is a daunting challenge to facing its political stability, namely the tension between modern forces known as reformist groups and traditional forces which have no idea about new models of global capitalism. In the light of existing tension over how to integrate Iran with regional and global economies, President Khatami's administration has managed to reduce government debts. At the end of 1999 Iran's debt to foreign banks was around $8.12 billion; the debt at the end of 2000 should reduce to $5.792 billion, including $646 million less than the previous year to foreign banks. Foreign banks lending money to Iran include Germany, with an outstanding loan of around $2.71 billion, and France, second highest lender with the figure of $1.359 billion. As far as the Islamic government is concerned the debt has been due to lack of economic policy in the past, and involvement in the conflict with traditional forces to the detriment of fostering foreign investment; the government could otherwise pay off the debts (*Ettelaat*, no. 1462, 4 June 2000). Iran is also suffering from a lack of 'know-how' (this extends to how to utilize its existing expertise to remain in government). There is also a lack of cohesion and coherent understanding among the reformist groups as to how to negotiate Iran's passage to global integration. Rather than promoting the understanding of global capitalism, the Islamic government is heading ever faster in the direction of fighting its internal enemies not to blackmail its daily running of the country.

In this part, Chapter 4 focuses on how economic globalization reduces a nation-state's ability to provide public goods. This process, which is harmful in the case of countries with a proper balance between the state and society, may in fact enhance chances for democracy in Iran by modifying the state's structure and function. Chapter 5's discussion is more concerned with the Iranian economy and international finance markets in the age of transition from capitalism to globalization. Currently the Iranian economy is in need of an infusion of capital and technology. Whilst the bulk of financial resources will be generated domestically – by both the government and private sectors – the role of foreign capital will be crucial to the Iranian economy. Every day close to one thousand billion dollars are moved across borders, which gives the order of magnitude of resources in international financial markets. Iran has not benefited from this source of finance. This chapter presents a complete picture of Iran's options vis-à-vis international financial markets. The strengths and the weaknesses of Iran's financial institutions are analysed and policies recommended for the optional utilization of international resources. In response to extensive changes in the international finance sector, for example, the Ministry of Posts, Telegraphs and Telephones recently established a data link between major Iranian banks with 60 countries for transferring data and financial transactions. Annual subscription to this service for the private sector is about $55 (*Ettelaat*, no. 89, 15 September 1994). Chapter 6 precisely summarizes the implications of Iranian economic policies in the past two decades, particularly the damage of the eight-year war with Iraq which resulted in one million casualties and tens of billions of dollars in structural damages. The economic embargo placed upon Iran by the United States reduced Iran's export market. There was massive immigration of refugees from Iraq and Afghanistan – according to official reports, 1.5 million Afghans and 400,000 Iraqis, plus a further 30,000 from Bangladesh and Pakistan, with only 5 per cent of the total housed in refugee camps. There are also 300,000–400,000 illegal Afghan refugees in the country (*Ettelaat*, no. 1464, 7 June 2000). With external as well as internal pressures mounting, the Iranian government was kept busy sorting out day-to-day problems. Consequently it failed to see the rapid changes emerging in the western world. Now, twenty years after the revolution, the Iranian government is facing the 'know-how' issue of how to go about the globalization process; but government officials are not aware that they are able to function effectively at home and abroad without attempting to reverse the brain drain and expertise in order to resolve the issues which are holding Iran back from the role it is actually able to play in the globalized world. The following chapters raise some of the problems that the Islamic Republic is facing now as a consequence. It is also important to note that the failure of economic policy in the past two decades has led the Minister of Agriculture himself to openly criticize the leadership's neglect and lack of planning policy on the agriculture sector. Official reports revealed that over eight years an annual four per cent growth in agricultural production attracted 2.7 per cent negative investment, which means that as demand is growing, actual production is decreasing. The lack of investment security and any clear economic policy remains an issue in this sector. There is also a serious failure to recognise agriculture as an important modern profession and a lack of incentive to invest in the sector. Ministers have suggested the growth rate is not sufficient: only three million people work in the agricultural sector which produces a 25 per cent share of GDP and accounts for 23 per cent of national employment. These figures far from satisfy national demand. In order to bring agricultural prices to a reasonable level for producers and consumers, a change of policy is essential, together with the allocation of greater investment to make the agriculture sector more attractive for farmers (*Ettelaat*, no. 890, 24 December 1997).

4 Economic globalization and the prospects for democracy in Iran

G. Reza Ghorashi

This chapter is an examination of the failure of democracy to prevail in Middle Eastern countries such as Iran, a problem arising out of modern statehood rather than Islam. Ghorashi, in this chapter, adopts the provision of 'public goods' as a means to describe the state's major function. He argues that as an economy develops, this function evolves and results in the democratization of the state. Due to the fact that the modern state in Iran was imposed from above, and oil revenues gave it financial autonomy, it did not follow this 'normal' path.

Economic globalization reduces the nation-state's ability to provide public goods. This process, which is harmful in the case of countries with a proper balance between the state and society, may enhance the chances for democracy in Iran by modifying the state's structure and function.

Background

The wave of democratization that started in southern Europe and extended to Latin America, eastern Asia and, with the collapse of Communism, eastern Europe, seems to have ignored the Middle East. This introduced the possibility of, and attempts to explain, the 'exceptionalism' of the Middle Eastern countries like Iran. The 1979 revolution overthrew an authoritarian monarch. Rather than establishing democracy it resulted in another authoritarian regime. The conventional explanation, relying upon the views of 'Orientalists' of the previous centuries, has been to consider Islam as the main culprit. The line of argument is simple: Islam is 'unique' in the sense that the prophet Mohammad simultaneously established a new religion and a new (city) state. The two are inseparable for true believers, to whom Sharia (Islamic law) is the only acceptable law. This, like any other religious law, discriminates between followers and non-followers (and male and female), and thus violates the principle of equal treatment of all citizens and universality of human rights. Therefore Islam, as a political doctrine, is inherently undemocratic.

A variety of criticisms had discredited this view and it would probably be extinct if not for the unexpected surge of militant political Islam (fundamentalism) about two decades ago. Its anti-Western (anti-modern, anti-secular) rhetoric revived Orientalist views and overshadowed moderate Islamists who for decades had argued, based on, for example, Sharia's treatment of religious minorities, that Islam was compatible with pluralism and democracy.

The 'uniqueness' of Islam, or more appropriately its differences with the 'Christian' Europe, although present, have been grossly exaggerated by the media and political leaders, while similarities, particularly in a historical context, have been ignored. But even if accepted at face value, do these differences explain the current pattern in the Middle East? The appeal of militants' rhetoric to the masses, more than its content, has been due to the failure of the alternative 'Western' (modern, secular) models, capitalism and socialism, in delivering the promised economic prosperity and political democracy. Since both have been advocated and monopolized by various modern states in the region, Islam has emerged as an alternative political theory that these states could not lay claims on. More importantly, its advocates are not responsible for corruption and failure of the (modern, secular) state. This means a more plausible explanation of the Middle East's 'exceptionalism,' therefore, must center around the role these modern (nation) states have played in suppressing attempts to achieve democracy in the region.

Provision of public goods

In a 'normal' setting states are, to take an economic approach, expected to provide the society with public goods. Public goods are goods and (mostly) services that are needed in order for the society, including its economy, to function. Although very much needed, they are not usually produced by the market mechanism because they are not profitable. Philip Cerny (1995) recognizes three categories of public goods.[1] They are 'regulatory', 'productive/distributive', and 'redistributive'.[2]

In the early stages of capitalist development, sustenance of a rapid rate of economic growth requires well-organized and centralized allocation of resources in favour of investment, mainly in infrastructure and basic industries. This is, necessarily, against immediate consumption. Under market mechanism resource allocation is decentralized. Besides, at this early stage markets are usually undeveloped, thus insufficient as well as inefficient. There is little choice for government but to become the main agent of resource allocation, i.e. provider of productive/distributive public goods. These governments, usually self-appointed, but even if elected, are generally authoritarian. This may help a forced allocation of resources. At this stage institutions of *modern* civil society,[3] such as unions, are non-existent or underdeveloped. Also, the sense of citizenship associated with the modern nation-state is weak. Thus there is little pressure on the state apparatus to behave democratically; that is, to provide 'regulatory' public goods. Since the economy is poor and pre-modern institutions of support such as extended family and religious endowments are still functional, little is expected from government in terms of the provision of 'redistributive' public goods.

With the growth of the economy the allocation of resources becomes a more delicate task beyond the capability of government bureaucracy and requires more entrepreneurship. Markets meanwhile are, or have the potential to be, developed and can play a more important role. Private, sometimes foreign, investors are willing to participate but require a safe and secure legal and political environment. All of this points to the increased necessity of provision of 'regulatory' public goods and a reduced government role in provision of productive/distributive public goods. At the same time elements of modern civil society have evolved and demand – and their further development requires – democratization of the state. In other words, unlike the earlier stage in which democracy was not a requisite and was perhaps even incompatible with the growth of the economy, here it is compatible and, arguably, a prerequisite. This may explain the inconclusiveness of studies attempting to correlate democracy with economic development.[4]

To the extent that the state's transition from an authoritarian to a democratic and representative entity is successful, the process of economic development will become self-sustained. In the past, many – particularly in the dependency school of thought – believed that the Third World countries with their 'dependant' capitalism controlled by the 'center' in the First World, would not succeed in completing this transition. However, in the past few years a number of developing countries have done so. The question, therefore, is why Middle Eastern countries like Iran have not succeeded in such a transition?

Iran's modern state

The modern (nation) state is an 'imported' concept that was introduced to Iran in the nineteenth century. It was imposed on, rather than evolving from, the existing (civil) society. The traditional civil society, dominated by religious and ethnic institutions, was segmented, parochial and conservative. There was little sense of nationhood and a degree of hostility toward the citizenship.[5] Colonialism was at its height and a brutal competition between Tzary Russia and Great Britain over the domination of Iran was underway. The influential minority of intellectuals and 'enlightened' who advocated the modern state were more concerned about independence, both political and economic, than democracy.[6]

The 1907 Constitutional Revolution[7] was apparently the triumph of modern nation-state over the traditional society. But the political elite very soon realized that due to lack of objective and subjective conditions, some degree of economic development and a modern civil society, they had no choice but to rely heavily on the state apparatus for delivery of the first two categories of public goods, which the old state and the traditional civil society were unable and unwilling to provide. Later on, substantial oil revenues and further shrinking of the traditional civil society made government the dominant provider of redistributive public goods as well. The authoritarian modern state's hostility towards institutions of modern civil society on one hand and its financial means on the other, convinced opposition figures that attempts to build such institutions were futile and must wait until they come to power. This reinforced the belief that only government can and should provide public goods. The only exception was religious fiefdoms and foundations. Although drastically reduced in size and domain of activities, they provided certain redistributive public goods. The 1979 revolution and the establishment of the Islamic Republic (IRI) changed the situation. Although increased in number and size, these are perceived as quasi governmental agencies. Like many government enterprises that provide productive/distributive public goods, these agencies are run by influential individuals closely associated with the government.[8]

Today's Iranian state is somewhere between the neo-Marxist concepts of Poulantzas-Miliband, and the state autonomy of Skocpol. The latter defines state apparatus as 'an institutional ensemble in its own right, independent of the society' and 'claiming control over territories and people … and [pursuing] goals that are not simply reflective of the demands or interests of social groups, classes, or society.'[9] The former believes in class orientation of the state. Yet it is different from the instrumentalist definition since it assumes some degree of autonomy for the state.

Poulantzas-Miliband considers 'two sets of impulses to state action: external (class interest) and internal (those generated within the state). The latter are of two types: the self-interest of state managers, and their conception of the national interest.'[10] Because of oil revenues the modern Iranian state has had little concern for the dominant (i.e. bourgeois) class. Yet it has not gone so far as to make it 'independent of the society' and the dominant class. Therefore, class orientation of the state is relevant but not determinant. More important are its self-interest and its perception of national interests. Needles to say the two are intertwined. At times one defines the other.

It may be argued that as a 'messianic' regime, economic development and prosperity is not a high priority for the IRI leadership. Waterbury (1994) questions the rationality, defined as desire to survive and hold on to power, of messianic movements.[11] Although remarks have been and are being made, though less frequently, that reinforce this perception, IRI leaders have behaved quite rationally whenever survival of their regime has been at stake. There are ample examples that suggest IRI leaders consider economic development and global integration a necessity for the survival of their regime.

Economic globalization

Developed countries

The impact of economic globalization[12] on the nation-state has been the subject of numerous studies in recent years. The literature is generally critical of this impact. The basic belief is that globalization hampers government's ability to provide public goods. Cerny (1995) for example, argues:

> In a globalized world, however, national states have difficulty supplying or fostering all of these categories of public goods. Regulatory public goods are an obvious case. In a world of relatively open trade, financial deregulation, and the increasing impact of information technology, property rights are more difficult for the state to establish and maintain.
>
> International capital flows and the proliferation of offshore financial centers and tax havens have rendered firm ownership and firms' ability internally to allocate resources through transfer pricing and the like increasingly opaque

to national tax and regulatory authorities. Traditional forms of trade protectionism, too are both easily bypassed and counterproductive.[13]

As Robert Reich (1991) has noticed, this has made capital (the private sector) an unwilling participant in the social affairs of the nation or even the city it operates from. There is little incentive for, or pressure on, the capital to respond to national governments. At the same time, particularly since the early 1980s and the triumph of 'Thatcherism' and 'Reaganism', the ability of national government to provide productive/distributive public goods has been drastically reduced. 'Free–marketeers' have successfully convinced many that governments are inherently inefficient producers of goods and services at an additional and unwanted cost to firms that hamper their competitiveness in a global market. The only form of government intervention acceptable to them is those that facilitate the process of globalization.

National governments' inability to influence capital and the drastic reduction in their ability to provide productive/distributive public goods have had major impact on provision of the third, redistributive, category of public goods.

In short, the balance between the state and society has been disrupted and it has lost its ability to enforce a 'social contract' that for many decades has brought peace and prosperity. The presumption here is that prior to economic globalization there *was* a more or less acceptable balance between state and society. This is probably true only for the relatively stable democracies of the advanced capitalist economies. For many less-developed countries, particularly in the Middle East, the 'balance' did not exist. Instead, there has been a lop-sided relationship between the state and society. Economic globalization, by forcing the state apparatus to a reduced role in the economy, may make this a more balanced one.

Developing countries

Up to the late 1970s the literature on the impact of economic integration on developing economies was dominated by those who would see no merits for the Third World countries' integration into the (capitalist) world economy. Indeed such integration was regarded as harmful, since international trade was the mechanism for unequal exchange and exploitation by the First World. These views are no longer prominent among policy-makers of the Third World, even the nationalists. This does not suggest that integration is beneficial at any cost and for all. As Baumol (1986) and later on Sachs and Warner (1995) have noted, a developing economy may benefit from global integration if it 'converges', that is, closes its gap with developed countries at a faster-than-average rate of growth. But not every country can do this. 'Convergence is a fact of life, but only among countries with a sound human capital base for using modern technology.'[14] Scully (1992) has developed a model that assumes 'the goal of economic development is to raise the capital–labor ratio (k) to a level beyond $k3$, that is, to move economies that are in a low-level equilibrium trap (for example, $k1$) and those that are developing but are unstable ($k2 < k < k3$) on a path of self-sustaining economic growth.'[15]

Definition of capital is important. Mankiw (1995) has noted that within the neo-classical paradigm:

> Traditionally, capital is thought to be tangible-it includes the economy's stock of equipment and structures. The return to capital is the profit received by the owners of equipment and structures.
>
> Over the past decade, a new view of capital has emerged. According to this view the return to capital is a much larger function of national income …'[16]

In addition to human capital it includes externalities of capital. Scully points out that an increase in k is achieved via higher capital formation. This requires an increased marginal propensity to save; which itself depends on socio-economic factors such as trust on government, optimism about future, and institutions of civil society. In other words, an economy must have passed a threshold level to benefit from integration into the global economy.

Impact of globalization on the Iranian economy

Objective criteria such as degree of urbanization, rate of literacy and higher education and the like suggest that Iran has reached the threshold. A supply of rich natural endowments and many decades of oil revenue have resulted in a decent infrastructure and fixed capital. An educated and skilled labor force, a large domestic market and favorable geographic location have provided all major pre-requisites for 'convergence' and the rise to a high-tech economy. Neither material nor human resources constitute the main bottleneck of the Iranian economy. Iran's modern-era governments have a dismal record in the provision of an economic approach for public goods. The IRI's recent inability to attract substantial foreign investment, although partly due to world and regional politics beyond its control, has been mainly due to a lack of clarity and stability of the legal framework required for long-term investment. Emphasis here is on clarity and stability, and not concessions, as has been feared by opponents of integration. Indeed, Iran's challenge is not to downgrade and erode institutions of civil society such as labor unions; it is rather to build them. Iran's economy has reached a level where among primary requirements for its further growth is provision of those regulatory public goods that necessitate state's accountability to the public.

While the economic approach for public goods suffers from inadequate supply, there is over-production of provision of public goods. Oil revenue has upended the state–class relations in Iran and turned it into a *rentier* state. Instead of depending on the tax revenues for its financial needs, the state has become provider of finance capital. As a result, proper connections with the state apparatus, rather than entrepreneurship, have become the main criterion for profitability of the private sector. Allocation of resources has been based on favoritism and political considerations. The result has been rampant corruption, inefficiency and low productivity. Moreover, as was mentioned earlier, government's omnipresence has made independent institution-building difficult and has reinforced the imbalance between the state and society.

Provision of redistributive public goods in Iran has started on a residual basis. That part of oil revenues not used to pay for the large government bureaucracy or to subsidize the economy has been devoted to this category of public goods. Here, too, political considerations and favoritism have been the main criteria. Due to the absence of independent social forces and institutions, government has not been accountable, nor has there been a long-term plan with clearly stated goals and means of coordinating the supply of this type of public goods with the rest of the economy. Frequently, such as in the case of subsidized basic necessities, government activities have hurt producers, particularly farmers. Little is known about the social consequences of the provision of these public goods (e.g. encouraging migration from rural to urban areas). Globalization may force a reallocation, rather than reduction, of resources due to a reconsideration of priorities. Beneficial would be more feedback and the direct involvement of non-governmental, grass-roots organizations.

Conclusion

Seldom, if at all, do those in positions of power willingly relinquish it. This is not confined to the state of Iran or the Middle East. The question, therefore, is why a 'rational' regime such as the IRI has not been forced to democratize? The conventional explanation points to the lack of socio-economic preconditions and the dislike of an authoritarian state for democratization. Since there has been no pressure on the state apparatus, primarily due to an undeveloped civil society, it has had no incentive to democratize. This approach has been deemed simplistic in light of the fact that in the past two decades countries with similar socio-economic foundations have had different results in their attempts to establish democracy. Zhang (1994) argues that due to 'failure of earlier attempts to find preconditions for democracy … [emphasis has] shifted to the dynamic aspects of transitions to democracy … The most important democratic transition theory … holds that the right decisions and choices by elites, both from authoritarian regimes and oppositions, are crucial to the outcomes of democratization.'[17] Dividing these elites into moderates and radicals, out of four possible outcomes only one that has moderates in leadership, both in power and in opposition, will likely result in a peaceful transition to democracy. Any outcome that has radicals in the leadership of one side will force radicalization of the other side and drastically diminish chances of a peaceful transition to democracy. Global economic integration and convergence of a moderately developed economy requires, and enhances the chances of, a moderate political leadership. This in turn increases the chances of a peaceful transition of an authoritarian regime to a democratic one.[18]

Notes

1 In a footnote (p. 608) Cerny acknowledges that he is 'borrowing freely from Theodore Lowi's [1969] three categories of public policy: distributive, regulatory, and redistributive'.

2 Regulatory public goods 'include the establishment and protection of private (and public) property rights, a stable currency, the abolition of internal barriers to production and exchange, standardization of weights and measures, a legal system to sanction and enforce contracts and to adjudicate disputes, a more specific regulatory system to stabilize and coordinate economic activities, a system of trade protection, and other systems that could be mobilized to counteract system-threatening market failures ... The second involves specific state-controlled or state-sponsored activities of production and distribution ... Among these are full or partial public ownership of certain industries, direct or indirect provision of infrastructure and public services, direct or indirect involvement in finance capital, and myriad of public subsidies. The third type ..., especially those resulting from the expanding political and public policy demands of emerging social classes, economic interests, and political parties and the responses of the state actors to those demands ... include health and welfare services, employment policies, corporatist bargaining processes ... and environmental protection – indeed, the main apparatus of the national welfare state.' (Cerny, 1995, pp. 608–9)

3 Civil society has been defined in a number of ways. Here we have the broadest concept in mind. Amirahmadi (1996, p. 88) defines it as 'the sphere of social discourses, trends, and autonomous social movements that attempt to regulate the society'. What necessities such a broad and inclusive definition is the dominance of state apparatus over society in one hand, and the limited range of civil society on the other. As civil society evolves and becomes more complex, the need for specification arises. Thus 'political society' – political parties with the express goal of gaining political power –, and 'economic society' are usually distinguished from civil society. Here we do not make such distinction.

The word 'modern' is emphasized to remind readers that in many cases, including Iran, there is a traditional civil society, which, like other aspects of pre-modern societies, is dominated by religious institutions. Modern civil society is generally understood, following Hegel and Marx, to be the one built by the bourgeoisie. Here we use it in contrast to the traditional one. The interaction and contention between the two is a major source of social tension in many societies.

4 See Prezeworski and Limongi (1993).

5 Even many years later Mr Khomeini, whose utopia was this pre-modern era, would prefer '*Ommat-e-Islam*' (People of Islam) over '*Millat-e-Iran*' (nation [citizens] of Iran) and was critical of nationalists. Only due to the need for support during the Iran–Iraq war did the Islamic leadership make a concerted effort to tap into people's nationalistic feelings. Ironically, at the same time, the nationalist, and presumably secular, Baathy regime of Iraq moved toward religion and 'God is Great' appeared on the Iraqi national flag!

6 Although both Pahlavi monarchs have mercilessly suppressed democratic forces, they were primarily criticized for the role that 'foreign' powers (UK and the US) played in their ascendance to the throne.

7 For an informative background on Iran's political history from this to the 1979 revolution see, Abrahamian (1982).

8 This is a major distinction between Iran on one hand and Egypt and Turkey on the other. Since the latter two do not claim to be theocracies, there is room for Islamic groups, such as the Muslim Brotherhood in Egypt, to establish an independent network to provide the redistributive public goods. It is not difficult to imagine how the political 'spillover' will help them, as it has in case of the Rifah party in Turkey. Lack of such independent networks, religious or otherwise, is an additional obstacle in the case of Iran.

9 Skocpol in Das (1996), p. 48.
10 Das (1996), pp. 32–3.
11 Waterbury in Salame (1994), p. 39.
12 By economic globalization we mean freedom of capital in all its forms (finance, productive, ...) from national restrictions. Thus from many attempted definitions of economic globalization, that of Ross and Trachte (1990) is closest to our purpose in this article, in which they attribute it to 'an international group of political economists variously associated with Clark University'. (footnote 10, p. 235). They define 'global capitalism' as a 'variant or submode of capitalism that can be distinguished from two other ... the competitive and monopoly variants'. It is a 'system of global production relations'. They refer to 'three strategic relations ... between capital and labor, between ... capital and capital ... , and between classes, especially the dominant class-capital, and the state'. (pp. 25–6). Here we concentrate on the third strategic relation.
13 Cerny (1995), pp. 609–10.
14 Sachs and Warner (1995), p. 41.
15 Scully (1992), p. 26. Scully uses this measure to divide developing countries into three categories of '(1) underdeveloped and stable or stagnant, (2) developing but unstable, and (3) developing and stable' (p. 29). Although Iran is not included in his tables, one may place it between the second and third categories.
16 Mankiw (1995), p. 289.
17 Zhang (1994), p. 110.
18 This is not to undermine the significance of socio-cultural and political consequences of global integration in the process of democratization. The increased level of telecommunications, for example, necessitates cultural tolerance and openness. These impacts are significant enough to require studies in themselves. Here we are concerned with direct economic consequences alone.

5 Iran and the global finance markets

Kamran M. Dadkhah

The Iranian economy is in need of an infusion of capital and technology. While the bulk of financial resources will be generated domestically – by both the government and the private sector – the role of foreign capital will be of crucial importance. Every day close to one thousand billion dollars are moved across borders, which gives the order of magnitude of resources in international financial markets. Iran has not benefited from this source of finance. The chapter aims at presenting a complete picture of the Iran's options vis-à-vis international financial markets. The strengths and weaknesses of Iran's financial institutions are analyzed and policies recommended for the optimal utilization of international resources. It is shown that among financing options, international borrowing, far from rendering any benefit, will only add to the economy's problems. Policy-makers' efforts should concentrate on strengthening institutions, laws and procedures that will increase direct foreign investment and investment through the Tehran Stock Exchange. The first order of policy measures involve clarity and sanctity of private ownership of financial capital, and reaching an understanding with the United States so that foreign firms and individual investors are not worried about the consequences of their decisions. Furthermore, small investors should be protected against actions of large domestic conglomerates – both public and semi-public – who may not feel accountable for their profits and losses. All these necessary steps, however, are not sufficient for attracting foreign capital and for the efficient functioning of domestic capital markets. In Iran, financial intermediation has never taken place. Banks are not instruments of intermediation in the money market, nor has the Tehran Stock Exchange played its role in marshalling funds for investment. Briefly, the reasons for this deficiency are: inflation, inadequacy of financial instruments (particularly bonds), and overvaluation of the rial against foreign currencies. These issues are analyzed and their policy implications are discussed.

Introduction

Iran is facing significant economic problems: inflation, stagnant per capita income, a growing labor force requiring jobs and amenities of life, low level of investment, and income disparity between rich and poor. Iran is in need of investment sources, both domestic and foreign, and an infusion of new technologies to pull the economy out of the morass. While economic, political, social, and even cultural issues are intertwined, and one cannot assign primacy to any of them, it is evident that without economic resources progress in other areas will be extremely difficult if not impossible.[1] The Iranian government has recognized these problems and for many years has tried a variety of policy initiatives. The last effort, entitled Economic Rehabilitation Plan, was announced recently.[2]

Regarding these efforts, three points have to be kept in focus. First, where should be the starting point? What decisions should have priority? There is no question that economic affairs are intertwined and one cannot consider a decision in isolation. Yet the foremost problem facing the government is marshalling resources for investment and introduction of the newest technologies into the economy. In this regard, while domestic resources – both government and private – have their place, the leading role can be assigned to foreign investment. Second, while government pronouncements address general directions, the devil is in the details. The real issue is to determine what policies, regulations and actions result in a move toward an economic objective. In particular, quite often governments state goals that are either inherently contradictory, or at least, given a particular time frame and limited resources, in conflict with each other. Finally, having a program, even if it is internally consistent and within the means of an economy, is no guarantee that it will be implemented. A will to carry out a plan is as important as having a plan. The government has to show determination and take steps to implement a policy. Moreover, it should possess the credibility to convince people of its seriousness of purpose. In a world of rational expectations and within a democratic system, people have to understand and believe in a plan and be ready to help carry it out.

The present chapter is concerned with the role that international financial markets can play in promoting the growth of the Iranian economy, and policies that the Iranian government can adopt to facilitate such a process.

The importance of foreign resources

From the basic national income identity we know that investment has to be financed from three sources: private savings, government savings, and foreign inflow of capital. To be sure, the bulk of resources for investment has a domestic origin. However, there are many reasons to believe that the future growth of the Iranian economy is dependent on foreign resources. First, in another paper, I have argued, I believe persuasively, that Iranians save a very small portion of their income. Marginal propensity to save in Iran is closer to that of the United States than Japan. Moreover, not all such savings are mobilized for investment. Government savings, with their origin in oil revenues, have been the main source of investment in Iran. Even the larger of private sector undertakings have been financed by government savings through industrial and agricultural banks. Far from mobilizing private resources, many specialized banks simply hand out government money to investors.

But government resources have been shrinking over the past decades. This statement does not particularly refer to the recent drop in oil prices. As Figure 5.1

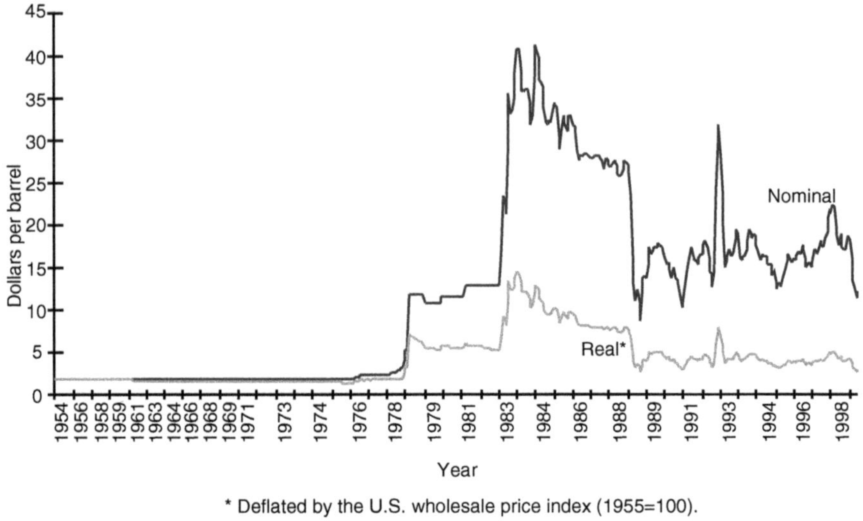

Figure 5.1 Monthly price of Iran light petroleum, 1955–97 (API = 33.9).

Source: OPEC Bulletin, different issues.

shows, since the heyday of the 1970s, and despite a few episodes of sharp increase, the real price of oil has been on the decline. To get an order of magnitude of this problem, observe that a barrel of oil sold today for $12 has the same purchasing power as $7.10 in early 1979 when the same quantity of Iranian oil sold for $17.15.

If the private sector is not saving enough, and if government revenues from oil are not keeping up with the international rate of inflation, then the impetus for growth has to come from foreign capital. But there is more to foreign investment than just providing financial resources. Foreign investment, it is hoped, will be accompanied by the transfer of technology. An advantage of not being the leader in technology is that for a long time the country can simply adapt technological innovations that other countries have paid to develop. This is not to say that technology transfer is a mechanical process. Research into ways of adapting new technologies, and means of introducing them into the Iranian economy, should receive high priority. This issue, nevertheless, is not the subject of this chapter.

A number of financing options are open to participants in international financial markets. Broadly, they include borrowing and investment. Borrowing could be short term and for commercial purposes. For instance, letters of credit for imports and exports are routinely used by all participants in the market. Long-term borrowing is used for financing investment projects or in times of emergency – Iraq, for example, borrowed to finance arms purchases during the 1980s. Long-term borrowing, in turn, may be resorted to by either the private sector or government. As long as a private loan does not involve government guarantees for the repayment of interest and principal, and the exchange rates are determined by the market, it differs little from borrowing by a company from a domestic bank. However, governments of developing countries such as Iran borrow large sums, and often guarantee the loans taken out by private companies.

International investment can take two forms: direct investment in a country by multinationals, or purchase by international investors of publicly offered shares of various companies in that country. The latter is a very important avenue for raising capital, and the Tehran Stock Exchange's role in marshalling domestic and foreign resources for investment in Iran is crucial.

The exchange can and should play a significant part in mobilizing both domestic and foreign funds for investment in Iran. Iran's financial markets, however, remain primitive. Despite considerable growth in recent years, the Tehran Stock Exchange has a negligible role in channelling funds toward investment. In 1996, the total value of shares traded was less than two percent of the GDP. A true bond market has never existed in Iran. But since 1984, with the implementation of the law of banking operations without interest payment and the prohibition against the sale of government bonds to the private sector, the secondary market for government bonds has ceased to exist. Perhaps with the development of a secondary market for 'bonds of national participation', the deficiency is partially remedied. Other financial markets have not fared any better. The foreign exchange market, outside the control of the government, is in the hands of moneychangers who remain fearful of a government crackdown.

Well-organized and efficiently functioning stock, bond and foreign exchange markets that are tied to the network of global financial markets and open to investors around the world are essential for mobilizing funds for investment in Iran. Such markets would provide a vehicle for the continuous evaluation of financial assets, thereby facilitating the attraction of foreign capital. They would eliminate the need for unduly restrictive government guarantees to investors, by providing for the smooth and orderly transfer of capital and repatriation of dividends. Moreover, such markets would safeguard the economy from shocks resulting from the transfer of large sums to and from the country. They would also make it possible for Iranians to use their savings in productive activities instead of clandestinely transferring them abroad or using them for unproductive domestic activities.

International borrowing

Table 5.1 shows the foreign debt of Iran from 1980 to 1997. It is noteworthy that despite military needs during the war, the amount of foreign debt remained constant and the long-term debt was reduced.

This was a restricting factor in Iran's military efforts but in the long run was a prudent decision. Iran came out of the war badly damaged but with a clean slate in terms of financial obligations. Contrast this with the situation of Iraq which owed billions of dollars to its Arab backers, Kuwait and Saudi Arabia, and to the West. Indeed, the burden of its debt might have been one reason for Iraq's ill-fated venture into Kuwait.

Table 5.1 Foreign debt of Iran, 1980–97 (billion US dollars)

Year	*Total debt*	*Long-term debt*	*Public and publicly guaranteed debt*
1980	4.5	4.5	4.5
1981	3.9	3.8	3.8
1982	8.2	3.5	3.5
1983	7.1	3.0	3.0
1984	5.2	2.5	2.5
1985	6.1	2.4	2.4
1986	5.8	2.4	2.4
1987	6.1	2.3	2.3
1988	5.8	2.1	2.1
1989	6.5	1.9	1.9
1990	9.0	1.8	1.8
1991	11.3	2.1	2.1
1992	16.0	1.7	1.7
1993	23.4	5.8	5.8
1994	22.7	16.0	15.6
1995	21.9	17.4	17.1
1996	16.8*	n/a	n/a
1997	11.6*	n/a	n/a

Source: The World Bank, *World Debt Tables*.

* *The Economist Intelligence Unit*, 2nd quarter 1998.

However, beginning in 1990, Iran started borrowing in the international financial markets in a big way. From $6.5 billion in 1989, the total debt reached $23.4 billion in 1993. At the beginning most of the debt was short term, but especially after rescheduling in 1993 and 1994, the borrowings were turned into long-term debt. Equally important, the bulk of long-term debt is owed by the government or is government guaranteed.

To get an order of the magnitude of Iran's foreign debt, consider Table 5.2. From a low of 4.8 percent in 1980, the foreign debt of the country swelled to more than 58 percent of GNP. Perhaps more revealing is the debt-to-exports ratio which rose from 32 percent in 1980 to more than 114 percent in 1995. The burden of this debt can be seen in the debt-service ratio. Table 5.2 shows that this ratio rose to more than 21 percent. In other words, every year the country was committed to spending one fifth of its foreign-exchange earnings on servicing its foreign debt. Add to this the military, food and industrial requirements of the country, and little room is left for any discretionary spending of the foreign exchange.

This situation was alarming, particularly because petroleum constitutes the bulk of Iran's exports. Dependence on a single product makes Iran's economic condition vulnerable to fluctuations in the international oil market – and even

Table 5.2 Long-term debt and debt service as percentage of GNP and exports, 1980–97

Year	*Total debt as % of GNP*	*Total debt as % of exports*	*Debt service as % of exports*
1980	4.8	32.0	6.8
1981	3.7*	29.4†	n/a
1982	6.2	38.2	5.4
1983	3.0*	31.1†	n/a
1984	2.0*	28.6†	n/a
1985	3.2	40.5	4.1
1986	2.7	74.9	7.3
1987	4.5	49.7	3.6
1988	4.6	52.2	5.6
1989	5.3	47.0	3.3
1990	7.6	44.7	3.2
1991	9.4	58.0	4.1
1992	14.7	77.4	5.2
1993	37.5*	121.0	9.3
1994	42.8*	113.5	21.6
1995	58.2*	114.6	n/a
1996	26.7*	n/a	n/a
1997	12.8*	n/a	n/a

Source: The World Bank, *World Debt Tables*.

* Calculated using official exchange rates.

† Calculated using the sum of exports of goods and services plus income.

more so when Iran needs a chunk of its oil revenue to service its debt. Such a vulnerability could conceivably have far-reaching economic and political consequences, as we have witnessed in other countries. Finally, at the risk of stating the obvious, one has to bear in mind that for Iran, exporting oil is equivalent to selling its assets. To sell assets to service foreign borrowing would make sense only if the funds borrowed have been used for extraordinarily productive projects. As will be argued below, even the existence of such projects is in doubt.

The government took heed of such a threat, and since 1995 has reduced the foreign debt considerably. In 1997, the total international debt stood at $11.6 billion and its ratio to the GDP was reduced to 12.8 percent. Although the ratio may be underestimated because of the use of the unrealistically low official foreign exchange rate. Despite this it behoves us to put to rest, once and for all, the false notion that international borrowing could foster economic growth. Below, I will succinctly enumerate my reasons.

The most important issue is that repayment of a foreign loan has to be financed by foreign exchange earned through exports of the products of the project financed by the loan. Put simply, the country borrows from abroad, sets up a factory, produces goods that are sold internationally, and earns enough foreign exchange to pay back the interest and principal of the original loan. I will argue that such a project, if it exists at all, is a rarity.

To illustrate this point, let us look at an example. Assume that the project costs $200 million, half of it financed by a 10-year foreign loan that charges 8 percent interest. The loan has a three-year grace period, during which interest accrues but no payment is required. That is, payment of interest and principal starts at the end of the third year and continues to the end of the tenth. Let us also assume that interest accrues on an annual basis and payments are made once a year. Such a loan requires the country to generate more than $20 million in exports beginning in the third year in order to pay the interest and principal. The question is: are there such projects?

Before answering let us rule out one possibility. In the case of oil-producing countries like Iran, sometimes a project is shown to be profitable only because oil is sold to the company in question at a concessionary price. Petrochemical projects are a good example. But if every input is valued at its market price it may be difficult to find a project of the type we are seeking here.

The proposition that such projects are rare can be made in a taxonomic fashion. For the country to produce exportable goods with such short notice, it must either have a comparative advantage in producing such a product, or gain it through the infusion of new technology or the discovery of a new resource. We may rule out the first possibility because if the country already had a comparative advantage in a product, there would be no need for government intervention. The private sector would have already exploited the possibility – or if private firms needed to borrow from abroad there would be no need for the government to guarantee such a loan. If the comparative advantage has to be created through the transfer of technology, it is an argument in favor of direct foreign investment. There is no question that foreign investment by a multinational company would be preferable to borrowing from abroad by the host government. The foreign firm has every incentive to make sure that the right technology is transferred, that investment has a fair chance of succeeding, and would make every effort to create a comparative advantage. It has to, because the firm is bearing the risk of the project. In the case of foreign borrowing the risk would be borne by the government as the borrower or the guarantor. The reason is that the loan is contracted in the foreign currency. Thus, depreciation of the rial will not have any effect on the amount of interest or principal that has to be paid in foreign currency.

Thus, the only instance where borrowing can be defended is the exploitation of a country's natural resources. Here, if the technology is known and the markets for the product are assured, a case can be made for borrowing. Since one can never be assured of the market and because the choice of technology is never quite clear cut, even in these cases a joint venture can be recommended.

Some may have reservations regarding the argument above. It is argued that based on a comparison of Iran's financial situation and those of other countries, Iran is not over-indebted and can borrow for some time to come. Indeed, this is no argument at all. It resembles the contention that, if a country or state has a tax burden that is less than the average for other countries or states, it should increase its taxes. The same kind of analyses were performed for Poland and Mexico in the 1970s and 1980s with disastrous outcomes. Moreover, Iran does not enjoy the kind of cordial relationship with other countries that can influence international financial markets. When the crisis comes, Iran can hardly expect the kind of help that Mexico received.

Direct foreign investment

There are two main advantages to direct foreign investment. First, the risk is borne by the investor and not by the host government. It is hard to imagine that government decision-makers, no matter how knowledgeable and well-intentioned, could accurately assess the risk in different investment projects, whether they are directly under government control or the government directs the private sector to undertake them. Second, a major issue for developing countries is the transfer of technology. Direct foreign investment by its very nature involves transfer of technology. Indeed, as a matter of simple economics, the foreign firm will choose the most appropriate technology. Should it fail to do so its investment will be in jeopardy. Nevertheless, the host government has nothing to worry about.

One aspect of the assumption of risk by the foreign firm relates to foreign exchange. The era of fixed exchange rates came to an end in 1971. There is little reason to believe that Iran, or any other country, can maintain a fixed exchange rate over a long period of time. Proof of this point is the failure of all the Iranian government's initiatives since the revolution to fix the rial's exchange rate. In the case of foreign investment, the cost of the foreign-exchange risk arising from market fluctuations would be borne by the foreign firm. Of course, this presupposes that the exchange rates are market-determined and reasonably stable.

The Iranian government has recognized the economy's need for investment and has taken a number of steps, including the establishment of free trade zones, to encourage foreign investment in Iran. Yet despite all of the Iranian government's efforts, the level of foreign investment has been negligible. Worse, in some cases government overtures have been turned down.

If it was true that the government had done everything possible and still foreign firms shunned Iran and refrained from investing in it, the answer would be that the country has to invest within the confines of its domestic resources. While this would impede economic growth, it is a better alternative than borrowing. However, it is doubtful that the government has done everything possible to encourage foreign investment. Though the government offers all kinds of guarantees regarding repatriation of profits and dispute resolution, the main concern of investors is uncertainty. The Iranian government has adopted policies and postures in the international arena that are not confidence-inspiring. In addition, many investors may be wary of alienating the United States. A policy of rapprochement with the United States would go a long way in this respect. Nevertheless, the government cannot hope for an immediate effect here. Iran has to show, through time, that it abides by the rules both domestically and internationally and that the rules of the game will not be changed.

Another set of obstacles in the way of foreign investment is the inadequacy of domestic financial markets. In the absence of a viable stock market in Iran, direct foreign investment has to be undertaken by a multinational company in cooperation with the Iranian government or a domestic firm. Such ventures are only within the means of large multinationals. Moreover, from its inception, such a project is an all-or-nothing proposition. There is no readily available means of valuation of the enterprise, nor do the investors have access to forward and futures markets to safeguard against future changes in the exchange rate. In addition to being a vehicle for foreign financial intermediation in the domestic capital market, an active stock market will be helpful in attracting foreign direct investment.

The role of the stock market in an economy

The importance of a stock exchange for the efficient working of an economy is self-evident to policy-makers, business, and the public in advanced countries. While some Iranian policy-makers recognize the benefits of the stock market for a functioning economy, it is doubtful that the public, many businesses, and some in decision-making positions appreciate its functions or trust the enterprise. Educating the public and building trust by establishing regulatory institutions and by passing laws and regulations are only the necessary conditions for the flourishing and widespread acceptance of stock exchanges.

The aim of this section is not to offer a comprehensive review of the role of the stock market in a developing economy. Neither do we have the space for such an indulgence nor is it needed. Rather I offer a brief review of the main functions of a stock market as a prelude to discussion of the shortcomings of the Tehran Stock Exchange, and the policies proposed to rectify them.[3]

The stock market brings together the sellers and buyers of stocks of different companies. Since supply and demand meet in the market, equilibrium prices are established for the shares traded. Unlike markets for housing and labor, financial markets enjoy instantaneous clearing. Thus, at every moment the price of traded securities, particularly when the market is not thin, reflects the investors' valuation of the assets being traded. This valuation is quite important because by their very nature capital goods once in place – in the form of buildings and factories – are prohibitively costly to move or divert to other uses. Thus, the undesirability of an investment that has turned out to be unprofitable is reflected in a decline in the price of its stock. The new buyers who pay far less for the factory or building may find the return quite acceptable. The reverse happens to the shares of a down-and-out company that experiences a change in its fortune, with the projects it has undertaken turning a profit. Those who made the right decisions are rewarded.

The market allows investors to move from one company to another. Thus, while the factory and buildings are tied up, the investor is not. This has several implications. First, the market participants will not be afraid that once they make a decision they will have to live with it for the rest of their lives, should they later find out that they made a poor investment. In this case they pay the penalty and get out. Second, financial resources are channelled toward projects with higher returns. Most important, however, is that a market attracts foreign capital. Without a stock market, the country can only hope that entrepreneurs and multinational firms will invest in it. A stock market open to international capital has the ability to furnish domestic entrepreneurs and companies with savings from abroad.

Allocation of investment resources is a crucial task for an economy. It is a link to the future. Investing in promising industries and paving the way for technologies of the future while pruning obsolete and inefficient enterprises are daunting yet absolutely vital tasks for an economy. Experience has shown that governments are the worst arbiters of such decisions. A stock market is not always correct in predicting the best investment projects. But through a process of trial and error it furnishes the economy with the best guide for such decisions. It should be noted that this function of the stock market does not require that all investment or even the bulk of it be allocated through the exchange. It is enough that the exchange reflects the free assessment of many buyers and sellers regarding different investment potentials.

A stock exchange facilitates the process of turning savings, particularly, moderately small amounts of it, into investment. This in turn encourages investment. Entrepreneurs and companies are not dependent upon personal fortunes or loans to finance their projects, nor are savers limited in their options for safeguarding their savings.

All these tasks require that participants in an exchange have a trust in its workings. The majority of people in many countries, including Iran, are unfamiliar with stock markets and the way they function. Even worse, they do not generally trust the market. Here is a task for the government: not to interfere in the workings of the market, but to set the rules and to guarantee that they will be changed only democratically and through due process. Furthermore, such changes should not go into effect retroactively. The government should also encourage the academics and journalists to educate the public regarding the stock exchange. Needless to say, neither building trust nor educating the public are tasks to be accomplished overnight.

The Tehran Stock Exchange officials and the Iranian government are well aware of these issues.[4] Nevertheless, implementing appropriate policies and putting in place the necessary machinery for the effective functioning of a stock exchange require a political consensus.

The Tehran Stock Exchange

Trading in the Tehran Stock Exchange started in early 1968. Compared to the established exchanges of advanced countries, its operation was minuscule. During its first seven years, fewer than 50 companies were accepted for trading. Yet it was a beginning for a developing economy. By 1978 and the start of the revolution, the number of companies had risen to 105. The growth of the value of shares transacted was even more impressive. From a low of 32 million rials in 1968, it grew to more than 23 billion rials in 1978 (Table 5.3).[5]

Table 5.3 Activities of the Tehran Stock Exchange, 1967–96

Year	*No. of accepted companies*	*No. of shares traded (1000 shares)*	*Value of shares traded (million rials)*	*Price of shares index*
1967	2		15.0	
1968	6		32.0	
1969	9		89.0	
1970	12		107.0	
1971	17		134.0	
1972	23		334.0	
1973	34		1,322.7	
1974	43		6,505.6	
1975	59		10,721.8	
1976	80	1,641.0	21,064.1	
1977	102		19,487.9	
1978	105		23,380.6	
1979			30.2	
1980	70		0.0	
1981	71		0.0	
1982			2.1	
1983	59		6.6	
1984	56	982.9	1,167.9	
1985	56		1,211.5	
1986	55		1,735.8	
1987	56	514.3	1,690.3	
1988	56	1,830.2	9,935.7	
1989	67	3,984.1	11,139.7	100.0
1990	95	13,314.3	64,687.3	184.3
1991	108	62,594.3	478,258.1	472.1
1992	121	49,755.8	352,072.1	435.1
1993	137	97,328.5	515,613.0	403.5
1994	163	149,237.2	793,401.8	694.3
1995	198	432,138.4	1,880,564.4	1549.4
1996		901,700.0	4,381,600.0	

During the 1970s, oil money was flowing into Iran, and the national income, both in real and nominal terms, was on the rise. Thus, despite the growth of activities in the Tehran Stock Exchange, its role in the economy remained unimportant. As Table 5.4 shows, the ratio of total value of transacted shares to GDP was 0.01 percent in 1968 and by 1978 it had reached 0.44 percent.

Table 5.4 Value of shares traded on the Tehran Stock Exchange and total investment as percentage of GDP, 1967–96

Year	*As a percentage of GDP*	
	Value of shares traded	*Total investment*
1967	0.00	21.51
1968	0.01	22.07
1969	0.01	23.27
1970	0.01	23.92
1971	0.01	22.80
1972	0.03	23.95
1973	0.07	21.81
1974	0.21	17.90
1975	0.32	28.07
1976	0.46	32.73
1977	0.36	33.26
1978	0.44	29.68
1979	0.00	19.09
1980	0.00	21.74
1981	0.00	19.08
1982	0.00	17.47
1983	0.00	21.45
1984	0.01	20.91
1985	0.01	17.49
1986	0.01	15.37
1987	0.01	13.35
1988	0.04	13.26
1989	0.04	13.35
1990	0.18	15.45
1991	0.95	21.64
1992	0.53	22.03
1993	0.55	22.07
1994	0.62	23.25
1995	1.02	23.69
1996	1.83	26.48

Government bonds were also traded in the Tehran Exchange. Prior to the revolution, government bonds never fared well in the Iranian economy. The reason was that the interest paid by the government hardly compensated for inflation, while the investor could easily find borrowers in the private sector who paid several times the interest rate paid by the government. Nevertheless, since some contractors dealing with the government purchased bonds, the volume of trade grew to about 25 billion rials in 1977 (Table 5.5). The revolution put an end to the growth of the bond market. Between 1979 and 1983, the value of transacted bonds continuously decreased. In December 1983 the Islamic banking law put an end to bond transactions in the Tehran Stock Exchange.

On the stock side, between 1979 and 1983, the value of stocks transacted was almost nil. There were some transactions between 1984 and 1987, but the renewed activity of the exchange waited until 1988.[6]

In 1988 the war with Iraq ended, and in the same year the first development plan (1988–93) of the Islamic Republic of Iran went into effect. This plan called for privatization of government-owned enterprises.[7] The election in 1989 of Ali Akbar Hashemi-Rafsanjani to the presidency of Iran meant that the mandate of the plan would be carried out. In 1990, stocks of government-owned companies worth 10.8 billion rials were offered in the Tehran Exchange. This figure rose to 166.6 billion rials in 1993.[8] Indeed, according to *The Economist*, 'Iran has voluntarily adopted the principle of IMF's restructuring rules, albeit without asking for IMF loans in return.'[9]

Not all the stocks traded on the Stock Exchange are bought by the private sector. The shares of the private sector purchase in the total value of stocks traded were 100 percent in 1989 and 1990, but in 1991 this share dropped to 79.3 percent, in 1992 to 53.2 percent, and in 1993 to 65 percent.[10]

The boom in the market came to a halt in 1992 due to the change in the foreign exchange policy of the government.[11] But in 1993 the market resumed its growth, which continues to this date.

Table 5.5 Value of bonds traded on the Tehran Stock Exchange, 1968–83 (million rials)

Year	*Value of bonds traded*
1968	92.0
1969	44.0
1970	15.0
1971	254.0
1972	865.0
1973	1,451.2
1974	4,456.6
1975	7,342.9
1976	17,191.9
1977	24,929.3
1978	10,824.7
1979	4,075.9
1980	538.0
1981	49.1
1982	48.2
1983	2.6

A better measure of the growth of the Tehran Stock Exchange and its relation to the Iranian economy is gained by comparing the value of transacted stocks to the GDP of the country (Table 5.4). In 1996, the ratio of the value of stocks traded to the GDP was only 1.83 percent. In the United States the comparable figure for 1995 was 48 percent of GDP.[12]

Also reported in Table 5.4 is the ratio of gross investment to GDP. This ratio has fluctuated between a high of 33 percent during the oil boom years of 1976–7 and a low of 13 percent during the last years of the war. In 1996 the ratio was 26.48 percent. It is clear that the Stock Market plays a negligible role in the mobilization of savings and the allocation of investment resources to different activities (Figure 5.2).

The daily activities of the Tehran Stock Exchange during May–August 1998 are depicted in Figures 5.3–5.5. Several features are noteworthy. The number of traders fluctuates between 55 and 426, and is 260 on average. The number of daily trades averages 693, with a high of 1,264 and a low of 118. What is quite remarkable is the volatility of both the total number and the aggregate value of shares traded (see Figures 5.4 and 5.5). For instance, in three consecutive trading days, 29 July, 1 August, and 2 August, the value of shares traded was respectively, 1.2 billion, 106.3 billion, and 1.0 billion rials. Such a volatility may be caused by the thinness of the market or by a few large players in it. Either way, it will not enhance the confidence of small investors in stocks or the exchange.

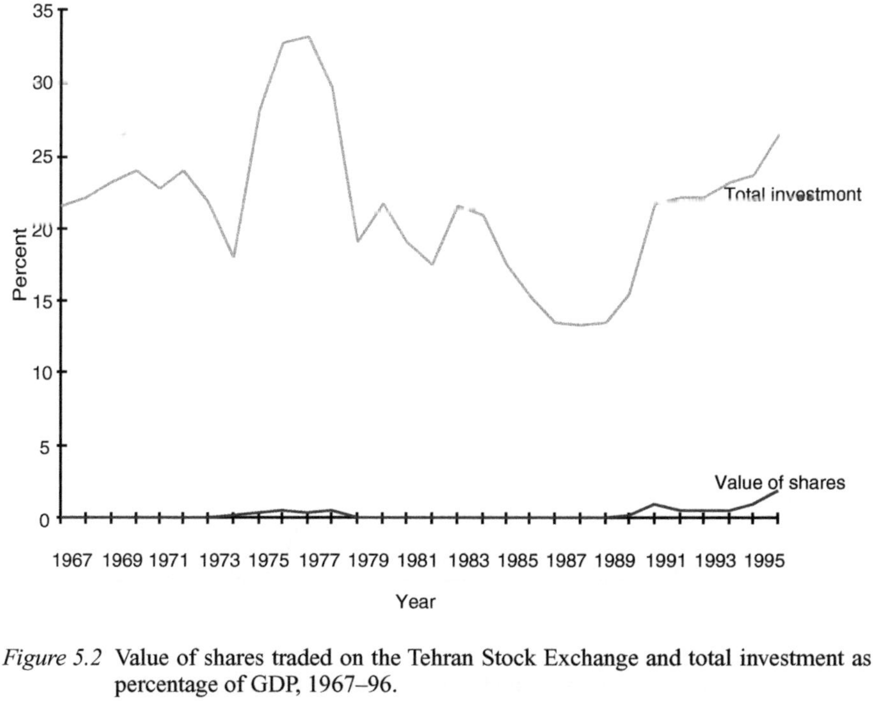

Figure 5.2 Value of shares traded on the Tehran Stock Exchange and total investment as percentage of GDP, 1967–96.

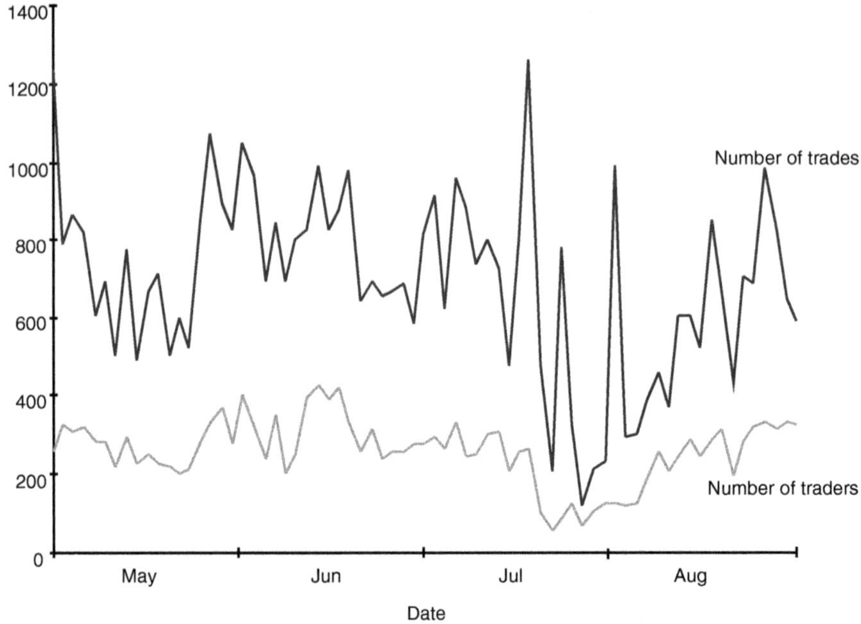

Figure 5.3 Daily number of trades and traders on the Tehran Stock Exchange, 1998.

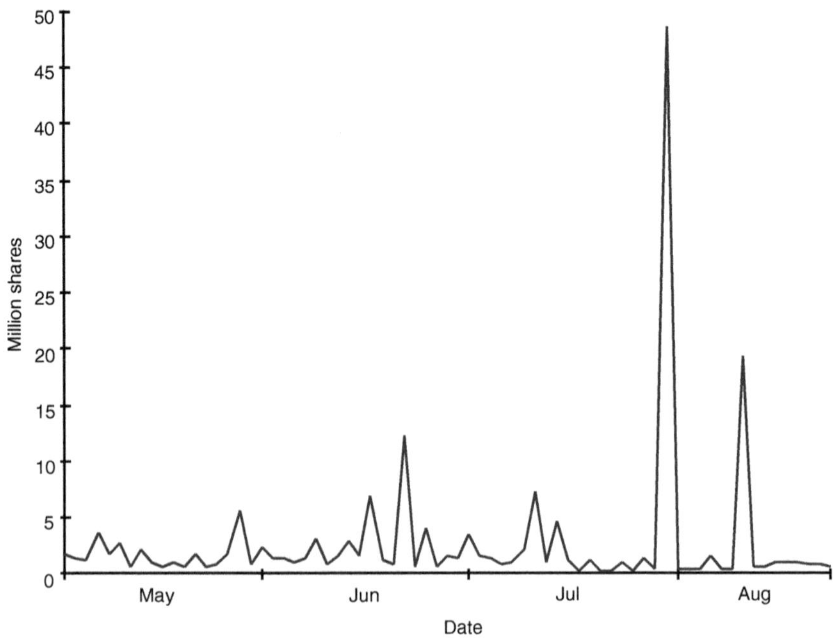

Figure 5.4 Daily number of shares traded on the Tehran Stock Exchange, 1998.

The source of these wide fluctuations needs to be investigated. There are a number of giant semi-governmental organizations in Iran, each consisting of a large number of companies. These organizations control vast financial resources and are usually not accountable to government officials. If these organizations are responsible for the volatility in the stock exchange, there is an additional incentive to break them up.

Earlier it was pointed out that the Tehran Exchange officials and the Iranian government are cognizant of the importance of the Stock Exchange and well aware of the prerequisites for its effective functioning. This can best be seen in the steps taken to equip the exchange with modern technology, to bring it to the attention of international investors, and to build investor trust.

The Tehran Stock Exchange has computerized its operations and has tried to extend to the provinces. In September 1990, the exchange joined the International Stock Exchange Federation. Since 1996, its daily operations have been reported on the Internet. Furthermore, the Stock Exchange is aware of the necessity to build confidence and to protect small investors.[13]

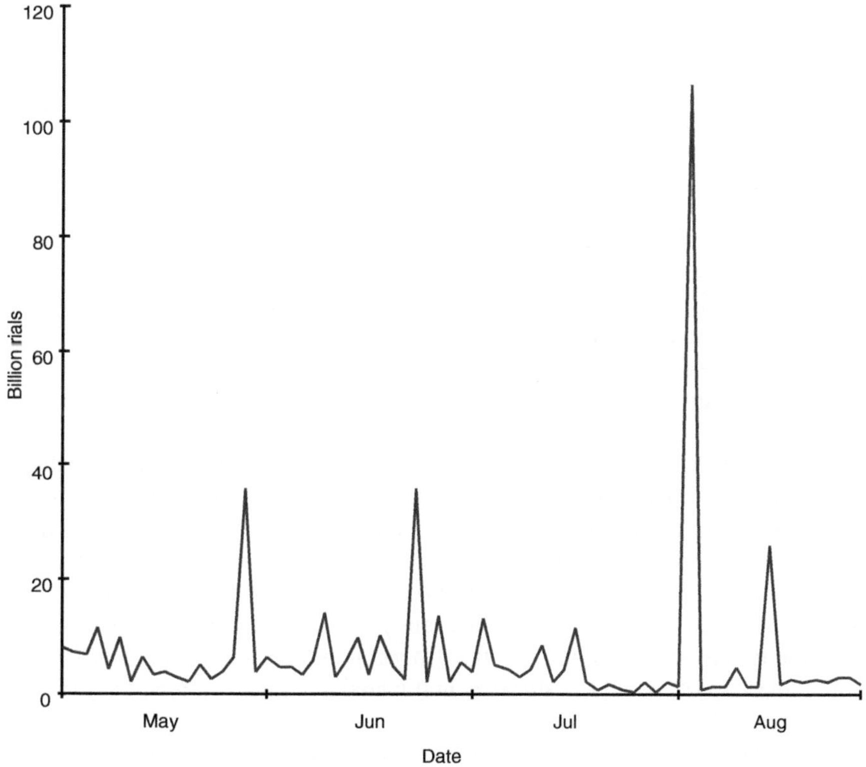

Figure 5.5 Daily value of shares traded on the Tehran Stock Exchange, 1998.

Prerequisites for an effective financial intermediary

Overall issues bearing on the operation of the Tehran Stock Exchange, and matters related to the standing of the Iranian government in the international community, were alluded to above. In the following I will concentrate on a few important macroeconomic and monetary policy measures that are urgently needed if the exchange is to play a constructive role in the Iranian economy. A characteristic of these policies is that they can be defended on their own and with no reference to their effects on the exchange. The fact that they would facilitate the mobilization of capital through the exchange is an added bonus. The crucial issue of the exchange value of rial against dollar, however, is discussed in the next section.

The first issue is reintroduction of government bonds into the Iranian economy. Bonds are needed to balance portfolios and to tie up investors when they feel they have to stay away from stocks. If government bonds find universal acceptance, they would add a new dimension to monetary policy in Iran. At present, open market operations are impossible, as they were during the previous regime. As a result, monetary policy is very much tied to fiscal policy. The way to increase money in circulation is to lend to the government, and decreasing money supply requires reducing government credit. When the government spends the new loan, the additional money finds its way into the economy. On the other hand, when the government refrains from some expenditures due to reduction in its credit, the money supply contracts. But since to policy-makers fiscal issues come first, monetary policy is determined as a by-product of fiscal plans. Similarly, any deficit spending by the government is reflected in an increased money supply.

The issue of bonds of national participation would go a long way in filling this void. It is necessary, however, that they receive widespread acceptance and, more important, that a secondary market for them is created.

A practical issue regarding the issuance of government bonds is the high rate of inflation in Iran. In order to induce investors to buy bonds, the government has to pay an interest rate on its bond that is equal to or greater than the rate of inflation. This in turn would add to the budget deficit. The solution is to reign in inflation.

The virtues of such a goal hardly need elaboration. But some may argue that in an inflationary environment investors may turn to the stock market as a safe haven. While the argument is correct in countries that are experiencing mild inflation but have had a history of stable prices, it does not apply to a country with skyrocketing prices. The reasoning in favor of inflation is flawed because it does not consider that inflation breeds uncertainty. If prices are rising so fast, when is the time to buy and when to sell? If a financial asset is sold, what is to be done with the proceeds? Wouldn't stocks denominated in a stable currency, say the dollar, be preferable?

As far as foreign investors are concerned, there can be no better reason to avoid stocks of a country than high rates of inflation. Between 1979 and 1997, the value of a dollar has risen from 70.48 rials to 3,000 rials (the official rate) and 5,500 rials (the black market rate). In other words, the rial has depreciated more than 4,100 percent officially and close to 7,700 percent unofficially. A foreign investor would have required an average annual rate of return of 21.8 percent officially and 25.8 percent unofficially to come out even with inflation. Considering the risk of the country and the usual returns obtained in advanced countries, demanding a 15 percent annual return on top of inflation is not unreasonable. Thus, Iranian stocks would have had to produce between 37 and 41 percent returns to stay on par with stocks of other countries.

I have argued elsewhere that inflation in Iran is a monetary phenomenon.[14] The government has to control the money supply, not allowing it to grow more that a few percentage points above the growth rate of the economy. Given the present condition of the economy, this may seem a tall order, but again the government is aware of its importance. From 1998 to 2000 inflation was reduced significantly. In this regard, a necessary step is to transform the Central Bank into an independent institution, mandated to stabilize the internal and external value of the rial.

If inflation is brought under control, inevitably the exchange rate of other currencies per rial would stabilize. In an environment of stable prices and exchange rates, the Tehran Stock Exchange has a good chance of flourishing.

The true value of rial per dollar

A historical problem of the Iranian economy has been the overvaluation of the rial. Yet whenever the subject has been raised false economic and political alarms have been sounded. Politically, it is assumed that a lowering of the value of the rial brings national humiliation. Economically it is claimed that it will cause higher prices and will be an imposition on lower income classes. The falsehood of such assertions needs no elaboration here. Indeed, only those with enough economic and political power to obtain foreign exchange at concession rates will be hurt by the devaluation of the rial.

To understand the problem, suppose for the moment that Iran did not have any oil to export. What would have been the exchange value of rial per dollar? That imaginary rate is the exchange rate that the productive capacity of the Iranian economy can support. To the extent that the dollar is sold at a lower price, Iranians are consuming at a rate they can afford only by selling national wealth. Overvaluation of the rial is nothing more than subsidizing the present at the expense of the future generations, and allowing the national wealth to be squandered. Consider the case that a commodity is subsidized. Demand for such a commodity is increased and most often it is put to wasteful use. The same is true about foreign exchange earned through the sale of oil.

The damage is not confined to wasting resources. The international value of the rial will be at the mercy of the vagaries of the international oil market. The only way for Iran to keep a stable foreign exchange rate is to keep huge foreign reserves. Iran neither has such a reserve nor, at present, can afford to have one. An overvalued rial and the fear of instability is a deterrent for foreign investors. In general, an undervalued dollar puts domestic production as well as exports at a disadvantage against foreign production and imports.

Sometimes, perhaps sarcastically, it is said that Iran would have been better off had it not had oil. This is wrong. If Iran did not have oil it would have had a fate similar to some of the neighboring countries. The problem is that the wealth has not been used economically.

The first step in establishing a realistic external value for the rial is to encourage the development of an organized foreign exchange market. Some recent decisions of the government point in this direction and are commendable. These include the extension of the grace period for selling of foreign exchange earned by exporters to the Central Bank, and allowing the banks to open bank accounts denominated in foreign currencies. But these measures do not go far enough.

Once such a market becomes operational the government should sell a limited amount of its foreign exchange in this market. The resulting equilibrium exchange rate should then be used as a basis for evaluating foreign exchange requirements of different governmental and quasi-governmental agencies, and for evaluating different public and private sector projects. Once the budget of an organization is determined in rials, then the government would sell the necessary exchange rate at the market price.

Allocation of resources can be made either on the basis of an objective function and by determining optimal quantities, or one can find the optimal prices and use them to evaluate different activities. So far, allocation of foreign exchange earned through oil exports has been based on rules of thumb and political haggling. Here, it is proposed to allocate this scarce resource on the basis of market-determined optimal prices.

Conclusion

The twenty-first century is upon us, and economies around the world are becoming increasingly interconnected. An economy that hopes to thrive needs to link itself with the global network of the world economy. World trade, the traditional link between countries, is increasing. At the same time, a new and more powerful connection is being forged through financial markets around the world. If Iran aspires to a place on the international economic map as something more than a seller of oil, it has to establish and develop its financial markets and link them to the international capital markets.

The argument can be extended to all financial markets – stocks, bonds, foreign exchanges and commodities. The present paper has the modest aim of studying the question of direct foreign investment and the role of the Tehran Stock Exchange, which is already established and has taken some steps toward realizing the above goal. The progress of the exchange, to this date, leaves much to be desired. It was shown above that its role in the economy of Iran is rather negligible. It does not play a significant part in mobilizing savings, allocating capital, or attracting foreign investment.

All evidence shows that Iranian decision-makers are aware of the imperative for the development of a viable stock market linked to the world economy. Yet they seem to be shackled by xenophobia and a preference for government ownership. Concentration of economic power in large conglomerates managing many state-owned enterprises has complicated matters. While the framework of economic activity in Iran needs rethinking and certain fundamental changes in laws and attitudes are required, medium-term macroeconomic policies also need to be addressed. In particular, a restrictive monetary policy with the goal of stamping out inflation and stabilizing the international value of the rial is recommended. Reintroduction of government bonds would provide monetary authorities with a tool for conducting such a policy. In addition, bonds would enrich the stock market with a new instrument and help investors better to balance their portfolios. Most important, the rial should be allowed to find its equilibrium value against foreign currencies, a value that is in line with production capabilities of the economy excluding oil.

Notes

1 In his first report to the Iranian people on the economy, President Khatami noted that 'economic issues are the most tangible and immediate concerns of every society ... Without economic capabilities we cannot have significant progress in political and cultural arenas.' He added that, 'we have spent more than one third of cabinet meetings on discussing economic issues.' *Ettelaat International*, 16 March 1998, p. 3.

2 *Ettelaat International*, 4 and 5 August 1998.

3 The interested reader is referred to William Baumol, *The Stock Market and Economic Efficiency* (New York: Fordham University Press, 1965), and James Tobin, 'Financial intermediaries,' in J. Eatwell, M. Milgate and P. Newman (eds), *Finance, The New Palgrave* (New York: W.W. Norton, 1989), pp. 35–52.

4 'An interview with the Secretary General of the Tehran Stock Exchange Organization (TSEO)', *Payam-e Safir*, May–June 1995, pp. 87–92.

5 Data source for 1973–95 is the Tehran Stock Exchange, and for 1967–72 Firouzeh Khalatbari, 'The Tehran Stock Exchange and privatization of public sector enterprises in Iran: a study of obstacles to the private sector development', in Thierry Coville (ed.), *The Economy of Islamic Iran: Between State and Market* (Tehran: Institut Français de Recherche en Iran, 1973), pp. 177–208. As mentioned in the text, the Tehran Stock Exchange commenced its operation in early 1968. Since the Iranian year starts on March 21, the data for 1968 refers to 21 March, 1968 to 20 March 1969, which corresponds to the Iranian year 1347. The figure for 1967 refers to the last months of the Iranian year 1346.

6 According to the Secretary General of the Tehran Stock Exchange Organization, the first flurry of activity in the market was due to the enactment of the new tax law in 1986. Shareholders transferred some stocks to their children and relatives to avoid paying taxes.

7 *Performance Report of the First Economic, Social and Cultural Development Plan of Islamic Republic of Iran 1989–1993 (preliminary)*, volume 11 of the documents of the second development plan, Plan and Budget Organization (1994), pp. 1-14–1-16.

8 Ibid., Table 15.

9 *The Economist*, op. cit., pp. 12–13.

10 Performance Report, op. cit., Table 16.

11 Interview with the Secretary General of the TSEO, op. cit.

12 In 1995, the market value of stocks traded on all exchanges was $3,507 billion (*Statistical Abstract of the United States* (1997), p. 527), and GDP in current prices $7,265.4 billion (*Economic Report of the President* (1998), Table B1).
13 See the interview with the Secretary General of the TSEO, op. cit.
14 Kamran Dadkhah, 'The inflationary process of Iranian economy: 1970–1980', *International Journal of Middle East Studies*, 17 August 1985, pp. 365–81, and 'The inflationary process of Iranian economy: a rejoinder', 19 August 1987, pp. 388–91.

6 The Iranian economy and the globalization process

Hamid Zangeneh

Since the revolution of 1979, many obstacles, both internal and external, have hindered the stability and growth of Iran's economy. While impediments to economic recovery and prosperity accompany revolutions in general (such as those which occurred in Algeria and Cuba, for example), states typically emerge with a uniqueness that is characteristic of the country and reflects the constellation of political, demographic, social, and economic factors coming into play at the time.

The case of Iran presents a prime example of how the sometimes self-inflicted, internal and external, economic and political conditions have impeded its attempts to emerge from a form of colonialism. It experiences internal rebellion and external sanctions and aggression as it attempts to achieve economic and political independence within a global political economy. Taken separately, each of the many hurdles to Iran's economic recovery would be somewhat daunting; taken together, they are formidable. Included among the major external factors are the following:

- The eight-year war between Iran and Iraq, which brought extraordinary calamity to the Iraqis and the Iranians, resulted in approximately one million casualties, and caused tens of billions of dollars in physical damage (Amirahmadi, 1988) to strategic industries as well as to the private property of ordinary citizens, hospitals, schools, etc.;
- an economic embargo placed upon Iran by the United States, effectively reducing a large market for Iranian exports;
- what might be described as less than favorable treatment of the country by other advanced industrial nations in regard to intermediate and long-term loans and so-called dual-use technologies;
- massive immigration of refugees from Iraq and Afghanistan. According to the United Nations, Iran was the largest recipient of refugees in the world during the 1980s;
- an oil price collapse in the mid-1980s, which cut Iran's oil revenues by more than 50 percent.

Equally formidable internal strife and economic mismanagement have accompanied the external obstacles just outlined. During and after the revolution, various political entities struggled to attain and maintain power by appealing to different factions in order to expand and solidify their power base. This resulted in a set of policies that have prompted rising domestic and international uncertainty. The major problematic factors that have been generated internally are enumerated as follows:

- unfulfilled promises to enhance social welfare programs;
- confiscation and nationalization of properties that, according to the revolutionary courts, had been illegitimately acquired by their owners;
- forced sale of some agricultural lands to the people who worked the land (Shaul Bakhash, 1989);
- nationalization of banks and establishment of Islamic banking in 1983–4;
- monetization of the government deficits. Government budget deficits were mostly financed by borrowing from the Central Bank (printing money), which added unneeded liquidity to an economy that was not capable of utilizing its capacity;
- a foreign exchange rate system characterized by too many new initiatives and policy reversals;
- sudden and frequent economic policy reversals in general;
- absence of the uniform application of laws and regulations. Legal and other official rulings depend on a form of patronage in which decisions are based upon one's identity and acquaintances;
- widespread corruption, rampant throughout the country;
- dwindling international trade (exports and imports) as a percentage of world trade.

During the uncertain economic times that have emerged, everyday citizens have had to hold more than one job in order to meet their financial obligations. This, in turn, has led to reduced efficiency and production as workers have not been able to perform their duties in a timely manner, if at all. Rules, regulations and red tape have characterized all aspects of life, personal and social. At all levels, bureaucrats have been unable or unwilling to make decisions that can stand the test of the day. Consequential decisions are not rendered because of either fear or corruption. The government as a whole has been irresolute and has not shown the ability to stay the course. It has reversed itself prematurely in the face of unexpected adverse outcomes. These sudden and frequent policy reversals have been a major cause of uncertainty among the private sector (Ghasimi, 1992), and, therefore, of the country's economic ills. The public sector itself has become a reluctant partner in the economic development of the country.

This chapter intends to set forth an empirical evaluation of Iran's economic performance and development in the years that have followed the revolution. Various socio-economic indicators will be presented and discussed. The next section is allocated to a discussion of international trade. In the last section some observations and conclusions are provided.

Empirical evidence

Demographics

The population of Iran rose from 18.95 million to 60.055 million between 1956 and 1996 (see Table 6.1). During the 20-year period between 1956 and 1976, the population growth rate was approximately 3.0 percent to 3.6 percent per year, while during the decade of 1976 to 1986 it jumped to almost 5 percent per year. However, during the early years of the 1990s, the average rate of growth declined to just over 1.5 percent. These population trends mean that just under half of the population is 20 years old or younger, and is in need of education, vocational skills and jobs.

As has been the experience of many countries, there has been a consistent migration of the population within Iran from rural to urban areas (see Table 6.2). Even though the rural population increased in actual numbers from 13 million in 1956 to about 23.6 and 23.025 million in 1991 and 1996 respectively, there was actually a decline in rural residents as a proportion of the nation's overall population. In terms of percentages, a smaller percentage of the total population was living in rural areas. Typically, urban migration places tremendous pressure upon a country's social service system, due to the higher visibility and concentration of urban problems, and as a result, greater attention and resources are expended by government on welfare and social service programs. Also, rural populations have traditionally been relatively self-sufficient in terms of food production and consumption. Migration to the cities changes their status from producers/consumers of foodstuffs to that of consumers only.

The literacy rate among Iranian men and women has continued to increase, following the trend that began before the revolution. However, in spite of the

Table 6.1 Total population (millions) and rate of growth (%), 1956–96

	1956	*1976*	*1986*	*1991*	*1992*	*1993*	*1994*	*1995*	*1996*
Total population	18.95	33.71	49.45	55.84	57.15	58.49	59.78	60.05	61.13
Growth	–	30.71	46.69	12.92	2.35	2.34	2.21	0.50	1.79

Source: Iran statistical yearbooks.

Table 6.2 Urban and rural distribution of population (millions), 1956–95

Year	*1956*	*1966*	*1976*	*1986*	*1991*	*1995*
Total	18.95	25.79	33.71	49.45	55.8	60.05
Urban	5.9	9.8	15.9	26.8	31.8	36.8
Rural	13.0	15.9	17.8	22.3	23.6	23.0
% of total in rural areas	68.6	61.6	52.8	45.0	42.2	38.31

Source: Iran statistical yearbooks.

continuing improvement in the literacy rate of the population as a whole, a sizeable portion (about 31 percent) is still illiterate. Also, as Table 6.3 indicates, a rather significant difference remains between the two genders. Men have achieved a higher literacy rate than women: 73 percent versus 64 percent, respectively. Nevertheless, in the absence of data to the contrary, these official numbers suggest, in general, high and improving literacy rates.[1]

Production (GDP)

After the revolution, during a period spanning approximately 10 years, the production of goods and services in real terms fell as long as the Iran–Iraq War continued. After the war, in 1989, production began to rise. However Iran's growth rate has not been large enough to spur a significant increase in per capita income. As shown in Table 6.4, per capita GDP had a decreasing trend for many years. In the first half of the 1990s, a modest upward trend in per capita GDP resulted in an increase of about 64 percent of its 1976 level.

One could identify several factors leading to the decline in income. One obvious factor, justifiably, was the country's preoccupation with its war efforts. For

Table 6.3 Growth in literacy of population aged six and over by gender, 1966–95 (millions)

	Men and women	*Men*	*Women*
1966	5.5 (28%)	3.9 (39%)	1.6 (17%)
1976	12.9 (47%)	8.2 (58%)	4.7 (35%)
1986	23.9 (62%)	14.0 (71%)	9.8 (52%)
1991	33.9 (74%)	19.1(81%)	14.9(67%)
1995	41.6 (69%)	22.5 (73%)	19.1(64%)

Source: Iran statistical yearbooks.

Table 6.4 Total population, real GDP and per capita GDP, 1976–95 (units unavailable)

Year	*Population (millions)*	*Real GDP*	*Per capita GDP*
1976	33.71	10,710	317.7
1986	49.94	8,672	173.6
1990	54.50	9,666	177.3
1991	55.84	11,010	197.2
1992	57.15	11,563	202.3
1993	58.15	11,894	204.5
1994	59.78	11,701	195.7
1995	60.05	12,200	203.1

Source: Iran statistical yearbooks.

years, the western and southwestern regions were repeatedly battered and overrun by the country's own tanks and warplanes as well as those of Iraq. Many economically prosperous towns and cities in Khozestan were completely obliterated.

Another reason for the economy's lacklustre performance was the collapse of oil prices in the mid-1980s.[2] The price of Iranian light oil fell an estimated 55 percent, from $28per barrel in 1986 to as low as $12.75 in 1989.[3] Iran's oil revenues took a tumble and fell to $9.673 billion in 1988, significantly reducing the country's purchasing power and mitigating Iran's plans for potential development and reconstruction of war-torn areas.

Agriculture

While villagers flocked to the cities, presumably in search of a better life,[4] total agricultural production increased in absolute real terms as well as on a per capita basis between 1976 and 1996 (see Tables 6.5 and 6.6). Per capita agricultural production increased from 50.6 to 63.3 over this period. This successful outcome was achieved through years of preferential treatment of agriculture in the budgetary process. Designated as high priority, agriculture was allocated a considerable amount of government resources every year until the 1990s when this tapered off to about 10 percent of total economic expenditure. Its share of the budget increased in real absolute terms every year and it accounted for a high percentage of the total budget. This is true in spite of the fact that government budget, as a percentage of total GDP, was, in real terms, declining.[5]

Table 6.5 Total real agricultural production and per capita agricultural production, 1976–96 (units unavailable)

	1976	*1986*	*1990*	*1991*	*1992*	*1993*	*1994*	*1995*	*1996*
Real agricultural output	1,706	2,651	2,968	3,120	3,352	3,536	3,690	3,739	3,869
Population (millions)	33.7	49.9	54.5	55.8	57.2	58.5	59.8	60.0	61.1
Per capita output	50.6	53.0	54.4	55.9	58.6	58.2	61.7	62.3	63.3

Source: Iran statistical yearbooks.

Table 6.6 Share of agriculture in economic affairs budget (million rials), 1976–96

Year	*1976*	*1981*	*1986*	*1990*	*1991*	*1992*	*1993*	*1994*	*1995*	*1996*
Economic affairs	451	626	597	1,382	1,954	2,082	7,128	11,102	15,350	12,109
Agriculture	57	74	109	236	312	384	1,087	1,421	1,647	1,357
Ratio (%)	12.7	11.8	18.3	17.1	16.0	18.5	15.2	12.8	10.7	11.2

Source: Iran statistical yearbooks.

Fiscal management

With the advent of the Islamic Republic, whose new constitution envisioned a government that was active in all facets of life, the role of government became more all-encompassing. In particular, the constitution specified that the government should design its budgets to ensure political and economic independence and more equitable distribution of income. In this context, taxes were not to be levied just for the sake of raising revenue for the government, but rather, they should be designed to enhance and improve the distribution of income and general welfare of the country.

In 1976, before the revolution, government expenditure was 37 percent of GDP while its revenue was about 39 percent (see Table 6.7). However, after the revolution, even though the government was at war, its total expenditure, including that earmarked for war purposes, constituted a much smaller percentage of real GDP than that during the pre-revolutionary years[6] (Amirahmadi and Zangeneh, 1997). Real government expenditure as a percentage of real GDP decreased to a low of 16 percent in 1991–2 and then rose to a high of 23 percent in 1994–5. Ratios of government revenues to real GDP followed the same pattern during the same period. This decline is mainly due to the decrease in oil revenue, which was both intentional and incidental. Oil revenue decreased due to the ravages of the eight-year Iran–Iraq war and its ramifications, and second to the national policy of economic independence and self-sufficiency. Before the revolution, Iran was exporting upwards of 5 million barrels of oil a day. The war destroyed the country's ability to extract and ship oil at a level near this magnitude. In the meantime, Iranian policy-makers were determined to limit oil and gas exports to expand non-oil exports in order to pay for imports. While oil exports were effectively limited, there was no corresponding increase in non-oil exports.

Table 6.7 Government revenue and expenditure in relation to GDP (billion rials), 1976–95

Year	*Revenue*	*Expenditure*	*GDP*	*Revenue/ GDP*	*Expenditure/ GDP*	*Def/sur*
1976	1,790	1,675	4,548	39	37	3%
1980	1,453	2,249	6,632	22	34	–12%
1981	1,975	2,707	8,009	25	34	–9%
1985	2,993	3,313	15,775	19	21	–2%
1988	2,513	4,210	22,304	11	19	–8%
1990	6,266	6,051	36,644	17	17	1%
1991	7,920	8,090	50,107	16	16	0%
1992	11,183	10,756	66,462	17	16	1%
1993	22,124	20,886	93,609	24	22	1%
1994	31,137	29,593	128,381	24	23	1%
1995	45,432	41,961	184,185	25	23	2%

Source: Economic and Social Time Series, *Planning and Budget Organization*, Tables 3 and 14.

Expansion of non-oil exports has not materialized yet. In actuality, such exports declined to about 2 percent of total imports.[7] As a result, total government revenue and expenditure declined. Although the direction of this trend seems to have shifted upward in 1993, revenue and expenditure as a percentage of GDP remain much lower than the 1976 levels. It seems unbelievable that the government has been running a growing surplus rising to as much as 2 percent of the GDP in the first half of the 1990s, despite the high rate of unemployment, both open and disguised, and the obvious need for growth and development.

Investment

Even though there might be several reasons for the 'sick' state of the Iranian economy, one could pinpoint and shorten the list by looking at one of the most important factors. The investment picture of post-revolutionary years has not been promising. The limited rate of investment explains the slow growth rate of GDP. The low investment rate has not been limited to the private sector, but also has been characteristic of the Iranian government. Both public and private sectors have been investing increasingly lower percentages of GDP in construction and machinery every year (see Table 6.8). In 1990, private investment in machinery and construction, as a percentage of the GDP, was 7.9 percent. The same scenario is true for government investment, which dropped to 7.9 percent as well. These figures are low by any standard, whether it be that of industrially

Table 6.8 Capital formation in relation to GDP, 1976–95 (units unavailable)

	1976	*1981*	*1986*	*1989*	*1990*	*1991*	*1992*	*1993*	*1994*	*1995*
1 Private investment	1,424	851	885	748	765	1,136	1,143	1,243	1,278	1,316
2 Machinery	515	144	43	198	231	493	506	580	562	569
3 Construction	909	707	842	550	534	643	437	663	717	748
4 Government investment	1,904	873	761	469	613	807	934	890	928	973
5 Machinery	388	282	277	154	230	287	344	283	303	312
6 Construction	1,516	591	483	314	373	519	590	607	625	660
7 Real GDP	10,710	8,180	8672	8,493	9,666	11,010	11,563	11,894	11,701	12,200
Investment as % of GDP										
8 (1/7)	13.3	10.4	10.2	8.8	7.9	10.3	9.9	10.5	10.9	10.8
9 (2/7)	13.3	10.4	10.2	8.8	7.9	10.3	9.9	10.5	10.9	10.8
10 (5/7)	17.8	10.7	8.8	5.5	6.3	7.3	8.1	7.5	7.9	8.0
11 ((1+4)/7)	31.1	21.1	19.0	14.3	14.3	17.6	18.0	17.9	18.9	18.8
12 (3/7)	8.5	8.6	9.7	6.5	5.5	5.8	3.8	5.6	6.1	6.1
13 ((3+6)/7)	22.6	15.9	15.3	10.2	9.4	10.6	8.9	10.7	11.5	11.5

Source: Social and Economic Time Series, *Budget and Planning Organization* (1997).

advanced countries or of newly industrialized countries. Investment on the part of both the private and government sectors has been higher in the area of construction relative to the resources going toward machinery.

These low levels of investment have alarming implications for the country's industrial capacity to maintain and expand production as well as to contain inflation. There is no doubt that these levels will not lead to a higher standard of living or to the prospect of a growth rate high enough for the economy to absorb current open and disguised unemployment as well as the estimated one million new entrants into the job market every year. The question then becomes, why such a low investment? The answer is the same. When there is uncertainty, there is limited or no investment in long-term projects. People will invest only in very liquid businesses so that they can cash in their holdings on short notice to avoid being caught with their wealth tied down in illiquid assets. Uncertainty due to social factors such as unrest, lawlessness, and lack of a protective civil society diminish the willingness of investors and frighten potential long-term investors; hence flight of capital to a safe haven and avoidance of long term commitment to any investment strategy.

Inflation

Table 6.9 shows annual inflation rates grouped into four different time periods. The first grouping covers the early years before the oil price rise. The second includes the years after the oil price increase and up to the revolution. The third period covers the post-revolutionary years, most of which were taken up by the Iran–Iraq war. Finally, the fourth period reflects the post-war and 'post-Khomeini' era. As Table 6.9 shows, prior to the 1970s and before the oil price rise, inflation in Iran was rather tame, with an average rate approximating 2.42 percent per year. However, this does not hold true for the subsequent three time periods.

Table 6.9 Inflation rates over four time periods (%)

											Average
1963–72	1963	1964	1965	1966	1967	1968	1969	1970	1971	1972	
	0.79	3.91	2.26	–0.74	1.48	0.73	3.62	2.1	4.11	5.92	2.42
1973–79	1973	1974	1975	1976	1977	1978	1979				
	9.94	14.69	12.81	10.92	27.56	11.73	10.50				14.02
1980–88	1980	1981	1982	1983	1984	1985	1986	1987	1988		
	20.50	24.27	18.7	19.69	12.57	4.38	18.40	32.94	22.17		19.85
1989–97	1989	1990	1991	1992	1993	1994	1995	1996	1997		
	20.38	17.10	25.70	21.20	31.50	49.66	28.91	17.20	19.41		25.67

Source: IMF international financial statistics.

Budgetary constraints became almost irrelevant to Iran's economic planning, at least for a short while, when huge oil revenues accrued due to the spiralling oil prices triggered by the Arab oil embargo in 1973. Prior to that year, the availability of foreign exchange dictated the government's project selection, and therefore, imported inflation was not a problem.[8] The tremendous increase in the price of oil gave the government an opportunity to engage in grandiose nationwide projects that were beyond the absorption capacity of the country. Iran's infrastructure was too limited to accommodate these new projects, and inflationary pressure started to mount.

In pursuit of rapid economic development, the government, on one hand, used the oil revenues to finance almost all of the old and new projects. This contributed to an increase in the monetary base and money supply (discussed below), and therefore in aggregate demand. On the other hand, due to the limited capacity, the higher aggregate demand could not be satisfied internally, hence goods had to be ordered from abroad. Due to the universal inflationary situation of the 1970s, all of the ordered materials carried with them an inflationary premium. Regardless of this, however, the open door policy was ineffective because of the inability of importers to bring their merchandise into the country due to inadequate port and transportation facilities. There was a waiting period of over six months for ships to unload their cargo in the port cities of the Persian Gulf. And when they did unload, they were unable to transfer the merchandise to its final destination. Since there were no storage facilities, the imported goods could not be safely stored in these port cities. As a result, the imported items were stored in open facilities located around the outskirts of the port cities, a practice which resulted in their ruin. Therefore, the inflationary pressure could not be eased by a greater volume of imports.

Another factor contributing to the inflationary build-up prior to the revolution was the higher per-capita income. As purchasing power trickled down to the masses, demand for goods and services increased, which in turn increased the intensity of inflation. Pre-revolutionary Iran provided a classic example of a country in which there were too many dollars chasing too few goods.

However, the revolution added a new dimension to the already festering inflationary problem. Besides fiscal and monetary policy mismanagement, many other conditions that tended to exacerbate Iran's inflationary problems can be identified: the eight-year Iran–Iraq war and its ramifications, the exodus of the managerial and industrial leadership strata of the country, the foreign embargo imposed by the United States along with unfavorable economic treatment by other nations, and a decline in oil revenues were among the major contributors to the problem.

Table 6.9 shows that in each of the time periods specified previously, the average yearly inflation rate was growing. The sudden rise in inflation immediately after the jump in oil prices jolted the economic system because people were not used to that magnitude of instability. However, the years following the revolution were not any better. Although inflation rates reported by official sources are high, unofficial anecdotal estimates are much higher. One must be cognizant of the fact that the official estimates include all of the prices that are controlled by the government directly or through its agencies, companies and *bonyads* (religious foundations). These goods and services, such as electricity, water, bread, tobacco and tobacco products, tea and sugar, are subject to government-mandated price controls. Even so, they continue to be included in the calculation of price indexes, upon which they have a biasing effect due to their combined magnitude. Therefore, when the controlled prices of these commodities are combined with the prices of other free market goods, this results in far more moderate official inflation rates. So, the question that remains to be answered is: what has been the main culprit(s) in causing price instability in Iran? Already mentioned within this paper have been various contributing factors, such as inadequate investment, decline in real per capita output, excessive population growth, urban migration, influx of international refugees, and the Iran–Iraq war. While these conditions have had significant direct and indirect impact upon the problem, all of them taken together could not have sustained inflation at such high rates without monetary accommodations.

Monetary and banking policy

Central banking in Iran is rather new. In 1928 the first government-owned commercial bank (Bank Melli Iran) was authorized to act as the nation's Central Bank. Before this time the Imperial Bank, a British-owned commercial bank, was performing as the central bank in Iran. The increasingly apparent conflict of interest between commercial banking enterprises and the central banking system paved the way for the creation, in 1959, of a central bank that was free from the influence of its own commercial banking activities. However, the Central Bank of Iran has never been an independent agency in setting monetary policy. It has been more subject to political control than other central banks such those in the United States, Germany, Japan, New Zealand and Great Britain. This is especially true under the government of the Islamic Republic, which sees itself and its organs as integral parts of one system and not independent of each other.[9]

During the years just prior to the revolution, Iran's banking system expanded very rapidly to satisfy the heightened volume of internal and external trade that was created by the oil boom. In a span of 6 years (1972–8), 10 new banks and 1291 branches of both old and new banks were added to the banking system. The system was neither experienced nor capitalized enough to withstand the bank runs of 1978–9 when the revolutionary movement threatened the safety of depositors who started to withdraw their assets from the banking system. The Central Bank did assist banks with an easy rediscounting policy in an effort to stave off open bankruptcy of these banks as they faced massive deposit losses. After the revolution, most of the banks (28 of 36) were nationalized.[10] The revolutionary government went one step further and merged these nationalized banks. As a result the number of banks was reduced to 6 commercial and 3 specialized banks, a total of 9 banks. Total branches were reduced from 8,275 to 6,581 by 1982.

It seems that during the post-revolutionary period, monetary policy was driven, on the one hand, by the Iran–Iraq war needs, the freezing of Iranian assets in the US, and large fluctuations in the crude oil prices, and on the other hand by the domestic policies which promoted nationalization and Islamicization of banking. In the early years of the revolution, these two domestic policies dealt a hard blow to the confidence of the public. The public's concern with the unknown environment led to the unusual withdrawal of resources from the banking system. In order to facilitate and support the newly inaugurated banking system, the Central Bank provided liquidity to ensure its survival. Meanwhile, the war, the freezing of Iranian assets by the US, and the sharp decline in oil prices, and most prominently, a sharp decline in output of goods and services (the tax base), increased government's need to borrow from the banking system to finance its deficits. Given that the Central Bank was not and is not free of government control, and has lacked a mandate to target economic variables such as prices and/or nominal income, it seems that its monetary policy has engaged in crisis management rather than economic management.

International trade

International trade has always been the centerpiece of economic development policies of many developed and newly developed nations during the post-Second World War period. For many countries, international trade has consistently grown faster than other sectors of the economy, providing them means of expanding their income and standard of living through outward-looking policies of economic integration. Greater openness and integration imposes a greater degree of competition which, in turn, leads to increased innovation, capital-deepening, and higher efficiency and productivity growth.

However, for the most part, trade policies of many less developed countries (LDCs) have taken a different route. They have revolved around protectionism and inward-looking policies. Proponents of protectionism are much more organized and clearly identifiable. Besides the nationalistic tendency of the public and self-interest of the rent-seeking groups (labor unions,[11] trade lobbies, industrial associations and government agencies as well as the old leftist guard who, for the most part, provided the intellectual ammunition[12]), protectionism has an inherent advantage for governments. Protectionism in LDCs with a less than adequate tax base or well-developed tax-collecting administration functions as a rather easy and cheap source of revenue for the government. Therefore, even though protectionism, in general, reduces the economic welfare of the country and the world as a whole, it is usually popular with the general public and the government. Also, those in the import competing industries are well financed, well organized, and ready to fight trade liberalization. The question one could pose is why have LDCs until recently, for the most part, chosen protectionism?

Why protectionism?

Protectionism could be defended on both economic and political grounds. In terms of economics, there are five reasons in favor of protectionism and promotion of import-competing industries. Terms of trade (TOT) argument (or export pessimism) was originated by Prebish (1952). He argued that if all countries engaged in international trade, supply of commodities to the market would increase. Assuming that demand for primary products grows at a slower rate (inelastic demand) than manufactured commodities, they will face an insufficient demand and, as a result, their exportable prices will fall and thence their TOTs will deteriorate. In order to avoid deterioration in international TOT and to launch successful industrialization, countries need to impose optimum tariffs and follow imports substitution policies rather than exports promotion policies. Another persuasive argument relates to protecting the balance of payment. If free-trade policies are enacted, increased imports will consume the precious little foreign exchanges that are necessary for economic development. This, coupled with inadequate foreign exchanges generated from exportables, leads to balance of payment difficulties. A third reason for LDCs' protectionism policies has revolved around the concept of self-sufficiency and protection of the country from exploitation by the powerful imperialists. A fourth reason is the cyclical behavior of demand for primary commodities. If LDCs use export-led development strategies, their economies will be subject to industrial countries' business cycles, rather than remaining balanced and healthy. Finally, economic theorists as well as policy-makers were intent on pursuing economic growth and development through import substitution policies and did not, in general, give liberalization of trade a chance.

Besides the theoretical economic arguments in favor of protectionism, there are political considerations as well. There is always a tug of war between what is good for a narrow interest group and what is good for the country. In the absence of an outside constraint such as membership in WTO, governments regularly give in to the demands and pressures of rent-seeking groups who favor protectionism policies and enact policies that promote economic rent for the powerful and well-financed interest groups. These can explain, to a large part, LDCs' reluctance to embrace GATT, trade liberalization, and export promotion policies.

Forms of protectionism

Protectionism comes in different forms and guises, including high average nominal tariffs and high quantitative restrictions. Among imported goods, there is less restriction on imports of capital goods. This means that the capital goods industries are left to compete with the foreign competitors and, therefore, must be able to produce comparable products at competitive prices. High tariffs are usually placed on imports of consumer goods that are produced domestically. Also, there is a high tariff on imports of nonessential products that are usually deemed to be wasteful. Therefore high incentives are given to domestic manufacturers to produce these import-competing goods domestically, i.e. domestic production of nonessential commodities is encouraged. This means that wasteful consumer goods are given protection. Therefore, given the less protection for capital goods and high protection against consumer goods, less developed countries actually undermine their industrialization policies. There is another source of distortion that negates the industrialization and incentives to produce essential products at home. Even though imports of essential products such as machinery are not protected, there are usually high tariffs on inports used by these machines which effectively nullify the protection provided to the intended industry.

In order to decrease the negative impact of protectionist polices on exportables, countries have a system of export incentives (see Clements and Sjaastad, 1984, Chapter 3).

Evidence against protectionism policies can be found in the performance of the Argentinian and Indian economies (see Balassa, 1977). Evidence of the benefits of liberalization can be found in the economies of Hong Kong, Singapore, Taiwan and South Korea (see Bhagwati, 1982, pp. 17–19), of Chile (see Congdon, 1985, pp. 36–45) and of Taiwan (see Little, 1979, p. 479).

Advantages of trade liberalization

There are many advantages to trade liberalization. In general, it is accepted that international trade increases international economic welfare by increasing choice, improving quality of goods and services, and reducing imports and import-competing goods prices which, in turn, leads to lowered cost of living. On the production side, higher exports necessarily mean higher growth, higher employment, and higher income for the exports sector as well for those sectors that have forward and/or backward links to it. For example, estimated impacts of the Uruguay Round on world income ranges from US $212 billion (see Nguyen, Perroni, and Wigle, 1993) to US $510 billion (see François, McDonald, and Nordstrom, 1994). Developing countries are expected to earn a significant fraction of this higher economic welfare. An OECD study (1993) estimated that LDCs will gain about US $86 billion while François, McDonald, and Nordstrom (1994) put the gain at $122 billion. Distribution of these gains among participating countries directly depends on each country's own commercial liberalization policies. Also, expansion and extension of the market increases competition and, as a result, increases economic efficiency. Potential foreign markets enable the country to specialize, innovate, and take advantage of increasing return to scale and scope, and to learn how to obtain and use information in the international market. This all leads to higher efficiency in resource allocation. Finally, openness imposes the global market tyranny. As a result, a liberalized country is no longer allowed to plunder its scarce resources in the production of commodities for which it does not have a clear international comparative advantage. International competition forces each country to be much more judicious, and a great deal less cavalier, in its choices of *what* and *how much* to produce.

Advantages of export-led development strategies

Export-led development would lead to a more complete utilization of resources required in the production of commodities over which the country has a comparative advantage (Kruegar, 1983). That is, resources that are not used due to insufficient domestic demand would be employed to supply international demand. Strategies involving export development could attract foreign direct investment if the economic–political climates are ripe for and conducive to such undertakings. The use of external capital for development makes it possible to foster economic growth and development without the potential associated problems of foreign debt creation and the burden of foreign debt services. Beyond these advantages, export development would have forward and backward linkage effects. Finally, it would increase the economy's ability to withstand external shocks by increasing its ability to switch from domestic to international markets and vice versa.

How to liberalize

Trade liberalization could take many forms. One form is to participate in a regional free-trade block. Second, rather than a piecemeal approach, the country could join a global network such as WTO. Problems with these regional free-trade blocks are several. One is the possibility that trade blocks could increase common tariffs such that there would be a diversion of trade from more efficient (low-cost) non-members to less efficient (high-cost) member countries. This is not only an inefficient way of conducting business, but subsidizes the inefficient producers and, simultaneously, leads to a loss of revenues for the governments. Another possibility is the erection of a large and fortified barrier against all other countries that could retaliate against the free-trade block such as is the case with the United States and the EU. Another potentially more damaging scenario is the possibility of denial of competitive trade with better-equipped non-member countries. Members of free-trade blocks could potentially limit their access to more advanced and better technologies from the rest of the world. This could result from the promotion of intra-block trade that usually is common and pushed by member country governments.

General agreement on trade and tariffs

As a consequence of the great depression, unambiguous theoretical and empirically verifiable advantages of free trade, and the desire to prevent another catastrophic global deflation, developed countries were eager to pursue an international organization that could oversee trade policies and attempt to liberalize trade. In pursuit of that desire, immediately after the Second World War, the General Agreement on Trade and Tariffs (GATT) was created. Its primary purposes were: 1) to set rules of conduct in international commerce; 2) to function as an arena for hearings to resolve disputes in international commerce; 3) to provide a forum for multilateral talks to lower protectionism. These general rules resulted in eight operational principles: 1) Trade barriers should be lowered. 2) Quotas should be eliminated. 3) Trade barriers should be lowered on a non-discriminatory basis (MFN basis). 4) Trade concessions could not be rescinded with compensations to the trading partners. 5) New non-tariff barriers could not be erected to replace lowered or eliminated barriers. 6) Trade disputes must be settled by consultation. 7) Internal taxes should apply equally to domestic as well as imported products (i.e. imported products should be treated 'no less favorably' than similar domestic products). 8) All rules and regulations with regard to custom procedures that impede imports such as rules of transit, custom valuation, custom fees and formalities, and markets of origin, should be formulated and applied in a transparent manner.

Problems with GATT–47

As with any multinational agreement, GATT–47 had problems. The first related to the loopholes such as voluntary export restraints (VER) that were found to impose new barriers on trade. A country with enough clout, such as the United States, could effectively erect a sufficiently high trade barrier against other less powerful countries without impunity. Trade skirmishes between the United States and Japan that resulted in VER are very recent examples of this loophole. The second problem of GATT–47 which occupied the center of the United States' trade concerns, had to do with restrictions in the service sector such as banking, securities and insurance. This is especially relevant to more mature economies that are changing their production mix from industrial to services. The third weakness of GATT–47 pertained to agriculture subsidies and restrictions that were of concern to the EU countries that had always maintained a high degree of protection for their agriculture sector. Finally, it contained no mechanism for enforcing and settling a trade dispute among nations. Since the final decision required approval by a unanimous vote, a country that was accused of trade violation was able to veto any decision indefinitely. Given these problems and the desire to improve the organization, a total of eight negotiation rounds was held.[13] Starting with the Kennedy Round, the focus shifted to non-tariff barriers (NTBs) and non-tariff measures (NTMs), such as anti-dumping codes, and agriculture issues. This refocusing trend continued in the Tokyo Round. Starting with the Tokyo Round, negotiations included topics that were not subject to GATT jurisdiction and discipline such as product standards and government procurement policies. The shift in attention to topics that were not in the purview of GATT continued further in the Uruguay Round, where trade in intellectual property, services, dispute settlement procedures, transparency and surveillance of trade policies, and rules of origin were discussed.

World Trade Organization

WTO,[14] established in 1995,[15] is an international organization[16] that administers multinational agreements pertaining to trade in goods (GATT), services (GATS), and intellectual property rights (TRIPs). WTO is essentially not concerned with private transactions. It only deals with government actions with regard to tariffs and non-tariff barriers and subsidies. It is a supranational regulator of international markets. Its operating costs are paid by membership dues that are assessed on each country based on the three-year average of the most recent trade data. If the average is less than 0.12 percent, a minimum contribution is assessed.

The basic underlying premise of the WTO is that open markets, global competition, and absence of discrimination in international trade will lead to economic growth and development and thence to higher world economic welfare. This is in contradistinction with the 'beggar-thy-neighbor' policies of mercantilists and projectionists who favor high and prohibitive or discriminatory trade barriers for international trade. WTO is charged with five functions. First, it is to facilitate the implementation of Multilateral Trade Agreements (MTAs). Second, it must provide a forum for negotiations. Third, the WTO is to adjudicate and administer any settled disputes. Fourth, it is to administer the Trade Policy Review Mechanism (TPRM).[17] Fifth, it must coordinate and cooperate with the International Monetary Fund (IMF) and the World Bank (WB) for congruous global economic policy decision-making.

WTO membership

The accession protocol is a set of steps that new members must take in order to bring their economic policies into compliance with the rules of the WTO. When a country is ready for membership, it must negotiate certain requirements which it must meet. These requirements are country-based; that is, they are tailored to the needs, realities and economic conditions of the country. During the period of negotiation, the country is given an observer status, which means it is allowed to participate in most functions without having a voice in decisions. In order to become a member, there are additional core requirements that must be met. The first is in regard to the transparency in the trade regime. That is, all rules and regulations with regard to imports and exports must be available, clearly stated, and followed. Second, economic policies must be adjusted to eliminate most direct export subsidies and direct production subsidies. Third, quantitative restrictions must be converted to tariffs, which must be bounded. Once set, these tariffs can only be reduced but not increased without receiving an exception from the WTO.

Advantages of membership

The estimated impact of the Uruguay Round on world income ranges from US $212 billion (see Nguyen, Perroni and Wigle, 1993) to US $510 billion (see François, McDonald and Nordstrom, 1994). Developing countries are expected to earn a significant fraction of this higher welfare. OECD's study in 1993 estimated that LDCs will gain about US $86 billion, while François, McDonald and Nordstrom (1994) put the gain at $122 billion. The distribution of these gains among participating countries directly depends on each country's own commercial liberalization policies.[18] However, given the high trade barriers that LDCs have faced in developed countries, any reduction in tariffs stimulates and creates exports opportunities for them.[19] The extent of these expansions, of course, depends on the country's comparative advantage and availability of resources that could be used for this purpose. This is a potential loss of trade because of trade diversion from those nations that are not members of the WTO to those who are members of the organization. Those with MFN and preferential treatment status, of course, will reap the benefits first. Whatever is left over, if any, will go to those outside the loop. Arguably, the most important advantage of membership in the WTO is the guarantee of MFN[20] (those who automatically are in the MFN loop) that puts the country on a par with other countries in international trade.

Besides the additional growth in output, income, and employment, as well as improvements in efficiency and proper allocation of resources that accompany trade liberalization, other advantages are:

- binding on tariffs that reduces rent-seeking by the domestic producers; that is, since a country must abide by the WTO rules which require each country to avoid unilateral trade restrictions without the consent of the WTO, its government is no longer forced to increase protection of its industry;
- access to the WTO dispute settlement body. This is very important for smaller and less powerful countries because this body must maintain its impartiality if it is going to retain its credibility. Therefore, it puts these countries in a better position to argue their case if and when a need arises;
- a voice in the creation of future rules. For many decades, international trade organizations such as GATT have been mainly within the realm of rich industrial countries. LDCs were marginally involved in the decision-making activities of those organizations and therefore rules of the game were set according to the needs of countries that had high volume of trade. This changed in the Uruguay Round of negotiations where LDCs became engaged and, as a result, received considerable presence and differentials;
- the country will have to make and maintain internationally acceptable economic policies. This is certainly a great incentive for the government to legislate and adhere to policies that are for the good of the public and not necessarily for the special interest groups represented by powerful lobbies;
- one country one vote. This is very different from the IMF and the UN Security Council where each country's vote depends on its economic or political might. WTO's decision-making is based, in general, on the GATT practice of decision-making by consensus. Therefore, unlike the IMF where one country's vote is proportional to its share in the fund, no one country has a larger vote than any other.

Consumer choice is another advantage that would lead to competition among domestic and foreign suppliers. As suppliers try to attract customers, they have to improve the quality of their products and sell them at a lower price. This leads to a better standard of living and lower cost of living for the masses.

Iran's trade in the post-revolution era

The Islamic revolution of 1979 washed over Iran with a tidal wave of anti-imperialism and anti-foreign rhetoric. The rhetoric of the revolutionary leadership called for freeing the country from imperialist domination and for redirecting the country's trade and cooperative ventures toward the oppressed and exploited Third World countries. By doing so, it was argued, Iran's resources would be immune from exploitation by the more powerful transnational and multinational corporations. At the same time, it would enhance Iran's prestige and leadership among other Third World countries while improving their prospects for prosperity, fair trade, and mutual cooperation. This, in turn, would promote Islamic ideology and an Islamic economic system that would better meet the moral, spiritual and materialistic needs of the deprived and repressed masses of the Third World. In practice, by choice or due to the US sanctions and unfavorable treatments by the industrialized countries, there has been a considerable shift in Iranian trade away from developed countries and in favor of other LDCs.[21] However, Iran's overall trade in general, and exports in particular, have not kept pace with the rest of world, in absolute as well as in relative terms (see Figures 6.1, 6.2 and 6.3). Total exports fell to a low level of US $8.15 billion in 1988, and ever since have inched upward to the 1977 levels. In the meantime, due to an increase in world trade (both imports and exports), Iran's share in world trade has been woefully declining to negligible levels. For example, in 1997 Iran's share of world exports was about 0.45 percent, while for imports and overall trade it was 0.26 percent and 0.36 percent, respectively.

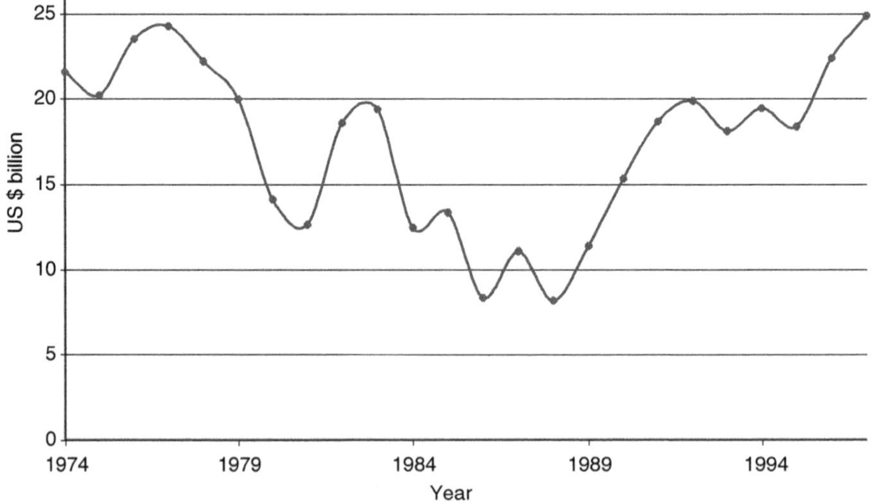

Figure 6.1 Iran's exports.

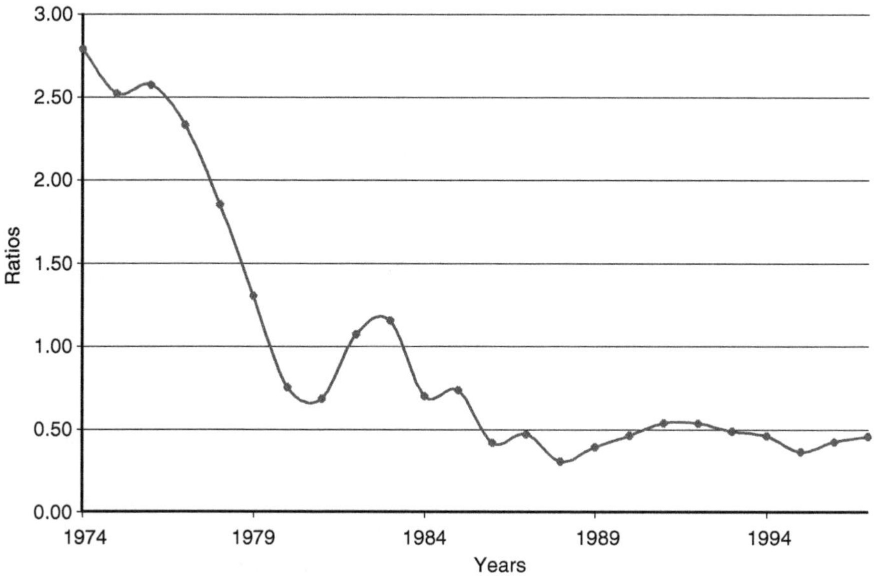

Figure 6.2 Ratios of Iran's exports to the world's exports.

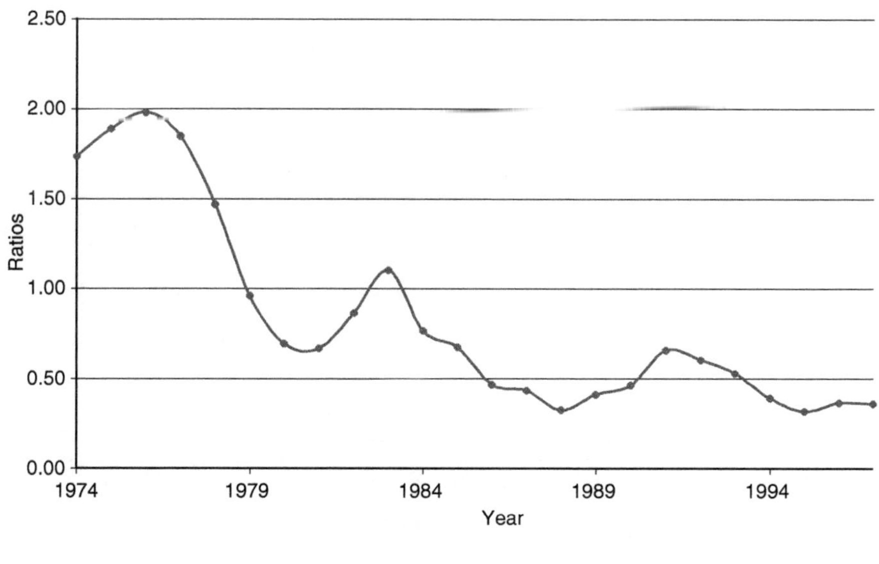

Figure 6.3 Ratios of Iran's total trade with the world.

Non-oil exports

In 1977 (1356) non-oil exports totalled $563 million. The best performance took place in the 1990s when Iran was able to pay for a relatively very large percentage of imports with revenues accrued from non-oil exports. The country had never achieved that level of performance. In 1974 (1353), the ratio of non-oil exports to total imports was at 9 percent. Even though this low ratio is understandable in the face of a sharp rise in imports due to a large increase in oil revenues, it never recovered to any significant degree until later in the 1990s, when draconian import restrictions were imposed.

The decline in the ratio of non-oil exports to total imports was at its worst throughout most of the post-revolutionary era (see Figure 6.4). For three years in a row, 1982–5 (1361–4) the ratio fell to about 2 percent. This situation is not surprising given the Iran–Iraq war, which caused much destruction and required the reallocation of resources to the war efforts. In the second half of the decade despite a better picture, there were many conditions to concern the Iranian government. Recently, the Deputy Commerce Minister stated that between 1986 (1365) and 1991 (1370) only 9 percent of the foreign exchange needs of Iran were paid by non-oil exports. This is an improvement over the 1982–85 (1361–64) period but it does not in any way show that the composition of non-oil exports, or its ratio to total imports, has improved to the point where the country is no longer vulnerable to cash problems and related consequences. As Figure 6.1 shows, there is a substantial increase in the ability of the country to

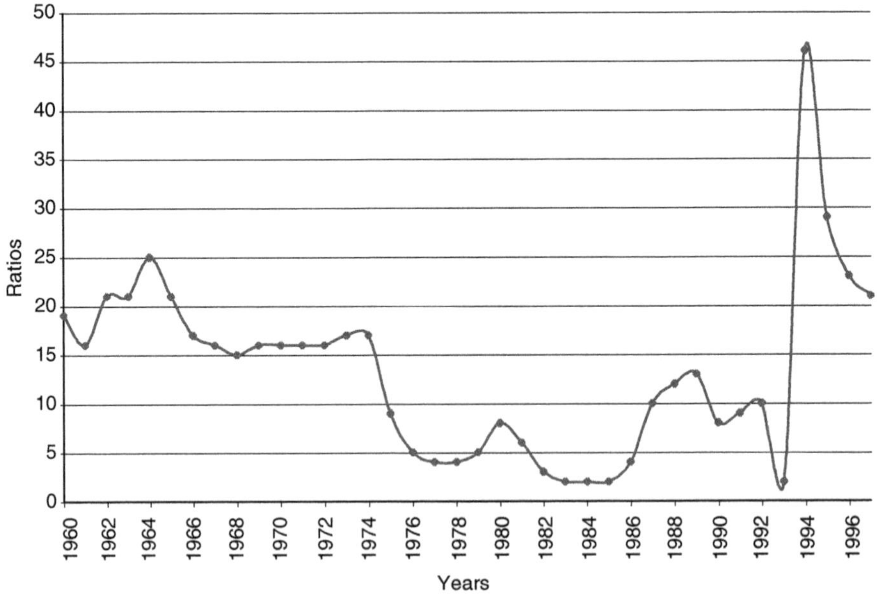

Figure 6.4 Ratios of non-oil ex/imports.

pay for its imports with non-oil exports. The ratio increased to 46 percent but fell back to a little over 21 percent by 1997. However, this was mostly artificial and due to 'the impact of an increasingly appreciated exchange rate, a weaker demand for Iranian products in some export markets, and anti-export bias in policy. In particular, the single largest component of non-oil exports – carpets – declined markedly to US $600 by 1996–7, compared with US $2.1 billion in 1994–5'.[22]

Observations and conclusions

For many decades, rich industrial countries have dominated international trade organizations such as GATT. Less developed countries[23] were only marginally involved in decision-making activities and therefore the rules of the game were set according to the needs of the industrial world – i.e. by those countries that had a high volume of trade. However, some rules, such as preferential tariff reductions or exemption from GATT rules, were instituted as aid and assistance for trade and development to LDCs. This power structure changed during the Uruguay Round of negotiations where LDCs became engaged and, as a result, received considerable presence and differentials. [24]

Iran's unimpressive economic performance came about as a result of the Iran–Iraq war and the inevitable collapse of oil prices, both of which were beyond the government's control, in combination with many self-inflicted and self-destructive policies. Many of the negative economic conditions could easily be reversed if Iran's ideological straightjacket were removed from the policy-making process.

Foremost among the self-inflicted and self-destructive wounds is the insecurity of individual citizens. Human rights violations are repeatedly acknowledged by officials of the UN and independent researchers, and are highlighted by the media with a troublesome frequency.[25] One could refer to the student unrest, and the arrest and imprisonment of prominent figures, as well as the serial killings of 1997–9.[26] Second is the ease and frequency with which laws and regulations are revoked and modified. It seems that when a law or regulation does produce instant results, it is changed. One case in point is the way the Central Bank dealt with exchange rates' another, the way the government dealt with trade liberalization in 1991. The government decided to open Iran's doors and allow importers to import freely to fight inflation. The importers knew that the open-door policies would not last and therefore brought home much more than was necessary. In other words, due to the uncertainty about the future course of action, they imported more than needed in order to have a stockpile of goods in the event of an anticipated policy reversal. And they were right. The government did not stand its ground and very shortly clamped down on imports when trade deficits emerged. Had the importers been certain that the government would not reverse its course, they most probably would have imported only the necessary commodities and would not have gone overboard to create such a large imbalance in the current account.

Third, one might not be able to depend, with certainty, on the laws of the land as the guiding principles. These laws may or may not stand the test of time: they may be dismissed as un-Islamic or against the interests of Islam. This came to the forefront in 1988. Ordinarily, when a bill is passed by the Majles[27] it must be signed by the President and approved by the Guardian Council. In the event of disagreement between the two, the bill does not become law unless the issues are resolved by the *Showrawye Tashkhis-e Mosalehat-e Nezam* (Council on the Discernment of Expediency), a body created by the late Ayatollah Khomeini in 1988 to resolve and mediate between the Majles and the Guardian Council. However, even when there is an agreement among the Parliament, the President, and Council of Guardians about a law, it is possible for it to be nullified by the Council on the Discernment of Expediency[28]. In the case of land reform, for example, the Majles, the President and the Council of Guardians could not agree on the definition of land ownership and property rights, therefore, an impasse was created which required the intervention of the late Ayatollah Khomeini in January 1988. He issued a *fatva* (finding) which draws on the authority of the Prophet of Islam. According to this *fatva*, issues that are not directly and explicitly addressed in the Quran, the holy book of Islam, can be decided by the present government. This unprecedented ruling gives the Islamic Republic's governmental authorities the right to act in ways that are above and beyond the normal mode of conduct and the country's constitution. According to this ruling, if there is overriding necessity, the government could 'unilaterally revoke any agreement with the people … prevent any matter, whether religious or secular, if it is against the interest of Islam. This includes the suspension of the five pillars of the Islamic faith including fasting, prayer and pilgrimage to Mecca.'[29] Khomeini reportedly backed away from this unlimited ruling later.[30] But the fact that such a ruling was made and the fact that it was not challenged on religious or constitutional grounds, provides a precedent that does not give solace or security to those who deal or expect to deal with the government or its representatives and institutions. It contributes to the sense of uncertainty about laws and regulations that is felt by potential foreign and domestic investors.

A fourth related problem, which would possibly explain the faltering private investment, is lack of uniformity in the application of the laws of the land and uncertainty due to political instability, and the sense of individual insecurity which these conditions instil. Court decisions as well as other official rulings depend on who you are, where you are, and with whom you are acquainted.[31] In Iran, individual government officials could and would interpret the law to suit the person and not the situation. For example, one person could obtain a permit to open a business while the next person with the same qualifications might be denied the permit.[32]

The fifth area of concern has to do with Iran's international relationships. The revolutionary zeal and fervour, which understandably were present at the beginning of the revolution, gave way to a more rational decision-making process. However, Iran's leadership has persistently clung to many tenets of the revolution, refusing to engage in rapprochement with the country's international adversaries and underestimating their willingness and ability to cause damage directly or through roundabout methods. The controversial positions taken by Iran in regard to various issues have often resulted in negative opinion within and throughout the international community. The direct damage of the eight-year Iran–Iraq war and the freezing of Iranian assets by the United States are self-evident and need little elaboration.

However, since the revolution Iran has been paying for its political leanings in other less quantifiable ways. An example of this has to do with the 'dual containment policy', by which Iran has been penalized persistently in at least three important and long-lasting ways. One punitive aspect, promoted by the United States, is the unwritten and circuitous international prohibition of the transfer of technology which might be considered as capable of serving dual purposes by the United States. Even though, on the surface, other countries do not directly subscribe to and participate in this prohibition, they have conducted business with Iran with a watchful eye on these transactions. This means that Iran cannot openly buy what it needs without a great deal of European and Japanese governmental red tape. This red tape and watchfulness is, of course, to protect the images of these countries as perceived by the international community. Japan and the European nations do not want to be accused of supporting or arming a 'rogue' nation. The second way that Iran is penalized by the 'dual containment policy' is that trading countries have raised the overall price of doing business. In the financial markets, Iran's credit rating is far lower than that which a country of its like should receive. There is not even one instance in which Iran has failed to pay its debt, even during those chaotic days of the hostage crisis and frozen Iranian assets. Yet, Iran must pay higher interest rates due to, among other things, low credit ratings and high country risk. Other examples abound. Iran has not been able to buy oil technology in a competitive way. The Conoco example, even though it is unique in its circumstances, is not an isolated one.[33] Third, the 'dual containment' strategy keeps foreign investors away.[34] Even though Iran has been trying to lure businesses to invest in the country proper or in the Free Trade Zone areas, the attempts have been less than successful.[35]

It is well established that Iran is a marginal country in exports and imports (total trade) relative to the world total trade. But her absence from international arenas denies her a forum to defend and protect her interests. One such example is the WTO. Being a member of WTO means participation in the decision-making process. WTO's decision-making is based, in general, on the GATT practice of decision-making by consensus.[36] This means that a decision is finalized not necessarily because all of the present members agree with it: rather, a decision may be made because those countries that are present and have reservations may not object strongly enough to the matter to block the passage of a given motion. By definition, in an organization that operates by consensus, presence means having the ability to protect one's interests. Those who are not present at the table do not have a voice and their interests may be infringed upon. Given Iran's faltering trade situation, she might badly be in need of trade partners and of becoming a part of the multilateral trade.

Another point that is important to reiterate is the impact of openness on the economy of a member state. Openness imposes the tyranny of the global market. The country is no longer allowed to plunder its scarce resources in the production of commodities that do not have clear international comparative advantage. International competition forces each country to be much more judicious and a great deal less cavalier in its choices of what and how much to produce.

Finally, from the discussion of output (GDP), faltering investment in machinery and construction, and spiralling inflation, it is apparent that monetary policy has not been effective in stimulating real economic activities, nor has it been used successfully to control the value of the currency. It has been employed in an on-again-off-again manner rather than as a tool for proactive decision-making. If this undesirable tendency (to use monetary policy in the regulation of short-run ups and downs) were to be overcome, it would require three initiatives. First and foremost, the Central Bank must be given independence and the authority to make monetary policy without regard to politics. Its authority and independence should be similar to those characterizing other Central Banks such as those of the United States, New Zealand and Germany. When the Central Bank is unencumbered by political considerations, the short-run vacillation in its monetary decisions would be eliminated or considerably mitigated. Second, given the limited usefulness of monetary policy in directing and influencing the real variables of the economy such as real output, and employment in the long run, the Central Bank must be directed to strive to achieve the one and only objective over which it has much control – price stability. This would enable the Central Bank to focus its resources and power upon a realistic and feasible outcome. Third, the Central Bank must adhere to a set of explicitly and publicly announced quantitative targets for inflation, and also, to a set of rules designed to achieve those quantitative targets. These would go far in cooling the speculative minds of the *bazaaris* (businessmen), who would no longer profit from hoarding and from speculation about future higher prices. Arguably most importantly, these changes would promote a considerable reduction in uncertainty, a problem that has been pervasive and harmful to the economy in the post-revolutionary Iran.

Notes

1 This might be true for all of the official statistics since there are no publicly available alternative sources of data.

2 This was considered a strategy of Iraq's allies to defeat Iran in the war. That is, by denying Iran revenues from oil, it was assumed, Iran would try to cut its losses and surrender or at least agree to a ceasefire.

3 Cyrus Bina, 'Global oil and the oil policies of the Islamic Republic', in Cyrus Bina and Hamid Zangeneh (eds), *Modern Capitalism and Islamic Ideology in Iran* (New York: St Martin's Press, 1992).

4 See Hamid Zangeneh, 'International trade in Iran: an appraisal', *Research in Middle East Economics*, Vol. 2, (1997).

5 For a discussion of government budget, see H. Amirahmadi and Hamid Zangeneh, 'Iranian government budgets: an analysis', *Journal of Public Budgeting, Accounting & Financial Management*, 9(2), Summer (1997), pp. 1–19.

6 One needs to be cognizant of the fact that many economic activities are undertaken by *bonyads* (religious foundations) that were created after the revolution. In some estimates, these *bonyads* are as large as the government itself. However, they are not subject to audit or supervision by the formal organs of the executive or legislative branches of the government.

7 See Hamid Zangeneh, 'International trade in Iran: an appraisal', *Research in Middle East Economics*, Vol. 2 (1997).

8 Under a regime of fixed exchange rates, inflation could be imported through several channels, including higher imported goods prices, monetization of foreign reserves by the central banks, and higher demand for exportable goods.

9 For a discussion of central banking and its function in an Islamic framework, see Hamid Zangeneh and Ahmad Salam, 'Central banking in an interest free banking system'. *Journal of Research in Islamic Banking* Vol. 5. (Center for Research in Islamic Economics, King Abdulaziz University) (1993), p. 26, and M.N. Siddiqi, 'Central banking in an Islamic framework,' paper submitted to the Royal Academy for Islamic Civilization Research, Amman, Jordan, and published in Arabic in *al Idara al Maliyah fil Islam*, Vol. 1, (1989) pp. 31–76. Arguably, the most important function of the central bank is the stability of the price level. This is more important in an Islamic welfare state than in other systems of governance. An Islamic government, by definition, requires a value-based economic system. Therefore, social justice is of paramount importance and must have a very high priority in all decisions. For a discussion of this point, see B. J. Reilly and Hamid Zangeneh, 'The value-based Islamic economic system and other optimal economic systems: a critical comparative analysis', *International Journal of Social Economics*, 17(10), (November 1990), pp. 21–35. It must design and pursue economic policies that lead to economic development and fair distribution of income. However, inflation is the cruellest and most capricious redistributive system. Obviously, it hurts most those who can least afford it.

10 Thirteen of these banks had some foreign partners and the other 15 were totally Iranian-owned.

11 Trade unions' objection to free trade and for protectionism in industrial countries with high capital intensity is based, to a large extent, on the Stopler–Samuelson theory that shows international trade benefits the abundant factor of production at the expense of the scarce factor.

12 There are those who religiously believe in the concept of imperialism and multinationals as their vanguard. However, these believers immediately change their minds about imperialism when the discussion comes to the United States. They ignore the fact that multinationals have always striven to make sure that the government does not have any capability to restrict 'unfair trade' practices. They, the multinationals, unlike the early years, do not need to be 'American' or helped by the American government.

13 Multilateral trade negotiation rounds under GATT were 1) The Geneva Round (1947), 2) The Annecy Round (1949), 3) The Torquay Round (1951), 4) The Geneva Round (1956), 5) The Dillon Round (1960–1), 6) The Kennedy Round (1964–7), 7) The Tokyo Round (1973–9), 8) The Uruguay Round (1986–94). The first five rounds basically dealt with tariff reductions.

14 The suggestion to create a single multilateral trade organization to encompass GATT, GATS and TRIPs was first suggested by Canada and endorsed by the European Union in 1990.

15 In December 1993, the Uruguay Round of multilateral trade negotiations was completed after seven years of arduous negotiations that started in Punta del Este, Uruguay. The final act, establishing the WTO, was signed in Marrakech on 15 April 1994. The last date that a country could enter the WTO as a founding member was 31 December 1994. The agreement took effect on 1 July 1995.

16 This is in contrast to GATT, which was not an organization; it was a treaty among parties involved.

17 This mechanism is designed to examine the impact and adherence of trade policies and practices of members on the trading system. These policy reviews are more frequent for the larger trading countries: every other year for Japan, Canada, the US and the EU; every 4 years for the next 16 largest countries; every 6 years or longer for developing countries. These trade policy reviews are based on the country reports and reports prepared by the WTO secretariat. This mechanism is an important instrument in assuring transparency in trade policies of the member states.

18 For a more detailed discussion of various studies of potential gains from trade liberalization, see Raed Safadi and Sam Laird, 'The Uruguay Round Agreement: impact on developing countries', *World Development*, Vol. 24, No. 7, (1996), pp. 1223–42.

19 Trade expansion depends on whether or not the country enjoys MFN or preferential treatment.

20 MFN requires every member of the WTO to treat each of its trading partners as well as it treats its most favored trading partner. Any special tariff cuts agreed to by, say the United States, in any bilateral negotiations would apply to the products of all other trading partners whom the US government had designated by most favored nation status.

21 For a discussion of Iran's trade philosophy as well as empirical evidence, see Hamid Zangeneh, 'International trade in Iran: an appraisal', *Research in Middle East Economics*, Vol. 2 (1997).

22 IMF Staff Country Report No. 98/27, International Monetary Fund, Washington DC, April 1998, p. 39.

23 Minsky has identified 'five stages in the US economy – merchant, industrial, banker, managerial, and money manager. Whalen noted that the United States may be on the verge of entering a sixth stage, which he termed global finance.'

24 These can be summarized 'under five general headings: 1) a lower level of obligations; 2) more flexible implementation timetables; 3) best endeavour commitment by developing countries; 4) more favorable treatment for developed countries; 5) technical assistance and training.' For details, see Bernard M. Hoekman and Michael M. Kostecki, *The Political Economy of The World Trading System: From GATT to WTO* (Oxford: Oxford University Press, 1995).

25 Debates about and research into the existence or lack of a civil society have become prevalent among Iranian scholars. For example, the Fifteenth Annual Conference of the Center for Iranian Research and Analysis (CIRA), held at Georgia Tech University, Atlanta, Georgia, 18–20 April 1997, was entitled 'Towards a civil society in Iran: prospects and obstacles'. Its six multiple-author sessions and panels convened around the question of civil society and an additional session focused upon human rights. On one hand, there is a serious attempt to portray the Islamic Republic system of governance as being neither monolithic nor immutable. There are instances where the Islamic Republic has had to change direction in the face of resistance from the public. An example of this was the government's unsuccessful attempt to do away with secular holidays such as New Year's celebrations (*norooz*) and replace them with religious events. Other examples, which advance this line of reasoning, abound, according to advocates of the existence of civil society in Iran. They list, among other things, public disagreement with the government and its policies by *Soroush* or others within the system as evidence in support of their argument. On the other side of the issue, critics of the Islamic Republic tend to reduce the system to the all-encompassing, omnipotent and omnipresent office of the *Faqih* (the supreme leader of the Islamic Republic). Even though there are some cracks in the walls of rules and regulations, it is argued, there is not much that could be done without the explicit or tacit acquiescence of the Faqih who either directly or indirectly controls all of Iranian affairs. This includes domestic as well as foreign policy of the country.

26 For a thorough discussion of the problems associated with student unrest, see *Journal of Iranian Research and Analysis*, Vol. 15, no. 2, November 1999.

27 In Iran, theoretically, there is one legislative body, the Majles (the Parliament). A bill passed by the Majles does not become law, even if the president signs it. It must receive the approval of the Guardian Council who study all laws passed by the Majles to assure their compatibility with Islamic codes. This council is comprised of 12 appointed members, 6 of whom must be clerics. However, even in this case one could not be well assured that the law is the law. The law can be pronounced null and void by the Council on the Discernment of Expediency or, in extreme cases, by the Faqih who could step in and reinterpret the issue.

28 The Council on the Discernment of Expediency has, according to the constitution, an advisory role and responsibility to the Faqih, the supreme leader of the country. It is comprised of a group of leaders who are appointed by the Faqih. Their function is to assess what needs to be done, i.e., initiate legislation, or to express an opinion (mediate) with regard to a bill that is held up by the Guardian Council when there is disagreement over the bill between the Majles and the Guardian Council. Their decision is final even if it is not in conformity with Islam or the constitution. This council includes ten ex-officio members: the president, the speaker of the Majles, the chairman of the judiciary, six clerical members of the Guardian Council (not any of its six lay members of the Council), the cabinet minister or government agency minister associated with the legislation before the council.

29 Shaul Bakhash, 'The politics of land, law, social justice in Iran', *Middle East Journal*, Vol. 43, no. 2, Spring 1988, pp. 186–201.

30 Ibid., p. 198.

31 It is similar to the old system of governance in Iran whereby regional chieftains ruled. In this case, chieftains are replaced with local or regional clergy.

32 It is commonly known and believed that in Iran nothing is impossible if one knows the right people and is ready to pay the price (bribe).

33 Spain, during the Iran–Iraq war, even refused to sell barbed wire to the Iranian government in the open market. They considered the wire as having a military purpose.

34 The 'dual containment' policy has, unfortunately, reinforced the hesitation of the foreign business community to invest in Iran. This hesitation was created in the early post-revolutionary years by Iranian laws of regulations.

35 See Hamid Zangeneh, 'International trade in Iran: an appraisal', *Research in Middle East Economics*, Vol. 2 (1997).

36 In cases where consensus can not be reached, votes, based on one-country-one-vote, will be taken. Unless it is specified in the WTO articles, a simple majority carries the motion. However, in issues of importance to the principles of the organization, much stricter voting rules are specified. For example, unanimity is required for amendments to general principles. A two-thirds majority is needed for amendments on issues other than WTO's principles. A three-fourths majority is needed for interpretations of agreements and a waiver of a member's obligations.

Part III

The global challenge for development

After the Second World War, the world divided into two camps: communist, under the leadership of Soviet Union, and capitalist, with the United States of America as a leading force for the Western world. The idea of development emerged out of a discussion between President Truman and his speech-writer over the presidential inaugural address on 20 January 1949. The main message in the President's speech later became known as the 'point-four program', and inaugurated the 'development age' which was to become the new mission of the US around the world. After rescuing Europe from Nazism, the US now aimed to help the free peoples of the world, through their own efforts, to produce more food, more clothing, more materials for housing and more mechanical power to lighten their burden, whilst claiming that the old imperialism had no part at all in this four-point program (Rist, 1997). Iran, considering itself protected from the capitalist world by virtue of its 2,000 km border with the Soviet Union, signed into the US development plan with no concern for social, cultural and religious traditions of its people. The lack of definition of what this development intended to achieve and for whom, together with the dismissal of the immediate needs of the people, produced a total setback of American development plans and furthermore interfered in the democratically elected government of Iran by destroying the positive view of development promoted by the leadership under Musaddeq. The outcome was the Islamic Revolution of 1979 and a return to nativism, accompanied by a resounding antipathy for American-style development.

Now, twenty years later, the Iranian people are again growing frustrated at the limits of a theocratic regime and the global challenge that face them. The following chapters in this section outline the various issues and paradoxes which Iran is currently encountering. Chapter 7 concentrates on the efforts to rebuild the war-damaged areas after the end of the eight-year war with Iraq. The urgent need for reconstruction meant that, despite attempts to survey existing patterns of settlement, development of the new villages did not follow existing patterns. The design of these new villages was based on the assumptions that urban dwellers had made about rural populations. The functional segregation of pedestrians and animals on the one hand and the urban character of the development on the other, reflected an environment perceived by the designers as desirable by the local people. Not dissimilar to the post-war reconstruction of Europe, when modernist development replaced the ruins of war, the destruction of these settlements was seen as an opportunity for improvement. Changes in traditional building materials and lifestyles were seen as inevitable. In the modernist spirit, the designers, therefore, took up the role of reformers.

By reviewing some of these developments, and evaluating their use by their inhabitants, this chapter argues that the designers' assumptions were not realistic and that the existing patterns of everyday life and spatial organization should have been taken into account in a systematic way. This chapter offers a brief account of these patterns, which were studied by the author during a two-year project funded by Iran's Building and Housing Research Center. It argues that there is an often urgent need to study such patterns before their disappearance in the modernization process. This chapter also argues that there has been a contradiction between revolutionary preference for traditional life patterns and the actual modernisation processes.

Chapter 8 examines how access to development is possible when the minds, attitudes and behaviours of its people are turned in the direction of development. It examines the ability of human resources in relation to the requirements of economic development and considers the main characteristics of human resources during the period 1976–91. Its focus is the trend of human resources as a whole, including both the economically active and economically inactive, and employment and its structure in particular. This chapter also investigates the shift of spheres of public and private-sector employment in the post-revolutionary period. To give a clear picture of the role of private and public sectors in running the economy, the major characteristics of employment in both private and public sectors are analysed. It explores the impact of the rapid growth of population on human resources structure and concludes that during 1976–91, the tendency of employment was oriented mostly towards unproductive activities: the work force (particularly in the private sector) lacked the necessary academic abilities to manage and run the country's economy. Finally, this chapter will highlight the fact that raising the capability of the population systematically across all sectors is an essential factor for the economic development of Iran. Chapter 9 in this part analyses the process of feminization and defeminization of the work force in Iran as reflected in data covering the period 1956–91. This chapter also examines the role of Islamic ideology in shaping the pattern of female employment in Iran, the process of nation-building and the period over which nationhood was redefined. In conclusion, it is suggested that the Islamic government is starting to promote the image of woman as an individual citizen rather than simply a mother and wife. It is possible that women's social participation, including their engagement in the formal world of work, may increase in the future.

7 Modernization and everyday life

Urban and rural change in Iran

Ali Madanipour

In this chapter Madanipour discusses aspects of modernization in Iranian society, drawing upon examples of change in the built environment. How modernization has penetrated the everyday life of the people, and how it has transformed the social and physical environment of the country, are the main focus of this chapter. He argues that the revolution in Iran, despite its traditionalist tones and appearance, is a new phase in a historical process of modernization. To illustrate this, he uses two examples of spatial transformation from Tehran and Khuzestan to represent urban and rural change. The case study of Tehran draws upon his book on Tehran, in which he presents a profile of the city and traces the process of urban development (Madanipour, 1998). The case study of Khuzestan is based on a two-year research project by a team of researchers, headed by the author and funded by Iran's Building and Housing Research Centre, on the typology of rural housing in Khuzestan. It also draws upon the author's involvement in the re-design of several war-damaged rural settlements in southwest Iran (Madanipour *et al.*, 1984, 1985, 1986; Madanipour, 1995).

Historical tensions of modernity

Discussions about modernization and modernity are not new in Iran. Ever since the early encounters with the industrialized West, the questions of how to modernize or how to avoid it have been on the agenda. In the early nineteenth century, the Russian and British Empires defeated Iran in several wars and conquered parts of the Persian Empire's territories. Iranians, who were shocked by the military might and the economic supremacy of the West, started a process of reform, realizing that change was inevitable. They wanted now to change institutions, appearances and environments to refashion the country in the image of the powerful West. This also triggered a reaction to such change, as it was found to be unpleasant or humiliating for some, and threatening for others. These internal tensions had a close link with external ones, in the context of expanding, capitalist economies of the West forcing to integrate Iran into a new world system as a peripheral partner. External and internal tensions of this kind lie at the heart, but are not the sole cause, of two revolutions and several upheavals during the past one hundred years.

For a while, it was felt that discussions and hesitations in relation to modernity were only a symptom of the so-called traditional societies, on the margins of the expanding West. These were thought to be sleepy societies that were being dragged into the modern age, and therefore some disruption was not only inevitable, but also healthy. Modernism was essentially based on the possibility and necessity of breaking with traditions and instituting new ways of living and thinking. It was therefore not expected to see these debates taking place in the heartland of modernity. But we have witnessed in recent decades heated criticisms of modernity and modernization processes in the West on similar grounds (see, for example, Berman, 1982; Harvey, 1989; Giddens, 1990; Touraine, 1995). As the prosperity and security that the post-Second World War period was offering began to fade, some of the earlier hesitations about modernity returned. These had dominated the fields of architecture and urban planning, with Jane Jacobs' (1961) book a classic example, and can be detected still in other fields in the humanities and social sciences, where a major battle is taking place between the legacies of the Enlightenment and its critics, between reason and unreason, between order and disorder, between modernization and everyday life.

The practices which have led to, and followed, the Iranian revolution can be studied in the light of these and similar debates. Ever since the eighteenth century, revolutions have been major vehicles of breaking with the past and of modernization. In this sense, the Iranian revolution was no exception. What made it exceptional was the use of traditional cultural forms for such a drastic break. The coexistence of breaking with the past and returning to the past, however, has created contradictions for the revolutionary practices and rhetoric. It has become conventional wisdom that the revolution in Iran took place in reaction to the forced modernization processes of the Pahlavi period, aiming to emancipate the everyday life practices and beliefs from such processes. What emerged, however, included some new forms of modernization or a continuation of the existing forms. The revolution may have protected some aspects of popular culture from a further encroachment of the modernization processes. It has, at the same time introduced strong elements of modernization in the social and political institutions as well as in the built environment.

During the last 150 years the political and economic contact of the country with the West has found a dual response in Iranian society, as best reflected in two distinctive strata: modern intelligentsia and traditional middle classes (Abrahamian, 1982). These both formed nationalist movements opposing foreign political interference and economic dominance, and the country's rulers whom they saw as responsible for the humiliating effects of such dominance. The two forces usually confronted each other, confrontation which could reach its peak during periods of political freedom such as the 1940s (Young, 1948). However, at two instances in the recent history of Iran, these two groups formed alliances, which led to the advent of revolutions in 1906 and 1979.

The modern intelligentsia was those intellectuals who, through travels, translations and new educational establishments, had adopted modern ideas, aspirations and values along Western lines. Initially, they came from different strata, from aristocracy as well as from the bazaar, and were too few to form a social class. In the twentieth century, however, resulting mainly from the expansion of the bureaucracy and the armed forces, they developed into a salaried middle class (Abrahamian, 1982). The constituent parts of the traditional middle classes were the clergy and the bazaar community of merchants and artisans who, before the impact of the West, practised a large degree of control over economic and social affairs. These traditional privileges of this group were lost through the establishment of new economic orders with predominance of foreign interests and their associates, and through secularization of the society by the government. Integration of the country into the world economy somewhat marginalized this group, who turned into a propertied middle class.

The modern intelligentsia, who gained the upper hand in the first revolution, believed that, to break the chains of royal despotism, clerical dogmatism and foreign imperialism, the solutions were liberalism, secularism and nationalism. They argued that, for a modern, strong and developed Iran, a radical transformation of society was required. To pave the way for a capitalist development, the country needed to be restructured in the image of the materialized example of industrial development, the West. Against this approach were the traditional middle classes, who gained the upper hand in the second revolution. They believed in a nationalism in which the political and economic independence of the country was sought through a return to the traditional values, as idealized in Islamic culture of the society, and through least possible contact with Western forces and values.

Both traditional middle classes and the modern intelligentsia, however, formed the country's elite and as such could be easily differentiated from the masses. On the surface, the modern intelligentsia was very distant from the masses, as it introduced alien forms and practices. It was, however, introducing reforms some of which were seen by the masses as necessary. It is true that the relationship between the traditional middle classes and the masses was rooted in long-standing cultural practices of everyday life. Here, however, the relationships of domination have also prevailed, as these common roots and narratives are constantly manipulated and have failed to help improve the living conditions of the impoverished masses. The urban and rural transformation of Iran can be studied against this background, where two sets of elites have competed to shape the society and space in their idealized images and where the social life of the masses has been kept in the background rather than actively participating in this shaping process. What links the two groups, however, is their shared tendency to radical change, a hallmark of all modernization processes. The underlying current for both groups, as evident in the two following cases of urban and rural transformation, has been modernization from above. Before the Islamic revolution, as always the modern intelligentsia had had the upper hand and the modernization processes were enforced, thus the traditional middle classes could claim to be protecting everyday life from such threats. With the establishment of the Islamic state, however, it became obvious that modernization was continuing, albeit, although not always, in different forms. The case of Tehran here signifies the pre-revolutionary trend but identifies how the trend has continued after the revolution. The case of post-war reconstruction, which happened after the revolution, is a clearer example of how modernization has continued to be the main approach to social and spatial change.

Urban transformation: the case of Tehran

Tehran was reshaped during two phases in the 1860s and1870s by Nasser-al-Din Shah and in the 1930s by Reza Shah. In the first phase, the sixteenth-century city walls were demolished to allow the growth of a larger city, to be enclosed within new walls and gates. New boulevards and new neighbourhoods were developed and the capital city found a new, semi-European image (Curzon, 1892). Later, in the 1930s, the city walls and gates were demolished to permit the imposition of a network of streets, an open matrix in which goods and services could circulate. These two phases of transformation laid the foundations of the post-war growth of the city, when it acquired most of its population. It is not surprising that the two phases of restructuring of Tehran were supported, or carried out, by the modern intelligentsia as a part of the process of recreation of society in a new image. The outcome of this transformation of society was to have no relationship with its predecessors, as traditions and everything associated with them were thought to indicate backwardness. This sharp break with the past meant that the new forms, of urban fabric as well as of economic activities and social norms, could not develop out of the existing ones. The existing institutions and practices were totally disregarded and a process of heavy borrowing from the West started. The new institutions and structures which were imported, therefore, were imposed on or juxtaposed to the existing social practices and physical environments, creating an uneasy coexistence of sometimes antagonistic entities. Iran had experienced this juxtaposition of old and new in various invasions of different cultures and armies, as best exemplified in the dual city tradition after the Arab conquest in the seventh century, when the new and old were first put together and were integrated later. The speed of change in our time, however, could not allow the combination to develop gradually into a new cultural tradition.

During the first three hundred years of Tehran's urban life, from the building of the walls in 1553 to the restructuring of 1868, the main approach, as regards the context of built space, was somehow based on consensus and conformity. Due to various constraints which limited the agents of production, every act of development had to be carefully set against its built context, and the outcome was usually respectful and adaptable to it. This contextualism, however, could not survive the two major phases of transition in the 1870s and 1930s. During the 1870s, it was tried to create a balance between the old and the new. Therefore, the new neighbourhoods were juxtaposed to the old ones without attempting to transform them. Here, a degree of respect for and adaptation with the past was at work. However, the extent of conformity to the old fabric was largely diminished. The new patterns of streets and buildings in the new quarters were put forward as a rival as well as a complement to the old ones. The break with contextual conformity, which created a dualism in the typology of physical fabric, was consistent with the break in social structure that was on the way. This cautious attempt at modernization still paid respect to traditions and the old urban fabric. The fierce attack on these two, however, came with the major attempt of the 1930s, which with a total disregard of the past, tore the old fabric apart. The new network of streets imposed on it was to build new facades as soon as possible to hide whatever remained of the old . The long-term trend was to eliminate the old parts of the city, to be replaced with a modern fabric with minimal relationship to what it succeeded.

The framework set by this cry for modernity provided the basis for the future development of the city. The sheer size of the post-war development of the urban fabric, in which the principle of minimal relationship with the past was maintained, reduced and virtually nullified the proportion of the old fabric to, and its impact on, new developments. After all, the pre-1868 Tehran forms only 0.7 per cent of the present-day urban area. Tehran grew for more than two decades without any major control by the government, before a planning system was devised. The rising oil revenues and the legal and bureaucratic tools that the municipal government had acquired seemed now capable of ensuring the city to become a symbol of modernity in the country.

Unlike many other countries of the Third World, these new forms were not directly introduced by Westerners, since Iran was never colonized. Instead, the agents of transformation here were the group who came to existence as a result of contacts with those powers. However, like many other colonized countries, the imposition of new institutions led to a crisis of cultural identity, and was partly instrumental in economic failure and political breakdown. Nevertheless, the coexistence of the new and old institutions resulted in the apparently permanent establishment of the new and the relative disappearance of the old. This was made possible by the direct intervention of the state in the creation and support of new institutions for most of the twentieth century. It was also supported by the apparent success of similar forms of institutions elsewhere, especially in the West. Urban form, especially in Tehran, whose transformation pre-dates other Iranian cities and whose old parts are proportionately smaller, appears to be the product of, and a contributor to, these new institutions.

In Tehran, the coexistence and duality of the old and new, of two modes of production and two cultures, found spatial manifestation in numerous aspects. The most obvious was the rivalry of two city centres: the old and a new city centre to the north. Whereas the new centre, housed in the new urban space, was encouraged by the state as a sign of modernity, the old centre, with the bazaar as its focus, was undermined and threatened to destruction. The outcome was hoped to be a unity and homogeneity of urban space. Nevertheless, as in many other cases, this threat did not materialize, leading to the coexistence of old and new, as the old was strong and deeply rooted enough to wage a war against the new. The battle between the old and new continues even after the apparent victory of the traditional values and forms heralded with the Islamic revolution. With the establishment of a religious government and the role of the clergy in judicial, legislative and executive branches of the government, it would appear that traditionalism has now won the battle. The reality, however, is that at all times and under any regime in the country, the battle between tradition and modernity has been fought, as both tendencies can be clearly traced in both modern intelligentsia and in traditional middle classes. The integrative nationalism of the Pahlavis was associated with the ancient political form of executive monarchy, as is now a modern republic associated with the ancient institution and traditionalism of the clergy. These contradictions are signs of tension inside both camps and represent a continuing struggle between tradition and modernity.

The new approaches to economic development and spatial transformation signify a rising strength of modernity. In Tehran today, a return to modernization tendencies by a clerical government is observable. The development of new motorways, mushrooming tower blocks, the encouragement of mass production of housing, the threat to the old core of the city by redevelopment, and some grandiose schemes (such as the crossing of the Alburz mountains by a straight motorway to link Tehran with the Caspian Sea) are all modernizing the capital. The concepts of space are once again modern, rather than traditional, images, although some attempts are made to reconcile the two. At the same time, there are strong reactions to these developments, which in due course may reverse the trend once again.

The revolution, therefore, took up once again the task of modernizing the city, rather than protecting it from radical change. After all, the revolution was all about radical change. As such, it has continued the century-long trends of urban transformation. The social life of the city is left to cope with such transformations imposed from above. Everyday life, whose protection from the brutal forces of modernization was apparently a major aim of the revolution, could not find a voice in the new practices. Democratic governance in general, and participation of the people in urban transformation in particular, were demands still on the agenda. Similar trends can be found in the countryside, which for long has provided classic cases of forced modernization.

Reshaping the countryside: the case of post-war reconstruction in Khuzestan

The long war between Iran and Iraq in the 1980s cost thousands of lives and ruined hundreds of towns and villages on both sides of the border. Major efforts were made in Iran to rebuild the rural settlements. A brief look at these new settlements will show how post-revolutionary practices are a continuation of earlier, modernist approaches. It will evaluate these new developments against traditional settlements, in their location, layout, house design, construction technology, and their subsequent use by people. It also looks at how these attempts relate to the previous experiences of post-disaster reconstruction in Iran.

The southwestern province of Khuzestan in Iran is formed of a vast plain, confined to the north and east by the Zagros mountains, to the south by the Persian Gulf, and to the west by marshlands on the international border with Iraq. There is a dramatic contrast between the mountains, where the average height is 1,500 metres above sea level, and the plain, which lies as low as only three metres above sea level. On their way from the mountains to the sea and marshes, several important rivers irrigate the hot, partly humid plain, affecting the settlement pattern of a large number of the province's 24 cities and 4,200 villages.

The majority of Khuzestan's rural population, almost three out of four, live in larger villages, mostly located around the centre and south of the plain near the larger cities. Around 70 per cent of all the villages, however, have populations of less than 50 households, with a total of only a quarter of the rural population. Whereas the cities here are often melting pots of various ethnic groups, the rural settlements are more ethnically homogeneous. The history of settlement in this region goes back several millennia to early Mesopotamian civilizations. However, in the recent past, apart from the old settlements in the northern parts of the plain, Khuzestan was dominated by nomadic tribes. These tribes have mostly settled during this century due to the central government's forced settlement policy and the establishment of oil industry in the area. Following their previous tribal territories, Arabs now live in their villages in the plain and Lurs and Bakhtiaris, the two main tribes of the Zagros mountains, in the piedmonts and highlands (see Madanipour, 1987). They have often created clusters of villages near water resources, with distances of up to three kilometres from each other, to ensure easy communication between former tribal camps and to maintain their close family ties and security needs.

After a long interval, the central government has once again shifted towards persuading the remaining nomads to settle down by developing tribal new towns. Some, mostly Bakhtiari, tribes still follow their nomadic patterns of living in traditional black tents, while some others prefer a half-settled pattern of moving between a village and pastures. Even most of the fully settled villagers have not forgotten their nomadic past. This is why they have at times shown a readiness to abandon their villages collectively and search for better locations. A constant concern with access to water has been a major cause for relocation. Another cause has been the increased importance of roads that allow easier access to urban job markets and to utilities and services.

With the advent of war in 1980, hundreds of villages were ruined or damaged. The settlement pattern in the west of the province was disrupted in an eight-year long conflict. The border's rural population suffered casualties and was eventually displaced for a long time. The first task in the reconstruction programme, which started during the war, was to rebuild these villages so that they could be inhabited as soon as the area was made safe.

In the reconstruction programme, the major aim was to rebuild the war-damaged villages on their former site to keep their previously established relationships with their water resources, farms and pastures, and neighbouring villages. Wherever the reuse of a village site was impossible due to heavy damage, the task was to seek an alternative site as close as possible to the original site, to avoid using prime agricultural land. In this respect, the reconstruction programme did not intend to change radically the settlement pattern of the area. It is not, however, clear how far the settlement pattern will be affected by the large-scale changes being made to the natural environment by drying out the marshes on the other side of the international border. In the 1960s and 1970s, the Iranian government tried to change the settlement pattern in some parts of Khuzestan by introducing large agribusinesses and by grouping smaller villages into larger ones. The latter formed part of a national strategy to 'rationalize' the rural settlement pattern to improve access to infrastructure and services. Such plans for large-scale intervention in countrywide spatial change were mostly shelved with the advent of the revolution in 1979. As compared to this background, the post-war reconstruction programme concentrated on keeping the overall spatial pattern intact but intervening on a smaller scale so that rebuilding schemes might be undertaken without delay.

The tribal origins of most of the villagers and their short history of settlement have been largely influential in the formation and organization of space in these rural settlements. The routines of nomadic life had formed tribal camps of small groups of extended households on the move. The relationships between these households were based on tribal hierarchy and family ties and their need to help each other in looking after their cattle and defending themselves against potential enemies. These relationships were evident in the layout of their temporary camps and have continued to be instrumental in their settlement forms.

One of the most distinctive features of these relatively new settlements has been their very low density, lacking the normal coherence and compactness of the built environment in the more established villages. In the north of the plain, where the villages are much older, compact fabrics have evolved over long periods due to the need for safety and security in the face of constant threats from other nomadic tribes, restrictions from landowners, an agricultural economy that is reluctant to use agricultural land for any other purpose, and a drier, hotter climate. The pattern of narrow winding alleys leading to cul-de-sacs, a hallmark of Middle Eastern settlements, can be seen in these older northern villages. In the villages of the nomadic tribes developed during this century, however, new patterns have emerged. Wide, irregular streets, vaguely defined open spaces, and an unclear relationship to the surrounding countryside are among the characteristics of these newer villages. Stretched along rivers, foothills and roads, these villages had no major difficulty in using the common tribal land that had not been used for agriculture. Without ties to any specific part of their territories, the tribesmen could decide to build their villages in the same temporary but spacious manner as their tents and camps. The street pattern is based on a free movement of pedestrians and their cattle heading towards or along their pastures, dry farming lands, water resources and roads. Streets and open spaces seem to have a minimal relationship to social organization of space. Public open space has not often found any formal recognition in the village space. This does not, however, imply an absence of public meetings, as this can happen inside the elders' guest rooms or mosques. Informal meetings can take place at street corners, but the elders of the tribes continue to dominate the social structure of the village, providing the necessary space for social and religious events and rituals.

Unlike its attitude towards the settlement pattern in the province, the post-war reconstruction programme intended to follow a modernist path in the design and development of the new settlements. The urgent need for reconstruction meant that, despite attempts to survey the traditional patterns of settlements in the war-damaged areas, the development of the new villages did not follow these patterns. One reason was the haste with which the process took place. Another was the general perception of poor quality of rural physical heritage in this part of the country, which apparently justified its disregard by designers. It was felt that the time had come for a radical departure from the past. The designs of the new villages, with their dry, rationalist tones, are a witness to this trend.

The main feature of these designs is their strict segregation of people from livestock in house design as well as in settlement layout to improve the hygiene conditions in villages, where animals were previously kept inside houses and the street system of the settlement was dominated by them. Previous post-disaster experiences in new village design by the authorities had shown the strong resistance of people to complete separation of livestock from the village. People preferred to live in their half-ruined villages to be able to keep an eye on their cattle. The main reasons for this attitude were the centrality of animal husbandry in the rural economy, as reflected in the importance of livestock as people's main belongings, and their methods of raising them which required constant attention and contact.

The idea of segregating animals and people seemed to be rational to the city-based planners and therefore expected to work. In practice, however, there have been major difficulties. The experience of the way people use the new villages shows that pedestrian routes are often left largely empty despite the protection they provide from the sun and wind. They seem to be so narrow and uninviting as to make informal meetings difficult. The streets are cut off from the village space by the walls of houses, reducing visibility in a village whose inhabitants were used to a spacious layout and open perspectives. In their old villages, the guest rooms of houses were so placed that they gave views of the entrance to the village or its main streets. Now, it is impossible to have a view of activities on the pedestrian side due to the limited width of the streets and therefore the limited perspective they offer. The design, therefore, has not taken into account how space was treated in the ruined villages, where mosques, guest houses and open spaces together created the public space of the village. In new villages, the designed public space does not correspond to the actual public spaces of the village.

The cattle routes, on the contrary, are the centres of activity. The daily routines of cattle-raising, the more spacious environment and the possibility of car access have all led to a wider use of cattle routes. Here people meet and, in the absence of high walls, have a view to the open countryside and to the entire unit of which their house is a part. They even use the cattle routes to build small structures such as mud ovens and to dry their cow dung, to be used as fuel.

The other major problem with the design of these settlements is their high density. The spacious, low-density village was perhaps not aesthetically comparable to the high-density villages of hot arid zones elsewhere in Iran, but it was what people here had built themselves and were used to living in. The higher densities introduced by the reconstruction programme, however, were based more on economic than aesthetic considerations. The allocation of space was determined as a government policy based on the available resources. The establishment of these new settlements was also determined by government policy, since the authorities felt responsible to undertake the reconstruction programme themselves. Rather than enabling the people to build for themselves by providing building materials and know-how, the government agencies took up the task. This was a political solution as the war and its consequences were seen as the responsibility of central government. It was also seen as an opportunity for improving the low standard of rural housing. What the programme failed to do was to look more carefully at the patterns of rural life, or to find out about the people's specific needs. The government's perception of rural life seemed to be affected by the general pattern in the country, where a long history of agricultural economy and a settled lifestyle have given the people a stronger attachment to a particular site and the villages a well-developed, compact fabric. It is true that, compared to previous experiences, which ended sometimes in disastrous responses from the rural recipients, this programme showed more sensitivity. In contrast to the previous experiences, for example, the necessity of incorporating livestock into the design was taken into account. But it still did not go far enough, and was limited due to scarcity of resources.

The designs of the new villages were based on the assumptions that the urban dwellers had made of rural populations. The functional segregation of pedestrians and animals on the one hand and the urban, or rather suburban, character of the development on the other, reflected an environment perceived by the designers as desirable by the local people. Not dissimilar to the post-war reconstruction of Europe, when modernist development replaced the ruins of war, the destruction of these settlements by the war was seen as an opportunity for improvement. It was thought that changes in traditional building materials and lifestyles were inevitable. In true modernistic spirit, the designers, therefore, once again took up the role of rationalizing everyday life from above.

The traditionalist revolution as a modernization process

The overall direction of the revolution in Iran was to revive traditions and guard against the modernism associated with the modernization processes of the recent past. By reinstituting many traditional practices in all aspects of life and by seeking a continuity with pre-modernization times, the revolution seemed to be worthy of its epithet of a guardian of traditions.

At the same time, however, there was an element of modernism in the act of revolution itself, turning the tide of events as it did and discarding the immediate past. The modernism that the revolution invoked is traceable in a whole range of ideas and practices. A prime example was the introduction of a new form of government, the republic, which was without precedent in Iran. Modernism in general has had a faith in the possibility of human emancipation through the use of technology and imposition of order on the disordered spontaneity of everyday life (Madanipour, 1995; 1996). The revolution in Iran, by its very nature, was a manifestation of these ideas in parallel with its preference for traditions as an external form.

Our cases in this chapter suggest that the revolution was a new phase of modernization in Iran, even if this appears strange to many who are accustomed to viewing the Islamic revolution as a traditionalist movement. It struggled against the executive monarchy and established a republic with a more active parliament. It was at the same time a postmodern movement, in that it challenged the humanist notions of reason and the modernist notions of progress, seeking a return to historically tested values. An explanation for this apparent contradiction is that the revolution was not a single event conducted by a homogeneous group of people. It was a major social movement that brought people with different expectations and approaches to social change. The social environment was so explosive that it created a fluidity of beliefs, identities and behaviour. Exposure to, and association with, the power of the revolution changed, at least temporarily, many characters, from liberal to radical, from modernist to traditionalist, and after a while, vice versa. Even individuals who were instrumental in the course of revolution played different, at times contrasting, roles in different moments, as exemplified by the first and last presidents of the republic. These show a multiplicity of agencies and a circumstantial fluidity that united only long enough to dismantle the political establishment, which was acting as an obstacle to the political modernization of the country.

It is not surprising, therefore, that the majority of modernist ideas continued to be practised after the revolution in Iran. It is true that most professionals had been trained in the modernist environment of the 1960s and 1970s and the revolution had not found time to train its own brand of traditionalist professionals. It is also true that the spirit of revolution encouraged modernist practices, especially in the areas that were seen as the realm of technology and/or the professions. In this way the revolutionary rhetoric and its apparent respect for tradition is placed in contradiction to the modernist practices which discouraged traditions and advocated dramatic changes, as evident in our study of the recent transformation of the capital city and the redesign of the war-damaged settlements. It is worth mentioning that the efforts of the reconstruction were not organized by liberal, Westernized professionals but by the mainstream revolutionaries. The design of the rural settlements attempted to impose a new order on the everyday routines of the people, a typical modernist intervention. This was expected to create a new pattern of life, a new identity for the village. As with many such attempts to impose order on the rich complexity of human life, it remained unsuccessful.

The juxtaposition of inherited and borrowed concepts of space, therefore, represent as much as stimulate the uneven coexistence of traditional, pre-capitalist life forms with modern, capitalist ones. A tense coexistence of old and new, in which they constantly struggle for domination, is a hallmark of the modern history of Iran and its capital Tehran. Urban and rural areas, both before and after the revolution, have undergone considerable change. The reconstruction programme that followed the long war between Iran and Iraq in the 1980s set out to improve the standards of housing in the war-damaged villages. This was, however, based on assumptions distant from the local population's practices, in their skills and productive capacities, their climate, and their preferred organization of space based on their patterns of daily life. Designers from the large cities once again assumed new identities for the local population or triggered social engineering by introducing new spatial relationships. The most important of these relationships was a segregation of living places and pathways of animals from people, an attempt that was unsuccessful for being too prescriptive. Thus the attempt to impose an order on the perceived disorder of rural life failed. Yet the impact of this, and of other interventions in towns and villages is long-standing, leading to major reorganization of these fabrics and life routines with unforeseen consequences. It is an example of the unresolved conflict that can be found at the intersection between modernization processes and everyday life practices.

Conclusion

Encounters with the West since the nineteenth century have pushed Iran into the global economy as a peripheral partner. External pressures and the internal multiplicity of reactions to such radical change have caused major political tensions, and led to social transformation and environmental change. The agents of these changes have often been the urban elite, forcing the modernization of the city and the countryside. These pressures for modernization have effectively aimed to change the everyday life of urban and rural populations. Even popular eruptions against such transformations, as exemplified by the Iranian revolution, have been channelled towards further modernization of the human world, despite some appearances of traditionalism. The example of Tehran shows how the capital of the country was the first place to undergo radical change. An example of post-revolutionary modernization is the reconstruction of the war-damaged areas in Khuzestan. Both cases show the tensions that can result from modernization from above, from expecting the social world to adjust to, rather than participate in, change.

8 Iran's economic development and structural change in human resources

Mohammad B. Beheshti

This chapter will focus on the issue of economic development in relation to human resources before and after the revolution. As we enter the new millennium, the problem of human resource development becomes more acute as a result of the lack of any policy initiative undertaken after the revolution. Beheshti carefully examines the ability of human resources in relation to the requirements of economic development. This study also evaluates the main characteristics of human resources during the period 1976–91. It sets out to consider the trend of human resources as a whole, including both the economically active and economically inactive sections of the population. Special attention is given to the issue of employment and its structure. In order to evaluate the potential capabilities of the work force, the literacy level of the employed population, defined by economic sectors, is considered. In order to present an accurate assessment of the abilities of both the private and public sectors in running the economy, and as an addition to the investigations on the changing patterns of employment occurring in the post-revolutionary period, the major characteristic elements of employment in the private and public sectors are analysed. After presenting the various characteristics of the unemployment phenomenon, the chapter goes on to examine the impact of the rapid population growth on the human resource structure and concludes that, during 1976–91, the tendency of employment was oriented mostly towards unproductive activities; the ability of the workers (particularly private-sector workers) to employ academic approaches in the production process was not high enough to be able to manage and run the country's economy.

Finally this study, through all its findings, highlights the fact that raising the capability of the work force, through a systematic approach that is related to all relevant systems, is an essential factor for the economic development of Iran.

Background

There are various internal and external reasons behind the underdevelopment of the Iranian economy. The tremendous power and influence wielded by foreign sources in the politico-economic fields since the beginning of the nineteenth century, and the enhancement of their interest in Iranian economic matters in the twentieth century with the advent of oil, together with the incapability of the shahs to rule the country, resulted in the change from a relatively strong traditional economy to an oil-dependent economy. Increasing dependency on oil revenues, while facilitating the starting of industrialisation through capital-intensive techniques did not, however, bring long-term economic growth to Iran. Instead, the oil-based economy created an anti-development attitude which sought maximum returns from easy-earning activities, and resulted in a lowering of attitudes towards innovation.

The nation's several uprisings against continuous external interference and internal dictatorship, finally resulted in the victory of the Islamic revolution in 1979. In the post-revolutionary period, the country was beset with many difficulties and obstacles, including an eight-year war imposed by Iraq that devastated the country and increased socio-economic problems. Although the country resumed development planning soon after the end of the war in 1988, the developing economy needs to find ad hoc solutions for the problems.

Apart from the impact of external factors on the underdevelopment of the Iranian economy, the key reason as to why the country's economy has not developed has been the omission, in almost all development plans or policies, to meaningfully develop the ability of the people. It has been forgotten that people are the centre of development, and that without orienting all minds, behaviours and attitudes towards an evolutionary, long-term process of development, successful development becomes impossible. The main reason is the low capability of the work force. It is because of this that a country such as Iran, despite having 50 years of development planning experience, has yet to witness any meaningful long-term economic development.

The experiences of developed countries confirms that their achievement in the development process originated from their people's capability in utilising their material resources towards development requirements. Unfortunately, Iran, ignoring this fact, always imitated other countries' development models and therefore could not attain any substantial achievements of its own.

Development economists have given various definitions of the term development. For example, Lewis (1954), in a dual model of development, states that development is equivalent to the gradual swelling of the modern sector and the gradual decline of the traditional one (Bigsten, 1983, p. 30). Chenery (1979, p. xvi), with a similar view to Lewis, considers that 'economic development can be viewed as a set of interrelated changes in the structure of an economy that are required for its continued growth'. Azimi's view is similar to their viewpoints, as he states that economic development is a set of five interrelated factors of: a) favourite culture, b) favourite education for development, c) capital accumulation, d) favourite management and economic system, and e) keeping stability in the system (1992, pp. 173–88). Economists such as Seers (1969, pp. 2–3), Meier (1984, p. 6), and Bhattacharya (1989, p.1) view development as much more than economic development. Some development economists, such as Schumacher (1973, p. 157), Sundrum (1983, p. 78), and Griffin and Knight (1992, pp. 576–8), give special priority to the issue of human development. Schumacher says that: 'development does not start with goods; it starts with people and their education, organisation, and discipline'. Sundrum's viewpoint is that: 'the pervasiveness of modern economic behaviour and the ability of people to absorb modern technology, depends on education, infrastructure and institutions'. Referring to the human development concept, Griffin and Knight state that: 'economic growth can be seen as a means to the end of enhancing people's capabilities'.

Regarding the various definitions given for development, and the experiences of the developed countries, we would say that, in fact, economic development is a long-run, evolutionary-indigenous process and human beings are the engine driving its development. Therefore, the capability of human resource is the essence of development. The capability of human resource, per se, is dependent on culture (beliefs, attitudes and behaviours), educational system and contents, health, and economic conditions.

The purpose of this chapter is to investigate the capability of the human resources in Iran in relation to development requirements, through a consideration of the properties of the labour force. In this study, the period 1976–91 is selected in order to use the most reliable and up to date data, the population censuses of 1976 and 1986, and the last population census of 1991. The major economic indicators to be examined are the consumption increase which occurred irrespective of production between 1976 and 1999, and the stagnant GDP in comparison to the 66.6 per cent increase in private consumption. The comparison of per capita GDP with per capita private consumption shows that the per capita GDP in 1991 was 61 per cent that of 1976, whereas the per capita private consumption in 1991 and 1976 remained almost the same (see Table 8.1). In other words, by decreasing the level of production the level of economic welfare did not decline, indicating that maintaining the stability of current economic welfare has been carried out at the expense of investment and future production.

The issue of decreasing productivity during 1976–91 must be seen as a direct result of the failure to increase GDP and the declining productivity of labour which had fallen by 30.9 per cent. The only sector enjoying steadily increasing labour productivity was agriculture, which grew by 59.2 per cent. The service industry lost almost half of its productivity, with industry losing some one third itself. Therefore the low and ever-decreasing productivity of labour was one of the main characteristics of the economy of the time.

As a result of the shift in the structure of the economy, due to the high dependency of the economy on oil revenues, the share of the secondary sector declined from 52.9 per cent to 39.7 per cent, whilst shares of the primary and tertiary sectors increased from 12.7 per cent to 23.3 per cent, and from 34.4 per cent to 37.0 per cent respectively. This shift also saw an expansion of the numbers employed. Employment figures for the tertiary sector increased from 30.9 per cent to 43.6 per cent.

The government budget in 1991 (at constant prices) was 41.5 per cent less than in 1976, reflecting a downward trend in the government's purchasing power. This was compounded by an inefficient administrative system which demonstrated the full extent of the governments ineffectiveness in implementing a sustainable programme of development. From an examination of the data, it can be seen that there was an improvement in the income (=expenditure) distribution factor, indicated by

Table 8.1 Some economic indicators of Iran in 1976, 1986 and 1991* (units unavailable)

	Year			*As a proportion (%)*			*Annual average growth rate (%)*		
	1976	*1986*	*1991*	*1976*	*1986*	*1991*	*1976–86*	*1986–91*	*1976–91*
GDP	13,131.4	10,692.5	13,264.1				–2.03	4.40	0.07
Agricultural production	1,706.2	2,650.5	3,120.2	12.7	24.7	23.3	4.50	3.32	4.11
Industrial production	7,128.4	3,435.7	8,318.7	52.9	32.0	39.7	–7.04	19.35	1.03
Service production	4,640.7	4,654.7	4,945.9	34.4	43.3	37.0	0.03	1.22	0.43
Private consumption	4,969.6	6,543.7	8,281.5	36.5	63.0	61.9	2.79	4.82	3.46
Government consumption	2,379.4	1,507.6	1,450.0	17.5	14.5	10.8	–4.46	–0.78	–3.25
Gross domestic investment	3,328.8	1,645.9	1,942.9	24.4	15.9	14.5	–6.80	3.37	–3.53
Population (000)	33,709	49,445	55,837	100.0	146.7	165.6	3.91	2.46	3.42
Per capita GDP	389.6	216.3	237.6	100.0	55.5	61.0	–5.72	1.90	–3.24
Per capita consumption	147.4	132.3	148.3	100.0	89.8	100.6	–1.07	2.31	0.04
Labour force (000)	8,799	11,002	13,097	100.0	125.0	148.8	2.26	3.55	2.69
Agriculture	2,992	3,191	3,206	34.0	29.0	24.5	0.65	0.09	0.46
Industry	3,012	2,781	3,616	34.2	25.3	27.6	–0.79	5.39	1.23
Service	2,721	4,670	5,713	30.9	42.4	43.6	5.55	4.11	5.07
Labour productivity	1,531.5	973.3	1,058.8	100.0	63.6	69.1	–4.43	1.70	–2.43
Agricultural sector	570.3	830.6	907.8	100.0	145.6	159.2	3.83	1.79	3.15
Industrial sector	2,365.9	1,235.9	1,581.1	100.0	52.2	66.8	–6.29	5.05	–2.65
Service sector	1,661.0	919.0	846.9	100.0	55.3	51.0	–5.75	–1.62	–4.39

Table 8.1 continued

	Year			*As a proportion (%)*			*Annual average growth rate (%)*		
	1976	*1986*	*1991*	*1976*	*1986*	*1991*	*1976–86*	*1986–91*	*1976–91*
Government budget	2,580.1	1,532.8	1,508.5	100.0	59.4	58.5	–5.07	–0.32	–3.51
Government budget deficit	404.5	874.4	302.2	100.0	216.2	74.7	8.01	–19.14	–1.92
as % of government budget	10.1	43.6	13.8				15.69	–20.57	2.06
as % of GDP	3.08	8.18	2.28				10.26	–22.55	–1.99
Income distribution:	1977	1986	1991						
Gini coefficient	0.515	0.466	0.456	100.0	90.5	88.5			
Share of lower 40%	11.36	12.71	13.43	100.0	111.9	118.2			
Share of middle 40%	31.32	36.51	36.64	100.0	116.6	117.0			
Share of upper 20%	57.32	50.78	49.92	100.0	88.6	87.1			

Source: Central Bank; Plan and Budget Organization of Iran.

* at 1982 constant prices

a decline in the Gini coefficient from 0.515 in 1977 to 0.456 in 1991. During this period, the share of the lower 40 per cent of the population increased from 11.36 per cent to 13.43 per cent, and that of the middle 40 per cent from 31.32 per cent to 36.64 per cent. However, in 1991 about half of incomes belonged to the upper 20 per cent of the population.

Accordingly, the dominant policy throughout the 1976–91 period was the maintenance of per capita consumption together with improving income distribution, in spite of the fact that GDP did not increase. However, the economically active population of Iran increased from 9.8 million to 14.7 million during this period, a growth rate of 2.76 per annum. (The census of 1976 and the last population census of 1991 recorded the economic activities of those aged 10 years and over; the census of 1986 set the limit at 6 and over). The economically inactive population, with a 4.04 per cent annual growth rate, increased to 23.9 million from 13.2 million, implying a reduction of the economically active proportion from 42.6 per cent to 38.1 per cent.

Over the same period, of a 22.1 million increase in the country's population, some 15.7 million were 10 years of age and under, with the total increase in the work force being confined to 4.9 million. This indicates that over time, the increase in the (potential) productive population was less than that of consumers (Table 8.2).

Gender comparison elaborates that there was a huge disparity between males and females, from the standpoint of economic activity, such that in 1991 the male work force was about 8 times that of the female, while the potential work force of males was only 7 per cent more.

Homemakers and students constituted a majority of the economically inactive population. The proportion of homemakers (out of the total economically inactive population), instead of showing a decreasing trend, rose to just over 50 per cent in 1991. The student figure was about 40 per cent. The increase in students had an effective role in the increase of the economically inactive population, especially among rural females.

The activity rate (the ratio of economically active to total population) dropped from 29.1 per cent in 1976 to 26.4 per cent in 1991. The male rate decreased from 48.1 per cent to 45.6 per cent, and the female from 8.9 per cent to 6.0 per cent. Meanwhile, the activity rate from 1986–91 improved slightly in comparison with the 1976–86 period (Table 8.3).

In 1976, each employed person had to provide food and other basic needs for 3.83 persons. By 1986, this number had increased to 4.49 but fell slightly to 4.26 in 1991. In the latter year, the dependency burden in urban areas was 4.18 and in rural areas 4.37, demonstrating that in this regard the employed population suffered more in rural than in urban areas (Figure 8.1).

Accordingly, during the period 1976–91:

1 The proportion of the economically active population decreased.
2 The increase in the (potential) productive population was behind that of consumers.

Table 8.2 Economically active and inactive population (aged 10 and over) by area and sex, 1976, 1986 and 1991

	Both sexes				*Male*				*Female*			
	Total population	*Aged 10 and over*	*Econ. active*	*Econ. inactive**	*Total population*	*Aged 10 and over*	*Econ. active*	*Econ. inactive**	*Total population*	*Aged 10 and over*	*Econ. active*	*Econ. inactive**
All areas												
1976	33,708,744	23,002,499	9,796,056	13,206,443	17,356,347	11,796,414	8,347,050	3,449,364	16,352,397	11,206,085	1,449,006	9,757,079
1986	49,445,010	32,874,293	12,820,291	20,054,002	25,280,961	16,841,418	11,512,379	5,329,039	24,164,049	16,032,875	1,307,912	14,724,963
1991	55,837,163	38,655,049	14,736,704	23,918,345	28,768,450	19,997,274	13,107,062	6,890,212	27,068,713	18,657,775	1,629,642	17,028,133
Change during												
1976–86	15,736,266	9,871,794	3,024,235	6,847,559	7,924,614	5,045,004	3,165,329	1,879,675	7,811,652	4,826,790	(141,094)	4,967,884
1986–91	6,392,153	5,780,756	1,916,413	3,864,343	3,487,489	3,155,856	1,594,683	1,561,173	2,904,664	2,624,900	321,730	2,303,170
1976–91	22,128,419	15,652,550	4,940,648	10,711,902	11,412,103	8,200,860	4,760,012	3,440,848	10,716,316	7,451,690	180,636	7,271,054
Annual average growth rate (%)												
1976–86	3.91	3.64	2.73	4.27	3.83	3.62	3.27	4.45	3.98	3.65	–1.02	4.20
1986–91	2.46	3.29	2.83	3.59	2.62	3.49	2.63	5.27	2.30	3.08	4.50	2.95
1976–91	3.42	3.52	2.76	4.04	3.43	3.58	3.05	4.72	3.42	3.46	0.79	3.78
Urban areas												
1976	15,854,680	11,427,977	4,335,564	7,092,413	8,291,451	6,017,794	3,846,266	2,171,528	7,563,229	5,410,183	489,298	4,920,885
1986	26,844,561	18,280,802	7,026,005	11,254,797	13,769,617	9,411,621	6,284,688	3,126,933	13,074,944	8,869,181	741,317	8,127,864
1991	31,836,598	22,483,337	8,488,622	13,994,715	16,435,244	11,664,532	7,530,080	4,134,452	15,401,354	10,818,805	958,542	9,860,263
Change during												
1976–86	10,989,881	6,852,825	2,690,441	4,162,384	5,478,166	3,393,827	2,438,422	955,405	5,511,715	3,458,998	252,019	3,206,979
1986–91	4,992,037	4,202,535	1,462,617	2,739,918	2,665,627	2,252,911	1,245,392	1,007,519	2,326,410	1,949,624	217,225	1,732,399
1976–91	15,981,918	11,055,360	4,153,058	6,902,302	8,143,793	5,646,738	3,683,814	1,962,924	7,838,125	5,408,622	469,244	4,939,378

Table 8.2 continued

	Both sexes				*Male*				*Female*			
	Total population	*Aged 10 and over*	*Econ. active*	*Econ. inactive**	*Total population*	*Aged 10 and over*	*Econ. active*	*Econ. inactive**	*Total population*	*Aged 10 and over*	*Econ. active*	*Econ. inactive**
Annual average growth rate(%)												
1976–86	5.41	4.81	4.95	4.73	5.20	4.57	5.03	3.71	5.63	5.07	4.24	5.15
1986–91	3.47	4.23	3.85	4.45	3.60	4.39	3.68	5.75	3.33	4.05	5.27	3.94
1976–91	4.76	4.61	4.58	4.64	4.67	4.51	4.58	4.39	4.86	4.73	4.58	4.74
Rural areas												
1976	17,854,064	11,574,522	5,460,492	6,114,030	9,064,896	5,778,620	4,500,784	1,277,836	8,789,168	5,795,902	959,708	4,836,194
1986	22,600,449	14,593,491	5,794,286	8,799,205	11,511,344	7,429,797	5,227,691	2,202,106	11,089,105	7,163,694	566,595	6,597,099
1991	24,000,565	16,171,712	6,248,082	9,923,630	12,333,206	8,332,742	5,576,982	2,755,760	11,667,359	7,838,970	671,100	7,167,870
Change during												
1976–86	4,746,385	3,018,969	333,794	2,685,175	2,446,448	1,651,177	726,907	924,270	2,299,937	1,367,792	(393,113)	1,760,905
1986–91	1,400,116	1,578,221	453,796	1,124,425	821,862	902,945	349,291	553,654	578,254	675,276	104,505	570,771
1976–91	6,146,501	4,597,190	787,590	3,809,600	3,268,310	2,554,122	1,076,198	1,477,924	2,878,191	2,043,068	(288,608)	2,331,676
Annual average growth rate (%)												
1976–86	2.39	2.34	0.60	3.71	2.42	2.55	1.51	5.59	2.35	2.14	-5.13	3.15
1986–91	1.21	2.07	1.52	2.43	1.39	2.32	1.30	4.59	1.02	1.82	3.44	1.67
1976–91	1.99	2.25	0.90	3.28	2.07	2.47	1.44	5.26	1.91	2.03	-2.36	2.66

Source: Iran's Census Centre (1980, pp. 52–4; 1988, pp. 114–16; 1993, p. 59).

* Includes 'not reported'.

Table 8.3 Activity rate of population by area and sex (%)

	Both sexes	*Male*	*Female*
All areas			
1976	29.1	48.1	8.9
1986	25.9	45.5	5.4
1991	26.4	45.6	6.0
Urban areas			
1976	27.3	46.4	6.5
1986	26.2	45.6	5.7
1991	26.7	45.8	6.2
Rural areas			
1976	30.6	49.7	10.9
1986	25.6	45.4	5.1
1991	26.0	45.2	5.8

Source: Calculated from Table 8.2.

3 There was a huge disparity between males and females from an economic activity viewpoint, at least as far as official measures were concerned.
4 Despite an improvement in the activity rate from 1986 to 1991, the rate in 1991 was lower than that of 1976.
5 Having increased in 1991, as compared with 1976, the dependency burden was higher in rural areas than in urban areas.

The upshot of all is that because of the youth population structure, higher population growth rates and the significant increase in the student population, the activity rate and participation rate were very low, especially amongst females. As a result, the dependency burdens (both real and nominal) were very high, particularly in rural areas.

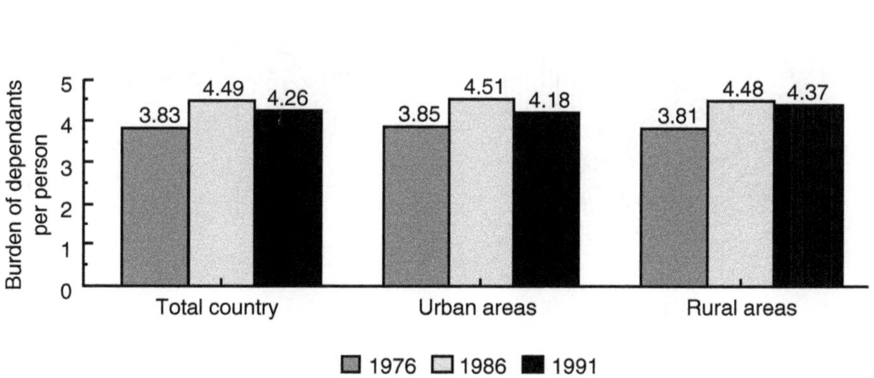

Figure 8.1 Dependency burden by area, 1976, 1986 and 1991.

General characteristics of employment

In 1976, 34 per cent of all employed persons were engaged in agriculture, 34.2 per cent in industry and 30.9 per cent in the service sector. In 1991, the contribution of agriculture dropped to 24.5 per cent, industry's share (including all subsectors except water, electricity and gas) fell by 6.6 per cent to 27.6 per cent, whereas service's share by increased 12.7 per cent (including all subsectors) to 43.6 per cent (Figure 8.2 and Table 8.4). According to Syrquin (1991, p. 241), in an oil-exporting country such as Iran, the decline in industry is the result of the oil boom–Dutch disease. With this in mind and conscious of the fact that, during the 1976–91 period, the proportion of the urban population increased from 47 to 57 per cent, it may be concluded that in Iran, urbanisation was directly correlated to the expansion of the tertiary sector rather than industrialisation.

In addition, the proportion of females in the labour force declined from 13.8 per cent to 9.4 per cent (urban from 11.2 per cent to 9.9 per cent and rural from 16.0 per cent to 8.7 per cent). In urban areas, about 65.9 per cent of new jobs for males were created in services sectors, and females by losing 50,337 jobs in the commodity-producing industries, gained 307,445 new jobs in the service industries. Likewise, in rural areas, 77.3 per cent of new jobs for males were created in the tertiary sector, and whilst females lost some 353,078 jobs in the primary and secondary sectors they gained a subsequent 28,194 jobs in the tertiary sector. The age median of the employed population increased from 32.4 years to 32.7 years (male from 34.0 to 32.2 years, while the female median increased slightly from 25.5 to 28.3 years).

As a whole, from 1976–91, some 1,009,712 employees were absorbed by the professional groups, with a total of 88.9 per cent of them engaged in community, social and personal services, 3.2 per cent in financial, 1.2 per cent in transport and communications and 0.6 per cent in the wholesale and retail trade. In other words, in the service sectors the number of professional employees increased by 947,726

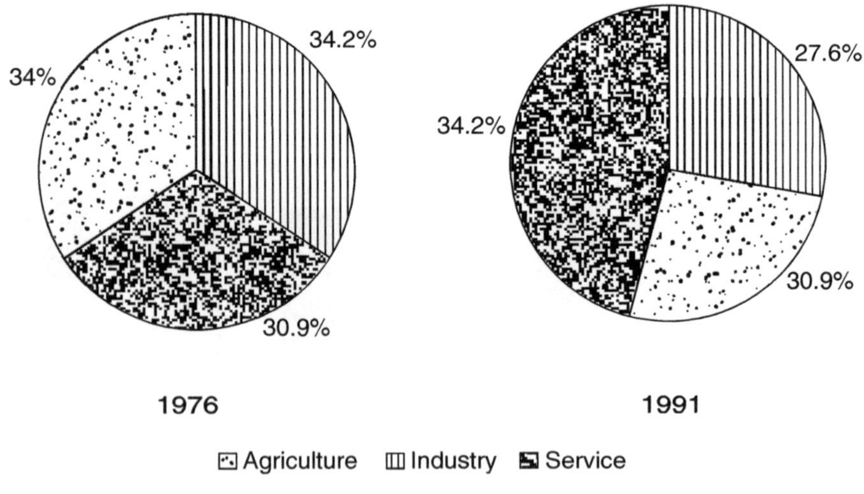

Figure 8.2 Contribution of major sectors to total employment, 1976 and 1991.

Table 8.4 Employed population by major industrial group, 1976, 1986 and 1991

		Total	Primary sector	Secondary sector					Tertiary sector					Other
			Agr.	*Total*	*Min.*	*Man.*	*Water*	*Cons.*	*Total*	*Trade*	*Trans.*	*Fin.*	*Com.*	
1976	No.	8,799,420	2,991,869	3,012,300	89,888	1,672,059	61,633	1,188,720	2,720,562	668,494	431,471	100,473	1,520,124	74,689
	%	100.0	34.0	34.2	1.0	19.0	0.7	13.5	30.9	7.6	4.9	1.1	17.3	0.8
1986	No.	11,001,551	3,190,764	2,781,012	32,370	1,451,333	91,044	1,206,265	4,670,048	875,458	630,547	114,288	3,049,755	359,727
	%	100.0	29.0	25.3	0.3	13.2	0.8	11.0	42.4	8.0	5.7	1.0	27.7	3.3
1991	No.	13,096,770	3,205,560	3,615,930	100,554	2,013,884	128,997	1,372,495	5,713,348	1,238,400	762,213	194,736	3,517,999	561,932
	%	100.0	24.5	27.6	0.8	15.4	1.0	10.5	43.6	9.5	5.8	1.5	26.9	4.3
Change during:														
1976–86	No.	2,202,131	198,895	–231,288	–57,518	–220,726	29,411	17,545	1,949,486	206,964	199,076	13,815	1,529,631	285,038
	%	0.0	–5.0	–9.0	–0.7	–5.8	0.1	–2.5	11.5	0.4	0.8	–0.1	10.4	2.4
1986–91	No.	2,095,219	14,796	834,918	68,184	562,551	37,953	166,230	1,043,300	362,942	131,666	80,448	468,244	202,205
	%	–100.0	–4.5	2.3	0.5	2.2	0.2	–0.5	1.2	1.5	0.1	0.4	–0.9	1.0
1976–91	No.	4,297,350	213,691	603,630	10,666	341,825	67,364	183,775	2,992,786	569,906	330,742	94,263	1,997,875	487,243
	%	0.0	–9.5	–6.6	–0.3	–3.6	0.3	–3.0	12.7	1.9	0.9	0.3	9.6	3.4
Ratio 1991:1976		1.49	1.07	1.20	1.12	1.20	2.09	1.15	2.10	1.85	1.77	1.94	2.31	7.52

Source: *Markaze Amar-e Iran* (1980, p. 73; 1988, p. 117; 1993, p. 155).

Agr. = Agriculture, hunting, forestry, and fishing; *Min.* = Mining; *Man.* = Manufacturing; *Cons.* = Construction; *Water* = Water, electricity and gas; *Trade* = Wholesale, and retail trade, etc.; *Trans.* = Transport, storage and communications; *Fin.* = Financing, insurance, etc.; *Com.* = Community, social and personal services; *Other* = Activity not adequately defined.

persons, which was 61,986 persons lower than all new employment opportunities (1,009,712) in professional occupations during the period. Except for the construction sector, which lost 43 per cent of its professional occupants, the professionalisation of occupations increased by 7.15 per cent per annum. Nonetheless, the growth rates for the professionalisation of the primary (0.86 per cent) and secondary sectors (2.59 per cent) were much lower than that of the tertiary sector (7.66 per cent). It clearly shows the tendency for professional workers to become employed in the service sectors, especially in community, social and personal services.

Therefore, it could be concluded that:

1 The structure of employment was not founded on academic approaches, traditional activities constituting a majority of the country's overall employment.
2 Despite the fact that the economy of Iran is highly dependent on oil, the contribution of the oil industry to Iran's total employment was a mere 1.4 per cent, indicating that producing and exporting crude petroleum for about 90 years could not transform the natural resource into physical or human capital in the service of developing the economy.
3 Although there was an improvement in the growth of some modern industries, particularly fabric metal production and equipment, during the 1976–91 period, the general tendency was for a reduction of commodity producing industries, on the one hand, and the increase of some service industries, on the other. Among the latter activities, the growth of wholesale trade and the expansion of the public sector's sphere in the post-revolutionary period were the most important factors. This trend is consistent with Halliday's argument that rent-based economies encourage the service sector at the expense of the production sector (1979, pp. 157–8).
4 In Iran urbanisation occurred without industrialisation; instead it established a direct relationship with the expanding tertiary sector.
5 The contribution of females to the employment sector decreased in commodity-producing activities but increased in services.
6 The age structure of the total employed population did not change considerably. In addition, in spite of the increasing age median of females, their median in 1991 was about four years younger than males.

Literacy of the employed population

Between 1976 and 1986, the literacy rate of the employed population increased from 40.7 per cent to 59.7 per cent. Agriculture, with an 82.3 per cent illiteracy rate in 1976 and 70.5 per cent in 1986, was ranked first. Meanwhile, 61.8 per cent of its literate workers in 1976, and 56.1 per cent in 1986, had attained only a primary education, whilst those employees with a higher educational attainment were minuscule, 0.5 per cent in 1976 and 0.6 per cent in 1986 (see Table 8.5). The literacy of the manufacturing sector increased from 38.6 per cent to 65.7 per cent, construction from 29.5 per cent to 41.0 per cent, community,

Table 8.5 Employed population by industrial group and educational attainment, 1976 and 1986

	Total employed population	*Literate*						*Illiterate*	*Not reported*
		Total	*Primary*	*Guidance*	*Secondary*	*Higher education*	*Other*		
1976	8,799,420	3,580,700	1,767,603	406,417	577,783	268,315	560,582	5,218,720	0
Agriculture etc.	2,991,869	529,043	327,173	19,640	8,607	2,890	170,733	2,462,826	0
Mining	89,888	58,088	27,764	7,179	11,534	6,114	5,497	31,800	0
Manufacturing	1,672,059	644,727	428,743	71,431	45,122	20,080	79,351	1,027,332	0
Construction	1,188,720	350,811	224,790	30,233	17,348	13,051	65,389	837,909	0
Water, electricity and gas	61,633	47,474	21,170	6,731	9,861	4,833	4,879	14,159	0
Wholesale and retail trade	668,494	354,066	192,147	46,575	33,150	7,197	74,997	314,428	0
Transport etc.	431,471	271,238	159,332	38,121	30,620	9,555	33,610	160,233	0
Finance	100,473	92,818	18,031	12,884	42,614	12,053	7,236	7,655	0
Community, social and personal services	1,520,124	1,189,423	353,528	167,706	370,722	186,611	110,856	330,701	0
Other	74,689	43,012	14,925	5,917	8,205	5,931	8,034	31,677	0
1986	11,035,962	6,580,982	2,551,516	1,005,096	1,826,316	497,286	700,768	4,450,443	4,537
Agriculture etc.	3,208,613	944,067	529,645	121,297	64,573	5,368	223,184	2,263,169	1,377
Mining	32,377	20,911	9,054	2,420	4,850	1,185	3,402	11,451	15
Manufacturing	1,460,132	958,505	482,871	151,518	174,109	24,744	125,263	501,108	519
Construction	91,064	72,773	25,150	8,353	26,217	7,545	5,508	18,276	15
Water, electricity and gas	1,207,459	494,777	280,920	77,148	54,056	13,115	69,538	712,186	496
Wholesale and retail trade	875,919	574,318	252,396	72,813	162,474	16,842	69,793	301,361	240
Transport etc.	630,704	465,888	222,655	63,989	125,773	12,488	40,983	164,684	132
Finance	114,302	109,305	15,218	8,586	68,333	13,601	3,567	4,982	15
Community, social and personal services	3,050,943	2,680,033	639,612	462,768	1,072,207	378,963	126,483	369,998	912
Other	364,449	260,405	93,995	36,204	73,724	23,435	33,047	103,228	816

Table 8.5 continued

	Total employed population	*Literate*						*Illiterate*	*Not reported*
		Total	*Primary*	*Guidance*	*Secondary*	*Higher education*	*Other*		
Change during 1976–86	2,236,542	3,000,282	783,913	598,679	1,248,533	228,971	140,186	–768277	4,537
Agriculture etc.	216,744	415,024	202,472	101,657	55,966	2,478	52,451	–199657	1,377
Mining	–57511	–37177	–18710	–4759	–6684	–4929	–2095	–20349	15
Manufacturing	–211927	313,778	54,128	80,087	128,987	4,664	45,912	–526224	519
Construction	–1097656	–278038	–199640	–21880	8,869	–5506	–59881	–819633	15
Water, electricity and gas	1,145,826	447,303	259,750	70,417	44,195	8,282	64,659	698027	496
Wholesale and retail trade	207,425	220,252	60,249	26,238	129,324	9,645	–5204	–13067	240
Transport etc.	199,233	194,650	63,323	25,868	95,153	2,933	7,373	4,451	132
Finance	13,829	16,487	–2813	–4298	25,719	1,548	–3669	–2673	15
Community, social and personal services	1,530,819	1,490,610	286,084	295,062	701,485	192,352	15,627	39,297	912
Other	289,760	217,393	79,070	30,287	65,519	17,504	25,013	71,551	816

Source: Iran's Census Centre (1980, p. 76; 1988, p. 129).

social and personal services from 78.2 per cent to 87.9 per cent, financial from 92.4 per cent to 95.6 per cent, and the remaining sectors (except mining which remained unchanged) all showed an improvement as well. The share of community, social and personal services, out of the total country's higher educated employees, increased from 69.5 per cent to 76.2 per cent. Male illiteracy decreased from 57.8 per cent to 40.8 per cent and females from 68.8 per cent to 36.0 per cent.

In 1976, out of the total literate employed female population, 16.5 per cent had attained a higher education and, 33.6 per cent a secondary education, whilst the corresponding figures for males were 6.4 per cent and 14.1 per cent respectively. The corresponding data for 1986 saw female figures increase to 18.0 per cent and 45.8 per cent, and males to 6.4 per cent and 25.8 per cent, indicating a relatively higher quality of females than that of males. Briefly, the employment factors can be summarised as follows:

1 The ability of the work force in the agriculture sector, which is the most important commodity-producing industry, was considered too low to be able to use academic approaches in production processes.
2 The number of those employed in community, social and personal services doubled, over the period of 1976–86; with a great majority of higher educated employees working in this sector.
3 The commodity-producing industries employed the lowest educational status workers, whilst the majority of literate people, especially the higher-educated employees, were absorbed by the service industries, particularly community, social and personal services.
4 During the decade from 1976 to 1986, the educational status of workers in all industries, except mining, improved.
5 The educational status of female employees, although they constituted a low proportion of the work force, was generally better than that of males, and their situation was enhanced as the period progressed.

Employment by private and public sectors

In 1976, out of 8.8 million workers, 2.1 per cent were employers, 31.9 per cent own-account workers, 34.9 per cent private sector wage and salary earners, 11.6 per cent unpaid family workers and 19.0 per cent public sector wage and salary earners. In 1991, the proportion of employers increased to 3.0 per cent, the share of own-account workers rose to 41.6 per cent and the public sector wage and salary earners to 32.2 per cent. In comparison the proportion of private sector wage and salary earners declined to 17.9 per cent and unpaid family workers to 2.6 per cent (see Figure 8.3 and Table 8.6).

The average number of workers per employer decreased dramatically from 16.9 workers in 1976 to 5.9 workers in 1991. The number of public sector wage and salary earners increased by 159.7 per cent, whereas that of the private sector declined by 23.6 per cent. Female employment in the public sector was 20.5 per

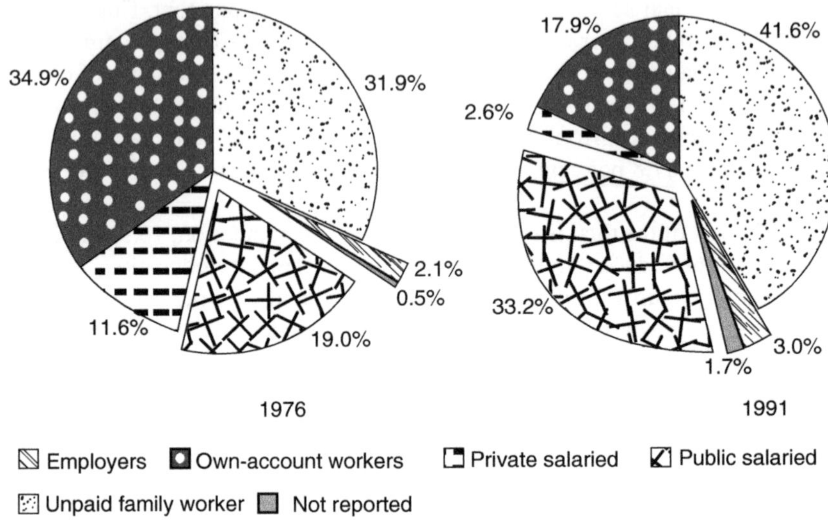

Figure 8.3 Employed population by employment status, 1976 and 1991.

cent in 1976 (male employment, 18.9 per cent) and increased to 53.6 per cent in 1986 (male employment to 31.8 per cent).

In 1986[1], the illiteracy rate of workers in the private sector was 54.2 per cent and in the public sector 13.6 per cent. Out of the total number of literate employees working in the private sector, 51.7 per cent attained primary education, 14.5 per cent guidance, 15.9 per cent secondary and only 2.1 per cent higher education. The corresponding figures for the public sector were 25.1 per cent, 15.3 per cent, 40.6 per cent and 13.6 per cent, respectively (see Figure 8.4 and Table 8.7, and Table 8.8). Only 13,006 employers in 1986 had attained higher education, and the total number of employers possessing secondary or higher educational attainments numbered only 59,659. The literacy rate of females was 64.0 per cent and that of males 59.2 per cent, but the literacy rate of females in the private sector (36.1 per cent) was much lower than that of males (46.5 per cent). In the public sector 87.5 per cent of literate female workers attained secondary (61.8 per cent) and higher education (25.7 per cent), while the related figure for males was 49.2 per cent (37.4 per cent and 11.8 per cent).

In 1986, of the 497,286 workers with higher educational attainment, 11.2 per cent graduated in educational fields, 11.0 per cent in human sciences, 10.8 per cent in natural sciences, 9.7 per cent in health and medical sciences, 7.8 per cent in social sciences, 6.3 per cent in mathematical and computer sciences, 6.1 per cent in commerce, 3.4 per cent (18,795) in agriculture and the rest in other fields.

Out of the 18,795 members of the employed population with higher educational attainment in agricultural fields only 1,106 (5.9 per cent) actually worked in agricultural occupations. In other words, 94.1 per cent of higher educated employees from agricultural fields engaged in occupations other than agriculture.

Table 8.6 Employed population by industrial group and employment status, 1976, 1986 and 1991

	Total employed population	*Private sector*					*Public sector wage and salary earners*	*Not reported*
		Total	*Employers*	*Own-account workers*	*Wage and salary earners*	*Unpaid family workers*		
1976	8,799,419	7,085,679	182,229	2,810,211	3,071,927	1,021,312	1,673,092	40,648
Agriculture etc.	2,991,869	2,952,334	35,784	1,705,756	623,364	587,430	38,708	827
Mining	89,888	19,884	312	1,068	18,434	70	69,951	53
Manufacturing	1,672,059	1,528,272	49,885	307,722	759,416	411,249	141,440	2,347
Water, electricity and gas	61,633	8,472	137	469	7,858	8	53,123	38
Construction	1,188,720	1,177,515	18,840	99,057	1,055,230	4,388	10,500	705
Wholesale and retail trade	668,494	649,385	47,052	432,602	157,710	12,021	18,851	258
Transport etc.	431,471	319,399	8,915	147,624	160,737	2,123	111,615	457
Finance	100,473	58,399	3,163	12,898	42,236	102	41,966	108
Community, social and personal services	1,520,123	337,973	15,965	99,252	219,704	3,052	1,180,247	1,903
Other	74,689	34,046	2,176	3,763	27,238	869	6,691	33,952
1986	11,035,962	7,117,480	341,301	4,397,897	1,881,682	496,600	3,454,437	464,045
Agriculture etc.	3,208,613	3,107,996	110,079	2,315,039	292,631	390,247	39,369	61,248
Mining	32,377	4,470	284	1,207	2,958	21	27,081	826
Manufacturing	1,460,132	1,007,621	66,007	439,393	428,540	73,681	389,543	62,968
Water, electricity and gas	91,064	13,528	902	4,188	8,352	86	74,760	2,776
Construction	1,207,459	1,100,019	42,747	388,517	663,904	4,851	60,547	46,893
Wholesale and retail trade	875,919	795,329	44,699	610,776	128,995	10,859	54,450	26,140
Transport etc.	630,704	462,130	12,005	336,861	110,618	2,646	149,026	19,548

Table 8.6 continued

	Total employed population	*Private sector*					*Public sector wage and salary earners*	*Not reported*
		Total	*Employers*	*Own-account workers*	*Wage and salary earners*	*Unpaid family workers*		
Finance	114,302	22,928	2,046	10,901	9,857	124	87,475	3,899
Community, social and personal services	3,050,943	418,877	32,494	205,399	173,530	7,454	2,448,834	183,232
Other	364,449	184,582	30,038	85,616	62,297	6,631	123,352	56,515
1991	13,096,910	8,534,053	395,866	5,453,175	2,347,919	337,093	4,345,757	217,100
Agriculture etc.	3,205,447	3,141,520	94,091	2,534,342	293,215	219,872	60,689	3,238
Mining	100,554	9,512	946	3,591	4,879	96	90,982	60
Manufacturing	2,013,767	1,472,593	92,850	657,583	629,650	92,510	539,425	1,749
Water, electricity and gas	128,997	11,896	831	4,167	6,857	41	117,030	71
Construction	1,372,467	1,271,611	51,031	525,668	692,510	2,402	99,476	1,380
Wholesale and retail trade	1,238,324	1,162,679	75,099	865,225	210,464	11,891	74,676	969
Transport, storage and communications	762,187	545,652	16,425	391,790	135,554	1,883	215,750	785
Finance	194,691	56,217	6,427	25,615	23,964	211	138,367	107
Community, social and personal services	3,517,937	654,971	48,471	342,149	258,035	6,316	2,858,820	4,146
Other	562,539	207,402	9,695	103,045	92,791	1,871	150,542	204,595

Source: Iran's Census Centre (1980, p. 82; 1988, p. 147; 1993, pp. 212–13).

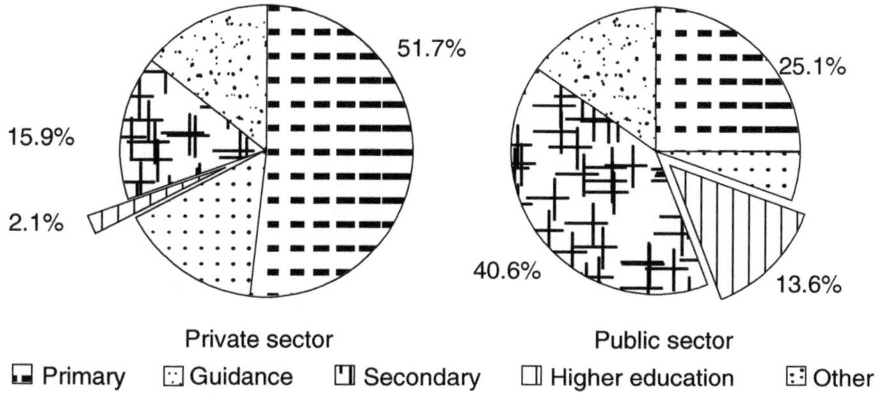

Figure 8.4 Educational attainment of literate employees in private and public sectors, 1986.

Furthermore, only 4,226 employees with higher educational attainment worked in agricultural occupations (Table 8.9). These figures vividly reveal the weak employment base of agriculture, as well as the unfair educational system of the country.

A further comparison between males and females indicates that a great majority of females, 90.4 per cent, were engaged in the professional occupations, while the corresponding figure for males was only 64.8 per cent. Meanwhile, the highest number of females graduated in the following areas, health and medical sciences (18.0 per cent), human sciences (15.7 per cent), education (14.3 per cent) and natural sciences (12.3 per cent). In comparison, engineering (22.2 per cent) constituted the highest participation rate for males, with education (10.3 per cent), human sciences (9.7 per cent) and natural sciences (7.4 per cent) following next.

Therefore, engaging a great majority of females in professional fields, with a particular concentration of graduates in the health and medical sciences, human sciences and natural sciences, characterised the higher educated employment of females. However, the proportion of professional occupations for males was lower than that for females, with engineering, education, human sciences and natural sciences constituting the main fields of entry.

Finally, having fully considered the employment records of both the private and the public sector it can be concluded that:

1 From 1976 to 1991, the structure of employment in the private and public sectors changed remarkably.
2 Apart from employees transferring from the private sector to the public sector, most of the new workers tended to be employed as own-account workers.
3 About half of the total workers did not have anything other than their labour power to provide their livelihood. Adding a majority of own-account workers and unpaid family workers to wage and salary earners, especially in the agricultural sector, implies the vulnerability of a great majority of employees (at least 73 per cent) to inflationary conditions.

Table 8.7 Employed population by sex, educational attainment and employment status, 1986

	Total employed population	*Private sector*					*Public sector wage and salary earners*	*Not reported*
		Total	*Employers*	*Own-account workers*	*Wage and salary earners*	*Unpaid family workers*		
Both sexes	11,035,962	7,117,480	341,301	4,397,897	1,881,682	496,600	3,454,437	464,045
Literate	6,580,982	3,253,689	202,691	1,861,642	953,469	235,887	2,982,881	344,412
Primary	2,551,516	1,683,226	95,216	974,312	477,318	136,380	748,130	120,160
Guidance	1,005,096	472,619	19,101	225,479	177,930	50,109	456,725	75,752
Secondary	1,826,316	517,815	46,653	292,121	161,279	17,762	1,210,499	98,002
Higher education	497,286	69,360	13,006	27,577	28,204	573	406,054	21,872
Other	700,768	510,669	28,715	342,153	108,738	31,063	161,473	28,626
Illiterate	4,450,443	3,861,220	138,525	2,534,772	927,507	260,416	470,735	118,488
Not reported	4,537	2,571	85	1,483	706	297	821	1,145
Male	10,048,859	6,608,887	327,582	4,216,711	1,781,844	282,750	3,046,803	393,169
Literate	5,950,298	3,070,442	196,746	1,797,226	906,276	170,194	2,591,776	288,080
Primary	2,433,395	1,600,265	93,714	943,316	460,350	102,885	727,062	106,068
Guidance	960,002	449,767	18,572	217,788	172,620	40,787	439,836	70,399
Secondary	1,537,347	491,699	44,502	283,681	148,453	15,063	968,844	76,804
Higher education	383,788	63,404	12,041	26,131	24,787	445	305,487	14,897
Other	635,766	465,307	27,917	326,310	100,066	11,014	150,547	19,912
Illiterate	4,094,966	3,536,224	130,755	2,418,143	874,938	112,388	454,288	104,454
Not reported	3,595	2,221	81	1,342	630	168	739	635

Table 8.7 continued

	Total employed population	*Private sector*					*Public sector wage and salary earners*	*Not reported*
		Total	*Employers*	*Own-account workers*	*Wage and salary earners*	*Unpaid family workers*		
Female	987,103	508,593	13,719	181,186	99,838	213,850	407,634	70,876
Literate	630,684	183,247	5,945	64,416	47,193	65,693	391,105	56,332
Primary	118,121	82,961	1,502	30,996	16,968	33,495	21,068	14,092
Guidance	45,094	22,852	529	7,691	5,310	9,322	16,889	5,353
Secondary	288,969	26,116	2,151	8,440	12,826	2,699	241,655	21,198
Higher education	113,498	5,956	965	1,446	3,417	128	100,567	6,975
Other	65,002	45,362	798	15,843	8,672	20,049	10,926	8,714
Illiterate	355,477	324,996	7,770	116,629	52,569	148,028	16,447	14,034
Not reported	942	350	4	141	76	129	82	510

Source: *Markaz-e Amar-e Iran* (1988, p. 240).

Table 8.8 Ratio of employed population by sex, educational attainment and employment status, 1986 (%)

	Total employed population	*Private sector*					*Public sector wage and salary earners*	*Not reported*
		Total	*Employers*	*Own-account workers*	*Wage and salary earners*	*Unpaid family workers*		
Both sexes								
Primary (as % of literate)	38.8	51.7	47.0	52.3	50.1	57.8	25.1	34.9
Guidance (as % of literate)	15.3	14.5	9.4	12.1	18.7	21.2	15.3	22.0
Secondary (as % of literate)	27.8	15.9	23.0	15.7	16.9	7.5	40.6	28.5
Higher education (as % of literate)	7.6	2.1	6.4	1.5	3.0	0.2	13.6	6.4
Other (as % of literate)	10.6	15.7	14.2	18.4	11.4	13.2	5.4	8.3
Illiterate (as % of total)	40.3	54.2	40.6	57.6	49.3	52.4	13.6	25.5
Not reported (as % of total)	0.0	0.0	0.0	0.0	0.0	0.1	0.0	0.2
Male								
Primary (as % of literate)	40.9	52.1	47.6	52.5	50.8	60.5	28.1	36.8
Guidance (as % of literate)	16.1	14.6	9.4	12.1	19.0	24.0	17.0	24.4
Secondary (as % of literate)	25.8	16.0	22.6	15.8	16.4	8.9	37.4	26.7
Higher education (as % of literate)	6.4	2.1	6.1	1.5	2.7	0.3	11.8	5.2
Other (as % of literate)	10.7	15.2	14.2	18.2	11.0	6.5	5.8	6.9
Illiterate (as % of total)	40.8	53.5	39.9	57.3	49.1	39.7	14.9	26.6
Not reported (as % of total)	0.0	0.0	0.0	0.0	0.0	0.1	0.0	0.2

Table 8.8 continued

	Total employed population	*Private sector*					*Public sector wage and salary earners*	*Not reported*
		Total	*Employers*	*Own-account workers*	*Wage and salary earners*	*Unpaid family workers*		
Female								
Primary (as % of literate)	18.7	45.3	25.3	48.1	36.0	51.0	5.4	25.0
Guidance (as % of literate)	7.2	12.5	8.9	11.9	11.3	14.2	4.3	9.5
Secondary (as % of literate)	45.8	14.3	36.2	13.1	27.2	4.1	61.8	37.6
Higher education (as % of literate)	18.0	3.3	16.2	2.2	7.2	0.2	25.7	12.4
Other (as % of literate)	10.3	24.8	13.4	24.6	18.4	30.5	2.8	15.5
Illiterate (as % of total)	36.0	63.9	56.6	64.4	52.7	69.2	4.0	19.8
Not reported (as % of total)	0.1	0.1	0.0	0.1	0.1	0.1	0.0	0.7

Source: Calculated from Table 8.7.

Table 8.9 Employed population with higher education by field of study and occupational group, 1986

Field of study	*Total*	*Professional, technical and related workers*	*Administrative and managerial*	*Clerical and related workers*	*Sales workers*	*Services workers*	*Agricultural, animal husbandry and forestry workers*	*Production and related workers*	*Not reported or classified*
All fields	497,286	351,238	16,773	31,976	14,965	4,878	4,226	22,124	51,106
General study	13,906	11,699	69	304	213	129	213	590	689
Education	55,697	52,240	189	858	182	65	103	228	1,832
Fine arts	2,874	2,294	50	140	92	23	18	133	124
Humanities	54,883	45,025	896	2,756	1,298	335	293	1,116	3,164
Religious	5,829	4,851	112	248	74	22	27	68	427
Social sciences	38,716	25,677	1,660	4,203	1,808	391	342	1,125	3,510
Commerce	30,415	16,782	2,787	4,501	2,132	313	249	1,039	2,612
Law	9,681	5,902	389	804	357	371	111	195	1,552
Natural sciences	53,467	39,679	1,297	2,839	1,434	485	335	1,913	5,485
Mathematical and computer sciences	31,273	22,419	709	2,022	1,077	227	184	1,268	3,367
Health and medical sciences	48,318	40,917	514	1,549	687	379	77	576	3,619
Vocational	2,929	2,536	30	83	39	6	6	128	101
Engineering	89,390	46,869	6,181	7,446	3,726	675	748	11,279	12,466
Architecture and urbanisation	3,405	2,083	281	264	113	18	22	338	286
Agriculture	18,795	11,139	832	2,057	794	183	1,106	749	1,935
House management	641	524	9	37	11	5	2	15	38
Transport and communications	531	222	13	66	14	24	8	24	160
Trade services	305	108	4	45	30	77	3	15	23
Librarianship and mass media	1,005	668	40	126	40	6	4	41	80
Other fields	11,841	4,479	136	316	209	751	58	208	5,684
Not reported	23,385	15,125	575	1,312	635	393	317	1,076	3,952

Source: *Markaz-e Amar-e Iran* (1988, p. 192).

4 Relatively more females were absorbed by the public sector; female activity in this sector was concentrated in professional and clerical areas, while in the private sector women were found more in production and agricultural occupations.
5 Many workers in the agriculture industry (peasantry) and manufacturing industry (mainly in carpet and rug handicrafts), because of economic difficulties, could not employ anyone other than their own family members and could not pay wages.
6 In the private sector, the literacy rate and educational status of literate employees was lower than in the public sector.
7 Having a labour force with a very low educational status (in terms of secondary as well as higher educational attainment), the private sector did not possess much potential capability in the areas of innovation and entrepreneurial skills. Added to this is the structure of the private sector in Iran, which is mostly based on extended kinship and family relations (Sami, 1983, p. 95), and is therefore limited in its efficiency. This shows that the concept of a private sector, in a developing country such as Iran, is considerably different from that of developed countries.
8 The literacy quality of females, especially in the public sector, was higher than that of males.
9 The engagement of a great majority of workers in professional occupations, the consigning of the least educated to the areas of agriculture, animal husbandry and forestry, as well as the inconsistency of the employed population as regards their educational attainments (particularly those who possess higher educational attainments in agricultural fields, the majority of whom are employed in other fields) not only indicates the weakness of the human resources of agriculture but also shows the inefficiency and inappropriateness of the educational system.

Unemployment

The unemployment rate increased from 10.1 per cent in 1976 to 16.0 per cent in 1986. In urban areas, the unemployment rate increased from 5.1 per cent (male 5.0 per cent and female 6.0 per cent) to 17.4 per cent (male 15.8 per cent and female 29.2 per cent), and in rural areas from 14.2 per cent (male 12.6 per cent and female 21.6 per cent) to 14.4 per cent (male 13.7 per cent and female 20.5 per cent). The age median of the unemployed population decreased by 3.70 years (urban by 3.37 years and rural by 11.1 years) to 22.19 years in 1986 (urban to 24.59 years and rural to 20.3 years). From 1976 to 1986, some 822,104 persons (males 726,488 and females 95,616) were added to the number of those classified as unemployed. The rise of unemployment in urban areas was 850,046 (males 662,870 and females 187,176); by contrast, the number of unemployed persons in rural areas declined by 27,942 to 745,766 (the reason for this change was the 91,560 reduction of females in rural areas while the number of males increased by 63,618).

In 1976, more than two-thirds of the unemployed population were illiterate, in 1986 this figure had declined to just one-third. In addition, in 1976, about 22.4

per cent of the unemployed population (males 25.5 per cent and females 12.4 per cent) resided in urban areas. In 1986, this changed, accounting for 59.0 per cent of the population (males 57.6 per cent and females 65.1 per cent).

Thus, the following may be concluded regarding the period 1976–86:

1. Both the absolute numbers of the unemployed and the percentage of unemployment (except among rural females) increased.
2. The age structure of the unemployed population became more youthful, with the 15–24 age group constituting the majority of the unemployed population.
3. The rate of urban unemployment (both male and female) exceeded the rural rate.
4. Rural–urban migration raised unemployment in urban areas.
5. The changes in the literate unemployed were consistent with the overall changes in the total literate population and the total literate employed population.
6. In 1976, a great majority of the unemployed population resided in rural areas, but in 1986, reversing the direction, a major part of the unemployed were job-seekers in urban areas. Nonetheless, in spite of the decrease in the relative proportion of illiterate unemployed in rural areas, a majority of the illiterate unemployed population lived in these same areas in 1986 (Tables 8.2 and 8.10).

By examining the rapid pattern of changes that occurred after 1976 the following conclusions can be made. First, the nature of the youthful age structure and the rapid growth of population, were achieved mostly as a result of decreasing the economically active proportion of the population, despite a considerable improvement in literacy and education from 1976 to 1991. The activity rate, the participation rate and the dependency burden all increased, and consequently consumers exceeded the increase of the productive population.

The second point to be considered here is that urbanisation had a direct relation with the expansion of the service sector, a fact which was inconsistent with the industrialisation process. In the post-revolutionary period, the tendency was towards a reduction of employment in commodity-producing occupations and an increase in employment in service occupations. The former was more likely the result of the investment decline that occurred during the Iraq–Iran war (1980–8) along with other socio-economic problems, and the latter was the consequence of a reduction in investment, extension of the public-sector sphere, easier access to high income in trade services, and the creation of jobs (even disguised unemployment) for a huge number of job-seekers, particularly in the service sector.

However, any change in the system was extremely difficult as the traditional approaches dominated the employment base in Iran. The overall ability of employees, especially those who had been employed in agriculture, and traditional and service industries, (particularly in trade), was too low to allow for training or an increase in their skills level to enable the utilisation of academic approaches in production processes. Another significant argument here was the

Table 8.10 Unemployed population by educational attainment, sex and area, 1976 and 1986

	All areas			*Urban*			*Rural**		
	Both sexes	*Male*	*Female*	*Both sexes*	*Male*	*Female*	*Both sexes*	*Male*	*Female*
1976									
Total unemployed	996,636	759,650	236,986	222,928	193,637	29,291	773,708	566,013	207,695
Literate	313,381	274,164	39,217	158,111	137,095	21,016	155,270	137,069	18,201
Primary	140,653	122,414	18,239	41,697	38,686	3,011	98,956	83,728	15,228
Guidance	37,809	35,265	2,544	26,267	24,413	1,854	11,542	10,852	690
Secondary	75,079	62,271	12,808	62,810	50,672	12,138	12,269	11,599	670
Higher education	11,365	9,402	1,963	10,757	8,824	1,933	608	578	30
Other	48,475	44,812	3,663	16,580	14,500	2,080	31,895	30,312	1,583
Illiterate	682,954	485,235	197,719	64,710	56,461	8,249	618,244	428,774	189,470
Not reported	301	251	50	107	81	26	194	170	24
1986									
Total	1,818,740	1,486,138	332,602	1,072,974	856,507	216,467	745,766	629,631	116,135
Literate	1,219,724	973,834	245,890	807,980	620,191	187,789	411,744	353,643	58,101
Primary	393,364	341,789	51,575	193,563	169,849	23,714	199,801	171,940	27,861
Guidance	257,085	223,854	33,231	154,506	131,696	22,810	102,579	92,158	10,421
Secondary	465,323	327,366	137,957	387,208	261,164	126,044	78,115	66,202	11,913
Higher education	33,110	25,358	7,752	31,186	23,632	7,554	1,924	1,726	198
Other	70,842	55,467	15,375	41,517	33,850	7,667	29,325	21,617	7,708
Illiterate	597,818	511,460	86,358	264,344	235,844	28,500	333,474	275,616	57,858
Not reported	1,198	844	354	650	472	178	548	372	176

Source: *Markaz-e Amar-e Iran* (1980, p. 136; 1988, pp. 243–5).

*Includes 'unsettled' population.

economic difficulties, which saw many workers in the agriculture sector (dominated by peasantry agriculture) and in manufacturing industry (mainly in carpet and rug handicrafts), unable to employ anyone other than their own family members or even pay wages.

The significant role of oil in the economy of Iran, and the contribution of the oil industry to employment, were tiny, demonstrating that exporting crude petroleum for about 90 years had done little to promote indigenous development. Almost half of all employees had nothing other than their own labour with which to provide their livelihood. If a majority of own-account and family unpaid workers are added to wage and salary earners, the great majority of employees would be vulnerable in inflationary situations. While the growth rate of professionalisation was higher than employment, the tendency was for professional employees to be engaged in the service sectors, especially in community, social and personal services.

Despite improvements, the literacy rate (as a prerequisite to academic-based production) of employees was generally low. In addition, the educational attainment of literate employees, the inappropriateness of the educational system for developmental requirements, and the employment of workers in occupations not related to their educational fields, as well as weaknesses in working consciousness and social discipline and the dominance of thinking only for one's own benefits rather than the national interest – all these imply that all the socio-economic systems of Iran have been inconsistent with each other. Most of the employed who held a higher educational attainment worked in service occupations, especially in community, social and personal services. Though the proportion of females in employment was very low, their age structure was younger, and they tended to be highly educated and largely professional. In addition, females working in the public sector were mostly engaged in professional and clerical occupations, whilst the most common occupations for women in the private sector were in the areas of production and agriculture.

Both the private and public sectors had structural problems, and the quality of the private sector's work force was much lower than that of the public sector, so much so that it could never possess the (potential) ability to manage and run the country's economy. In other words, without substantial wholesale changes the private sector will not be able to play its role in the country's development process. The increase of rural–urban migration saw a rapid increase in unemployment in urban areas, with the 15–24 age group constituting about half of the total number unemployed.

In concluding this chapter it must be reiterated that the most important reason for the underdevelopment of the Iranian economy is the low capability of the work force. We must look at the causes and effects of Iran's low capability and the implications of the policy procedures put in place to improve the situation before we can assess the prospects for future development.

In Iran, the causes of the low capability of human resources can be attributed briefly to a number of factors. First is a weak work consciousness, poor social discipline and the lack of a scientific approach to the whole issue, together with the inadequacy of the education system in training the work force for economic development requirements. Moreover, there was always a point missing in the five-year development plan and budget report, namely the requirements and characteristics of human resources for the achievement of the plan's objectives. The education system teaches literacy but does not prepare students to be able to carry out development needs. The content of textbooks, especially at advanced levels and even in the modern sector, has not changed according to the national need and development plan objectives. Students, especially in schools, are taught subjects that encourage rote-learning and memorising. In the meantime, the inconsistency of the Western-style academic calendar year with the Iranian national calendar, particularly in higher education, together with other socio-political problems, results in a low student attendance (usually in the second semester). In certain instances actual classroom attendance is about 40 per cent lower than required. The authoritarian teaching methods limit the flexibility of minds and curtail critical and abstract thinking (Sami 1983, pp. 83–5). The educational system of Iran does not train students to solve problems through thinking and utilising their abilities, but instead by using guidebooks or copying from others. Perhaps this suggests why the country usually looks outside for help in solving its problems. As a result of about 2,500 years of despotic rule, a monopolistic spirit pervades most aspects of socio-economic life, including education, which restricts the enthusiasm for acquiring knowledge and experience, and weakens the notion of working in groups.

Originating from the nature of Iran's administrative system itself, the education system does not place enough trust in teachers and pays them only a negligible salary. Thus, most teachers, even university lecturers, have to work overtime in order to meet their basic needs. Over-employment or multiple-job holding have contributed to inefficiencies in the educational system (Sami, 1983, pp. 83–5).

Generally, the ultimate goal of education is perceived to be getting a degree in order to be eligible for higher income and a privileged position (Sami, 1983, p. 83). As a consequence of a dominating employment structure based on traditional approaches, low value and low pay of technical schooling are commonplace, especially in the private sector, vocational and technical education areas. Generally speaking, in the education system of Iran, technical and vocational training is not a priority, nor is it financially feasible. The education system, which covers about one-third of the country's population, is not in harmony with other social systems, economic, cultural or political.

One of the major contributory factors to the low capability of the work force can be seen as the continued underdeveloped state of the economy. As a consequence of the low capability of most workers the development strategies and policies of the country have failed to change accordingly.

Low labour productivity and the inefficiency of the administrative system are other important factors contributing to the incapability of the work force. This is perhaps most evident in their failure to create a consistent set of social systems.

The education system, which is the most important factor in terms of meeting the development requirements, has remained inconsistent, ineffectual and weak.

It is important to note that the last, but by no means least, major obstacle effecting the low capability of human resources is the lack of any interrelationship between industries and the education system.

What are the implications?

In general, economic development is a long-run, evolutionary–indigenous process and human beings are the engine of development. As regards the characteristics of human resources, Iran's economic development is dependent on a major structural change occurring in these resources. In order to achieve structural changes, we need to adopt the following recommendations:

1 Defining the relation of, and the extent of, the 'individual' and 'society'.
2 Defining and establishing all social systems based on the determination of the individual and the concept of social relations.
3 Creating a scientific-based approach in executing affairs, such that illiterate people will not be employed, under any circumstances, in any form of employment.
4 Setting up a payment system based on educational attainment, level of skill and productivity, in both public and private sectors.
5 Carrying out a one-job policy for all workers so that every worker will be able to provide his/her basic necessities through his/her earnings.
6 Changing the existing education system to one that is efficient and can prepare the work force for their development requirements.
7 Establishing a new technical and vocational education system which will be able to train a skilled labour force (other than the higher-educated) for all non-professional occupations. This policy should be accompanied by one in which all employees should either attain a higher education qualification or be trained in technical and vocational education.
8 Decentralising the educational management system in accordance with the managerial capability of institutions, especially changing the existing centralised management of universities to an 'auto-management' system.
9 Paying adequate attention to the importance of management in allocating resources and implementing projects, especially changing the existing role of management in universities from secondary job[2] to the main job and paying managers on the basis of academic position and productivity.
10 Teachers as the engines of development should be capable and competent in their position. For this: i) teachers' salaries should be of a level that meets all their basic necessities, ii) all employed teachers should be retrained, iii) all functions related to teaching tasks such as teaching methods, examination, and textbook preparation should be delegated to teachers. In other words, teachers should be trusted and feel free to do their job to the best of their ability.
11 To increase the purchasing power of teachers the structure of the government budget needs to change so that the education budget is increased through: i) increasing the share of direct tax revenues in the government

budget, and ii) increasing the share of non-government institutions including households in financing the education budget.

12 Increasing the capability of managers by appointing them according to their educational attainment, speciality area, effective work experience and talent. In short and medium terms, present managers should be retrained effectively.

13 Improving the capability of managers and all workers through on-the-job training and establishing an effective productivity evaluation system, for organisations, managers and employees.

14 Determining national standards in all possible production levels and paying adequate attention to the quality of production in all industries. In education, the emphasis should be concentrated on carrying out the entire curriculum, both quantitatively and qualitatively.

Notes

1 In the 1976 census the literate population was not recorded by private and public sector.

2 In Iranian universities, except for a few administrative and financial positions, managers are appointed from academic staff who hold their academic job as primary and their management role as secondary. The only advantage of this approach is appointing academic skills to management, but it has several disadvantages such as: 1) creating short-term management views, 2) creating conservative morale in management, 3) decreasing the quality of education, since managers are inevitably engaged in managerial fields.

9 The feminisation of the labour force in Iran

Parvin Alizadeh and Barry Harper

This chapter consists of five sections and an introduction. Sections two and three provide a review of the literature and an examination of Iranian data respectively. It is shown that the process of economic development in Iran during the 1980s and 1990s has been accompanied by de-feminisation and increased occupational sex segregation. In this respect the pattern of female employment in Iran diverges from the 'normal' or expected pattern. In section four a summary of current debates on female employment in Iran is presented. Section five focuses on the relationship between women's social position in Iran and the process of nation-building. Discussion in this part provides an alternative explanation for the changing pattern of female employment in Iran during the 1980s and 1990s.

Introduction

The basic proposition raised in this chapter is that the control of women's social position is central to processes of nation-building. The state is essentially implicated in gender relations, which are defined here as the socially constructed power relationship between men and women. Hence, each state embodies a specific gender regime. Women on the one hand bear the burden of being 'mothers of the nation', a duty that is ideologically defined, reflecting the ideological orientation of the state. On the other hand, women as mothers and educators transmit culture and tradition and subsequently reproduce the boundaries of ethnic/national groupings. The role and social position of women, therefore, has specific importance in relation to the process of nation-building or redefinition of nationhood.

It is in this context that the establishment and consolidation of the Islamic Republic has played a decisive role in shaping the form and the extent of women's social participation in Iran. This study in particular is concerned with the changing pattern of female employment since the Islamic revolution of 1979.

Factors affecting the pattern of female employment

What factors affect female employment? Is there a positive relationship between the process of economic development and female employment? Does the level of female employment alter with the level of economic activities?

Studies by Boserup (1970, 1990), Tilly and Scott (1987), and Cagatay and Ozler (1995) indicate that the relationship between the long-term process of capitalist development and women's labour force participation is U-shaped. Accordingly, women's participation rate in the labour force during the initial stages of commercialisation and capitalist development decreases and then increases with increased urbanisation and further economic development.

In a pioneering study, concerned with female employment in a historical perspective, Boserup (1970, 1990) argued that in the early phase of capitalism and economic development women's share of the labour force declines. This is because of men's monopolistic control over technology and education inherited from the previous mode of subsistence economies. In subsistence agricultural economies the use of improved techniques is usually monopolised by the men. The skills gap between women and men widens during transition to capitalist development. 'Boys get systematic training as apprentices in family enterprise, while girls continue to be taught only simple household and agricultural operations by their mothers' (Boserup, 1990, p.19). Hence the skills gap between the sexes widens at the early stage of capitalist development and industrialisation. Furthermore, education systems everywhere have started with the schooling of boys, particularly those from the upper classes. Hence the early stage of urbanisation and economic development are associated with the downward portion of the U curve.

However, beyond the early stage of capitalist development women's share of the labour force increases. Expansion of industrial activities is concurrent with the growth of urbanisation, increased female education, falling fertility rates and commodification of domestic labour. Hence women's share of employment expands. This more mature phase of capitalist development coincides with the upward portion of the U shape.

This relationship between the process of economic development and female employment is known as feminisation U. Feminisation in this context refers to an increase in the share of the female labour force. De-feminisation has the opposite meaning.

Historical studies concerned with development of capitalist production organisations in France and England support the feminisation U hypothesis (Tilly and Scott, 1987). The fact that female employment increases with the growth of urbanisation, decline in fertility rate and increased female education is reflected in noticeable growth of female employment in OECD countries since 1950s (Howes and Singh, 1995). For instance, in advanced industrialised countries of the northern hemisphere the ratio of women's to men's labour force participation, on average, increased from 36.8 per cent in the 1950s to 55.6 per cent in the 1980s (Blau and Ferber, 1992: 300–304, Table 10.1)[1].

Furthermore, it has been shown that the countries of east Asia, the Caribbean and Latin America, as well as most eastern European countries, experienced a significant increase in female employment over the period from the 1950s to the 1980s (Blau and Ferber, op. cit.). In east Asia the ratio of women's to men's labour force participation increased from 45.8 per cent in the 1950s to 56.6 per cent in the 1980s. For Caribbean countries, on average, this ratio increased from 53.6 per cent to 63.7 per cent over the same period, although for individual countries like Jamaica the increase in female employment was much faster; from 54.2 per cent in the 1950s to 82.8 per cent in the 1980s (Blau and Ferber, op. cit.). The share of female employment in Latin America is below those of east Asia and the Caribbean. However, female employment in Latin America has increased moderately from 21.5 per cent to 33.1 per cent over the same period.

Another group of countries with a high level of female participation are the eastern European countries. For these countries the ratio of women's to men's labour force participation increased from 56.7 per cent in the 1950s to 75.1 per cent in the 1980s (Blau and Ferber, op. cit.).

The Middle East and North Africa are known to have a relatively low level of female labour force participation (Moghadam, 1993). This paper is not concerned with the underlying factors for lower level of female labour force participation in this region. Nevertheless, even in this group of countries female employment, on average, experienced a modest increase from 15 per cent in the 1950s to 19.2 per cent in the 1980s (Blau and Ferber, 1992: 300–304, Table 10.1).

In other words the empirical evidence indicates a global upward increase in female employment since the 1950s. Hence, the second part of the twentieth century corresponds to the upward segment of the U shape in female employment for most countries.

Cagatay and Ozler (1995) have highlighted other factors, including change in industrial policy and ideological factors, that have also influenced the growth of female employment. For example, the change of trade and industrial policies, from import substitution to export-oriented strategy, has often been cited as an important factor for the rise in the share of female labour in several developing countries (Wood, 1991; Joekes, 1987; Pearson, 1992). The growth of labour-intensive manufactured exports from developing countries in several instances, although not universally, has increased demand for female labour. In this respect increased female employment has arisen from the intensity of global competition and employers' search for lower wages (Standing, 1989). Women are usually seen as 'cheap' and 'flexible' workers, easily substituted for men.

Ideological factors have also been important in influencing the extent of feminisation. This is reflected, for instance, in the high levels of female employment in ex-socialist countries, which placed a high priority on female social participation. Similarly the potency of the 'male breadwinner' ideology is often discussed as impediment to feminisation process in Muslim and Catholic countries (Cagatay and Ozler, 1995).

However, the overall picture that emerges from the literature is that the 'expected' pattern of female employment usually follows a U shape.[2] Furthermore, capitalist development in developing countries is far beyond its early and initial stage and consequently, the current pattern of female employment in these countries is expected to correspond to the upward portion of the U curve.

In the next section we will analyse the assembled Iranian data in order to examine the extent to which the pattern of female employment in Iran diverges from, or converges towards, the 'normal' pattern.

Feminisation, de-feminisation and economic development in Iran, 1956–96

Feminisation, as was mentioned earlier, is defined here as a rise in the share of female labour in the total labour force. De-feminisation on the other hand implies a reduction in the share of the female labour force.

The years covering 1956 to 1996 can be divided into two distinct periods (see Table 9.1). The first period extends from 1956 to 1976 and the second covers the years 1976 to 1996. The dividing line between the two periods is the popular revolution of 1979, which was followed by a radical change in state ideology. The data in Table 9.1 are based on figures from the population census that takes place every 10 years. Table 9.1 provides a broad overview, which is accompanied by more detailed and explanatory data in Tables 9.2a and 9.2b.

The salient feature of the first period (1956–76) is the continuous rise in the share of female employment, from 9.7 per cent of total employment in 1956 to nearly 20 per cent in 1976 (see Table 9.1). The first period can be considered the period of feminisation. The second period (1976–96), however, witnessed a sharp decline in the share of female employment from nearly 20 per cent in 1976 to around 12 per cent in 1996.

The main decline in the share of female employment occurred over the period from 1976 to 1986. However, since then the share of female employment has increased slightly, from 9.7 per cent of total employment in 1986 to 12.1 per cent in 1996 (Table 9.1).

It is necessary to compare these figures with those from other countries similar to Iran. Table 9.3 provides data on female employment in four Muslim countries, namely Turkey, Egypt, Pakistan and Malaysia. Iran, Turkey and Egypt have comparable population levels. In the mid-1990s the populations of these three countries were around 65 million, 60 million, and 57 million respectively (World Development Report, 1995). Pakistan's population was 123 million while that of Malaysia was only 19 million. Iran and Turkey are classified by the World Bank as lower middle income countries, whilst Egypt and Pakistan are low

Table 9.1 Gender composition of employment, 1956–96

	Females (%)	*Males (%)*
Feminisation period		
1956	9.70	90.30
1966	13.27	86.73
1976	19.46	80.54
De-feminisation period		
1986	8.94	91.06
1996	12.10	87.90

Source: Statistical Centre of Iran, National Census of Population and Housing, 1976, 1986, 1996; Plan and Budget Organisation, 1985, 1988, 1997; International Labour Office, *Yearbook of Labour Statistics*, (Retrospective Edition on Population Censuses 1845–1989, Geneva, 1991).

Table 9.2a Gender composition of employment by activity, 1956–76

	1956		*1966*		*1976*	
	Males %	*Females* %	*Males* %	*Females* %	*Males* %	*Females* %
Professional	80.77	19.23	74.29	25.71	66.22	33.78
Administrative	97.42	2.58	96.74	3.26	96.66	3.34
Clerical	95.58	4.42	93.18	6.82	85.52	14.48
Sales	98.50	1.50	98.90	1.10	98.60	1.40
Services	76.08	23.92	78.02	21.98	84.27	15.73
Agriculture	95.21	4.79	93.60	6.40	77.19	22.81
Production	80.32	19.68	74.96	25.04	80.24	19.76
Miscellaneous	99.57	0.43	93.61	6.30	92.43	7.57
All activities	90.30	9.70	86.73	13.27	80.54	19.46
Total employed (000)	5,334.30	573.30	948.40	909.90	7,649.70	1,848.30
Unemployed as % of active population	2.80	0.40	9.60	8.90	2.00	6.90

Source: As Table 9.1.

Table 9.2b Gender composition of employment by activity, 1986–96

	1986		*1996*	
	Males	*Females*	*Males*	*Females*
Professional	67.43	32.57	67.10	32.90
Administrative	96.55	3.45	87.20	12.80
Clerical	87.27	12.73	83.00	17.00
Sales	98.51	1.49	94.90	5.10
Services*	92.96	7.04		
Agriculture	91.93	8.07	91.10	8.90
Production	93.67	6.33	89.00	11.00
Miscellaneous	95.97	4.03	94.70	5.30
All activities	91.06	8.94	87.90	12.10
Total employed (000)	10,048.80	987.10	12,808.40	1,763.10
Unemployed as % of active population	12.90	25.20	8.40	13.30

Source: As Table 9.1.

* Classification of occupations changed to combine sales and services.

income countries, and Malaysia, with a higher level of income, is an upper middle Income country (World Bank, 1997).

The data in Table 9.3 indicates that female employment in Turkey as well as in Malaysia has been always much greater than that in Iran. Nevertheless the gap in women's share of employment between Iran and the above-mentioned two countries has widened since 1976. The share of female employment in Turkey in the 1990s was two-and-a-half times greater than that of Iran: female employment accounted for 31.8 per cent of total employment in Turkey in contrast to only 12.1 per cent in Iran (Table 9.3). Similarly, the share of female employment in Malaysia is nearly three times greater than that in Iran. In fact the share of female employment in Iran is similar to that of a low income country like Pakistan and is even below that of Egypt.[3]

The changing structure of female employment

The process of de-feminisation has also been accompanied by the changing structure of female employment. A closer look at the data covering the period 1976 to 1986, the period of a sharp decline in female employment, reveals that the fall in female employment, by more than 860,000, is highly concentrated in the agriculture and production-based industries. This is presented in Table 9.4. Occupations classified under production consist of blue-collar jobs in manufacturing activities. The data also points to the growth of female employment in professional and technical occupations, which in absolute terms increased by 155,109 between 1976 and 1986. In other words, the process of de-feminisation

Table 9.3 Share of female employment in total employment (%)

Upper middle income country				
	1957	1970	1980	1993
Malaysia (10+)*	24.6	31.3	33.3	34.2
Lower middle income countries				
	1966	1976	1986	1996
Iran (6+)*	13.3	19.5	8.7	12.1
	1965	1975	1985	1990
Turkey (12+)*	40.2	35.6	36.4	31.8
Low income countries				
	1966	1976	1986	1992
Egypt (6+)*	6.4	6.6		21.2
Pakistan (10+)*	8.9	4.9	3.5	14

Source: As Table 9.1; International Labour Office, *Yearbook of Labour Statistics 1996* (Geneva, 1997).

* The number in bracket refers to the age of the active population who seek employment.

Table 9.4 Distribution of female employment by activity, 1976–86

	1976	(%)	*1986*	(%)	*Change 1976–86*
Professional	188,164	(10.2)	343,273	(34.8)	155,109
Administrative	1,356	(0.1)	1,534	(0.2)	178
Clerical	63,538	(3.4)	46,787	(4.7)	–1,675
Sales	8,391	(0.5)	11,329	(1.1)	2,938
Services	68,286	(3.7)	32,052	(3.2)	–36,234
Agriculture	822,771	(44.5)	263,175	(26.7)	–559,596
Production	658,945	(35.7)	230,823	(23.4)	–428,122
Miscellaneous	36,840	(2.0)	58,130	(5.9)	21,290
All activities	1,848,291	(100.0)	987,103	(100)	–861,188

Source: As Table 9.1.

has been accompanied by a substantial decline of female employment in agriculture and manufacturing activities. These are the blue-collar occupations in which female employment has experienced a sharp decline. Simultaneously the share of female employment has increased in professional and technical occupations.

By 1996 about 32 per cent of total female employment was concentrated in professional and technical professions in contrast to only 10 per cent in 1976. (See Tables 9.2a and 9.2b.) In fact, female employment has moved away from productive activities like agriculture and manufacturing, and has been directed towards professional and technical professions. This trend towards de-feminisation and the changing composition of female employment will be thoroughly discussed later in this chapter.

Occupational sex segregation

A number of indexes have been developed to measure the extent to which particular social groups are concentrated into specific sectors or occupations in the labour market (Watts and Rich, 1993, Jacobson, 1994). The most commonly used index to measure sex and race segregation is the Duncan index of dissimilarity. The index ranges from zero to one hundred. The former is complete integration and the latter is complete segregation. The index is based on the implicit definition of integration as a situation where the proportional representation of each sex is the same in all occupations as in total employment. Zero segregation is defined where each occupation has the same gender proportion of the employed labour force in aggregate. For instance, if 20 per cent of the total employment consists of women, then the index would be zero only if 20 per cent of employment in each occupation consists of women.

The index measures the proportion of total employment that must relocate, with full replacement by the opposite sex, to achieve zero segregation. An interpretation of the index is that it shows what percentage of men or women would have to switch occupations in order to achieve zero segregation. If the index equals 20, for instance, either 20 per cent of men would have to switch into relatively female-dominated occupations or 20 per cent of women would have to switch into male-dominated occupations in order to achieve zero segregation. In other words, ID index points to those occupations in which male/female employment is concentrated as well as the extent of that concentration.

We have measured the index of dissimilarity (ID) for occupational segregation in Iran between 1976 and 1996. This is presented in Table 9.5. The overall ID has increased from 14 per cent in 1976 to 29 per cent in 1986 and 31 per cent in 1996. This is a substantial rise in occupational segregation. Most occupations are now considered as male-dominated, as the share of female employment in these occupations has declined considerably since 1976. In fact, with the exception of professional and technical as well as clerical occupations, all other occupations are now male-dominated.

This data indicates that agriculture and related work, and to some extent production (manufacturing), which were female-dominated in 1976 are now male-dominated. It should be emphasised that 'female/male domination' in the present context does not imply domination of employment by one gender over another. Instead female/male-dominated occupations are those in which the share of female/male employment is higher than that in total employment.

These data also indicate that currently female employment is heavily concentrated in professional and technical areas. The ID index of female employment for professional and technical work, (5 per cent in 1976) had increased to 30 per cent by 1996.

Alizadeh and Harper (1995) have calculated a more complicated index of segregation, the IP index, to measure the extent of labour market sex segregation in Iran arising from the 1976 and 1986 population census data. Their results are in conformity with present results and confirm that there has been a sharp rise in occupational segregation since 1976.

To sum up: the trend in female employment in Iran since the late 1970s points to two distinct developments. First, there has been a sharp rise in the de-feminisation of employment since 1976, particularly over the period 1976 to 1986. Secondly, there has been a continuous increase in occupational sex segregation since the revolution.

The debate on female employment in Iran

A number of studies, with varying emphasis, have paid attention to the changing patterns of female employment in Iran (see, for instance, Afshar, 1985; Moghadam, 1989, 1991; Fatemeh Moghadam, 1994; and Alizadeh and Harper (1995)). These studies have identified a number of factors as explanatory variables. These factors include: decline in economic activities, methodological bias, demographic trends and ideology. Here we shall briefly refer to these debates before providing an alternative explanation.

A number of adverse external shocks in the aftermath of the revolution influenced the level of economic activities, including investment and employment (Karshenas, 1995a). A sharp decline in oil demand and later the fall in the price of

Table 9.5 Employment adjustment required for zero segregation in female-/male-dominated occupations, 1956–96

	1956		*1966*		*1976*		*1986*		*1996*	
	*F-dom.**	*M-dom.*	*F-dom.*	*M-dom.*	*F-dom.*	*M-dom.*	*F-dom.*	*M-dom.*	*F-dom.*	*M-dom.*
Professional & technical	2		3		5		28		30	
Administrative & managerial						<1		<1		<1
Clerical & related		2		2		1	1		1	
Sales		5		8		7	6			7
Services	12		6			1		<1		2
Agricultural & related		31		27	8			3		10
Production	27		30		<1			11		10
Miscellaneous		3		2		4		8		1
All activities	41	41	39	39	14	14	29	29	31	31

Source: As Table 9.1.

* *F-dom.* = female-dominated; *M-dom.* = male-dominated.

oil reduced the level of foreign exchange earnings upon which the economy is highly dependent. The shrinkage of oil revenue was combined with the protracted and costly war with Iraq, economic sanctions from the West, political uncertainty, the rapid increase in the working age of the population and the increasing flood of refugees from Afghanistan (Amirahmadi, 1990; Karshenas, 1995a).

The decline in investment and the rising rate of unemployment in the post-revolutionary period are in sharp contrast to the rapid growth of the economy that was experienced during the 1960s and 1970s. Unemployment figures are presented in Tables 9.2a and 9.2b. It is clear that unemployment in 1986 increased sharply to 14.1 per cent from only 3 per cent in 1976 (see Tables 9.2a and 9.2b).

The rapid growth of the economy in the pre-revolutionary period was accompanied by the implementation of a vigorous policy of import substitution which was financed and fuelled by increasing income from oil exports as well as easy availability of foreign aid and loans (Alizadeh, 1985).

Moghadam (1989, 1991) and Alizadeh and Harper (1995) have acknowledged the importance of economic conditions. However, the question remains as to why a deterioration in economic circumstances should lead to a subsequent decline in female employment. In fact the deterioration of economic conditions in many developing countries has been accompanied by the replacement of male workers with 'cheap' female workers. The literature on feminisation also points to this conclusion. It is well known that with a worsened economic situation more family members, particularly among the low income groups, are forced to seek paid employment to compensate for declining family income (Cagatay and Ozler,

1995). Deterioration in economic conditions can, however, affect female employment, particularly in circumstances where the ideology of 'male bread winner' is deeply ingrained.

It has been suggested that the sharp decline in female employment in the post-revolutionary period might be largely due to the prevalence of 'methodological bias' in census data (Moghadam, 1991), where a large number of women, particularly in agriculture, may not be counted and are consequently underrepresented in the employment data. While this possibility cannot be totally ruled out there is no indication that the methodological procedure used in the 1986 census differed in any way from the earlier period. Furthermore, the decline in female employment in the production and agriculture sectors was not, on the whole, incompatible with the pattern of output in these sectors (Alizadeh and Harper, 1995).

Another explanation given for the changing pattern of female employment after the revolution is government demographic policies (Afshar, 1985; Moghadam, 1991; Alizadeh and Harper, 1995). The rapid increase in the fertility rate and the subsequent population explosion was induced in response not only to the state's increased ideological emphasis on 'motherhood' but also to the government's opposition to family planning, which continued up until the late 1980s (Moghadam, 1991). There was a sharp decline in the activity rate of women of child-bearing age over the period 1976–86. Nevertheless it is difficult to identify the direction or causation of this phenomenon and to assess the extent to which the lack/reduction of employment opportunities for women contributed to the increased population growth. In the absence of employment opportunities women depend on motherhood for status and on child labour as a strategy for survival (Ward, 1984; Moghadam, 1991).

The role of ideology in the process of nation-building

The role of Islamic ideology in shaping the pattern of female employment in Iran has been acknowledged by Afshar (1985), Moghadam (1989, 1991), Fatemeh Moghadam (1994) and Alizadeh and Harper (1995). In particular, Fatemeh Moghadam puts the focus of her analysis on the role of Islamic ideology. She argues that in Islam female sexuality is treated as a tradable object. 'In a Muslim marriage the buyer (the man) and the seller (the woman or her guardian) should agree voluntarily on the terms of the contact and on the price for her female sexuality, *mehr* … Once the transaction is completed, the owner has complete and monogamous right to the object' (op. cit., p. 84). She argues that the process of modernisation in the pre-revolutionary period was an important step towards the deregulation of female sexuality and that it had a positive impact on female employment and female social participation. The modernisation process overshadowed a long tradition of sex segregation and the seclusion of women. With the triumph of the Islamic revolution and the imposition of forced veiling in 1980 the state regulated female sexuality and undermined the earlier trends directed towards its deregulation. In her analysis, female employment is closely related to the treatment of female sexuality in Iran.

The approach to the issue of ideology in this paper does not contradict the above approach but rather has a different emphasis. The potency of the Islamic ideology will be discussed here with regard to the process of nation-building and the period in which nationhood is redefined.

Let us first clarify the relation between the role of women and Islamic ideology in the aftermath of the Iranian revolution. It is important to examine and highlight those issues, related to the position of women in society, which were raised in the Constitution drafted shortly after the revolution.

The role of women in the Islamic republic was specified in the constitution, although the constitution itself does not provide an interpretation of Islamic law (Paidar, 1995, pp. 256–67). The constitution considered the family as the main element in the identity of the Islamic nation. The constitution emphasised that the family is the fundamental unit of the Islamic society. Hence all laws and regulations should facilitate the foundation of a family and protect its stability and sanctity. In this context, as Paidar has pointed out,

> women as citizens and political beings were subjugated to women as mothers. Since the woman's role within the family was a special one, motherhood was not considered equal in status with other dimensions of womanhood. Motherhood was the essence of a woman's being and as a result all other dimensions of womanhood were conditional upon it (op.cit., p. 259).

Furthermore, the role of the state in the constitution is to act as the creator of an Islamic society which, among other things, ensures the conformity of women's position with Islamic Law. However, Islamic law was not clearly defined. As a result, women's constitutional rights were left to be determined by the state, outside the boundaries of the constitution (op. cit., p.261).

In this chapter we concur with the views of Kandiyoti (1991), Najmabadi (1991) and Paidar (1995), that the social position of women, and the form and extent of their social participation, have all been shaped by the process of nation-building and the ideological orientation of the nation-state. We further contribute to this debate by proposing that the importance of the 'women's question' diminishes with the relative developmental maturity of the nation-state.

In the process of nation-building women are likened to the mother of the nation. They are the transmitters of tradition and culture and the educators of children. Thus their social role is intimately linked to the ideological orientation of the state. However, the emphasis on the 'motherhood' aspects of the social position of women decreases as the process of nation-building proceeds and the ideological orientation of the state becomes more established.

The modern nation-state and the changing social position of women in Iran 1900–41

For centuries, women in Iran worked at home as seamstresses, spinners and weavers, or in other people's homes as maids, nannies, midwives, healers, educators, matchmakers, weavers, etc. (Paidar, 1995: Chapters 3 and 4). However, the social participation of women in education and employment, and indeed their presence in desegregated public spaces, is closely interwoven with the process of modernisation which swept through the Middle East in the nineteen and early-twentieth centuries (Jayawardena, 1986; Najmabadi, 1991; Paidar, 1995). In the late nineteenth/early-twentieth centuries, the era of progress and modernisation, the 'women's question' was central to the emerging climate of political ideas and concerns (Najmabadi, 1991; Kandiyoti, 1991).

The first drive towards modernisation in Iran found its manifestation in the constitutional revolution during the period 1905–9.[4] The Constitutional Revolution, which was driven by an urban intelligentsia derived from diverse social groups, challenged the operation of an incapacitated pre-capitalist state ruled by Qajar monarchs.[5] Constitutionalists called for a wide range of economic and social reforms which encompassed a general move towards secularism and included women's emancipation. As elsewhere in the Middle East, reformers of women's conditions emerged from the ranks of an educated, nationalist male elite (Kandiyoti, 1991). The upper-class women followed their menfolk in founding and joining secret societies and writing and delivering speeches on constitutionalism and women's emancipation. One of the principal activities of these women's groups was propaganda regarding the need for the education of girls and the establishment of all-girl schools (Jayawardena, 1986; Paidar, 1995).

Although the Constitutional Revolution succeeded in creating a system of parliamentary government, this was not accompanied by the implementation of social and economic reforms. The operation of the parliament (Majles) as legislator was seriously crippled by the absence of a strong executive power (Paidar, 1995). The number of girls' schools, however, increased, reflecting the concern with female education.

The second step towards modernisation and the emancipation of women came to the fore during the 1920s and up until the early 1940s, when the state acted as an instrument of social reforms. Reza Khan, a military man, who came to power in 1921 through a bloodless coup, deposed the Qajars in 1925 and a year later made himself king. He crushed all opposition and created a monolithic power structure with which to control the population.

Reza Shah, who ruled until 1941, established the first modern centralised state in Iran, which provided a contextual base for capitalist development. He embarked on a series of programmes of reforms aimed at modernising the economy. These reforms included; the establishment of a strong central government; establishment of a basic infrastructural network; legal and administrative reforms, including the secularisation of education and the judiciary, both of which were monopolised by the clergy during the Qajar period; and compulsory unveiling of women.

Compulsory unveiling, which was made official state policy in 1936, was done to integrate women into society and to strengthen the image of a modern nation (Paidar, 1995). It was accompanied by a series of measures to increase women's education and employment opportunities. The number of girls' schools increased considerably after the 1930s. Female employment, however, was primarily concentrated in teaching and midwifery (Paidar, 1995). No reform was introduced in the electoral law and the state did not grant suffrage to women. The extent of reform in the areas of family and marriage codes also remained limited during Reza Shah's reign.

Nevertheless, the state policy of opening the public space to women was rooted in the ideology of modernisation. Ironically the Shah's policy of crushing all opposition was executed simultaneously with his effort to 'emancipate' women.

However, the centrality of the 'women's question' during Reza Shah's reign, as well as in the earlier period of the Constitutional Revolution, coincided with the process of nation-building in Iran (Najmabadi, 1991; Paidar, 1995). The language of nationhood revolved around the notion of national progress and women's position was defined in terms of national interest. Women were linked to the nation distinctively differently from men. Paidar has elaborated this point clearly: 'Women were likened to the nation in a way different from men. Nation was automatically taken to include men and the interest of the two merged inseparably. The link between women and nation, however, had to be specified' (Paidar, 1995, p. 101). The role of women as the main pillar and the firm foundation of ethnicity, religion, language, culture and national heritage implied that they could exert enormous influence on the education of the new generation.

In other words, during the process of nation-building the role of women as biological reproducers of the nation, educators of children and transmitters of culture is central to the definition of any society.

Women's social position, 1941–79

With the forced abdication of Reza Shah in 1941 the power of the central state weakened and with it came the disintegration of the discipline that had been imposed on the female dress (Afkhami, 1994). Some women who had been forced to unveil previously, reverted to the veil. However, during the 1940s and 1950s a number of women's groups and associations were established which had the support of a growing number of urban, educated, middle-class women.

Nevertheless the 'strong state' re-emerged in 1954, following a coup which ousted the democratically elected government of Musaddeq (Katouzian, 1981; Abrahamian, 1982)

Women were given the right to vote in 1963 although the dress code remained lax. Reforms in the marriage and family codes during the 1960s and 1970s benefited urban middle-class women although the 'trickle down' effects to the majority of rural and urban women have remained controversial to this day (Afkhami, 1994).

Female employment increased rapidly in the 1960s and 1970s. This was a period of rapid economic growth which was accompanied by the implementation of a policy of import substitution due to the increasing availability of oil revenue.

However, what distinguishes this period is that, despite the implementation of various reforms to increase women's social participation, the issue of 'women' was not as central as during Reza Shah's rule. This is due to the fact that the modern state had already been formed and with it a clear definition of the social position of women. Furthermore, reforms of the family code and marriage code in the 1960s and 1970s strengthened the position of women as individual citizens rather than the 'mothers of the nation'.

The popular revolution of 1979 and the redefinition of nationhood

The most significant and long-lasting impact of the popular revolution of 1979, and indeed its aftermath, was the redefinition of nationhood, which was simultaneously accompanied by the Islamicisation of gender relations. The decline in female employment opportunities in Iran in the post-revolutionary period is a clear reflection of this change.

The change in state ideology heralded by the Islamic republic was accompanied by the redefinition of the role and the position of women within the society. The Islamic constitution which was ratified in 1980 articulated the concept of women's rights within an Islamic context. Article 20 of the constitution specified that men and women enjoy equal protection under the law in keeping with Islamic principles (Esfandiari, 1994). The terminology 'inkeeping with Islamic principles', as was mentioned earlier, was not clearly defined. However it was interpreted at the time to indicate that Islam bars women from serving in certain professions, such as the judiciary, and from occupying any leadership positions. The theological reasoning behind this interpretation is that there are 'natural' differences between the sexes which should be taken into consideration. That is, the conformity of Islamic law with the purpose of divine or natural creation requires the acknowledgement of 'natural 'differences between the sexes (Afkhami, 1994).

One of the most significant changes to occur after the revolution was the enforcement of an Islamic dress code for women in offices and public places. The forced veiling has remained intact to this day. The Islamic republic, once firmly established, showed enormous concern with the Islamicisation of women and the reinforcement of the various aspects of Islamic gender relations, including safeguarding the Islamic family and legitimising gender-based discrimination in employment and education (Paidar, 1995). The total exclusion of women from employment was not politically feasible. This was partly because of their active role during the revolution, partly because their social support was essential for the preservation of the Islamic state during the protracted war with Iraq (which ended in 1988) and partly because of the skills requirements of a modern Islamic state (see below).

Furthermore, the acute skills shortage which has prevailed since the revolution, following the flight of many skilled and educated people from the country, made female employment in white-collar occupations indispensable for narrowing the skills gap.

Nevertheless, women were excluded from certain fields of employment and education. A large number of university fields of study were closed to women. Also, women working in factories were dismissed or encouraged to quit their job after the revolution (Moghadam, 1992). Women in the civil service who had a senior decision-making position were soon purged or given early retirement after the revolution (Esfandiari, 1994). The new labour law in 1982 also made female employment conditional on the husband's consent unless a woman had been in employment prior to marriage and the prospective husband had agreed to the continuation of her employment.

Attempts to segregate public spaces and the enforced veiling of women in the Islamic Republic are reminiscent of the desegregation of public sphere and enforced unveiling of women during the Reza Shah's reign. In both instances, change in the social position of women has been central to the redefinition of nationhood and the nation-state.

Islamic ideology and occupational sex segregation

How can the heavy concentration of women in the professional and technical areas of the work force be explained? Why has the decline in female employment been concentrated in agriculture and manufacturing sectors?

The lack of segregative data does not allow for the study of the structure of occupations within each major category. Casual empiricism, however, indicates that female employment within professional and technical occupations has been increasingly redirected towards certain professions and away from others. There are numerous examples of female engineers, architects, agronomists and judges who have been unable to find employment in their field and have turned to the teaching profession instead (Paidar, 1995). Nevertheless, the complete physical segregation of occupations has not been feasible due to the skills shortage.

Indeed, 'selective discrimination' has been an important factor in shaping the pattern of female employment during the post-revolutionary period. Selective discrimination has also been vigorously applied to the area of female education. Women up until recently were barred from studying in most fields of engineering and agronomy, which were considered incompatible with a woman's role as wife and mother. These are occupations which required substantial direct contact with men. Women are still considered unsuitable (i.e. too emotional) to take up judiciary occupations, although recently, they have been allowed to become assistant judges. In contrast, women's education and employment in certain fields such as teaching, nursing, midwifery, medical practice and social work has been actively encouraged.

The most likely reason for the deliberate encouragement of these occupations amongst women is that these are indispensable for the reproduction of physical sex segregation in the context of a modern economy (Alizadeh and Harper, 1995; Paidar, 1995).Training women to train other women is indispensable for preserving sex segregation. For segregation to be operational there is an acute need to train women teachers, doctors, nurses, midwives, social workers, etc., to serve other women. These are also occupations in which sexual segregation does not pose a heavy cost on employers. For example, female teachers are appointed to teach in girls' schools.

In the manufacturing and agriculture sectors segregation of male and female workers is costly at plant/farm level since it entails duplication of machinery and equipment, workshops and supervisors. Therefore women are either discouraged from taking up employment in these fields, are pressurised to quit their jobs or are provided with financial incentives to retire early.

Conclusion and recent trends

This study has indicated that the process of feminisation/de-feminisation in Iran has been closely interweaved with the process of nation-building /redefinition of nationhood. It was shown that a sharp rise in the de-feminisation of employment, which has been concurrent with a continuous increase in occupational sex segregation, has altered the structure of employment and occupations since 1976. However, more recent trends point to a modest increase in female employment.

What about the future? There is general consensus that the question of 'women' and their social position is still central to the Islamic Republic. However, recent trends indicate that selective discrimination against women's employment and education is on the decline. In fact a large number of university fields which were previously closed to women since the revolution have recently been reopened to them. Also, recent enthusiasm concerning women's participation in sports events in the Islamic Republic indicates that the image of women as individual citizens, rather than simply mothers and wives, has started to emerge. It is likely that women's social participation, including their engagement in formal employment, will increase in the future. However, it remains to be seen whether or not increased feminisation will reduce occupational segregation. Recent legislation concerning gynaecological problems aims at the medical segregation of women. Women should be treated by female gynaecologists unless under very special circumstances (*Zanan*, 40, 41). This trend, if it prevails, surely points in the direction of further sex segregation.

Notes

1 For certain individual countries like Sweden and the USA this ratio increased much faster than the average and for countries like Greece the growth of female employment lagged behind. For Sweden and the USA, over the period 1950 to 1980, the ratio of women's to men's labour force participation increased from 35.9 per cent to 76.5 per cent and 39.1 per cent to 67.7 per cent respectively. For Greece this ratio increased from 27.7 per cent to 34 per cent over the same period (see Blau and Ferber, 1992: 300–4, Table 10.1).

2 Feminisation is not a universal phenomenon. See, for instance, Cagatay and Berik (1991), and Elson (1996). However it can be considered as an 'expected' pattern of female employment.

3 In a study of female employment in the Middle East and north Africa, Karshenas has shown that the level of female employment in Iran is below that of several other Middle Eastern and north African countries (see Karshenas 1995b).

4 During the age of expansion of imperialist power in the nineteen century, Iran was not a formal colony. However, the expansionist ambitions of the Russian imperial power in

central Asia and the determination of the British to protect their interests in India (which then bordered with Iran) turned Iran into a sphere of influence and domination by these foreign powers. The Constitutional Revolution stemmed from the twin roots of this relationship with the West, which on one hand resulted in domination and manipulation of the Iranian economy and polity and on the other generated enthusiasm for Western institutions and technical progress (Paidar, 1995; Abrahamian, 1968, 1982).

5 Monarchs of the Qajar, who ruled Iran from 1796 until 1925, faced several military defeats which undermined their sovereignty and independence. Consequently they granted increasing concessions to European traders which undermined the interest of Persian merchants and handicraft producers (Abrahamian, 1982). Qajar monarchs were incapable of: preserving national sovereignty; safeguarding the interest of Persian merchants against European traders; shielding home industry from foreign competition; catering for the basic infrastructural needs of the economy and providing an institutional framework for economic progress (Abrahamian, 1968, 1982).

Part IV

The limits of theocracy

The globalization process is moving rapidly forward. The European Union is a case in point; however, the single currency debate amongst a few European countries has not yet been settled. The paradox between modern and traditional forces remains, precariously balanced because the traditional structure of power politics would generally prefer the status quo and is very uncertain about losing its grip on the present system. Changing the business structure of traditional societies and integrating them into the wider world is not an easy task. In the process of change, traditional forces will become more transparent and gradually, for their own survival, may destabilize government or resort to serious struggle in order to reinforce the status quo. Iran as a developing nation is in the process of experiencing such a challenge between the forces: those crying out for reform and the dominant forces who are against losing their control on society.

Since the election of President Mohammad Khatami in May 1997, the conflict between the two forces is apparent. The reformists consist of at least 16–17 political groups, they are more or less educated and are flexible in terms of Iran's development. They are very much for change and modernization: the main aims of all these groups are consistent with President Khatami's election campaign. In other words, the voice of all these groups can be categorized as the voice of liberal democracy in Iran. They are concerned with Iran's modernization process and its role in the international community of nations. They would like to improve Iran's image in the world and employ all their efforts to stop the brain drain and persuade the exiled Iranians to come back home and contribute to the development of Iran. Opposing them are the conservatives or traditionalists, comprising various right-wing conservatives and orthodox Islamicist groups with very traditionalist views of business and bazaar. They are supporters of the black-market, of a price-fixing monopoly on export and import of basic necessities, and are extreme in their religious attitude.

In this part, Chapter 10 focuses on Iranian return migration as it is perceived by Iranians in southern California. The results of the study showed 17.2 per cent of respondents who had no problem living in the United States never considered returning or decided to return home to Iran.This may seem to be a rational response. Yet it is interesting to point out that 41.4 per cent of the respondents who were encountering one or two serious problems whilst living in the United States still did not consider returning home as a realistic and viable option. The possible explanation for this is that although those problems may have been serious enough to be considered as a serious 'push factor' for return migration, yet 'pull factors', on the part of the Iranian government have not been strong enough to make return migration for these Iranians a realistic option. Despite numerous appeals from the Iranian authorities, calling for the return of Iranian professionals, no response is forthcoming. The Iranian government does not seem to have a policy on return migration or for the reintegration of returnees within Iranian society.

Chapter 11 argues that Iran's political maturity demands political parties as a necessity for political development. The 23 May 1997 election result was a clear message from the people who peacefully and effectively expressed their discontent over their government's shortcomings. This chapter also attempts to analyse the importance of political parties as a crucial instrument for people to convey their messages to candidates and thus for voters' views to be reflected in the Majles. The Islamic Republic's evolution toward democracy will depend on the establishment of fully functioning political parties and the institutionalization of political pluralism. While the constitution of the Islamic Republic guarantees the existence of parties, the ruling clerics have prevented them, for being a potential threat to the existing order. Chapter 12 examines the development of political groups, the process of the election of the sixth Majles deputies, and looks at the reformist groups who supported Khatami during his campaign and how they gained an upper hand in the Majles election. Now their mandate from the people is to improve the economy and help the government, through new legislation, provide jobs for approximately three million unemployed young people. This chapter also provides a survey of the various political groups and their backgrounds, and an evaluation of the election techniques of the conservative groups.

10 How Iranians view their return migration to Iran

Hossein Adibi

After the cessation of the Iran–Iraq war by the UN Security Council in August 1989 and Rafsanjani's first-term of presidency, there was a genuine attempt by the ruling clergy not only to improve the image of the Islamic Republic in the world, but also to light the candle of hope and create a climate of trust and reconciliation for millions of Iranians who were forced into exile. It is estimated that about four million Iranians have scattered around the Western world since the revolution of 1979. The involuntarily migrated Iranian has played a significant role in the poor image of the Islamic Republic at home and abroad. The largest migrated Iranian community is concentrated in the state of California. In this chapter Adibi provides us with a precise picture of Iranians' perception of the compulsion to return to Iran. In so doing, his study highlights one of the major stumbling blocks that remains to improving the image of the Islamic government in the face of all the recent global changes: the need for highly qualified workers to secure development. The evidence given here indicates that the Islamic Republic has failed even to gain the trust of those who might be encouraged to return to Iran.

The chapter primarily focuses on the perceptions of Iranians living in southern California. The principal research method was a lengthy, detailed self-administered questionnaire containing 94 questions.

Using a process of accidental sampling, 116 respondents from various professional, religious, social and cultural organisations as well as the business community participated in the survey. However, there are reasons to believe that the members of this sample are reasonably representative of in the broader population of professionals in the United States.

The results of this study indicate that 17.2 per cent of respondents who had no problem living in the United States never considered returning home. This may seem to be a rational response. Yet it is interesting to note that 41.4 per cent of the respondents who were encountering at least one or two serious problems whilst living in the United States did not consider returning home as a realistic, viable option. The possible explanation for this is that although their problems were serious enough, as is explained in the paper in full detail, and could be considered as serious 'push factors' for return migration, yet the 'pull factors' from the Iranian society and Iranian government were not strong enough to make return migration a realistic option. Despite appeals from the Iranian authorities from time to time calling for professionals to return, the Iranian government does not seem to have a policy on return migration, or indeed for the reintegration of returnees with Iranian society.

Background

Migrations are as old as human history, but they took on a new form and volume as the capitalist world market began to emerge. Early colonialism led to the emigration of Europeans to the New World, as well as to forced movements of labour: slaves or indentured workers for the plantations, mines and construction projects of the Americas, Africa and Asia.

Most studies on migration tend to focus on immigrants in the host countries where issues of alienation and assimilation predominate (Eisenstadt, 1954; Gordon, 1964; Bownkerk, 1974; Bottomley, 1992; Hannerz, 1992; Basch *et al.*, 1994). However, in the past few years, social scientists have increasingly noted that immigrants live their lives across borders and maintain ties to home, even when their countries of origin and settlement are geographically distant. Thus, study of return migration has become a distinct field in the contemporary world.

Return migration is not a new phenomenon. In 1885 Rawnstein proposed his laws of migration indicating that migrants move from areas of low opportunity to areas of high opportunity. Rawnstein (1885) further observed that each stream of rural–urban migration produces a counter-stream of return migration back to rural areas.

Although migration in the contemporary world may have different features, the process is very similar and taking place on a larger scale as international or transnational migration (King, 1986). Return migration has always been part of the process. In fact, immigrants have been heading back to Europe from the earliest days of the rush to the New World. Between 1908 and 1923, there were 9,949,740 immigrants from many countries of the world entering the United States and 3,498,185 leaving the country. Wyman (1993, p. 11) suggests that the return rate among all groups was 35 per cent for the period.

Today, at the dawn of the twenty-first century, not only is this trend continuing, but it has become one of the major population movements due to globalization and transnationalism.

Mass migration and growing ethnic diversity are changing the contemporary world. The central idea is that these developments cannot be understood as a number of isolated events or situations, but rather as Castle and Miller (1993) put it, as part of an overall global system, in which population movements are closely linked to economic, political and environmental changes. Therefore, population movement is an integral part of globalization, in constant interaction with the economic, political, cultural and other aspects.

Thus, one of the current debates in sociology of migration deals with globalization of cultures (Stahl *et al.*, 1993), the breakdown of the 'grand narrative' of the Enlightenment (modernity, liberalism and socialism) and the emergence of multiple identity based on gender, ethnicity, sexual preference and other criteria (Giddens, 1991).

In this context the idea of the diaspora is important in understanding changes in identity and culture brought about by migration. Increasingly, it is being used in relation not only to historical diasporas like those of the Africans, Jews, Greeks, Armenians, Assyrians and Kurds, but also to refer to other national groups such as Iranians who migrated to various destinations around the world. The concept of diaspora implies that migrants do not simply assimilate, even over long periods, but maintain long-lasting personal, cultural and economic links with each other and with the homeland.

It is in this context that the author endeavoured to study Iranians' return migration. The aim of the study is to describe, analyse and document the views of the Iranians living in Southern California, on their return migration to Iran.

Theoretical framework

In studying international migration there have been two approaches. The first perspective has considered the social elements of migration in isolation of one another. The elements have not been viewed as parts of a single, integrated complex of changes acting together to produce a particular outcome.

For example, the demographic approach deals with fertility, mortality and other demographic indicators, while the economic approach treats the potential migrants as economically rational actors and migration as a means of allocating workers between areas of low and high wages (Todaro, 1976). The cultural approach considers cultural complexes as prime determinants of behaviour; the historical approach treats migration as an evolutionary phenomenon; the psychological approach deals with individuals' motives to migrate.

None of these theories, however, is dealing specifically with international migration and providing an operational approach to study the growing international migration. Most of the existing migration models (such as Rawnstein's Laws of Migration, 1885; Lee's Theory of Migration (push–pull factors), 1966; and Todaro's Model of Rural–Urban Migration, 1976) aim to analyse the movement of relatively unskilled workers based on the following grounds:

1. existence of marked differences in labour market conditions between countries of origin and destination;
2. modes and standards of living;
3. desires and attitudes of migrants to improve the quality of their lives.

Although these theories provide a broad framework to understanding the general trend in population movement, they are inadequate for explaining the migration of highly skilled and qualified people in an international context and of Iranian migrants and refugees to the US.

The international migration of highly skilled people has been described in various terms, such as 'brain drain' which is regarded as a more or less permanent move (Barry and Goodin; 1992, Davis; 1982, Ghosh, 1985). 'Brain exchange' is also used, by Salt and Findlay (1989) to describe the movement of a large number of highly skilled workers. Thomas-Hope (1986), Bartlett and Sumantra (1989), and Appleyard (1989) use 'professional transients' to describe this movement. Ghosh (1985) distinguishes between brain overflow and brain drain: conditions for brain overflow occur where the country trains more people than it can effectively employ; this brain overflow may be good for a developing country with high educated unemployment while brain drain may be bad for a country with manpower shortages, and especially for a developing country.

Although these theories may deal with the present international migration in some ways, providing adequate explanation of the Iranian return migration requires the adaptation of a different theoretical framework. The Iranian immigration, in addition to its demographic and substantive significance, provides a theoretically interesting, deviant case of immigrant adaptation without a visible residential or commercial centre in southern California.

The second approach to the study of international migration provides clear direction for adequate explanation and considers international migration as a dynamic and cumulative process originating in structural transformation of sending and receiving societies (Massey, 1987).

This approach has been considered as the major theoretical framework for studying Iranian migration to the United States. The major components of this approach include:

a structural change of Iranian society;
b cumulative and social networks of Iranians in the US.

The structural change of Iranian society relates to the speeding pace of modernisation and economic development in Iran in 1960s and 1970s and the substantial change of the political structure in 1979 as the Islamic government came to power.

In the 1960s and 1970s a growing number of the Iranian new middle class had the opportunity to visit Western countries for the purpose of undertaking undergraduate or graduate studies, or a short holiday. This initial stage was very important, allowing a large number of people to experience aspects of living in a different society (Gilanshah, 1986). Later, these experiences were used as social capital in making the decision to migrate. This led to the second component, the creation of social networks which became central for sustaining the Iranian migration.

Kamalkhani (1988) explains low chain migration took place in the larger Iranian families, with the first members leaving home for Europe sometime in the early 1970s. The parents and older family members preferred to stay behind and, if forced to leave, were at first reluctant and felt more isolated abroad than the younger migrants. Having a close relative abroad strengthens the motivation for other family members who have been living under various constraints either to join the migrants or to ask for their support.

The Iranian mass migration of the 1980s eventually developed a social infrastructure that enabled movement on a mass basis (Ansari, 1992). The range of social contacts in this network expanded with the entry of each new migrant. Thus, Iranian international migration has become more widely accessible and increasingly adopted by families as part of a wider strategy for survival. Today Iranian migration to the United States has become a self-sustaining social process.

In analysing the state of Iranian migration including return migration, to a larger extent if not totally, the emphasis has been put on the first component of this framework: namely, the structural change of Iranian society (Lorentz and Wertime, 1980; *Iran Times*, 1984; Bozorgmehr, 1992). Thus it is the contribution of this study to provide an answer to why Iranian return migration is not occurring in significant numbers. While the framework acknowledges the importance of the structural change in Iranian society, it focuses on the significance of social capital network and the process of self-sustainment of the international migration of Iranians. Based on this framework, it is possible to foresee that even with the desired structural change in the political power relation in Iran, the rate of return migration will not be great. Within this context, it is necessary to understand why Iranians who may face great difficulties living in the United States prefer not to return to Iran so long as the present state of affairs endures.

Population sample

Iranians residing in southern California constitute the study population. It was not possible for this study to have a probability sample, because an ideal sample design would have been to select Iranian households in an area probability sample of housing units. Assuming that Iranian families constitute less than one per cent of housing units in the Los Angeles–Long Beach area, there was a need to screen at least 100,000 housing units in order to obtain a probability sample of about 1,000 Iranian families. Therefore, my population sample is based on what is called 'convenience sampling' by Camilleri (1941) or 'accidental sampling' by Dane (1990). That is, my population sample is based on self-selective respondents and not on probability sampling.

In this study 116 respondents – 72 male and 44 female participated in completing a questionnaire containing 94 questions. I also conducted informal interviews with more than 100 people including academics, students, housewives, businesspeople, medical practitioners, young people, journalists, the elderly, taxi drivers, the unemployed, labourers and professionals. Participant observation was also used throughout the course of investigation with the intention to use this opportunity to observe the intimate relationships and community life of the immigrants. I also made contact with 39 Iranian cultural, educational, religious, community and professional organisations in southern California for the purpose of gathering information.

Instrument

The principal technique for research in this study was a lengthy, detailed self-administered questionnaire, containing 94 questions. These were divided into sections on psychological problems, educational concerns, push and pull factors in emigration decisions, demographic data, future plans, and views on return migration.

Hypothesis

I was attempting to test the following hypothesis:

1 When migration as a process takes place, the process becomes a self-sustaining one. That is to say, during the settlement phase many immigrants may find adjustment to be a very painful process. However, once they have a feeling that they have been relatively adjusted, it is not easy for them to make a decision to return home, even though there may be good news about their home country.
2 If migrants are facing difficulties in establishing and adjusting to their new lives in the host country, it is more likely that they will consider and make the decision to return to their home country.
3 If the situation in the home country is not encouraging and there is no attraction to return, the migrants, despite having difficult times, prefer to face and tolerate difficulties in the hope for a better future in the host country, and not make the decision to return to the home country.

Describing data

The general characteristics of the sample population were as follows:

Gender Iranian immigrants who participated in this study comprised 62 per cent male and 38 per cent female.

Age The age distribution of sample members reveals that 63 per cent of the respondents were in the age group of 36 to 55; 18.2 per cent between 25 to 36; and 18.8 per cent over 55 years of age.

Employment 62 per cent of respondents were employed, 5.2 per cent were unemployed, 8.6 per cent were retired, and 24.1 per cent did not respond to this question. Comparing the unemployment rate with the general unemployment rate in the US (10 per cent) and that in Australia (12 per cent), or with the unemployment rate of Iranians in Australia (30 per cent) this figure is particularly low. However, compared with the unemployment rate of 1.9 per cent in the 1988 Survey of Iranian Migrants Economy, it is nearly three times higher (Bozorgmehr and Sabagh,1988).

Marital status 16.4 per cent of respondents were single, 58.6 per cent were married, 17.2 per cent divorced (20.4 per cent of women and 15.2 per cent of men), 3.4 per cent separated, 1.7 per cent widowed and 1.8 per cent cohabiting.

Religious affiliation Of the sample 50 per cent were Muslim, 8.6 per cent Jewish, 0.9 per cent Christian, 3.4 per cent Zoroastrian, 3.4 per cent Baha'i, 25 per cent had no religious belief and 2.6 per cent believed in God only.

Income 27.6 per cent of the respondents had annual income of $26,000 and less, 24.1 per cent between $26,001 and $50,000; 33.6 per cent, $50,000 and over, and 14.7 per cent did not respond to this question (see Table 10.1). Of particular interest is the upper sample: 33.6 per cent with an income of $50,000 and above. This becomes very pronounced when we compare it with Iranians in Australia, where only 0.3 per cent had an annual income of $50,000 and above (Adibi, 1994). In order to investigate the relationship of income with education, occupation, residency period, home ownership and other factors, further analysis has been carried out.

Educational attainment 24.1 per cent of the respondents had PhD/MD qualifications, 56 per cent had a university degree (BA, BS or MS), 4.3 per cent had Associate Diplomas, 9.5 per cent graduated from high school and 6 per cent did not respond to this question.

In order to test the assumption that there is a strong association between income and educational attainment and qualifications, the author attempted to cross-tabulate these two factors. By cross-tabulating income by educational qualifications, it became evident that 3.6 per cent of those who attained a university degree or above had an annual income of $50,000 and over; and 63 per cent of high-school graduates had an income of $26,000 or less. Table 10.2 provides information on income distribution by education. It shows that only those participants who held a university

Table 10.1 Annual income of sample population of Iranians in southern California

	Female		*Male*		*Total*	
		(%)		*(%)*		*(%)*
$0–$8,999	4	(9)	8	(11.1)	12	(10.3)
$9,000–$17,999	4	(9)	7	(9.7)	11	(9.5)
$18,000–$25,999	3	(6.8)	6	(8.3)	9	(7.8)
$26,000–$39,999	4	(9)	11	(15.2)	15	(12.9)
$40,000–$49,999	6	(13.6)	7	(9.7)	13	(11.2)
$50,000+	14	(31.8)	25	(34.7)	39	(33.6)
No response	9	(20.4)	8	(11.1)	17	(14.7)
Total	44	(100)	72	(100)	116	(100)

Table 10.2 Annual income of sample population by education (%)

	University degree and higher	*Associate and high school diploma*	*Total*
Up to $25,999	20.6	6.9	27.5
$26,000–$49,999	19.8	4.3	24.1
Over $50,000	33.6	–	33.6
No response	4.7	10.1	14.8
Total	78.7	21.3	100.0

degree or higher had an annual income of over $50,000. The table also shows that 20.6 per cent of those with a university degree had an annual income of $26,000 or less; the remaining 19.8 per cent holding a university degree had an annual income between $26,001 and $49,999. Another observation that can be made is that those who did not hold a degree had an annual income of $50,000 or less.

Considering income and age, data reveals that one fifth of respondents with $50,000 annual income were in the age range of 36–55 years.

This data, however, does not indicate whether people with higher qualifications had occupations related to their university studies. On the other hand, the strong relationship between higher qualification and income indicates that, even in the cases where higher qualification was not related to occupation, it was nevertheless indirectly related and resulted in higher income. This seems to confirm the findings of previous studies (Askari *et al.*, 1977; Ansari, 1977) and is borne out by other immigrant groups (Bean and Browning, 1984; Light and Bonacich, 1988).

Discussion

In studying the views of Iranians on their return migration, several questions were asked of the respondents. The aim was to test the hypothesis and identify the forces influencing people's attitudes and views towards return migration.

It was assumed that Iranians who are facing difficulties and hardship living in the United States are more likely to consider the decision to return home than those who have fewer difficulties.

The problems centred around six significant areas including: language, housing, employment, income, communication and social isolation, and family. The respondents were asked to indicate if they are facing any of the above problems. The responses were as follows:

- 17.2 per cent of respondents stated that they had no problem;
- 54.3 per cent had faced only one problem;
- 16.4 per cent had faced two problems;
- 11.3 per cent had faced three or more problems;
- 0.8 per cent did not answer this question.

Table 10.3 Migrants' inclination to return by number of difficulties faced

	Consideration of/decision to return									
Difficulties	*Once*		*Few times*		*Often*		*Never*		*Total*	
		(%)		*(%)*		*(%)*		*(%)*		*(%)*
None	1	(0.9)	3	(2.6)	2	(1.7)	20	(17.2)	26	(22.5)
1	11	(9.5)	6	(5.2)	3	(2.6)	37	(31.9)	57	(49.1)
2	2	(1.7)	3	(2.6)	3	(2.6)	11	(9.5)	19	(16.4)
3	2	(1.7)	2	(1.7)	5	(4.3)	5	(4.3)	14	(12)
Total	16	(13.8)	14	(12.1)	13	(11.2)	73	(62.9)	116	(100)

Table 10.3 examines whether there is any meaningful association between experiencing problems and returning to Iran. As the table indicates, 17.2 per cent of respondents with having no difficulties did not consider returning, nor make any decision to return, to Iran.

This supports the earlier assumption and seems to be a rational decision. However, it is interesting to observe that 31.9 per cent of respondents were having a major difficulty and 9.5 per cent who faced two major problems had not made any decision to return to Iran.

One explanation for this would be that although any of the six areas could give rise to serious problems and exercise great pressure on migrants to return to Iran in search of a better alternative, there was a lack of incentive on the part of Iranian society.

Since the migrants were not political asylum-seekers, other factors must have been discouraging them to return. It appears that existence of the dress code and a lack of social freedom could be considered as the major barriers in this respect.

The responses to the questionnaire indicated that 62.1 per cent of participants considered the lack of social freedom and the existence of the dress code, especially for women, as serious factors and barriers for not considering returning home. This would seem an expected, logical explanation. However, it must be emphasised that 37.9 per cent of participants did not consider lack the of social freedom and the existence of the dress code as a significant factor influencing their views towards their return.

Since the dress code for women has been highlighted and discussed so much in the Western media, giving the impression that it is the most important factor barring Iranian women's return to Iran, it was decided to test the validity of this prevailing belief. Thus Table 10.4 has been constructed to document and compare the views of Iranian women and men on the dress code: *chador*.

As the table indicates, 66 per cent of women and 59.5 per cent of men considered the female dress code and the lack of social freedom as major barriers to considering and making a decision to return home. On one hand, this supports the prevailing belief in the West. On the other hand, there is strong evidence that the climate of opinion is changing.

Table 10.4 Sample population considering female dress code as a barrier to returning home

	Considered as a barrier		*Not considered as a barrier*		*Total*	
		(%)		*(%)*		*(%)*
Female	29	(65.9)	15	(34.1)	44	(100)
Male	43	(59.7)	29	(40.3)	72	(100)
Total	72	(62.1)	44	(37.9)	116	(100)

As the table indicates, 34.1 per cent of females and 40.1 per cent of males did not consider women's dress code and the lack of social freedom as a major obstacles to returning to Iran. There are two possible explanations for this – the first is that this group of respondents held Islamic values, therefore did not constitute a serious barrier for them in adjusting to the new environment. The second explanation is that this group of respondents is concerned with more pressing matters of everyday life than the existing dress code.

In analysing the 'push factors', it was intended to test if there is a relationship between the level of job satisfaction and the decision to return. The data indicates that 12.1 per cent of respondents were very satisfied with their jobs, 43.1 per cent were satisfied, 18.1 per cent were dissatisfied and 6.9 per cent were very dissatisfied. A further 19.8 per cent did not respond to the question of job satisfaction. In all 52.6 per cent of all categories had not considered returning or made any decision to return to Iran. Thus, the data shows that there is no significant relationship between the level of job satisfaction and the decision to return.

It was also considered that home ownership may have an influence on the decision to return. Data indicates that 50 per cent of respondents owned their accommodation, 34.5 per cent were tenants, and 15.5 per cent were living with family or friends, or did not provide information in this area.

Data also shows that 63.2 per cent of landlords did not make a decision to return. In contrast, 36.8 per cent of landlords did consider and make a decision to return, but none was carried out. It is also interesting to note that 42.5 per cent of tenants did not make any decision to return. Analysis of data indicates that home ownership has exercised some influence on views of not returning. However, home ownership cannot be considered to be a major determining factor and barrier for the participants to return home.

The study also intended to explore the level of agreement between spouses in relation to return migration. The responses showed that 23.3 per cent of respondents were in complete agreement on considering and making the decision to return or not to return to Iran. However, there was no agreement between 24.1 per cent of couples. A further 41.4 per cent of respondents did not respond to this question, of whom 40.5 per cent were single, divorced or separated from their spouses. Thus, the data indicates that one of the major sources of arguments between one third of the respondents was related to the issue of whether or not to return to Iran.

In fact, the arguments were not a recent phenomenon – rather they began from the outset as participants started to establish their lives in the United States. About 31.9 per cent of respondents were hoping to return to Iran during or after the first year of living in the US. About 17.2 per cent were hoping to return to Iran after two years, and 28.4 per cent were hoping to return after five years. Only 17.8 per cent, while hoping to return to Iran, did not plan any specific duration for their stay. Among all respondents, only 14.7 per cent never hoped or considered returning to Iran.

This data suggests that a great majority of respondents left Iran with the intention of returning in the near future. It is interesting that while this psychological state has significantly influenced their adjustment process (Hojat and Herman, 1985), the intention in most cases was never fulfilled.

In terms of how this psychological state influenced immigrant's views about their future, responses to the questionnaire indicate that 19 per cent believed they were certain to have a very bright future in America. A large number, some 41.4 per cent, believed they would have a relatively certain future; 31.9 per cent perceived their future in America to be uncertain; and 6.9 per cent responded that they held no idea or hope hope for their future.

The data further indicates that 38.8 per cent of respondents were confused about their future and saw it as gloomy with no plan. It seems logical to assume that this group would be more willing to return to Iran than submit themselves to an uncertain future by living in America. Table 10.5 tests this assumption. A few observations can be made from this table.

The first observation is that only one-third of the respondents had considered and attempted to reach a decision on returning home, or made a decision to return home, but not carried it out.

Second, about one-third of people with uncertain futures considered and made the decision to return home but did not carry it out.

Third, only a quarter of those with no idea about their future attempted to make a decision about returning but again none was fulfilled.

One of the explanations for this is that although people faced gloomy and uncertain futures living in the United States, the 'pull factors' and attractions of Iranian society have not been strong enough to seriously encourage Iranian professionals to make the decision to return home.

Table 10.5 Future expectations of sample population in relation to decision to return home

Type of future	*Considering return*		*Not considering return*		*Total*	
		(%)		*(%)*		*(%)*
Very certain	7	(6)	16	(13.8)	23	(19.8)
Relatively certain	15	(12.9)	33	(28.5)	48	(41.4)
Uncertain	16	(13.8)	21	(18.1)	37	(31.9)
Don't know	2	(1.7)	6	(5.3)	8	(6.9)
Total	40	(34.4)	76	(65.6)	116	(100)

The discussions in the chapter can be understood in the context of what Giddens (1991: pp. 32–3) describes as the two poles of the dialectic of the local and global in which the situations in America are constantly remaking their identity, as a part of a reflective process of connecting personal and social change. This type of analysis indicates that such processes effect everybody including Iranians in the contemporary society of mass migration, and provides a necessary context for understanding the effects of immigration on identity and culture.

Conclusion

Mass migration and growing ethnic diversity are changing the contemporary world. The central idea is that these developments can not be understood as a number of isolated events or situations. Rather, they are closely linked to economic, political and environmental changes.

The early migration of Iranians to the United States, which was due to the fast modernisation of the 1960s and 1970s, began in a relatively narrow and distinct segment of the population. However, in the early 1980s, structural transformation within Iran created an extremely volatile political economy. In contrast to the mostly upper-class origins of the first group of Iranian migrants to the United States, the majority of migrants in the post-Islamic era are drawn from more diverse origins, with many coming from the new middle class which is well integrated into the international migratory system.

Thus, the emergence of Iranian mass migration during the 1980s to the United States was made possible only by the prior development of a complex social structure that supported and encouraged it. In the post-Islamic era, many of the Iranian migrants began their trip at some point in the past and then subsequent journeys brought them up to the present. The Iranian migrant networks have been gradually built up and elaborated over the years. In the initial phases, social ties to people in the United States were few in number. Starting from this small base, they extended slowly at first, but the number of connections between the Iranian migrants and others in the community expanded rapidly. Now every Iranian migrant in the United States can claim social ties with other Iranian migrants through either kinship, friendship, '*hamshahri*' or '*hamvatan*' (fellow countrymen).

Just as dicussion of the causes of Iranian migration covers a broad range, from political persecution at home to economic migration abroad, so are the causes of return migration just as numerous.

From this study the following general points can be made:

1 In the minds of the majority of Iranian migrants themselves, the intention of returning to Iran has been present from the beginning, although the date for this return has never been defined with sufficient precision, and varies in accordance with a complex set of variables. For the majority of participants in this study, it has been a project that is continually postponed. It is important to note that the future of Iran is uncertain.

2 Repatriation is the dream of a great number of Iranian migrants, but various objective conditions and subjective situations play their part in turning this into a realistic option.
3 It is believed that a number of Iranian migrants return because of failure abroad. Unemployment, racial prejudice, increasing violence, not feeling safe on the streets at night, being caught in the 'rat-race', and personal problems also push people home. Also some of the Iranian migration was precipitated by personal crisis: the breakup of a marriage, the death of a spouse, trouble with children, or ill health. Some attribute their return more to family and personal reasons than to economic or occupational ones. Overall, it is believed that the underlying reason for most of the Iranians who express the wish to return to Iran is unsatisfactory social, cultural and economic integration in the United States.
4 Those who acquire a good occupational qualification and are entirely satisfied with their lives rarely uproot themselves and do not tend to return to Iran. This is due to the fact that migration also generates expectations of upward mobility. It should be emphasised here that continuing economic and social integration of many Iranians in the United States makes it fairly improbable that a massive return migration will flow to Iran.
5 Data presented in this chapter indicates that one-quarter to one-third of Iranian professional migrants living in the United States have considered and even made the decision to return to Iran, often more than once, but have never carried it out.
6 Although there have been a number of appeals by the Iranian authorities requesting Iranian professionals to return home, it seems no action has been taken. Both the economic and the social reintegration of returnees and the making of simple provisions for return are being hampered by a lack of understanding, at very least, of the issues of emigration and return on the part of the Iranian government. The reintegration process is taken for granted, and masked by a lack of planning and the absence of any formal policy. This has influenced re-emigration of the returnees to the United States and to other countries. However, this is not unique to Iranian migrants: other migrants from many countries have gone through the same experience (Bhach, 1985; Lieberson, 1989; Gmelch, 1992).

But one significant point in the case of Iranians should be noted: namely, the uncertainty of the Islamic government, its lack of clear policy toward returnees and its behaviour in the context of the international system. One of the crucial problems of the Islamic Republic in terms of its international image is the four million or so involuntary exiles living in the West and their perception of the Islamic government. It is quite clear, that there exists a combination of social, political, economic, professional, cultural and educational factors that together constitute a 'vocabulary of motive' for their non-return. The dilemma facing Iranian migrants is that while they may be absorbed professionally in Iran, they risk marginalisation and serious difficulties in all major spheres of life, political, social and even cultural.

11 Theocracy versus democracy

Iran considers political parties

Stephen Fairbanks

This chapter is essentially a discussion on the nature of, and the need for, political parties in Iran. So far the ruling clergy has resisted the establishment of a political platform for debate and rational discourse whereby government may be led to choose or adopt a policy in tune with public opinion. They believe that the system established by President Kohmeini based on the theory of '*velayat-e faqih*' (supreme revolutionary jurisprudence) is far superior to existing modern political systems because the power comes from God, not people.

The 1997 presidential election in Iran showed pluralism and democracy developing to an extent that many Westerners found surprising. There were limits, to be sure: the Guardian Council had to vet the candidates, approving only four out of nearly 240, and there was no room at all for secularist candidates. But beyond that, the regime was not able to control the outcome, and quite clearly the winner was not the one whom the authorities had in mind. The 23 May election result was a clear message from the people, who peacefully but effectively expressed their discontent over their government's shortcomings.

But the evolution of the Iranian system toward a fuller version of democracy will depend on the establishment of fully functioning political parties, which would institutionalize political pluralism. The constitution of the Islamic Republic guarantees the existence of parties, but the ruling clerics have long prevented them as a potential threat to the existing political order. The president, Mohammad Khatami, and other politicians supported their establishment during the election campaign, as did other politicians during the previous year's Majles (parliamentary) elections. Authorities of the regime were faced with the dilemma of how to respond to broad popular demands for a party system without losing control of the political process. If there were to be parties, who was to form them – the people or the government?

The demands of an expanding electorate

The enthusiastic participation of a new generation of voters in 1997 increased the pressures for political pluralism. Iran's youth, many previously either too young to vote or alienated from the political system, made up a large part of the 20 million who gave Khatami his surprise victory. They were joined by unprecedented numbers of women. Both groups perceived Khatami to be an agent for change. That they believed they could achieve change by means of the existing political system speaks well for the democratic process in Iran.

Khatami's backers used opinion polls – in itself a good example of Iran's democratic trend – to gauge the concerns and voting strength of the populace.[1] Since declaring in January 1997 that he would run as an independent candidate, Khatami had a much better sense than his rivals about what the voters wanted. They seemed to be weary of revolution and tired of the regime's slogans, particularly its exhortations to confront the West's 'cultural onslaught'. The polls suggested that the government was not in touch with the concerns of the people.

One such poll, published in a newspaper sympathetic to Mr Khatami, showed that voters in Isfahan were concerned more about the economy than hard-line, anti-Western values. Those polled said the government's priorities should be to ensure social justice, tackle high inflation and joblessness, and address the problems of Iran's youth. Only 15 per cent of those polled felt that it was important for Iran's leaders to confront the 'cultural onslaught' and resist accommodation with the United States.[2]

Young Iranians now sensed the possibility of having a voice in their political destiny. They could now consider the system 'as their own', observed Faezeh Hashemi, daughter of former president Ali Akbar Hashemi-Rafsanjani.[3] Khatami frequently spoke at universities, promising a 'better tomorrow' for the frustrated, jobless young. He said that a 'fresh approach to the youth issues' is one of the 'main duties of the Islamic state' – otherwise, the youth will cause serious problems for society in the future.[4] Khatami distanced himself from the faltering and unpopular campaign to 'Islamicize' the universities, a goal of the conservative faction of his chief election rival, Majles Speaker Nateq-Nuri.

Khatami also sought the increasingly important women's vote. He proclaimed women should be active in all social, political and economic activities, and said he would welcome qualified women in his cabinet if he should win the presidency.[5] 'Efforts should be made to do away with male supremacy,' he told women, contrasting himself to those who 'do not approve of this approach.'[6] Nateq-Nuri was unable to shake a reputation that he advocated stricter social and employment restrictions on them. Vicious rumors even compared him to Afghanistan's Taliban in his regard toward women. Iran's Leader of the Revolution, Ayatollah Khamene'i, favored Nateq-Nuri but seemed to sense that Iranian women voters were discontented with the status quo he represented. Khamene'i tried to allay their concerns by telling them in a nationally televized speech that women had 'permission' to become involved in all spheres. He assured them that whosoever said otherwise 'has spoken against Islam'.[7]

Great numbers of women, like the nation's youth, placed their hopes in Khatami as someone who could open up the system. His ability to signal change, no matter how cautiously, distinguished him in an election where all four candidates pledged loyalty to the system and its Leader. All four championed social welfare, promised to continue President Rafsanjani's economic policies, and studiously avoided foreign policy issues. But the always smiling Khatami gave the impression that, compared to the rival candidates, he represented a less restrictive side of Islam. His supporters believed he would improve freedoms for the media and arts and would, for example, relax the ban on home satellite dishes. And under him, his allies and supporters were certain, the Islamic Republic would also be opened to broader political participation.

A new stage in Iran's political evolution

One distinguishing aspect of the 1997 presidential election was that the major candidates were backed by quasi-party political organizations. These were not formal political parties, but their participation in the 1997 presidential election was an important step toward the eventual formation of real, functioning political parties. Along with, and probably contributing to, the greatly expanded public participation, this made the 1997 election a new stage in the evolution of the Iranian political system.

In previous presidential elections in the Islamic Republic, the candidates ran without formal, party-like affiliations. In 1993, for example, Rafsanjani ran against three little-known others, all supposedly above factional identity and not representing formal political groupings.

In 1997 the candidate favored to win the presidency, Nateq-Nuri, had been formally chosen by the most powerful political organization of clerics, the conservative Tehran Militant Clergy Association (JRM, for *Jame'eh-ye Rowhaniyat-e Mobarez*).[8] At that time, deputies associated with the JRM constituted the majority faction in the Majles, and Ayatollah Khamene'i and President Rafsanjani were prominent members.[9] Nateq-Nuri was also backed by the JRM's *bazaari* ally, the Islamic Coalition Society (*Jam'iyat-e Mo'talefeh-ye Eslami*), as well as by the Qom Theological Lecturers Association and numerous smaller clerical, professional and trade organizations.

Mohammad Khatami announced his candidacy as an independent, but picked up important endorsements from major political groupings. The Militant Clerics Society (MRM, for *Majma'-e Rowhaniyun-e Mobarez*) was the first of these. The MRM, considered 'leftist' on the Islamic Republic spectrum for its statist economics and egalitarian socialism, is not to be confused with the right-wing Militant Clergy (JRM).[10] Even further to the left, but non-clerical, the Mojahedin of the Islamic Revolution Organization and related 'Imam's Line' groups also declared support for Khatami. More important, the moderate technocrats known as the Kargozaran, established by key officials of the Rafsanjani administration, eventually declared their support for Khatami.

A third candidate, former minister of intelligence Mohammad Reyshahri, also claimed the backing of a political organization, the Society for the Defense of the Values of the Islamic Revolution. His 'society', however, had few members and appeared to be something of his own creation started shortly before the 1996 Majles elections in order to make more viable his run for the presidency. The fourth presidential candidate, Seyyed Reza Zavare'i, had no organization behind him, and garnered even fewer votes than Reyshahri.

Several of the political groups mentioned above exhibited some of the practical attributes of parties, particularly in their efforts to mobilize support for the candidates they favored. Several have their own newspapers: *Salam* serves as the organ of the Militant Clerics and *Resalat* as the mouthpiece of the Militant Clergy, and the offices of those two papers at times resembled campaign headquarters for the two leading candidates. The Kargozaran's newspaper, *Bahman*, was closed down during anti-'liberal' backlash in 1996. In 1997, though, several papers, among them *Ettela'at*, *Akhbar*, *Iran*, *Iran News*, *Tehran Times* and *Hamshahri*, in 1997 clearly favored Khatami and the positions of the technocrats even if they lacked formal affiliation. Other party 'organs' include the Mojahedin of the Islamic Revolution Organization's biweekly *'Asr-e Ma*, the Society for the Defense of the Values of the Revolution's rather sporadic organ, *Arzesh-ha*, and the Islamic Coalition Society's *Shoma*.

The political parties law

Article 26 of the Islamic Republic's 1979 constitution provides that the 'formation of parties, societies, political or professional associations, as well as religious societies, whether Islamic or pertaining to one of the recognized religious minorities, is permitted provided they do not violate the principles of independence, freedom, national unity, the criteria of Islam, or the basis of the Islamic republic.' In the tumultuous first two years of the revolution nearly a hundred political organizations suddenly sprung into being where none (other than the Shah's official parties) could function legally during the latter years of the monarchy. Their number and variety threatened to undermine the Islamic Republic, and several, such as the Tudeh Party and the Mojahedin-e Khalq Organization, opposed the clerical regime altogether. After a severe crackdown on parties authorized by Ayatollah Khomeini, a political parties law was written in 1981 to stipulate what constitutes a political party, and if and how it can function.

The new law was meant to harmonize party activity with the Islamic regime by making party formation dependent on obtaining a permit from the Ministry of the Interior. Article 10 of the law established a commission of the ministry, comprising two Majles deputies, two representatives from the judiciary and one from the Interior Ministry, that was to issue the permits. The commission was also supposed to supervise the activities of the parties and organizations it approved, and order the dissolution of parties engaged in activities contrary to the law. Offenses included activities that would undermine the foundations of the Islamic Republic or Iran's independence, or intensify conflicts within the Iranian nation.[11]

Most parties had been declared illegal well before the political parties law was passed in September 1981, and Iran had already become a one-party state under the ruling Islamic Republic Party. The IRP, which had been founded during the revolution, itself voluntarily dissolved in 1986, when its leaders, then-president Khamene'i and then-Speaker Rafsanjani, declared it no longer had any useful function. A senior founding member, Asadollah Badamchian, subsequently explained that the IRP had served its purpose, which was to save people from 'falling into the trap of the parties' at a time when political pluralism appeared to pose a mortal threat to the fledgling republic. The party was closed when there was 'no longer a need to oppose groups that were hostile and in opposition to the government and the revolution'. Also, said Badamchian, the party's three major factions – the left, the right, and a third that 'worked between the other two groups' – were finding it impossible to work together.[12]

Mehdi Bazargan's Freedom Movement (*Nehzat-e Azadi*) was allowed to continue to exist, but after the first Majles (1980–4) did not field candidates for elections. Other Islamic organizations, such as the Mojahedin of the Islamic Revolution Organization and the Islamic Coalition Society (*Jam'iyat-e Mo'talafe-ye Eslami*) ceased their activities at various times but eventually resumed a quasi-party status.

The parties law was to permit and regulate, not prevent, activities, but its implementation was continually postponed. In 1988, Interior Minister Mohtashami blamed the delay on the eight-year war with Iraq, citing 'dire and difficult circumstances in which the nation's entire power, ability, and potential was directed toward the national struggle and defense'.[13]

Once the war ended, the Interior Ministry, under pressure from the Majles, declared that parties could submit their applications for permits to the Interior Ministry from 30 December 1988 to 20 March 1989. Each group was to submit its platform and constitution. The basic requirements were allegiance to the Islamic Republic's constitution and an absence of foreign ties, but a senior ministry official also said that former SAVAK members, Freemasons, ministers of the Shah's government or officials of the Shah's Rastakhiz Party, and 'those who have lost or will lose their social rights according to court rulings based on Islamic codes' were ineligible to establish parties.[14]

Within two weeks some 28 groups had sought recognition from the Interior Ministry, including Bazargan's Freedom Movement, the Women's Society of the Islamic Republic (headed by Khomeini's daughter, Zahra Mostafavi), numerous newly formed groups such as the Islamic Jihad Party and the Islamic Futurist Party, and the Martyr Navab Safavi Party, whose members were followers of a major Islamic guerrilla group of the early 1950s.[15]

The promise of a new political era of active parties failed to materialize, however. Despite the periodic meetings of the Article 10 Commission and its announcements that various small organizations had been granted permits, as of the 1997 presidential election parties were still not a reality.

Eventually it seemed to make little difference whether a group applied for an official permit or not. The Kargozaran, for example, were active in the 1996 Majles and 1997 presidential elections without having received a permit from the Article 10 Commission. Commission head (and Islamic Coalition Society head) Asadollah Badamchian complained that the Kargozaran lacked a central council or assembly, and had no provincial branches, or even any identifiable membership. Badamchian was more lenient, however, toward Reyshahri's Society for the Defense of the Values of the Islamic Revolution, granting it a permit even though it lacked a central council or constitution.[16]

The dominant political group, the conservative JRM, functioned more like a party than any other organization, but it never bothered to apply for a permit from the Article 10 Commission. This had been a source of complaint as early as 1989, when Interior Minister Mohtashami declared that the JRM 'indulges in political activity' and was therefore required to obtain a permit.[17] Seven years later *Salam* complained that the JRM still considered itself above the law and that it considered applying for a permit to be beneath its dignity.[18]

Adding to the confusion, a member of the Article 10 Commission, 'Ali Movahedi-Savoji, said that political parties were free to be active whether they had a permit or not.[19] Ebrahim Yazdi, secretary-general of the Freedom Movement – which was barred from the 1996 and 1997 elections – scoffed at the idea that groups were free to be active without a license from the Interior Ministry. He said that freedom without security is meaningless, since unnamed 'pressure groups' effectively prevent the free activity of groups such as his.[20]

Pluralism versus monopolism in the Majles

Despite such ambiguities in party activities, several groups functioned as quasi-parties in the 1992 and 1996 Majles elections, building up precedent for the organizational support for candidates that featured in a presidential election for the first time in 1997. Majles factional politics have been described adequately elsewhere,[21] but a brief review of the organized factional role in the previous two Majles elections is needed here as a context for the trend toward forming parties in 1997.

By the 1992 Majles elections, the two major factions of political clerics, the conservative JRM and its left-wing offshoot the MRM, had organized rival campaign headquarters. Each published a list of its favored candidates for the Majles and took on at least some of the characteristics of a political party.

But political pluralism was dealt a severe blow that year when the Guardian Council decided that most of the candidates favored by the MRM, including Majles Speaker Karrubi and numerous deputies up for re-election, were unqualified to run for the Majles. President Rafsanjani was probably behind this development, intending to eliminate the 'radicals' who were blocking his free-market economic reforms.

The rout of the left-wing MRM in 1992 elections resulted in the right-wing JRM becoming a huge majority in the 1992–6 Majles. The JRM, as its opponents in the MRM and other groupings charged, became increasingly 'monopolistic' and sought to eliminate rival factions from Iranian politics. The JRM had key allies in the Guardian Council, the judiciary, and above all Ayatollah Khamene'i, who used the conservative Majles to exert his personal dominance over Rafsanjani. The conservatives also controlled three ministries vital for domestic affairs – Interior, Intelligence and Security, and Culture and Islamic Guidance – and controlled the state radio and television.

When the MRM declared the atmosphere 'unfavorable' and declined to run in the 1996 Majles elections (other than for a few provincial seats), the JRM and allied conservative groups looked forward to a lock on power. They were confident of a single-faction Majles in 1996 whose leader, Speaker Nateq-Nuri, would be elected president in 1997. Both branches of the government would be in line with the Leader, Khamene'i, the Guardian Council, and the judicial branch.

Political pluralism suddenly seemed a viable prospect again on 17 January 1996, when a hastily formed group of technocrats challenged the conservative monopoly and announced their support for Rafsanjani's policies, promising change and reform. Originally calling themselves the 'Servants of Construction' (*Khedmatgozaran-e Sazandegi*), they included 10 currently serving cabinet ministers, four of Rafsanjani's vice presidents, four vice presidents, the mayor of Tehran, and the governor of the Central Bank. The 10 ministers withdrew in view of the constitutional ban on executive interference in legislative elections, and the group's name eventually became *Kargozaran-e Sazandegi* ('Executives of Construction') – although the 'Servants of Construction' name stuck in English.

In behavior that somewhat resembled that of parties, the Kargozaran, the JRM and several minor groups published official lists of candidates they endorsed for the Majles elections. But in a maneuver meant either to gain wider acceptability or to enable them to claim success no matter who won, the Kargozaran included many on their list that were on the JRM's as well – including Nateq-Nuri. Reyshahri's Society for the Defense of the Values of the Islamic Revolution published a similar list that overlapped with the others. Only the leftist Mojahedin of the Islamic Revolution Organization published a slate of recommended candidates that were not on any other group's list.

The Kargozaran articulated few policies but the group's formation was clearly meant to stop the JRM – Nateq-Nuri juggernaut. The Kargozaran's unexpected successes in first round of the elections on 8 March shook the right wing. Nateq-Nuri only barely won a Tehran seat by edging out Rafsanjani's daughter Faezeh Hashemi, a newcomer who drew the women's vote and Rafsanjani supporters. In the provinces, most of the candidates recommended by the JRM did not go on to the second round.

The factional disputes that led up to the first round of voting created considerable excitement among the electorate, encouraging many new voters to participate and foreshadowing in important ways the 1997 presidential election. Some 25 million voters – 71 per cent of those eligible and the highest voter turnout ever for a Majles election – participated in the first round. The potential of the youth vote became apparent, as well as the mobilization of women voters. As in 1997, many new voters were drawn in by debates over social and cultural freedoms, and by the calls from the leftist and moderate politicians for political pluralism and the establishment of parties.

The right-wing 'monopolists' tried to crush the budding political pluralism in the wake of the Kargozaran's impressive first-round showing. The Council of Guardians annulled results in Isfahan and several other constituencies without giving reasons. Many voters believed the Council acted at the JRM's behest, and because victories by women in Isfahan and Malayer were annulled, women concluded the JRM stood for male domination – an important element in Nateq-Nuri's 1997 defeat.

The conservative counterattack centered around branding the Kargozaran candidates as 'liberals', a label until then used only for members of the late Mehdi Bazargan's relatively secularist Freedom Party. Its users vaguely defined 'liberalism' to imply counter-revolutionary, Western values. Speaker Nateq-Nuri led the charge, claiming that liberals wanted dialogue with the United States and softer positions on the Rushdie affair and the Middle East peace process. He called liberalism a serious threat to the revolution and actually called on the Basij mobilization forces to 'destroy' liberal thinking.[22]

The campaign against the 'liberals' was accompanied by the harsh violence of the Ansar-e Hezbollah, bands of street thugs whose patron was Guardian Council spokesman Ayatollah Jannati. They were also linked in the public mind with the JRM. They attacked cinema-goers and women whose veiling did not live up to the Hezbollah's standards, and broke up political discussions at universities. In particular, they harassed the popular philosopher 'Abdolkarim Sorush. They urged voters to support 'fundamentalists' and to oppose liberals, in the second round of Majles voting on 19 April.

The crude, anti-liberal tactics of the JRM and their Ansar-e Hezbollah allies soured many voters. Turnout for the second round was light compared to the first. The JRM boasted victory, but the Kargozaran claimed that they and non-affiliated deputies in the Majles were together greater in number than the JRM.

The ugly atmosphere continued even after the elections were over. The Ansar-e Hezbollah demanded that some newly elected 'liberal' deputies be expelled as incompetent and 'deviant' – a charge, countered the liberals', that amounted to a slur on the Guardian Council for having failed in its duty to screen candidates.[23] Tehran deputy Morteza Nabavi, who sometimes functioned as a JRM spokesman, blamed liberals for the continuing Western 'cultural onslaught', the decadent behavior of the young, and for trying to start talks with the United States. He also warned that the liberals' ultimate goal was to take over the Iranian economy.[24]

Such was the atmosphere six months before the 1997 presidential election. Prospects had dimmed for political pluralism, and Nateq-Nuri and the 'monopolists' appeared destined to prevail. The conservatives had embarked on a new wave of repression based on raising public fears about the supposed threat posed by pro-Western liberals. Politicians of the JRM and affiliated right-wing groups were determined to protect the status quo – that is, their political power and access to wealth – by preventing moderate challengers from gaining ground. Whether they sincerely believed so or not, they portrayed political pluralism and democracy as an insidious plot of the West aimed against the faithful.

The political atmosphere had calmed sufficiently by October 1996 – to the extent that the Militant Clerics (MRM) announced that conditions were sufficiently favorable for them to return to politics after a hiatus of nearly five years.[25] It is not yet clear just why the repressive atmosphere that followed the Majles elections dissipated within a few months. It is likely that the right-wing JRM felt blithely confident that they faced no serious contest in the 1997 presidential election and so could afford to loosen up and allow competition. Their leaders publicly and magnanimously welcomed the return of the MRM as affording healthy competition. It is also quite possible that Ayatollah Khamene'i and other leaders felt that the actions of the 'monopolists' had gone too far and that the security of the regime would be endangered if the political landscape offered no outlet for a discontented populace to let off steam.[26]

In the improved atmosphere in the fall of 1996, the use of the pejorative 'liberal' became rare, and the much ballyhooed plan to 'Islamicize' the universities never got much beyond the discussion stage. The Ansar-e Hezbollah, so active earlier in the year, fell out of favor. When Mohammad Reyshahri was running for president he was criticized for turning against them after embracing them the year before,[27] and an Ansar-e Hezbollah member complained about 'the lack of judicial support and government protection for those who enjoin good' after a mob beat and 'martyred' a member who had been trying to 'advise' a young couple.[28]

New demands for party formation

With the freer atmosphere in late 1996, political leaders who were not part of the conservative 'monopoly' called for the legalization of parties just as they had prior to the Majles elections. Only with parties and party platforms, they argued, could the public understand what, if anything, the various politicians actually stood for. They had no obligation to the people at large since they were not required to present election platforms and manifestos. If politicians came to power on the basis of party platforms, optimists argued, 'it would be easier to assess and scrutinize their behavior after the elections,' and that would 'automatically lead to accountability of parties and party members to the nation'.[29]

The quasi-parties then in existence amounted to little more than pressure groups which functioned only to further the interests of their members. They spent most of their energies vilifying each other and so, argued the *Tehran Times*, 'parochial group interests become the ultimate goal of political groups … even at the expense of national interests'.[30]

Opponents of the 'monopolists' envisioned a party system as drawing in groups and individuals otherwise alienated from the system. Morteza Alviri, an unsuccessful Kargozaran candidate for the Majles, argued that 'groups which have despaired and felt hopeless' about their opportunity to participate in political activities should be allowed into the arena; otherwise, they 'will sink into their shells and become indifferent and alienated from the political issues and the fate and future of the country'.[31]

Hopes rose considerably when Rafsanjani himself, on 24 January, announced that he favored party formation. His precise wording (*tahazzob*) made it ambiguous as to whether he meant several parties or just one.[32] Khomeini, he said, had approved 'party formation', referring to the single Islamic Republic Party. This suggests that Rafsanjani at that time may have had in mind a single-party system such as Iran had under the IRP. In fact, in early 1996 there had been talk that he intended to head a revived Islamic Republic Party.[33]

Khatami was among those who advocated parties, though he did so with the same sort of caution that he showed on other issues in an apparent desire not to alarm defenders of the status quo. But on several occasions he said that if properly formed – that is, not imposed from above or planted from the outside – parties were important. A 'self-sufficient and advanced society,' he said, 'cannot last without civil societies, which include political parties.'[34] Khatami's impressive election victory created, noted one Tehran daily, an atmosphere of 'great expectations' in which people were 'assuming that the system will permit re-establishment of political parties and application of democratic process in politics.'[35]

After sixteen years of prohibition, there was intense excitement in seizing the Khatami momentum and forming parties – perhaps before the regime tried to impose its own terms on party formation. 'Just about every political faction and group within the system, sensing the shifting winds, clambered to get themselves organized and readied for registration as a political party,' wrote *Iran Daily*, which predicted there would be 'as many applications for new parties as there were self-appointed nominees for the presidential election!' Everyone was jumping on the bandwagon, with 'old hacks preparing to revive old parties, and new opportunists planning to start new ones.'[36]

The Article 10 Commission continued to claim it was busily granting permits, but none was to any group of substance. On 30 July, for example, it gave permission to 'nine political groups and guilds': the Islamic Association of Athletes, the Society of Followers of the Imam's Line, the West Azarbaijan Association of Graduates, the Khorasan Construction Servants, the Association of Retirees from the Tehran Educational Department for Children with Special Needs, the Association of Industrial Hygiene Experts, the Cooperatives Islamic Movement, the Association of Urban Engineers and the Welfare Workers Association of Retirees.[37]

But several important political groups did announce their intention to become formal parties. It appeared, thought, that they would have to wait for regime leaders to decide just how a party system was to be established. In the wake of Khatami's victory the Kargozaran formulated a constitution and manifesto with the intention of submitting them to the Article 10 Commission, and its six founders added new members that included Fa'ezeh Hashemi and 'Abdollah Nuri (soon to become interior minister). They planned to seek representatives throughout the country.[38]

A new group calling itself the Independent Hezbollah Association, whose more than 50 members comprised independent deputies from the Majles, several technocrats and journalists, and other non-affiliated activists (including former presidential candidate Mohammad Reyshahri, whose 'Society for the Defense of the Values of the Revolution' now appeared defunct), announced it was completing formalities to form a party.[39] A political party for workers was also being urged by the organization Worker's House which publishes the Tehran daily *Kar va Kargar*.[40]

One of the key political groups in the 1997 presidential election, the Militant Clerics Association (MRM), would not be transformed into a fully fledged political party, according to its secretary-general, Hojjat ol-Eslam Karrubi. He stated no reason, but the likely reason is that the MRM is an organization of politically active clerics and would therefore be unable to draw membership from society at large. Similarly, its rival and parent organization, the Militant Clergy (JRM), had no way to function as a broader, inclusionary political party. Karrubi hoped that others with views similar to the MRM's would form a party, and suggested the former prime minister, engineer Mir Hoseyn Musavi, as the right person to do so. He also said people from 'other factions' such as former foreign minister 'Ali Akbar Velayati, should start parties, too.[41]

Fear of parties

The inability of the two major groups of political clergymen, the JRM and the MRM, to form political parties that could claim any sort of membership amongst the population at large points to the most likely reason why the Islamic Republic regime has been so reluctant to allow party formation.

Parties open to public membership represent an alternative path to power that threatens the clerics' grip on power. The Islamic Republic in 1997 was still an oligarchy, controlled by a network of Shi'ite clerics who were disciples of Ayatollah Khomeini. In effect, they were a professional fraternity bound together by ties forged in the seminaries and by intermarriage, an exclusive network in distinctive clothes who could easily bar outsiders. They were not about to give up their grip on power easily.

President Rafsanjani admitted that the clerics, whom he called the 'main guiding force for political activity in our country,'[42] discouraged the formation of parties. He told journalists on 12 February, 1997 that the reason for parties not developing in Iran is that there are 'centers of power such as the clergy which overshadow parties.'[43] Article 10 Commission Chairman Badamchian explained that the people do not have much need for parties because they already have 'groups that enjoy public trust, such as the clergymen'.[44]

The regime's reluctance to allow parties stemmed from the clerical leadership's increasing feelings of insecurity as its role in government came more openly under criticism. The outspoken religious intellectual 'Abdolkarim Sorush had gained widespread audiences in recent years with his criticisms of the ideological platform of the state and his assertions that the clerical establishment must cut its links with the government.[45] Condemned by the highest level of the religio-political leadership, harassed and threatened, his university lectures disrupted by the Ansar-e Hezbollah (who called him a 'pseudo-religious intellectual, mercenary pen-pusher'[46]) Sorush struck a deep chord with the many Iranians who resented the clerics' domination of power and with those who felt that Islam itself would suffer as the government's failures were blamed on the clergy.

The anti-clerical atmosphere was such that the Leader, Ayatollah Khamene'i, may well have feared that if a non-cleric presented a viable presidential candidacy he would openly attract anti-clerical sentiment and undermine the state – or at least the clerics' domination of it. And so, when the MRM returned to politics in October 1996, and immediately proposed the former prime minister Mir Hossein Musavi as its presidential candidate, Khamene'i opposed his candidacy.[47] He subsequently allowed the MRM's Mohammad Khatami, a cleric and a *seyyed*, to run. It was nevertheless clear to many voters that Khatami was an intellectual and progressive cleric of a new generation and did not represent the conservative clerical establishment.

When Khatami won the presidency the clerical establishment tried to portray it as a great victory for the clergy, one that reaffirmed the people's faith in their leadership. Khamene'i called Khatami's election a 'referendum of the Iranian nation and an act of reiteration of the people's loyalty to Islam, the clergy and the religious system of government.' That system, based on the principle of *velayat-e faqih* (rule by an authoritative jurisconsult), was the 'most progressive political system in the world,' because it meant 'rule by someone who knows about Islam and is familiar with the methods of government.' Western political systems, on the other hand, separate religion from politics and are based on 'false democracies and deceitful propaganda.'[48] Other leading clerics of the regime expressed a greater sense of threat than Khamene'i – particularly Ayatollah Mohammad Yazdi, chief of the judiciary, who declared that non-clerics should stay out of politics.[49]

Apparently for Khamene'i, parties did not have a place in 'the world's most progressive political system'. In his message for Khatami's inauguration ceremony on 3 August, he thanked the Almighty that the Iranian nation had once again displayed its 'political maturity' without having had to follow political parties and their 'materialistic leaders'.[50]

Parties – from above or from below?

There is only one party, the Party of God; There is only one leader, Ruhollah (Khomeini) – revolutionary slogan, Tehran, 1979.

In numerous round-tables and newspaper interviews in 1996 and 1997, Iranian politicians, theorists and experts discussed at length why parties have had difficulty taking root in Iran throughout the twentieth century. They often cited the Pahlavi monarchy's monarchical despotism, which prevented parties under Reza Shah or resulted in artificial, regime-imposed parties under Mohammad Reza Shah. During the turbulent and unrestrained party activity of 1941–53 numerous parties had organizational and financial difficulties or suffered from a tendency to form around ambitious individuals rather than a program or purpose. Then, too, there is the legacy of distrust from the early years of the revolution, when numerous small parties clashed with each other and several leftist parties turned against the new state, leading Khomeini to turn against all parties other than the Islamic Republic Party. Some warned of the danger of foreign connections, citing British and Russian manipulation of parties particularly the pro-Soviet Tudeh communist party.

In their opposition to party formation, right-wing clerics, usually from the JRM, frequently said they wanted no repeat of the experiences of the aftermath of the 1906 Constitutional Revolution.[51] The clerics who led that revolution eventually found themselves displaced by secularists who had organized themselves into parties modelled along Western lines. The revolution lost much of its Islamic character and the clerics returned to the mosques.

Both the left and the right point out that parties are a Western concept. Right-wing opponents of party formation argue that there is therefore no place for them in Iranian culture; others argue that parties are needed, provided they develop in a genuinely Iranian form from within the culture. Khatami, for example, maintained that since the idea of the political party came from Europe rather than from Iran's own social and historical circumstances, efforts must be made to nurture parties on the basis of existing institutions and philosophical tendencies.[52]

In 1997, those in the middle to left-wing side of the political spectrum, including President Khatami, were much more inclined toward the development of parties stemming from the people themselves. But the right wing, the 'monopolists' as they were called until Khatami's election, more inclined toward state-created parties.

A system of government parties would satisfy those who contend there is a theoretical incompatibility between theocracy, where a government derives its legitimacy from God, and true democracy, where a people legitimize their government. If there are to be parties, they should be created by the state in order to carry out God's will.

In the system of the Islamic Republic, power comes from God through the supreme jurisconsult (*vali-ye faqih*) – currently Ayatollah Khamene'i, the Leader of the Revolution. He is therefore the source of legitimacy and, for true believers in the system, parties should originate with him. Parties should act as the 'eyes, ears, and arms' of the Leader, receive their legitimacy from him, and implement their policies within a framework set by him, according to one proponent of this theory.[53] Article 10 Commission head Badamchian explained that the supreme jurisconsult is the 'nurturer', and parties the 'instruments for nurturing the masses.'[54]

The creation of one or more parties as arms of the state would really be no different from what Mohammad Reza Shah had done. The various government parties of the last 20 years of his reign, from the Melliyun and Mardom parties to Iran Novin and Rastakhiz, were meant to give an illusion of popular support for the government and to avoid the destabilizing effects of democratic elections. The government parties, recruited mainly from the ranks of the civil servants, were used as instruments to shape pro-government sentiments, to eliminate alternative paths to power, and to carry out government programs.

Such state-run parties, however, rarely generate strong public attachments. As Marvin Weinbaum observed about Iran Novin, that party 'found no substitutes for the historical traumas, charismatic leadership, or ideological appeals that have elsewhere welded popular allegiances to political parties.'[55]

The 'twenty-million strong army for change,' as Khatami's voters have been called, ushered in a principle of people's government and a demand for the institutions of civil society. Those ideas are difficult to reconcile with theocracy: can an Islamic government also be an Islamic republic? With no easy answer in sight, the question of whether parties are to arise from the people or be imposed by the regime promised to be one of the most divisive issues for the Khatami era, and as it remains unsettled so will questions over the validity of Khomeini's theory of *velayat-e faqih* and the role of clergy in the government.

During Khatami's administration numerous newspapers and magazines, all pro-liberalism, emerged. Many editors and managers were imprisoned or fined by conservative courts, but the same forces supported Khatami to win the election; they continued to support his election campaign goals to an extent that 18 political groups – the so-called 'second of Khordad Front' – emerged to support candidate of sixth Majles election in order to establish Khatami's reformist plan and the process of liberalization.

The struggle between conservative and liberal forces is close to flashpoint. It remains to be seen who will win the next election. At this moment, the future is very much dependent on the fate of Iraq.

Acknowledgements

Stephen C. Fairbanks, a senior analyst in the office of Near East and South Asia Analysis at the US State Department, wrote this chapter while a guest scholar at the Woodrow Wilson International Center for Scholars in Washington, DC, on sabbatical from the State Department.

Notes

1 See, for example, *Akhbar*, 8 June 1997, and *Hamshahri*, 18 March 1997. One 'election watcher,' however, cautioned that Iran lacks the experience and 'technical know-how' to conduct reliable opinion polls, and complained that those conducting the polls are usually affiliated with one political faction or another (*Iran News*, 30 April 1997).
2 *Iran*, 4 February 1997, as cited in *Ettela'at-e Bein al-Mellali*, 5 February 1997.
3 *Akhbar*, 8 June 1997.
4 *Hamshahri*, 6 March 1997.
5 In fact, no woman was on the cabinet list that he presented in August 1997, though he did name a woman to the post of vice-president for environmental protection and claimed she would have 'cabinet status.'
6 *Keyhan International*, 23 February 1997.
7 *Resalat*, 11 March 1997.
8 *Iran News*, 2 November 1996. The best-organized political organization of clerics, the JRM, is also the oldest, originating in 1936 as a means to organize the clerics against Reza Shah. It helped unite clerical forces behind Khomeini in his 1963 uprising against Mohammad Reza Shah and in the 1978 uprisings that eventually toppled the Shah (*Iran Focus*, 'Special report on the 1996 Majles Elections', March 1996).
9 There was some controversy over whether Rafsanjani had acquiesced in the JRM's selection of Nateq-Nuri as their candidate. Some JRM members maintained that his presence during the JRM central council meeting when Nateq-Nuri was selected was proof of Rafsanjani's support. But Rafsanjani several times declared his impartiality, saying he would not even disclose his preference to his own children (*Iran News*, 19 May 1997).
10 True leftist, secular organizations such as the Tudeh communist party and the Mojahedin-e Khalq have been barred from participating in the Islamic Republic's electoral politics.
11 Asghar Schirazi, *The Constitution of Iran: Politics and State in the Islamic Republic*, trans. John O'Kane (London: I.B. Tauris, 1997), pp. 126–7.

12 *Kar va Kargar*, 5 October 1996.
13 Tehran radio, 14 December 1988, in FBIS-NES-88-241.
14 Islamic Republic News Agency (IRNA), 25 December 1988, in FBIS-NES-88-248
15 IRNA, 14 January 1989, in FBIS-NES-89-011
16 *Akhbar*, 21 January 1997.
17 *Resalat*, 28 January 1989, in FBIS-NES-89-021.
18 *Salam*, 13 March 1996, in FBIS-96-053.
19 IRNA, 8 August 1995, in FBIS-95-153
20 *Resalat*, 21 August 1995, in FBIS-NES-95-168.
21 See particularly Bahman Baktiari, *Parliamentary Politics in Revolutionary Iran* (Gainesville: University Press of Florida, 1996)
22 *Iran News*, 1 May 1996.
23 *Jomhuri-ye Eslami*, 25 May 1996; *Akhbar*, 24 April 1996.
24 *Resalat*, 16 May 1996.
25 The MRM did not explain how conditions had improved. MRM Secretary General Karrubi only said that the propagandist attacks and accusations against the group had been proved to be fallacious (*Hamshahri*, 15 October 1996). The MRM probably felt its chances had improved when it became apparent that President Rafsanjani would not seek a third term. Also, there was some speculation at the time that the Kargozaran had appealed to the MRM to return, arguing that together they could defeat Nateq-Nuri (*Iran News*, 16 October 1996).
26 Avoidance of the 'liberal' label continued throughout the months leading to the 1997 presidential election. A noteworthy exception was when the Ansar-e Hezbollah's patron, Ayatollah Jannati, declared in a Friday sermon on 28 February that Ayatollah Khamene'i had said that no candidate for the presidency should be a liberal (*Resalat*, 1 March 1997). Khamene'i did not confirm Jannati's remarks.
27 *Jomhuri-ye Eslami*, 22 January 1997.
28 *Kar va Kargar*, 14 October 1996.
29 *Tehran Times*, 21 February 1996.
30 *Tehran Times*, 16 October 1996.
31 *Iran*, 22 October 1996.
32 *Jomhuri-ye Eslami*, 25 January 1997; *Ettela'at-e Bein al-Mellali*, 27 January 1997
33 *Tehran Times*, 21 February 1996.
34 *Iran*, 16 March 1997.
35 *Iran Daily*, 11 August 1997.
36 *Iran Daily*, 11 August 1997.
37 *Iran News*, 31 July 1997.
38 *Akhbar*, 14 June 1997.
39 *Iran News*, 3 July 1997.
40 *Kar va Kargar*, 8 May 1997.
41 *Iran News*, 7 August 1997.
42 *Tehran Times*, 16 February 1997.
43 *Resalat*, 13 February 1997.
44 *Akhbar*, 21 January 1997.
45 See Valla Vakili, *Debating Religion and Politics in Iran: The Political Thought of Abdolkarim Soroush* Studies Dept Occasional Paper Series, No.2 (New York: Council on Foreign Relations, 1996).
46 *Salam*, 9 May 1996.
47 Though the Leader is supposed to be above politics and has no official role in vetting candidates, Khatami and the three other candidates who ran for president all reported having first met with Ayatollah Khamene'i to secure his approval. The Guardian Council would not have approved a candidate that Khamene'i disliked.
48 *Resalat*, 24 July 1997.
49 *Salam*, 10 July 1997.

50 *Resalat*, 4 August 1997.
51 See, for example, Ayatollah Mahdavi-Kani's interview in *Abrar*, 21 May 1997
52 *Iran*, 16 March 1997.
53 *Keyhan*, 12 February 1997.
54 Ibid.
55 Marvin G. Weinbaum, 'Iran finds a party system: the institutionalization of *Iran Novin*', *The Middle East Journal* 27, no. 4 (Autumn 1973), p. 453.

12 The sixth Majles election and the prospects for democracy in Iran

Ali Mohammadi

Since the election of President Khatami in May 1997, numerous changes have emerged in Iran. One of the most important is the actual formation of political parties. The various political groups that supported President Khatami's election platform or his rival candidate can be divided into three groups. This chapter sets out to define each of these in terms of their purpose and political objectives. Of the three, the group with a more or less defined policy for the country's development and with clear foreign policy objectives is the conservative group, whose candidate Nateq-Nuri lost in the landslide victory of President Mohammad Khatami, whose election manifesto had its basis in the rule of law, freedom of expression and development of civil society. These slogans were exactly what the people had been crying out for since the revolution but had been denied for the past two decades.

It is interesting to note that when the conservatives failed to gain the support of the people, particularly women and the younger generation, they resorted to various tactics to destabilize Khatami's election campaign. One significant instance was the response of conservative groups to student demonstrations at Tehran University.

The brutal midnight attack on students in their dormitory and its aftermath is rather complicated. Tehran University has been the centre of political movement in Iran since Musaddeq's nationalization movement during the 1950s. The true national liberation front and freedom movement began at Tehran University with the first of gathering of the National Association of University Lecturers in October 1977. They demanded basic freedoms of expression and thought. However, they were suppressed by the late Shah's military government. Later, in a similar manner, basic human rights and the process of democratization were betrayed and suppressed by various religious and traditional groups that emerged during the revolutionary process. Then, gradually, a new religious zealotry, the *Hojjatolislam* cadre, penetrated into the leadership of the revolution. By seizing the US embassy and taking American diplomats as hostages, they not only betrayed the aspirations of their fellow Iranians, they also damaged international sympathy towards the Iranian revolution and forced approximately four million professional and well-to-do Iranians into compulsory and voluntary exile.

Twenty years later the very same aspirations and sentiments of betrayal re-emerged. But this time they were pronounced by the children of the founding members of the movement of 1977. The disappointed children of the revolution, now university students, gathered late on Thursday, 8 July 1999, in front of the student dormitory to manifest their anger at and disapproval of the proposed tyrannical press bill and the closure of the *Salam* newspaper for printing government secrets. Before a day-by-day analysis of the student unrest, the responses of President Khatami in general and the security force in particular, it is necessary to reveal the secret government parallel to the elected government of Mohammad Khatami in May 1997.[1]

Government within the government

First, who comprises this secret government within the official government of the Islamic Republic? How do they operate? Who provides their finance and how do they influence, promote or neutralize the official government policy? How do they penetrate foreign policy and undermine national interests for their own personal gain or the group interest, planting their agents in powerful positions within the nationally elected popular government?

Every secret force in order to operate needs finance, obedience and loyal agents. Furthermore, it needs access to intelligence data to plan strategies and design plots for creating crises to sabotage and prevent the national government carrying out its duty and achieving its campaign goals. The legitimate source of income always plays a critical role in covering the financial affairs of an extensive intelligence operation. Such an operation is very costly, since it is necessary to buy out privileges or to silence rival groups by means of nepotism or organized crime through what is commonly known as Mafia-type action.

The most important criteria for recruitment are family ties, religious group membership, and business partnerships and networks. These have three significant characteristics in common: a) providing financial help for Khomeini during exile and helping to collect the religious donations; b) providing facilities for effective networking among Khomeini's students and political activists inside and outside Iran; c) organizing secret meetings among various factions in Qom, Tehran and Mashhad, establishing a united front against the late Shah, and encouraging competition with each other for further privileges or influence.

Various secret active religious groups which organized financial support for Ayatollah Khomeini during his years of exile in Turkey and Iraq subsequently claimed legitimacy and have held the upper hand. They have the ability to obtain with ease foreign trade and monopoly licenses from the Islamic government. Among them are the following organizations, which are very active in secret government.

Motallefeh

The most powerful group in commerce and business, with extensive influence in Bazaars throughout the country, is known as Motallefeh. This group is the amalgamation of various religious factions, whence its acquired name which means 'to connect'. It is also known as Askaroladi's group in Iran. Their outlook is based on extreme religious and business conservatism. In order to promote their brand of religious and economic orthodoxy, they put together a monthly magazine called *Shoma*. The main focus of their paper is to promote economic conservatism against any liberalization policy and to support extreme religious forces against civil or civic projects in Iran. The Motallefeh are against the restoration of law and order in the economy, foreign policy and internal affairs because the rule of law would jeopardize the extensive privileges that they enjoy.

Habibollah Askaroladi-Mosalman, the figurehead of the group, was born into a very religious merchant family in Tehran in 1932. He did not gain a high-school diploma; he can read Arabic and knows basic arithmetic. He became known as an active member of *Fadaiyan Islam* (Martyrs of Islam) and provided financial support for its members. Later, he became a member of the Supervisory Council of Ayatollah Khomeini's Relief Aid Committee and the director and founder of 15th Khordad Foundation, which allocated $2 million for the assassination of Salman Rushdie, the Muslim British writer accused of and condemned to death for blasphemy by Ayatollah Khomeini. During 1980–1 he became a member of the Islamic Council and then deputy Speaker of the Majles. He was also Minister of Commerce during 1981–3 and finally a presidential candidate. He is the most powerful businessman in Iran. His business operates in a tribal manner. His brother, Assadollah Askaroladi, is, arguably, the richest merchant in Iran.[2]

Second in command of this group is Assadollah Badamchian, who controls the Persian carpet business at home and abroad, as well as much else that is beyond the limits of this chapter.

The third most powerful man in this network is Mohsen Rafighdoust, who drove Imam Khomeini to Beheshte Zahra, the well-known cemetery in Tehran, on the first day of his return from exile, where Ayatollah Khomeini gave his first speech. Rafighdoust gained his popularity as a shrewd businessman during a long period as director-general of the Bonyad-e Mostazafin Foundation, one of the largest foundations established after the revolution. The holdings of Bonyads consist of various real estate, industrial centres, manufacturing factories, and agribusinesses formerly owned by the late Shah's regime.[3]

Mr Rafighdoust was born in 1940 in Tehran. He had a high-school education and was a member of the Coalition of Islamic Mourning Groups in 1962. He was influenced by Ayatollah Beheshti and was co-founder of Refah Islamic School. He went on to become a member of the Islamic Revolutionary Guard and the administrator of that force during 1982–8 and adviser to the acting commander-in-chief, President Rafsanjani, on the armaments industry, logistics and supplies to the armed forces. During this period he was less involved with the politics of Motallefeh and more active in the expansion of his own business empires, involving almost every member of his family and close associates in his fruit and vegetable market known as *Meidan*. He became a wealthy businessman with some help from Rafsanjani during the war with Iraq. He featured frequently in the headlines of *Jame'eh* newspaper when interviewed about the ills of the Iranian economy, and his controversial views on the hidden role of various foundations in official economic policy. He was one of the important figures of the secretive government during the scandal over foreign exchange embezzlement.

During the eight-year war with Iraq, Rafighdoust and his partner Rafsanjani had full control over armed forces procurement. During these critical years, the very foundations of tribalism were established in politics and business – extending far beyond the family tree – and the basis of a secret government was laid with the co-operation of Rafsanjani. Despite the seniority of Askaroladi and his extraordinary influence in the bazaar, the network of secrecy would not have been possible without the co-operation of Rafsanjani and his partners.

The Motallefeh group, with the co-operation of the Special Prosecutor of the Religious Court, initiated the tyrannical press bill and closure of *Salam* newspaper and triggered political unrest in Tehran. They had three ulterior motives in mind. First, to warn the reform-minded groups around President Khatami that they were able to destabilize the government and, by coup d'état if necessary, bring their business partner Mr Rafsanjani to power, at least temporarily. As evidence in the conservative press suggests, they would not allow pro-Khatami groups to win elections without considering their interests in the future government. Their second motive was to test the level of crowd mobilization and the efficacy of their existing hand in the security apparatus of the government. The third was an examination of Khatami's willpower and reaction to unrest.[4]

After one week of student unrest and the barbaric attack on their dormitory, 1,500 students were arrested. The conservative and liberal papers all focused on Rafsanjani as the future Speaker of the Majles and indirectly asked the Khordad Front (reform-minded supporters of President Khatami and arch-enemies of the conservatives) to endorse Rafsanjani among their candidate list for the next election. They refused outright and Rafsanjani decided not to run for election or, for the time being, to postpone his decision. Motallefeh, with the cooperation of other groups, decided to prolong the crisis to persuade reform-minded groups to resort to violence. The reaction of Makkarem Shirazi to the small student journal called *Mouj* is a case in point.[5]

The Reyshahri group

The second group with unlimited secret power in the security apparatus as well as enormous influence on Khamenehi is the group lead by Hojjatolislam Mohammad Mohammadi Nik Reyshahri (the former Minister of Intelligence and the architect of dismantling Ayatollah Montazery's power). He is a member of the Council for Determination of Exigencies, a member of the Assembly of Experts for Tehran, a representative of the Vali-ye Faghih, the head of the Iranian *Hajj* (Mecca) pilgrimage, and secretary-general of the Society for the Defence of the Values of Islamic Revolution. He is known among theologians as 'Colonel' Reyshahri. He was born in 1946 in Tehran, schooled in Qom and was detained in Mashhad when Prime Minister Hasan-Ali Mansoor was assassinated in 1965. He then went to Najaf in Iraq and Qom to study and to teach. After the revolution he suddenly became a judge in the Islamic Courts and later became the chief architect of the

Revolutionary Courts for the Armed Forces. He was appointed the first Intelligence Minister from 1984 till 1989. He was State Prosecutor General, Special Prosecutor of the Tribunal for the Clergy, and presidential candidate in May 1997. His published works include: *Mizanolhekmeh* (*Balance of Judgement*), a 10-volume book on judicial matters, and the two-volume *An Introduction to Knowledge of God*. Reyshahri also has a monthly paper called *Arzeshha*, the major focus of which is based on supporting *velayat-e faghih* and the rule of *Foqaha* (learned clergy) and *Shari'a* on all aspects of society. As the first Minister of Intelligence he wrote his memoirs in order to justify the dismissal of Ayatollah Montazery and the execution of his son-in-law, Mehdi Hashemi.[6] As a consequence of those executions, he gained enormous power within the Islamic system. It is important to note that he is also the son-in-law of Ayatollah Meshkini, the Speaker of the Assembly of Experts, known as the *Khebregan*. He is an extremist and one of the problems in the way of limiting the power of the supreme leader, Ayatollah Khamenehi.

The revenue from confiscated real estate and personal wealth of previous regimes as well as those of radical groups finance Hojjatolislam Reyshahri and his group. For instance, he has confiscated the residence of former member of the first Assembly of Experts, Mr Rahmat-e Maraghei. Despite the Islamic court order, he has refused to vacate the property for the past 16 years. He also still has influence in the rank and file of the security apparatus. His group is very hostile to President Khatami's reform, as he lost in the election and has no chance of being elected because of his conservative views of Islam and his extraordinary cruelty in the Military Court of the Armed Forces. He also will fight Khatami's planned law enforcement because he, like many others, would lose his financial base in the present politics of Iran. He is the closest ally and patron of Ayatollah Khamenehi and a very influential figure inside the Leader's office. He is known as an Islamic canonist and a close associate of Ayatollah Kani and is also popular for his mysterious image.[7]

Tehran Militant Clergy Association

The other conservative group is called Tehran Militant Clergy Association (Rouhaniyat-e Mobarez Tehran), led by Ayatollah Mohammad Reza Mahdavi-e Kani. He studied theology in Tehran and Qom and is, in principle, against the democratization process in Islam. Ayatollah Kani, on various occasions, has explicitly stated that 'Islam and democracy are not compatible'. He is also head of the erstwhile Management Institute established by the previous regime in order to train new managers for industry. He has changed the name of the Institute to Imam Sadeq University but its function remains the same. His influence is considerable since he trains the new Islamic cadre, selectively chosen from the elite of religious families, for the Islamic government. He also has gained support for the school from the Islamic business elite and important merchants. Ayatollah Kani was against Khatami's election as president as he supported the rival candidate, Nateq-Nuri. Since the landslide victory of President Khatami, Ayatollah

Kani can be found continuously politicking behind the scenes to ensure President Khatami is not successful in his plans.[8]

Among many clergy in Qom and Tehran Ayatollah Kani is known as a mysterious figure. He was also one of the close associates of Navab-e Safavi, the founder of *Fadaiyan Islam* (Martyrs of Islam) in 1949. It should be noted that, since his youth, Kani has always been active in clergy politics. During the nationalization of the oil industry by Dr Musaddeq, Kani was detained in the city of Isfahan following the 1953 coup d'état. He resumed his political activities in Tehran, and subsequently taught theology and mass prayers in Tehran. He was imprisoned several times prior to the revolution. He is the founder of the Tehran Militant Clergy Association. During the revolutionary process he organized the revolutionary council. Following the revolution, the late Iranian revolutionary leader assigned him to supervise the Islamic Revolution Committee. As well as playing various important roles in establishing today's Islamic government, he served as Interior Minister at a very critical embryonic point in the development of the Islamic Republic, and then formed an interim government for two months in September 1981 when former prime minister Bahonar was assassinated. Ayatollah Khomeini in his final days displayed his trust of Ayatollah Mahdavi Kani by appointing him to the Constitutional Review Panel and getting his will read after his death. Since 1982 Kani has been occupied with Imam Sadeq University. At present he has no official position in the government apart from being a member of the Council for Determination of Exigencies. Yet it cannot be overlooked that since the birth of the Islamic Republic Ayatollah Mahdavi Kani has held enormous undefined powers. One significant reason lies in the fact that he held many meetings with the US Ambassador to negotiate the transfer of power from the Army and other loyal organizations of the former regime to the Revolutionary Council. Ayatollah Khamenehi appointed him as the director of mosques in 1989, which many experts on Iranian affairs acknowledge as the most powerful position with regard to dealing with the clerical community. Besides Kani, the group has a handful of powerful clergy members, such as Nateq Nuri, the speaker of the Majles, Hashemi-Rafsanjani, Imami-Kashani, Movahedi-Savoji, Movahedi-Kermani, Jannati and many more of the conservative clergy. Their views on culture, politics and economics can be summarized as follows:[9]

Culture

The conservative clergy support:

- traditional values in cultural policies;
- any policy against cultural exchange in any shape or form;
- any policy by the government to further control on cultural activities;
- censorship and harsh surveillance of movies, plays, books, magazines and publications;
- maintenance of cultural activities under direct control of religious leaders.

Politics

The conservative clergy believe that:

- the West has a grand plan to overthrow Islamic culture;
- the people should not have the power to choose their religious leaders; the Assembly of Experts might search for a Vali-ye Faghih, but his selection is up to the wishes of Almighty God;
- the Vali-ye Faghih is above the constitution;
- the legitimacy of all social institutions is dependent on the Vali-ye Faghih;
- Almighty Islamic Justice should be established in place of the republic;
- the *Rouhaniyat* (religious clergy) should be in control of the whole community;
- absolute traditional values must be adhered to;
- no group should be allowed to function outside this spectrum;
- the clergy cannot be criticized and they are not responsible to the people;
- political participation is not to be supported, nor the principle of a civil society;
- the Islamic Revolution is to be supported beyond the Iranian borders;
- religious commitment is to be supported in favour of professional integrity.

Economics

The conservative clergy support:

- privatization of the economy;
- economic balance in various sectors of the national economy.
- the idea that economic development should not be in conflict with Islamic values according to their views of Islam;
- priority of social justice over development;
- priority of imports over industrial development;
- priority of trade and business over development.

There are numerous foundations and organizations outside government control which support the conservative forces against the law and order policy and the democratization process. These groups include: the Society of Militant Clergy, 15th Khordad Foundation, Mostazafin Foundation, Shahid Foundation, Emdade Imam Foundation, the Radio Television Organization, the Guardian Council, the judiciary system, the commanding chiefs of the Revolutionary Guard, the security forces, Imam Reza Foundation, the Association of Lecturers and Theologians of Qom, special forces within the Ministry of Intelligence, and the Association of Friday Prayers Imams. Their papers are as follows: *Kayhan* newspaper, *Resallat*, *Jumhury Islamy*, and *Abrar*; and many weeklies such as *Shoma*, *Jaam*, *Jebheh*, *Sobh*, *Pasdar-e Islam*, *Nesarol Hussein* and *Entekhab*. All these forces support traditional and conservative Islam. They are all against civil society and individual rights as well as human rights and what is known as secular and open society. They are all united in maintaining power and they would employ whatever instrument they can to create crises for President Khatami, in order to prevent the realisation of his election campaign goals.[10]

There are other political groups whose policies are not clear. They can be clustered together as political opportunists or Party of Wind groups (*Hezb-e bad*). One of these groups (known as the 'Policy-Maker'), is the Kargozaran Party, initiated by the imprisoned former mayor of Tehran, Karbaschi, and Rafsanjani's group of supporters. Rafsanjani has not clarified his position within this group: he never officially defended his close associate and friend in a very political and biased court trial.

Association of Militant Clergy

Another fairly powerful political group is known as the Association of Militant Clergy. The major founders of this group are Hojjatolislam Mehdi Karrubi and Hojjatolislam Musavi-Khoeiniha. Mehdi Karrubi was custodian of the Hazrat-e Abdolazim seminary and a member of Majles for Aligoudarz. From the start of the Iran–Iraq war, he was Speaker of the Majles, and later became the head of a foundation called Bonyad-e Shaheed. Musavi-Khoeiniha is a member of the Assembly of Experts and was a student mentor during the occupation of the US embassy. The other controversial figure in this group is Hojjatolislam Mohtashemi. Their views are drastically different from the groups mentioned above.

Politics

The militant clergy support:

- limitations on the role of the *Vali-ye Faghih*;
- elections in the absence of the Imam;
- equality of the Islamic system with the republican system;
- the idea that political Islam is flexible and adaptable to the progress of time and space;
- the need for political parties;
- freedom of political activities and expression according to the constitution;
- freedom and liberty as rights, not as privileges;
- compatibility of Islam with democracy;
- the institutionalization of political participation;
- a voting system as the people's right;
- expansion of the Islamic Revolution to other parts of the world;
- further development of relations with the East;
- alliance with independent governments to take advantage of the conflict between major powers.

The militant clergy also resist US hegemony and the necessity of establishing a political relationship with the US. Nor are they fond of international organizations. They express suspicion and doubt towards international organizations as the fifth column of rich and affluent countries.

Economics

The militant clergy support:

- direct government control of basic industries and economic strategies;
- a recognition of the inefficiency of the bazaar economy in relation to the complexity of the Iranian economy;
- the prioritizing of development for its relation to independence and social justice;
- co-operative institutions;
- an economy of self-sufficiency as the economic model;
- self-sufficiency in agriculture;
- a long-term industrial plan for the development of the country;
- social justice after economic independence as an important priority;
- a mixed economy as the model for development;
- foreign borrowing with certain conditions.

In step with their welfare-state outlook on the economy, they deny that privatization would help to remedy the ills of the economy.

Culture

The militant clergy support:

- supervision of cultural products after publication or distribution;
- control of excessive production of cultural products;
- government control over expansion of cultural activities and assurance of individual rights;
- equality of cultural taste;
- investment and subsidies for the cultural sector;
- internal forces against penetration of foreign culture;
- a preference for a shortfall of internal forces in relation to cultural pathologies rather than destructive external forces in culture;
- the improvement of the country's social and political status for improvement of cultural ills;
- cultural exchange and selection and the modification of cultural values;
- the use of culture as a coercive force;
- a policy of cultural protectionism;
- authenticity in culture and avoiding the influence of alien culture.

Haghani graduates

This last group emerged prior to the presidential election and came to prominence during the controversial trial of the mayor of Tehran, Gholamhossein Karbaschi. Its members are known as Haghani graduates, after the wealthy businessman who built the school with a new approach to teaching theology. The founders of the new method were the following: the late Dr Beheshti, the late Ayatollah Ghodousi, Ayatollah Jannati, and Ayatollah Mesbah Yazdi. Many theologians were sensitive to the teachings of Dr Shariati and other religious intellectuals outside the theological circle – the non-turbaned academics. The most conservative of all was Mesbah Yazdi, who continues to reject any democratization or modification of Islam in the globalized world.[11]

As a consequence of various approaches to theology, the outcomes of their teachings are critical. Their Islamic views have been formalized to correspond, to a certain degree, to the modern world. However, their readings of Islam reinforce an outmoded orthodoxy. They are very critical of Western political philosophy, basically re-emphasizing classical methods of reading Islam.

In economics, they are also conservative and advocate privatization based on payment of harsh religious duties and support of religious charities. The Foundation of *Farman-e Imam* (Imam's Command) identifies the property of those individuals who have not paid their religious dues. With no recourse to the judicial system, this property can be confiscated or heavy and unrealistic levels of religious taxes levied which the owners are unable to pay. As a result, they have divided the community into two – insiders and outsiders. The definition of insider is based on those who have paid their religious dues and are supporters of the Islamic system; outsider relates to those who do not support the arbitrary process of the Islamic system based on the Haghani school of theology. Since 1989 the impact of Imam's Command, together with the biased Islamic judiciary system and other factors, has become an incentive for the emigration of many middle-class families for the first time in the history of modern Iran.[12]

Haghani graduates are against election to or any sort of consultation about the *velayat-e faghih*. Instead they support appointment. In order to achieve their objectives in an Islamic system, this particular group, according to present evidence, has employed various clandestine tactics to push their members into key positions of government during Rafsanjani's and Khatami's administrations. The dirty trick of using cultural invasion during Khatami's time as Minister of Cultural Affairs and the denial of a vote of confidence to Mr Nateq-Nuri as Minister of Interior Affairs are cases in point.

In politics, this group is extremely protagonist and anti-Western. At the present time they are led by Ayatollah Mesbah Yazdi and Ayatollah Jannati. In day-to-day politics, their agents have occupied key positions in important organizations of the country. In the office of Ayatollah Khamenehi are Aliasghar Hejazi and his close associates Fallahian, Moezi, Hosseinian, Razini, Azheiie and Akbariyan. In the Ministry of Foreign Affairs can be found Hojjatolislam Saremi; in the Ministry of Intelligence, Hojjatolislam Raissi, Poormohammadi and Shafiie and many others. These figures have occupied the most important positions in

Khatami's government and they run a secret government against the national interests of the popularly elected government. They all were supported by and served under Khamenehi's leadership.

According to the Islamic Republic's constitution, the Supreme Leader (Vali-ye Faghih) has the authority to veto the plans of the nationally elected President. In other words, people's votes have no value. This is a major part of the problem in Iran. These crises will recur regardless of the personality and political and ideological views of the president, as long as the power of veto, control of the armed and security forces, the judiciary, and foreign affairs remain with the permanent and directly unaccountable Supreme Leader and not the elected president. In the May 1997 election, the majority said 'No' to the choice of the Vali-ye Faghih but he still disrespects the majority vote and continues to support a handful of political groups which cause incredible harm to a democratically elected government.[13]

The student unrest at Tehran University was manipulated by the security agency to cause serious problems for President Khatami. The evidence in various newspapers, from extreme right to reformist, clearly shows the hand of security everywhere in the student demonstrations. Even the official investigative report by the High Council for National Security, published on 15 August 1999 in most Tehran dailies, indicated the extensive role of the security forces in inflating the crisis out of all proportion. The reaction of Khamenehi to the student crisis is worthy of note. He spent a week with *Basijie* (hooligan) forces to the south of Tehran. Later he travelled to Mashhad and supported the Mesbah Yazdi line on the riot, showing the very deep involvement of the intelligence faction of his office.

The question that remains unresolved is the degree to which the conservative gatekeepers of Iranian society are willing to open the gate. How much are they ready to compromise with Khatami's chosen candidates for the election of the sixth Majles members? President Khatami holds the trust of the majority of the population as he won 70 per cent of the vote in the May 1997 election. To what degree does he compromise the people's trust by sharing power with the conservative forces who have sacrificed the national interest for their individual gain and group interest? After the obvious role of the security forces in crushing the student uprising, all political groups – particularly those pro-Khatami, known as the reformists – have deployed their own methods to win the sixth parliamentary election.[14]

The sixth Majles election: the campaigns

My aim now is to analyse the methods of these various political groups and their attempts to attract the voting power of active participants in the sixth Majle election. In order to evaluate the various methods and policy lines in terms of campaigns and publicity, it is necessary to look at the different tactics each group used and the active part played by the print media in the election campaign.

Apart from radio and television, which are in the hands of far-right conservative clerics in Iran, the press was more or less free to cover the election campaign as it wished.

Since 1980, the press has played a crucial role in Iranian parliamentary elections in terms of introducing the candidates and presenting discussion of the new Islamic Council (*Majles Shoraye Islami*). In the first Islamic Council after the revolution, only half of the eligible voting population participated in the election of the Majles: 51 per cent out of 20 million voters. This was perhaps due to the fact that the concept of the Islamic Council Assembly was new and the war with Iraq was beginning. In the second Majles this figure increased to 65 per cent. The majority of voters were stimulated by the collective identity arising out of the war, in spite of conflicting views towards the *velayat-e faghih*. Yet it gradually became clear, after the second Majles election, that the voting population was becoming disillusioned with their treatment at the hands of the Majles and the government. The major slogan of the election was unity and support for President Khamenehi, avoiding any argument which might weaken the government against the enemy. Despite the special circumstances of the war period, voters slowly discovered that the major concern of the Majles and the government was to protect themselves against the enemy instead of relieving the people's anxiety about the war. As a consequence of this lack of attention to people's basic needs, there was a sudden marked decrease in support for the third Majles election. The voting figures dropped to 58 per cent. The public was disillusioned by the nepotism, corruption, black-marketeering, and price-fixing of basic everyday essentials. Rafsanjani, an important actor during the war with Iraq, changed his position to become a man of peace and reconstruction. He relinquished his seat as Speaker of the Majles to become the only candidate for the presidency. But the constitutional changes, that would have made him the first president without a prime minister, had a negative impact on voters' perceptions. His personal physiognomy was another contributing factor, as he is short and not particularly photogenic, with an unkind face with Mughal features. Furthermore he lacks charisma, which had a further devastating impact on voters' opinions. In the modern world of media, celebrity, fashion and style, presence in front of the camera is of vital importance, as television is a transparent medium.[15]

The lack of alternative policies and absence of alternative candidates also contributed to voters' apathy towards the fourth Majles. After the death of Ayatollah Khomeini in 1989 and Rafsanjani's election to the presidency in August 1989, he employed all his efforts to demystify Islam and turn Islamic politics into a politics of pragmatism. His major message to the Iranian people and to the international community was the reconstruction of Iran and full co-operation with the outside world. He also changed the revolutionary slogan to a less aggressive tone and insisted 'the introduction of revolution without interfering in the affairs of others will be continued'. From 1989 to 1993 Rafsanjani's administration provided an important framework within which the government could embark on a programme of economic reform, including privatisation of large industries and mines, the revival of the Tehran Stock Exchange, the abolition of the multiple exchange rate mechanism and its replacement with a single market rate, the founding of a number of free trade zones and the encouragement of direct foreign investment. Furthermore, he encouraged skilled Iranians residing abroad to return to Iran. Despite all his good intentions, his development plan did not persuade the voting population to support him for a second term in office. The increase in turnout was minimal – from 58.6 per cent to 58.9 per cent – reflecting a lack of enthusiasm for Rafsanjani's development package. What was significant here was the decrease in voters for Rafsanjani's second term in office, from 15.5 million to 10.6 million, which clearly indicates not only a lack of support for his policies, but that people were also searching to identify themselves with someone else who more accurately reflected their wishes.[16] The term 'identization' is borrowed from Alberto Melucci (1992) and has a very complex meaning, as Melucci suggests: 'collective identity is becoming the product of conscious action and the outcome of self-reflection more than a set of given or "structural" characteristics. The collective actor tends to construct its coherence and recognise its self with limits set by the environment and social relations' (Melucci, 1995).[17]

In the context of press coverage of the sixth Majles election and an examination of the people's previous voting patterns, I have applied the definition of collective identity in the way Melucci suggests: 'collective identity is a concept, an analytical tool, not a datum or an essence, not a "thing" with a "real" existence. In dealing with concepts, one should never forget that we are not talking of "reality", but of instruments of lenses through which we read reality' (ibid.).[18]

In the 1996 Majles election and the 1997 presidential election, the use of campaign literature to reflect the people's demands became very transparent and the split between the two ruling elites in the Islamic Republic became apparent; consequently the sloganeering became very specific, even among the various politically active religious groups. Almost four months prior to the sixth Majles election, *Hamshahry* newspaper, reviewing the slogans of the different political groups, briefly summarised each group based on their speeches or interviews with various newspaper reporters. Rasul Montakhabnia, member of the Central Council of Majmae Rouhaniyat-e Mobarez (MRM), suggested that in order to identify the various groups they should be known collectively as the '*Dovvom-e Khordad*', or the supporters of the May 1997 election: they numbered 17 in all.

It is interesting to note that before the serious electioneering began, MRM and the 17 recognized groups all clearly defined their remit as being based on the Imam's line. The 17 identified groups were quickly labelled as the evolutionary product of Imam Khomeini's line. Adopting this tactic meant that far-right conservatives could not label them as liberal or revisionist or, in other words, take the initiative. Among the MRM there were only three active and known political figures: Musavi-Khoeiniha, the former managing editor of the banned *Salam* newspaper; Mohtashemi, former Minister of the Interior, and Karrubi, former Majles Speaker. None of them was close to the office of Ayatollah Khamenehi, the *Rahbar*, nor were they equal in terms of political weight to Majmae Rouhaniayat-e Mobarez Tehran (MRMT).

The MRM was politically aware enough to judge the public mood and see the people's enthusiasm towards the May election movement, Dovvom-e Khordad. Compromising their militant views to President Khatami's election platform and those of the 17 political groups, they speedily adopted a tactic of 'non-endorsement' towards other political groups such as Rafsanjani's Kargozaran. When Rafsanjani became president in August 1989, among the many promises he made in his inaugural speech was the establishment of political parties. In his second term, he tried to initiate a political group called Kargozaran and later asked Karbaschi to be general-secretary – as he saw himself as the king-maker, not a democratically elected party leader. This king-making tendency, with his nose everywhere, supports the dominant view among Iranian affairs analysts that Rafsanjani, like Kani, is not in favour of democracy and democratic practice in Iran. From the first day of the revolution, Rafsanjani's political activities have always suggested that he is an opportunist rather than a political leader. In the past two decades, his political performance has indicated that he is a political entrepreneur rather than a thinker. Even in his memoirs, his journalism in *Maktab Islam* periodical, and his book about Amirkabir, he refers to others instead of revealing what he himself thinks. After Karbaschi's imprisonment, Rafsanjani's brother in-law, Hossein Marashi, became caretaker of the Kargozaran group. He suggested that the group should participate in the sixth Majles election under the banner 'Security, Welfare and Freedom'. According to in depth interviews, Marashi promised people that the Kargozaran candidate policy would be based on this selfsame slogan, with its aim to create a balance between political and economic development. There is in Iran a common expression, which draws on the French wrench, a spanner which can change its size and shape easily. It is often used to refer to political opportunists who, in order to make the headlines, modify their position or politics. Kargozaran is such a group – its social and political focus capable of change without explanation, covering all directions at once without accepting blame or responsibility, rather like Rafsanjani himself.[19]

By contrast, the policies and aims of the other newly established political groups are very transparent and clear.

- Mohsen Mirdamadi, one of the members of Jebheh-Mosharekat (Participation Front Party), Khatami's group, suggested in an interview that political development provided the basis of his party and that candidates should be elected on the principle of political development.
- Ghandhari, the general-secretary of the Islamic Iran Solidarity Group, argues that the aims of this group are based on coalition with the Dovvom-e Khordad group. His group proposed a list of candidates for the sixth Majles.
- Hassan Ghaforifard, the general-secretary of the Association of Islamic Engineers, related to Hamsou groups and other Motallefeh groups, argues in an interview that the major slogan for participation in the election is to defend values in line with Ayatollah Khamenehi, the Supreme Leader.
- Soheyla Jeludarzahdeh, members of Hezbeh Islami Kar (Islamic Workers' Party), nominated with the support of the Dovvom-e Khordad group, are concerned with three principles: to protect the right to work, to solve unemployment and to continue and protect political development. These are their major slogans for the election.

Hamid Reza Taraghi, who was responsible for the Khorasan branch of the Motallefeh group, stated in relation to the sixth Majles election that all the Hamsou groups and Rouhaniyat-e Mobarez groups, despite lengthy discussion, had been unable to agree on slogans which represented their principles in the coalition. They had no slogan or message for voters. It is interesting to note that Hojati-Kermani criticized the entire Rouhaniyat after the revolution for its basis in traditional leadership. They wanted an organisation above the law, he said, and at the same time desired to act like a political party; they wanted the people to vote for them, but they divided political groups into insider (*Khodi*) and outsider (*Nakhodi*), whilst in Islam all people are brothers and sisters, and there is no division between friend and stranger. In other words, he continued, we as spiritual leaders of society must act according to Islamic constitutional law. All people are Iranian and equal according to the constitution, thus there is no place for a distinction between friends and strangers.[20]

Despite this critical article by Hojati-Kermani, Ayatollah Mahdavi Kani, the general secretary of Majmae Rouhaniyat-e Mobarez Tehran (MRMT), clearly suggested in an interview that MRMT was not a party but was above the party system. They needed to facilitate communication among the conservative elements in Qom seminaries, he said, and he drew distinctions between his group and other political groups in Iran. He was frank in adopting a tactic of secrecy and re-emphasising the policy of insider and outsider (*Khodi va Nakhodi*). It is important to note that Payam Azadi, in a critical review of MRMT policy, raised the concepts of friend and stranger and asked of Musavi-Khoeiniha and Nuri, were they friends or strangers? He criticized the MRMT platform and questioned their stand on various issues. MRMT remained silent in a manner that suggested no one had the authority to criticize or ask questions of them. The only source for an examination of the tactics of this group is the output of Ayatollah Kani on various occasions, which reinforces the climate of secrecy that surrounds them. This lack of any clear policy line was demonstrated a very sinister way by one of the group's members, Ayatollah Movahedi-Savoji, in an interview with CNN reporter Christiane Amanpour.

In order to define the method and tactics of various active political groups it is necessary to examine briefly various newspapers that have been published since Khatami's election, such as *Aftab-e Emruz*, *Arya*, *Azad*, *Gozaresh-e-Rouz*, *Hamshahry*, *Iran*, *Jahan-e-Islam*, *Jame'eh*, *Tous*, *Khordad*, *Neshat*, *Akhbare-Eghtesadi*, *Sobh-e-Emrouz*, *Zan*, *Mosharekat*, *Bayyan* and *Fath-e*.[21] Most of these were published off and on in response to social and political conditions that prevailed within the context of the *velayat-e faghih*. When conservative forces feel their authority is under threat, they take the law in their own hands and shut down newspapers. So far, the new newspapers are the reflection of social and political demand – they represent the public's cry for freedom, as is revealed by an examination of the conservative press, such as *Kayhan*, *Abrar*, *Jomhurieyeh Islami*, *Tehran Times*, *Entekhab* and *Resalat*, and the slogans and posters of the sixth Majles.

There are three kinds of slogans and messages for the voters. First, the messages of the conservative forces in the election can be summarized in a speech of the general-secretary of the Motallefeh groups, Habibolah Askaroladi. In it he refers to Ayatollah Khomeini, points out that the nation's vote is final and suggests that we respect the people's vote and should ask the sixth Majles not to change the concerns of the fifth Majles. The conservative groups' messages are based on reinforcing the status quo, resisting change and ignoring the demands of the young population calling for progress and reform. Conservative slogans continuously refer to past traditions, Islamic values and traditional models of communication, and they preach about and warn against reform and change, which they argue are foreign conspiracies and a threat to national security.[22]

It is interesting to compare the approaches of two candidates, one from the conservative camp and the other reformist. The conservative candidate introduced himself as a follower of the Imam line, a believer and supporter of *velayat-e faghih*, a supporter of Islamic values and the renaissance of Islamic culture and civilization. He was the candidate of Hezbeh Tamadon Islami, Chekad Azad Andisheh, Hezbeh Eatedal va Tousaeh and Hezbeh Islami Refahe Kargaran. In contrast, the reformist candidate's message to voters was based on the concepts of Iran for all Iranians, justice for all, a future for the young, respect for human beings, and management and administration by experts. The reformist candidate's message was quite transparent and clear, and appealed to all Iranians. The conservative message, however, was unclear and did not address any particular group.

Outlined in Table 12.1 on page 244 are the major slogans and keyword statements promoted by each group to entice voters.

Notes

1 *Neshat* newspaper, no.101, Vol. 1, 19 July 1999.
2 Various interviews with analysts and researchers of Iranian affairs.
3 F. Moin, *Who's Who in Iran*, (Bonn: Media & Book Co., 1998).
4 Interviews with government officials.
5 *Sobh-e-Emruz* newspaper, no.157, 10 July 1999.
6 *Who's Who in Iran*, (Bonn: Media & Book Co., 1998).
7 Interview with expert on Iranian affairs.
8 *Who's Who in Iran*, (Bonn: Media & Book Co., 1998).
9 Interview with various researchers of Iranian affairs.
10 *Iran Farda*, no.54, June 1999; *Azad* newspaper, 29 June 1999.
11 Interview with religious affairs specialist in Qom.
12 Interview with judiciary affairs specialist in Tehran.
13 *Khordad*, Iranian independent daily paper, 12 July 1999.
14 Nasser Hadian, *Sixth Majles Election in Iran: Dynamic and Assessment*, (Oxford University, February, 2000).
15 See Nasser, Hadian for further analysis.
16 See Nasser, Hadian, *Sixth Majles Election*.
17 Albert Melucci, in Hank Johnston and Bert Klandermans, (eds), *Social Movements and Culture* (University of Minnesota Press, 1995).
18 See Albert Melucci for further discussion.
19 See *Ettelaat* newspaper, no.1410, 3 March 2000 and no.1406, 28 February 2000.
20 *Fath-e* newspaper, no.1420, 19 February 2000.
21 *Mosharekat* newspaper, no.40, February 2000.

22 *Aria* newspaper, national security report, about the attack at the student dormitory, 15 August 1999. For further analysis see *Roozegare Now*, no.216, Vol. 12, February 2000 and *Rahe Azadi*, February 2000, *Ettelaat*, no.1374, 13 January 2000; *Ettelaat* no.1409, 2 March 2000, *Hamshahry* newspaper, no.2054, 16 February 2000.

Table 12.1 The principal election campaigns for the sixth Majles election

Conservative groups: Hamsou/ Motallefeh	*Kargozaran group*	*Participation Front (Jebheh Mosharekat)*
Message: Vague – lack of defined policy – re-enforce the present – refer to Islamic values – uphold the *Velayat-e Faqi* – boast of candidates' status yet fail to state their political achievements – lack transparency with regard to membership/titles – ally themselves with Imam Khomeini or Ayatollah Khamenehi	*Message*: Provide broadsheet and poster biography of each candidate – personalised letter/poster sent to 7 million voters in Tehran (the most expensive publicity campaign of the election) – still lack focus and clear policy line – opportunistic	*Message*: Peace, happiness, freedom. Today reform is the only way to rescue Iran – People's support for Khatami – 29 Bahman is the day people will rule – To ban varying approaches and to ignore the rights of others will ruin our country – voting is a duty – a conscious vote is the symbol of the people's rule
Tactics for election: Policy of secrecy – keeping information to themselves – making use of connection with office of *Rahbari* – avoiding public lectures or interviews – avoiding debate with other groups (on the grounds that they are unequal)	*Tactics for election:* Releasing Karbaschi from prison – using posters/ pictures to make most of link with Imam Khomeini – using inflated titles such as *Sardare Sazandegi* (Leader of Construction and Development) – making mileage of Rafsanfani's interview with the press in which he claimed 'My memory is the secret box of the regime', and with various political groups	*Tactics for election*: Honesty – straightforwardness – invitation for a brighter future – clear policy lines – using concerts to influence young voters for the first time in Islamic elections – responding to people's wishes – most most importantly, acknowledging Ayatollah Khamenehi for his support – 29 Bahman is the day for people to rule

Bibliography

Abrahamian, Ervand, 'The crowd in Iranian politics 1905–1953'. *Past and present: A journal of historical studies*, no. 41, December (1968).

Abrahamian, Ervand, *Iran between Two Revolutions* (Princeton, NJ: Princeton University Press, 1982).

Adibi, Hossein, 'Iranian in Australia', paper presented to the Australian Sociological Conference, December (1994).

Afkhami, M., 'A future in the past: The pre-revolutionary 'women's movement', in B. Morgan (ed.). *Sisterhood is global* (Middlesex, England: Penguin Books Ltd., 1984).

Afkhami, M., 'Women in post-revolutionary Iran: A feminist perspective', in M. Afkhami and E. Friedl (eds), *In the eye of the storm* (London: I.B. Tauris, 1994).

Afkhami, Mahnaz, *Hoghoghe Zan dar Iran* (Women and the Law in Iran, 1967–1978), (Washington, DC: Women's Center of the Foundation for Iranian Studies, 1994).

Afshar, H., 'Women, state and ideology in Iran', *Third World Quarterly*, vol. 7 no. 2 (1985).

Alizadeh, P., 'The process of import substitution industrialization in Iran', unpublished PhD thesis (Sussex University, 1985).

Alizadeh, P., 'Industrial development in Iran', *Middle East Study Series*, no. 31 (Tokyo, Japan: Institute of Development Economics, 1992).

Alizadeh, P. and Harper, B., 'Occupational sex segregation in Iran 1976–1986'. *Journal of International Development*, vol. 7, no. 4, (1995), pp. 637–51.

Amirahmadi, Hooshang, *Revolution and economic transition: The Iranian experience* (New York: State University of New York Press, 1990).

Amirahmadi, Hooshang, 'Economic cost of the war and reconstruction in Iran', in Cyrus Bina and Hamid Zangeneh (eds), *Modern Capitalism and Islamic Ideology in Iran* (New York: St. Martin's Press, 1992), pp. 257–82.

Amirahmadi, Hooshang, 'Emerging civil society in Iran', *SAIS Review*, 16 (2), (Summer–Fall 1996), pp. 87–107.

Amirahmadi, Hooshang and Zangeneh, Hamid, 'An analysis of Iranian government budgets', *Public Budgeting and Financial Management*, vol. 9, issue 2 (1997).

Amuzegar, Jahangir, 'The Iranian economy before and after revolution', *Middle East Journal*, 8, 3 (Summer 1992), pp. 413–25.

Amuzegar, Jahangir, *Economy under the Islamic Republic* (London and New York: 1993), p. 195.

Ansari, M., *The Making of the Iranian Community in America* (New York: Pardis Press Inc., 1992)

Ansari, M., 'A community in process: the first generation of the Iranian professional middle-class immigrants in the United States', *International Review of Modern Sociology*, 7, January–June (1977), pp. 85–101.

Appleyard, R., *The Impact of International Migration on Developing Countries*, OECD Publication (1989).

Askari, H. *et. al.*, 'Iran's migration of skilled labour to the United States', *Iranian Studies*, 10, Winter–Spring (1977), pp. 3–39.

Askari, Somayeh, 'Women, main victims of suicide in Iran', *Farhang-e Tose'e*, a monthly cultural, social, political and economic journal published in Tehran and banned 1999, 21 February–20 March, (1998).

Azimi (Arani), Hossein, 'Madarhay-e toseeh nayaftagi dar eghtesad-e Iran' [The Circles of Underdevelopment in the Economy of Iran], (Tehran: Nashr-e Ney, 1991).

Bakhash, Shaul, 'The politics of land, law, social justice in Iran', *Middle East Journal*, vol. 43, no. 2, Spring (1988), pp. 186–201.

Baktiari, Bahman, *Parliamentary Politics in Revolutionary Iran* (Gainesville: University Press of Florida, 1996).

Balfour, J.M., *Recent Happenings in Persia* (London and Edinburgh: Blackwood and Son, 1922).

Bank-e Markazi Jomhooriy-e Eslami-e Iran 1993, Hessabhay-e Melli-e Iran, 1370 [National Accounting of Iran, 1991], (Tehran: Edarey-e Hesabhay-e Eghtesadi, 1993).

Bank-e Markazi Jomhooriy-e Eslami-e Iran 1994, Barrasiy-e Moghaddamatiy-e Hesabhay-e Melli dar 1372 va Natayej-e Tafsili-e Hesabhay-e Melli dar 1371 [An introductory estimation of national accounting of Iran in 1993 and the detailed national accounting in 1992), (Tehran: Edarey-e Hesabhay-e Eghtesadi, 1994).

Bank-e Markazi Jomhooriy-e Eslami-e Iran 1994, Hessabhay-e Melli-e Iran, 1353–1369 [National Accounting of Iran, 1974–1990], (Tehran: Edarey-e Hesabhay-e Eghtesadi, 1994).

Barber, Benhamin, R., 'Jihad vs. McWorld', *The Atlantic*, (March 1992), pp. 53–63.

Barnet, Richard J. and Cavanagh, John, *Global Dreams: Imperial Corporations and the New World Order* (New York: Simon and Schuster, 1994).

Barraclough, Colin, 'Iran confronts a long-hidden problem: drugs', *New York Times*, 29 August, 1999.

Barry, Brian and Goodin, Robert (eds), *Free Movement: Ethical Issues in the Transnational Migration of People and Money* (University Park: Penn State University Press, 1992).

Bartlett, Christopher and Sumantra, Ghoshal, *Managing Across Borders: The Transnational Solution* (Boston: Harvard University Press, 1989).

Basch, L., Glick Schiller, N. and Blanc-Szanton, C., *Nations Unbound* (Pennsylvania: Gordon and Breach, 1994).

Baumol, William, *The Stock Market and Economic Efficiency* (New York: Fordham University Press, 1965).

Baumol, William, 'Productivity growth, convergence, and welfare: what the long-run data show', *American Economic Review*, 76(5), (1986), pp. 1072–85.

Bayat, Assef, *Workers and Revolution in Iran* (London: Zed Books Ltd., 1987), p. 107.

Bean, Frank and Browning, Harley L., 'The sociodemographic characteristics of Mexican immigrant status group', *International Migration Review*, 18 (1984), pp. 672–91.

Behdad, Sohrab, 'The post-revolutionary economic crisis', in Saeed Rahnema and Sohrab Behdad . Iran *After the Revolution; Crisis of an Islamic State* (London and New York: I.B. Tauris. 1995), pp. 97–128.

Berman, M., *All that is solid melts into air: the experience of modernity* (London: Verso, 1982).

Bhach, Parminder, *Twice Migrants: East African Sikh Settlers*, (London and New York: Tavistock, 1985).

Bhattacharya, Debesh, *Economic Development and Underdevelopment* (Sydney: Australian Professional Publications, 1989).

Bigsten, Arne, *Income Distribution and Development, Theory, Evidence, and Policy* (London: Heinemann, 1983).

Bill, James A., 'Modernization and reform from above: the case of Iran', *Middle East Journal*, 27 (February 1970).

Bina, Cyrus and Zangeneh, Hamid (eds), *Modern Capitalism and Islamic Ideology in Iran*, (New York: St. Martin's Press, 1992).

Blau, F.D. and Ferber, M.A., *The economics of women, men, and work*, (New Jersey: Prentice-Hall, 1992).

Boserup, E., *Women's role in economic development* (New York: St Martin's Press, 1970).

Boserup, E., 'Economic change and the roles of women', in I. Tinker (ed.), *Persistent inequality: Women and world development* (New York: Oxford University Press, 1990).

Bottomley, G., *From Another Place: Migration and the Politics of Culture* (Cambridge: Cambridge University Press, 1992).

Bownkerk, J., *The Sociology of Return Migration* (The Hague: Mouton, 1974).

Bozorgmehr, Mehdi, 'Internal ethnicity: Armenian, Baha'i, Jewish and Muslim Iranians in Los Angeles', PhD dissertation (Los Angeles: University of California, 1992).

Bozorgmehr, Mehdi and Sabagh, George, 'High status immigrants: a statistical profile of Iranians in the United States', *Iranian* (1988).

Brecher, Jeremy and Costello, Tim, *Global Village or Global Pillage: Economic Reconstruction from the Bottom Up* (Boston, Mass.: South End Press, 1994).

Brendan, Martin, *In the Public Interest? Privatisation and Public Sector Reform* (London: Zed Books, 1993).

Cagatay, N. and Berik, G., 'Transition to export led growth in Turkey: Is there a feminisation of employment?', *Capital and Class*, no. 43, Spring (1991), pp. 153–77.

Cagatay, N. and Ozler, S., 'Feminisation of the labour force: the effects of long-term development and structural adjustment', *World Development*, vol. 23, no. 11, November (special issue on Gender, adjustment and macroeconomics), (1995), pp. 1883–95 .

Calabrese A. and Redal W., 'Is there a US foreign policy in telecommunications? Transatlantic trade policy as a case study', IAMCR, 19th General Assembly, Seoul, Korea, 3–8 July 1994.

Camilleri, Santo F., 'Theory, probability and inaction in social research', *American Sociological Review*, 6 (February 1941).

Carnoy, Martin, Castells, Manuel, Cohen, S. Stephen and Cardoso, H. Fernando, *The New Global Economy in the Information Age* (Pennsylvania: Penn State University Press, 1993).

Castle, S. and Miller, M.J., *The Age of Migration: International Population Movements in the Modern World* (London: Macmillan, 1993).

Cerny, Philip, 'Globalization and collective action', *International Organization*, 49(4), (Autumn 1995), pp. 595–625.

Chenery, Hollis, *Structural Change and Development Policy* (New York: Oxford University Press, 1979).

Clurman, M. Richard, *To the End of Time, The Seduction of a Media Empire* (New York: Simon and Schuster, 1993).

Cooper, Richard, 'National economic policy in an interdependent world', in Richard Cooper (ed.), *Islam and Modernity: Muslim Intellectuals Respond* (London: J.B. Tauris, 1998).

Curzon, G., *Persia and the Persian Question* (London: Longmans Green, 1892)

Dadkhah, Kamran M., 'The inflationary process of the Iranian economy, 1970–1980', *International Journal of Middle East Studies*, 17 (1985), pp. 365–81.

Dane, F. *Research Method* (Wadsworth Inc., 1990).

Das, Raju, 'State theories: a critical analysis', *Science & Society*, 60 (1), (Spring 1996), pp. 27–57.

Davis, Kingsley, 'International inequality and migration in the Middle East and north Africa: an analysis of trends and issues', in *International Migration in the Arab World*, (United Nations Economic Commission for Western Asia, 1982).

Djavad, Salahi-Isphahani, 'The Iranian economy since the revolution', in S. Hunter (ed.), *Internal Development in Iran* (Washington, DC, 1982), pp. 25–48.

Drucker, Peter, *Post-Capitalist Society* (Harper Business, 1993), p. 9.

Drucker, Peter, *The New Realities* (Harper and Row, 1989), p. 69.

Eisenstadt, S.N., *The Absorption of Immigrants* (London: Routledge and Kegan Paul, 1954).

Elson, D., 'Appraising recent developments in the world markets for nimble fingers', in A. Chhachhi and R. Pittin (eds), *Confronting state, capital and patriarchy: Women organizing in the process of industrialisation* (Macmillan Press Ltd., 1996).

Esfandiari, H., 'The Majles and women's issues in the Islamic Republic of Iran', in M. Afkhami and E. Friedl (eds), *In the Eye of the Storm* (London: I.B. Tauris, 1994).

Esfandiari, Haleh, *Reconstructed Lives; Women and Iran's Islamic Revolution* (Washington, DC: The Woodrow Wilson Center Press and The Johns Hopkins University Press, 1997).

Fallaci, Oriana, 'The Shah of Iran', *New Republic*, no. 1 (December 1973).

Fallaci, Oriana, *Interview with History* (Boston: Houghton Mifflin, 1976).

Finger, J.M. and Olechowski, Andrzej, *The Uruguay Round: A Textbook on the Multilateral Trade Negotiation* (Washington, DC: The World Bank, 1987).

Fukayama, Francis, 'The end of history', *The National Interest* (Summer 1989).

Ghasimi, M.R., 'The Iranian economy after the revolution: an economic appraisal of the five-year plan', *International Journal of Middle East Studies*, 24 (1992), pp. 599–614.

Ghosh, B.N., 'Brain migration from the Third World: an implication analysis', *Rivista Internationale di Scienze Economiche Commerciali*, vol. 34, no. 1 (1985).

Giddens, Anthony, *A Contemporary Critique of Historical materialism* (London and Basingstoke: Macmillan, 1981), pp. 91–7.

Giddens, A., *The Consequences of Modernity* (Cambridge: Polity Press, 1990).

Giddens, A., *Modernity and Self-Identity* (Cambridge: Polity Press, 1991).

Gilanshah, F., 'Iranians in the Twin Cities', *Journal of the Institute of Muslim Minority Affairs*, vol. 7, January (1986), pp. 117–23.

Gmelch, G., *Double Passage: The Lives of Caribbean Migrants Abroad and Back Home* (University of Michigan Press, 1992).

Goldblatt, D., Held, D., McGrew, A. and Perraton, J., 'Economic globalisation and the nation state: The transfomation of political power?' *Soundings: A Journal of Politics and Culture,* issue 7, Autumn (1997).

Gordon, M.M., *Assimilation in American Life: The Role of Race Religion and National Origins* (New York: Oxford University Press, 1964).

Griffin, Keith and Knight, John, 'Human development: the case for renewed emphasis', in Charles, K. Wilber and Kenneth, P. Jameson (eds), *The Political Economy of Development and Underdevelopment* (New York: McGraw-Hill, 1992).

Hadian, Nasser, 'Majles Election in Iran: Dynamic and Assessment' (February 2000).

Haeri, Shahla, *Law of Desire; Temporary Marriage in Shi'i Iran* (Syracuse, NY: Syracuse University Press, 1989).

Halliday, Fred, *Iran: Dictatorship and Development* (New York: Penguin Books Ltd., 1979).

Halliday, Fred, 'The politics of Islamic fundamentalism: Iran, Tunisia, and the challenge of the secular state', in Akbar Ahmed and H. Donnan (eds), *Islam, Globalization and Postmodernity* (London: Routledge, 1994).

Hannerz, U., *Cultural Complexity: Studies in the Social Organisation of Meaning*, (New York: Columbia University Press, 1992).

Harandi, Hussein Saffaar, 'Economic security from three perspectives', *Kayhan*, 7 Shahrivar 1378 (29 August 1999).

Harney, Desmond, 'The Iranian revolution ten years on', *Asian Affairs*, vol. 20, June (1989), pp. 153–64.

Harvey, D., *The Condition of Postmodernity* (Oxford: Blackwell, 1989).

Hepworth, Mark, *Geography of the Information Economy* (London: Pinter, 1989).

Hill, Jill, *Deregulation Telecommunications* (London: Pinter, 1996).

Hirst, Paul and Thompson, Grahame F., *Globalization in Question* (Cambridge: Polity Press, 1996).

Hoekman, Bernard M. and Kostecki, Michael M., *The Political Economy of The World Trading System: From GATT to WTO*, (Oxford: Oxford University Press, 1995).

Hojat, M. and Herman, Mary, 'Adjustment and psychological problems of Iranian and Philipino physicians in the US', *Journal of Clinical Psychology*, January 1985, Vol. 41, no. 1, (1985), pp. 130–136.

Howes, A. and A. Singh, 'Long-term trends in the world economy: the gender dimension', *World Development*, vol. 23, no. 11, November (special issue on Gender, adjustment and macroeconomics) (1995), pp. 1895–1913.

Inkeles, Alex, *One World Emerging* (Bolder, Colorado: Westview Press, 1998).
International Labour Office (ILO) *Employment, income and equality: A strategy for increasing productive employment in Kenya* (Geneva, 1972).
International Labour Office (ILO), *Yearbook of Labour Statistics* (1985).
International Labour Office, *Yearbook of Labour Statistics* (retrospective edition on population censuses 1945–1989) (Geneva, 1991).
International Labour Office, *Yearbook of Labour Statistics 1996* (Geneva, 1997).
Iran Times, 'Iranians in America: more professional, better educated, very Californian', 14(34) 1–2 (1984).
Jacobs, J., *The Death and Life of Great American Cities* (New York: Vintage Books, 1961).
Jayawardena, K., *Feminism and Nationalism in the Third World*, (London: Zed Books Ltd, 1986).
Jazani, Bizhan, *Capitalism and Revolution in Iran* (London: Zed Books, 1981).
Joekes, S. with Moayedi, R., 'Women and export manufacturing: a review of the issues and AID policy', paper prepared for US Agency for International Development (International Center for Research on Women, Washington, DC, 1987).
Johnston, Hank and Klandermans, Bert (eds), *Social Movements and Culture* (Minnesota: University of Minnesota Press, 1995).
Kafka, Franz, *The Castle*, 1962.
Kafka, Franz, *The Trial*, 1962.
Kamalkhani, Zahra, *Iranian Immigrants and Refugees In Norway*. (Department of Social Anthropology, University of Bergen, 1988).
Kandiyoti, D., (ed.), *Women, Islam and State* (London: Macmillan Press, 1991).
Karshenas, M., *Oil, State and Industrialization in Iran* (Cambridge University Press, 1990).
Karshenas, M., 1995a, 'Structural adjustment and the prospects of Iranian economy', working paper series no. 57 (Department of Economics, School of Oriental and African Studies, University of London, 1995).
Karshenas, M. 1995b, 'Economic liberalization, competitiveness and women's employment in the Middle East and north Africa', paper prepared for the seminar on Economic liberalisation and women's employment in the Middle East and north Africa (Nicosia, 10 November 1995).
Katouzian, Homa, *The Political Economy of Modern Iran, Despotism and Pseudo-Modernism 1926–1979* (London, 1980).
Katouzian, Homa, *The Political Economy of Modern Iran* (London: Macmillan, and New York: New York University Press, 1981).
Katouzian, Homa. 'The Aridisolatic society: a model of long term social and economic development in Iran', *International Journal of Middle East Studies* (July 1983).
Katouzian, Homa (ed.), *Musaddiq's Memoirs* (London: Jebheh, 1988), Book 1.
Katouzian, Homa, *Khatarat-e Siyasl-ye Khalil Maleki*, 2nd edn, (Tehran: Sherkat-e Enteshar, 1368 [1989]), introduction, chapter 2.
Katouzian, Homa, 'Oil and economic development in the Middle East', in Georges Sabagh (ed.), *The Modern Economic History of the Middle East in its World Context* (Cambridge: Cambridge University Press, 1989).
Katouzian, Homa, 'Islamic government and politics: the practice and theory of the guardianship of jurisconsult', in Charles Davies (ed.), *After the War: Iran, Iraq and the Arab Gulf* (London, 1990).

Katouzian, Homa, *Musaddiq and the Struggle for Power in Iran* (London and New York: I.B. Tauris, 1991).

Katouzian, Homa, *Sadeq Hedayat: The Life and Literature of an Iranian Writer* (London and New York: I.B. Tauris, 1991).

Katouzian, Homa, 'The execution of Amir Hasanak the Vazir', Pembroke Papers (1993).

Katouzian, Homa, 'Eqtesad-e Siyasi-ye Iran', author's introduction to the second edition of the Persian translation (Tehran: Nashr-e Markaz, 1372 [1993]).

Katouzian, Homa, 'Demokrasi, Diktatori, va Mas'uliyat-e Mellat', *Ettela'at-e Siyasi Eqtesadi*, 67–68 (April–May 1993).

Katouzian, Homa, *Estebdad, Demokrasi va Nehzat-e Melli* (London and Washington: Mehregan, 1993, and Tehran: Nashr-e Markaz, 1994).

Katouzian, Homa, 'Nameh-resani va Maquleh-ye Siyasat', *Adineh* (September 1372 [1993]), reprinted in *Chahardah Maqaleh dar Adabiyat, Ejtema' Falsafeh va Eqtesad* [Fourteen Lectures on Literature, Society, Philosophy and Economics], (Tehran: Nashr-e Markaz, 1995).

Katouzian, Homa, *The Coup d'état of 1921 in Iran*, forthcoming.

Keddie, Nikki R. and Yann, Richard, *Roots of Revolution* (New Haven, Conn.: Yale University Press,).

Khalatbari, Firouzeh, 'The Tehran Stock Exchange and privatization of public sector enterprises in Iran: a study of obstacles to the private sector development', in Thierry Coville (ed.), *The Economy of Islamic Iran: Between State and Market* (Tehran: Institut Français de Recherche en Iran, 1973), pp. 177–208.

King, R. (ed.) *Return Migration and Regional Economic Problems* (London: Croom Helm, 1986), pp. 47–57.

Kooroshy, J., 'Land tenure under Shiite Islam', *Quarterly Journal of International Agriculture*, vol. 26, no. 4, October–December (1987), p. 391–397.

Kooroshy, Javad, *Wirtschaftsordnung der Islamischen Republik Iran, Anspruch und Wirklichkeit* (Hamburg, 1990), p. 178 ff.

Kooroshy, J., *Mabaniye eqtesad-e eslami* [The Basic Elements of the Islamic Economy] (Tehran: Daftar-e hamkariye houzeh wa daneshgah (The Bureau of Coordination between the Theological Institution and the University): 1992), Chapter 5.

Lee, E.S. 'A theory of migration', *Demography*, vol. 3, no. 1 (1966), pp. 47–57.

Lieberson, Stanley and Waters, Mary C., *From Many Strands: Ethnic and Racial Groups in Contemporary America* (New York: Russell Sage, 1989).

Light, Ivan and Bonacich, Edna, *Immigrant Entrepreneurs*, (Berkeley: University of California Press, 1988).

Lorentz, J.H. and Wertime, J.T., 'Iranians', in Stephen Thernstrom (ed.) *Harvard Encyclopedia of American Ethnic Groups* (1980), pp. 521–4.

Lowi, Theodore, *The End of Liberalism: Ideology, Policy, and the Crisis of Public Authority* (New York: Norton, 1969).

Lubbers, R.F.M. 'Globalization: an exploration', *Nijenrode Management Review*, no 1 (November 1996).

Lyon, David, *The Information Society, Issues and Illusions*, (Cambridge: Polity Press, 1988).

Madanipour, A., Davoudi, S., Mahmoodi, M. and Mojtabavi, J. (Akhir Consultant Engineers), *Guneh Shenasy-e Maskan-e Rustaii-e Khuzestan: Masaleh va System-ha-ye Sakhtemani* (Typology of Rural Housing in Khuzestan: Building Materials and

Systems) Markaz-e Tahghighat-e Sakhteman va Maskan (Iran's Building and Housing Research Center), (Tehran 1984).

Madanipour, A., Davoudi, S., Mahmoodi, M. and Mojtabavi, J. (Akhir Consultant Engineers), *Guneh Shenasy-e Maskan-e Rustaii-e Khuzestan: Baft* (Typology of Rural Housing in Khuzestan: Regional and Settlement Fabric), Markaz-e Tahghighat-e Sakhteman va Maskan (Iran's Building and Housing Research Center), (Tehran, 1985).

Madanipour, A., Davoudi, S., Mahmoodi, M. and Mojtabavi, J., (Akhir Consultant Engineers) *Guneh Shenasy-e Maskan-e Rustaii-e Khuzestan: Vahed-e Maskooni* (Typology of Rural Housing in Khuzestan: The Dwelling Unit) Markaz-e Tahghighat-e Sakhteman va Maskan (Iran's Building and Housing Research Center), (Tehran, 1986).

Madanipour, A., 'Postwar reconstruction in southwest Iran: new settlements or new identities?', in Eric Watkins (ed.), *The Middle Eastern Environment* (Cambridge: St Malo Press, 1995), pp. 209–19.

Madanipour, A., 'Reading the city', in P. Healey, S. Cameron, S. Davoudi, S. Graham, and A. Madanipour, (eds) *Managing Cities: The New Urban Context* (Chichester: John Wiley, 1995).

Madanipour, A., *Design of Urban Space* (Chichester: John Wiley, 1996).

Madanipour, A., Entries on 'Bakhtiaris', 'Lurs', and 'Arabs of Khuzestan', in Paul Oliver (ed.), *Encyclopedia of the Vernacular Architecture of the World* (Cambridge: Cambridge University Press, 1997).

Madanipour, A., *Tehran: the making of a metropolis*, World's Cities Series (Chichester: John Wiley, 1998).

Mahdavy, Hossain, 'The pattern and problems of economic development in rentier states: the case of Iran', in M.A. Cook, (ed.), *Studies in the Economic History of the Middle East* (New York und Toronto, 1970), 428–67.

Mahdi, Ali Akbar, 'The Iranian struggle for liberation: socio-historical roots to the Islamic revolution', *The Review of Iranian Political Economy and History*, vol. IV, no. 1, Spring (1980).

Mahdi, Ali Akbar, 'Reconstructing gender in post-revolutionary Iran: transcending the revolution?' *Middle East Insight*, vol. XI, no. 5, July–August (1995).

Mahdi, Ali Akbar, *Farhang-e Irani, J'ame'eh-ye Madani, va Daghdaghe-ye Demokr'asi* [Iranian Culture, Civil Society, and Concern for Democracy] (Toronto: Javan Publications, 1998).

Mankiw, N. Gregory, 'The growth of nations,' *Brookings Papers on Economic Activity*, 25th anniversary issue (1995) pp. 275–325.

Markaz-e Amar-e Iran, Sarshomariy-e Omomiy-e Nofos va Maskan Aban-e 1355, Koll-e Keshvar [National Census of Population and Housing, 1976], Shomarey-e 186 (Tehran, 1980).

Markaz-e Amar-e Iran, Shakhes-hay-e Nabarabariy-e Tozi-e Daramad dar Iran [The indexes of income inequality distribution in Iran], Barrasiy-e Shomareh 63, Modiriyyat-e Amarhay-e Mali va Mohasebat-e Melli (Tehran, 1983).

Markaz-e Amar-e Iran, Shakhes-hay-e Nabarabariy-e Tozi-e Daramad dar Koll-e Keshvar, Manategh-e Shahri va Rustaei, 1361–65 [The indexes of income inequality distribution in Iran, urban and rural areas, during 1982–1986], Barrasiy-e Shomareh 108, Modiriyyat-e Amarhay-e Mali va Mohasebat-e Melli (Tehran, 1987).

Markaz-e Amar-e Iran, Sarshomariy-e Omomiy-e Nofos va Maskan Mehr-e 1365, Koll-e Keshvar, Natayej-e Tafsili [National Census of Population and Housing, 1986], Shomarey-e 6 (Tehran, 1988).

Markaz-e Amar-e Iran, Salnameh Amari-e Keshvar 1369 [Iran Statistical Yearbook 1990], (Tehran, 1991).

Markaz-e Amar-e Iran, Gozareshi dar Zamineh Shakhes-hay-e Nabarabary-e Tozi-e Daramad dar Iran: Salhay-e 1368, 1369 va 1390 [A report on the indexes of income inequality distribution in Iran in 1989, 1990 and 1991], Daftar-e Hesabhay-e Eghtesadi (Tehran, 1992).

Markaz-e Amar-e Iran, Amargiriy-e Jari-e Jameyyat 1370, Natayej-e Omomi [The current population census, 1991], Shomarey-e, 1-25 (Tehran, 1993).

Markaz-e Amar-e Iran, Salnameh Amari-e Keshvar 1371 [Iran Statistical Yearbook 1992], (Tehran, 1993).

Markaz-e Amar-e Iran, Amargiriy-e Jari-e Jameyyat 1370, Natayej-e Tafsili [The current population census, 1991], Natayej-e 2, (Tehran, 1994).

Massey, Douglas, *Return to Azilan* (University of California Press, 1987).

Massey, Douglas 'Understanding Mexican migration to the United States', *American Journal of Sociology*, 92 (1987), 1372–1403.

McGrew, A., 'A global society?', in Hall, Stuart., Held, David and McGrew, A. (eds.), *Modernity and its Futures* (Cambridge/Oxford: Polity/Open University Press, 1992), pp. 61–102, especially p.92.

Meier, Gerald M., *Leading Issues in Economic Development*, 4th edn (New York: Oxford University Press, 1984).

Melucci, Alberto, *Nomads of the Present: Social Movements and Individual Needs in Contemporary Society* (London: Hutchinson Radius, 1989), p. 75–8.

Mittelman, James H. (ed.), *Globalization: Critical Reflections* (Lynne Rienner, 1996).

Moghadam, F., 'Commoditization of sexuality and female labour participation in Islam: implications for Iran, 1960–1990', in M. Afkhami and E. Friedl (eds), *In the eye of the storm* (London: I.B. Tauris, 1994).

Moghadam, V.M., 'Zan, kar va ideology', *Nimeye Digar*, no. 10, Persian quarterly (1989).

Moghadam, V.M., 'The reproduction of gender inequality in Muslim societies: a case study of Iran in the 1980s', *World Development*, vol. 19, no. 10 (1991).

Moghadam.V.M., *The political economy of female employment in the Middle East* (Helsinki: World Institute for Development Economics Research (WIDER), 1992).

Moghadam, V.M., *Modernising Women: Gender and Social Change in the Middle East* (Boulder and London: Lynne Rienner Publishers, 1993).

Moghissi, Haideh, *Populism and Feminism in Iran: Women's Struggle in a Male-Defined Revolutionary Movement* (New York: St Martin's Press, 1994).

Moss Kanter, Rosabeth, 'Thriving locally in the global economy', *Harvard Business Review*, September–October (1995), pp. 151–60.

Mostawfi, Abdollah, *Sharh-e Zendegani-ye Man*, vol. 3 (Tehran: Zavvar, 1360 [1981]).

Najmabadi, A., 'Hazards of modernity and morality: Women, state and ideology in contemporary Iran', in D. Kandiyoti (ed.), *Women, Islam and state* (London: Macmillan, 1991).

Nashat, Guity, 'Women in pre-revolutionary Iran: a historical overview,' in Nashat, Guity (ed.), *Women and Revolution in Iran* (Boulder: Westview Press, 1983).

Negrine, Ralph and Papathanassopoulos, Stylianos, *The Internationalization of Television* (London: Pinter, 1990).

Ogilvy, James, 'This postmodern business', *The Deeper News*, vol. 1, no. 5 (1989).

Pahlavi, Mohammad Reza, *Besu-e Tamaddon-e Bozorg* [Towards the Great Civilization], (Tehran: Sherkat-e Offset-e Sahami-ye Amm, 1978).

Paidar, P., *Women in Political Processes of Twentieth Century Iran* (Cambridge: Cambridge University Press, 1995).

Pakizegi, Behnaz, 'Legal and social positions of Iranian women'. in Louis Beck, and Nikki Keddie, (eds), *Women in the Muslim World* (Cambridge, MA: Harvard University Press, 1978).

Papanek, Hanna, 'The woman and the ideal society: control and autonomy in the construction of identity', in Valentine Moghadam (ed.), *Identity Politics and Women: Cultural Reassertion and Feminism in the International Perspective* (Oxford: Westview Press, 1994), pp. 42–75.

Pearson, R., 'Gender issues in industrialization', in Hazel J. Hewitt and D. Wield (eds), *Industrialization and Development*, (Oxford: Oxford University Press, 1992), pp. 222–47

Pesaran, M.H. 'The Iranian foreign exchange rate policy and the black market for dollars'. *International Journal of Middle East Studies*, vol. 24 (1992).

Prezeworski, Adam and Limongi, Fernando, 'Political regimes and economic growth,' *The Journal of Economic Perspective*, 7(3), (Summer 1993), pp. 51–69.

Rashidi, Ali, The economical change after the Islamic revolution 1357–1361 [1978–1982], in *Etelaat Siyasi wa Eqtesadi*, no. 67/68, p. 78.

Rawnstein, E.G., 'The laws of migration', *Journal of the Royal Statistical Society*, vol. 48, part 2, (1885), pp. 167–277.

Reich, Robert, *The Work of Nations: Preparing Ourselves for Twenty-First Century Capitalism* (New York: Knopf, 1991).

Rist, Gilbert, '"Development" as part of the modern myth: the Western socio-economic dimension of "development"', *European Journal of Development Alternatives,* vol. 2, no.1, (1990), pp.10–21.

Ross, R.J.S. and Trachte, K.C., *Global Capitalism: The New Leviathan* (Albany, NY: SUNY Press, 1990).

Rouleau, Eric, 'Iran: an economy in need of reform'. *Middle East Economic Survey*, vol. XLII, no. 27, July (1999).

Rowbotham, Sheila, *Beyond the Fragments: Feminism and the Making of Socialism* (London: Merlin Press, 1979).

Roy, Oliver, *The Failure of Political Islam* (London: I.B. Tauris, 1994).

Sachs, Jeffrey, and Warner, Andrew, 'Economic reform and the process of global integration', *Brookings Papers on Economic Activity*, 25th Anniversary Issue, #1 (1995), pp. 1–95.

Sadr, Mohammad Baqer, *Our Economy*, vol. I, p. 331.

Safadi, Raed and Laird, Sam, 'The Uruguay Round Agreement: impact on developing countries', *World Development*, vol. 24, no. 7 (1996), pp. 1223–42.

Sahabi, Azat, 'There is no other way except working and not consuming' (in Farsi), *Kayhan Havai*, no. 935, 19 June (1991).

Salame', Ghassan (ed.) *Democracy Without Democrats?* (London: I.B. Tauris, 1994).

Salt, John and Findlay, Allan, 'International migration of highly-skilled manpower: theoretical and developmental issues' in Reginald Appleyard, *The Impact of International Migration on Developing Countries* (OECD Publication, 1989).

Sami, Mohsen, 'The role and impact of education on the economic and political development of Iran', PhD thesis, the University of Nebraska (1983).

Samuelson, Huntington, *The Clash of Civilization, The Remaking of World Order* (New York: Simon and Schuster, 2000).

Sazman-e Barnameh va Budgeh, Majmoeh Ettelaati: Seri Zamani Amar-e Hesabhay-e Melli, Pooli va Mali [Time Series National Accounting, Monetary and Financial Data], Moavenat-e Omoor-e Eghtesadi, Daftar-e Eghtesad-e Kalan (Tehran, 1994).

Schiller, I. Herbert, *Communication and Cultural Domination*, (New York: International Art and Science Press, 1976).

Schiller, I. Herbert, *Who Knows Information in the Age of the Fortune 500*, (New Jersey: Ablex, 1981).

Schirazi, Asghar, *The Constitution of Iran: Politics and State in the Islamic Republic*, trans. John O'Kane (London, I.B. Tauris, 1997), pp. 126–7.

Schlesinger, Philip, R., 'Europe's contradictory communicative space', *Daedalus, Journal of the American Academy of Arts and Science*, vol.123, no. 2 (1994), pp. 25–52.

Schumacher, E.F., *Small is Beautiful: A Study of Economics as if People Mattered* (London: Blond and Briggs, 1973).

Scully, Gerald, *Constitutional Environment and Economic Growth* (Princeton: Princeton University Press, 1992).

Seers, D., 'The meaning of development' in International Development Review, vol. 11, no. 2–4', in Sundrum, R.M. 1990, *Income Distribution in Less Developed Countries* (London: Routledge, 1969).

Stahl, C., Ball, R., Inglis, C. and Guyman, P., *Global Population Movements and Their Implications for Australia* (Canberra: AGPS, 1993).

Standing, G., 'Global feminisation through flexible labour', *World Development*, vol. 17, no. 7 (1989), pp. 1077–96.

Statistical Centre of Iran, 1363 (1985), National Census of Population and Housing 1976, (Iran: Plan and Budget Organization 1985).

Statistical Centre of Iran, 1366 (1988), National Census of Population and Housing 1986, (Iran: Plan and Budget Organization 1988).

Statistical Centre of Iran, 1376 (1998), National Census of Population and Housing 1996, in Farsi, (Iran: Plan and Budget Organization 1998).

Strong, Maurice, 'The new south', *The World Today*, November (1995), pp. 215–9.

Sundrum, R.M., 'Development economics: A framework for analysis and policy' (London: Wiley, 1983), in Arndt H.W., *Economic Development: The History of an Idea* (Chicago and London: University of Chicago Press, 1987).

Sussman, Gerald and Lent, A. John (eds), *Transnational Communications, Wiring the Third World* (London: Sage, 1991).

Thomas-Hope, E., 'Transients and settlers: varieties of Caribbean migrants and the socio-economic implications of their return', *International Migration*, 24 (1986) pp. 559–70.

Tilly, L.A, and J.W. Scott, *Women, Work and Family*, 2nd edn, (New York: Routledge, 1987).

Tobin, James, 'Financial intermediaries', *Finance, The New Palgrave*, edited by J. Eatwell, M. Milgate, and P. Newman, (New York, W.W. Norton, 1989), pp. 35–52.

Todaro, P., *International Migration in Developing Countries* (Geneva: International Labour Office, 1976).

Touraine, A., *Critique of Modernity* (Oxford: Blackwell, 1995).

Vakili, Valla, *Debating Religion and Politics in Iran: The Political Thought of Abdolkarim Soroush*, Occasional Paper Series, no. 2, New York: Council on Foreign Relations, Studies Department, (1996).

Valibeigi, Mehrdad, 'The private sector in Iran's post-revolutionary economy', *Journal of South Asian and Middle Eastern Studies*, vol. XVII, no. 3, Spring (1994), p. 8.

Waldman, Peter, 'Mullah keep control of Iranian economy with iron hand', *The Wall Street Journal*, 5 May 1992.

Ward, K., *Women in the world system* (New York: Praeger, 1984).

Watts, M.J. and Rich, J., 'Occupational sex segregation in Britain, 1976–1986: the persistence of sexual stereotyping', *Cambridge Journal of Economics*, vol. 17, no. 2, June (1993).

Weinbaum, Marvin, G., 'Iran finds a party system: the institutionalization of *Iran Novin*', *The Middle East Journal* 27, no. 4, Autumn, (1973), p. 453.

Wison, Dizard P., *The Coming Information Age* (New York: Longman, 1985).

Wood, A., 'North–south trade and female labour in manufacturing: an asymmetry', *Journal of Development Studies*, vol. 27, no. 2 (1991).

World Bank, *World Development Reports 1995, 1997* (Washington DC, 1995, 1997).

Wolf, Martin, 'Why trade liberalization is a good idea,' in J.M. Finger and Andrzej Olechowski (eds), *The Uruguay Round: A Textbook on the Multilateral Trade Negotiation* (Washington, DC: The World Bank, 1987), pp. 14–21.

Wyman, Mark, *Round-Trip to America: The Immigrants Return to Europe* (Cornell University Press, 1993)

Young, T.C., 'The problem of Westernization in modern Iran', *The Middle East Journal*, 2, Washington, (1948), pp. 47–59.

Zanan, monthly women's magazine, no. 40, 10 & 11, 1376 (January/February 1998)

Zanan, monthly women's magazine, no. 41, 12, 1376 (February/March 1998)

Zangeneh, Hamid and Salam, Ahmad, 'Central banking in an interest-free banking system', *Journal of Research in Islamic Banking*, vol: 5 (Center for Research in Islamic Economics, King Abdulaziz University, Jeddah, 1993), pp. 25–35.

Zangeneh, Hamid and Moore, Janice M., 'Economic development and growth in Iran', in Hamid Zangeneh (ed.), *Islam, Iran, and World Stability*, (New York: St Martin's Press, 1994), pp. 201–16.

Zangeneh, Hamid, 'International trade in Iran: an appraisal', *Research in Middle East Economics*, Vol. 2 (1997).

Zhang, Baohui, 'Corporatism, totalitarianism, and transition to democracy', *Comparative Political Studies*, (27 (1), April 1994), pp. 108–36.

Zonis, Marvin, *The Political Elite of Iran* (Princeton: Princeton University Press, 1971).

Zysman, John, 'The myth of a 'global economy': enduring national foundations and emerging regional realities'. *New Political Economy*, vol. 1, no. 2 (1996).

Index

For Product Safety Concerns and Information please contact our EU
representative GPSR@taylorandfrancis.com
Taylor & Francis Verlag GmbH, Kaufingerstraße 24, 80331 München, Germany

www.ingramcontent.com/pod-product-compliance
Ingram Content Group UK Ltd.
Pitfield, Milton Keynes, MK11 3LW, UK
UKHW021246190926
475569UK00001BA/30
9780415308274